CRITICAL
PSYCHOLOGY
AND PEDAGOGY

Critical Studies in Education Series

CRITICAL PSYCHOLOGY AND PEDAGOGY

Interpretation of the Personal World

Edmund V. Sullivan

Introduction by Henry A. Giroux and Paulo Freire

CRITICAL STUDIES IN EDUCATION SERIES

BERGIN & GARVEY PUBLISHERS

NEW YORK • WESTPORT, CONNECTICUT • LONDON

Library of Congress Cataloging-in-Publication Data

Sullivan, Edmund V.
　　Critical psychology and pedagogy : interpretation of the personal
　world / Edmund V. Sullivan ; introduction by Henry A. Giroux and
　Paulo Freire.
　　　　p.　cm.—(Critical studies in education series)
　　Includes bibliographical references.
　　ISBN 0-89789-213-5 (lib. bdg. : alk. paper)
　　　1. Educational psychology.　2. Education—United States—
　Philosophy.　3. Educational sociology—United States.　I. Title.
　II. Series.
　　[DNLM:　1. Psychology, Educational. LB 1051 S949c]
　LB1051.S7488　1990
　370.15—dc20　　　　　　　　89-18635

Library of Congress Catalog Card Number: 89-18635
ISBN: 0-89789-213-5

First published in 1990

Bergin & Garvey Publishers, One Madison Avenue, New York, NY 10010
A division of Greenwood Press, Inc.

The paper used in this book complies with the
Permanent Paper Standard issued by the National
Information Standards Organization (Z39.48–1984).

10 9 8 7 6 5 4 3 2 1

Copyright Acknowledgments

The author and publisher are grateful for the use of the following material:

Edmund V. Sullivan, Sergio Martinic, and Horacio Walker, "Critical Interpretation:
A Comparison of Two Ethnographies," *Phenomenology + Pedagogy: A Human
Science Journal* 5, no. 1, 1987.

Horacio Walker Larrain, "Popular Education: The Soup Kitchen Study" (Ph.D. diss.,
University of Toronto, 1986).

TO

ANGELO DANESINO,

MY FIRST MENTOR,

IN LOVING GRATITUDE

Introduction: Toward a Critical Psychology of Schooling

Educational psychology has exercised a powerful influence on the theory and practice of American schooling. Whether in its cognitive, humanist, or behaviorist versions, the discourse of psychology has focused almost exclusively on the isolated, self-contained individual as the unit of analysis while simultaneously presenting a view of psychological life that is largely ahistorical and apolitical. Removed from the categories of ideology and power, the discourses of psychology have largely failed to engage critically the relationship between individuals and the wider social order, particularly around race, gender, and class considerations. Operating under the basic tenets of the natural sciences, the dominant discourses of educational psychology have defined themselves primarily through an appeal to science, objectivity, prediction, and control. While there are strong differences among these discourses, they all share assumptions, methods, and findings that reinforce a reductionistic emphasis on neutrality, objectivity, and instrumentality. More importantly, American educational psychology plays a major role as a discourse of social and cultural reproduction. That is, educational psychology has functioned primarily as a hegemonic discourse that actively serves to adapt students to existing relations of power in American schools through the use of its power to discipline, test, sort, and label. In effect, educational psychology in the latter half of the twentieth century has emerged as a technology of power legitimated, in part, by removing itself from the sphere of political discourse and recasting its project in the alleged neutral, value-free language of science. Psychology's subject as well as its methodologies are designed primarily to serve ideological purposes. For example, at the risk of great simplification, it is important to note that the cognitivists have generally functioned to idealize and operationalize consciousness in the interest of creating pedagogies and learning styles that largely ignore the historical, social, and cultural formations that operate within different relations of power in and out of schools to privilege some groups over others. Not only is difference in the cognitivist view reduced to a matter of will and style, but its goal of self-actualization also lacks any reference to the reconstruction of democratic public life. The recognition that individuals are socially and historically constructed within diverse social relations and subject to different resources and possibilities is stripped of its political implications and collapses into a reductionist notion of the individual as a unique and transparent subject who can shape, exclusively through the power of human will, his or her life and the larger world.

Though operating from a different set of theoretical assumptions, behaviorist psychology in education clings to similar political and ideological illusions. That is, though the behaviorists ignore questions of intentionality and will, they also remove their study of the individual from larger social and political forces. In doing so, behavioral psychology generally reifies human beings as objects to be manipulated, categorized, and controlled. Within this discourse there is little concern with how individuals come to be constituted as subjects of their own experiences; instead, individuals are treated as objects fashioned within the language of inputs and outputs, subjected to rules of scientific investigation whose language is commensurable with the logic of mathematics and physics.

It is important to note that both of these paradigms in psychology have played a major role in legitimating the current widespread emphasis on testing in American education, in developing ideological rationales for the apparatuses of tracking, and in providing the ideological legitimation for configuring culture and power through school practices that infantilize, subjugate, and oppress.

While dominant versions of humanist psychology have played a much less influential role in American educational psychology, its various discourses have also largely served to legitimate forms of social and cultural reproduction. By failing to provide a dialectical view of the relationship between the self and the social, the discourses of humanist psychology have treated politics as an obstacle to its goals and in doing so have ignored how the social and historical are implicated in the construction of individual "problems." What disappears in this perspective is the ground of community, the primacy of the social, and a public philosophy that rejects an overdetermining notion of private destiny for a broader sense of collective engagement and ethics based on the responsibilities of civic courage and democratic public life. *Critical Psychology and Pedagogy* is invaluable for understanding the ideological interests and practices that are at work in these various discourses. Although he does not address specific theoretical assumptions that characterize the various discourses of educational psychology, Edmund Sullivan's analysis of traditional psychology contains many insights for critical educators that relate directly to the ideological, social, and political practices of psychology at work in American schools.

Sullivan undertakes in this important book not only a devastating critique of the various dimensions of traditional psychology, but also attempts to develop an alternative, critical, and emancipatory notion of psychology that can play a vital role in expanding our understanding of a theory and practice of critical pedagogy. But Sullivan does more than merely draw an association between the discourse of critical psychology and critical pedagogy; he also provides detailed examples of how the discourse of critical psychology can be used within particular pedagogical practices. In this sense, Sullivan rewrites the theory and practice relationship in terms that ground particular pedagogical practices in theoretical principles that expand and deepen the existing literature on critical pedagogy.

It is worth mentioning that Sullivan organizes this book around a number of theoretical concerns that make it invaluable for educators. First, Sullivan rejects the notion of the autonomous individual and provides the theoretical basis for understanding how the "personal" as a historical and social construction can be understood in its dialectical relationship with broader social and cultural processes. Second Sullivan links the construction of the personal sphere with an ethical discourse that raises questions about how authority and power provide various subject positions through which people from different social and cultural formations construct their sense of self, place, and identity. The construction of personality and experience is not innocent and, in this case, must be understood as part of a wider political process that in complex and diverse ways serves to empower and disempower specific groups and individuals. In this sense, Sullivan claims that any study of psychology is basically ethical in nature because it cannot escape how dominant relations of power actively function in society to constitute human agents within different languages, ideologies, and social practices. But Sullivan is concerned with more than the role that psychology plays in understanding how subjectivities are regulated, transformed and limited by historically-produced social forms; he is also concerned with the social and political function of those who practice psychology. Describing psychology as an ethical enterprise, Sullivan raises important questions regarding the political responsibility of those intellectuals who engage in forms of social and moral regulation. There is no neutral ground in this perspective, and educators should take note that even a field like educational psychology, with its inflated appeal to science and objectivity, cannot cover up the deeply embedded ideologies and values that structure its assumptions, methodologies, and practices. Third, Sullivan develops a discourse of human agency without reproducing the theoretical pitfalls associated with the humanist construction of the subject. At the same time, he refuses to assign human agency a passive place within a poststructuralist theory of signs and effects. Instead, Sullivan places great emphasis on treating human action as a text that can be resymbolized and understood through the power of self-reflection and analysis.

In effect, Sullivan develops in this work an important notion of identity theory that is similar to views currently being advanced by a number of feminist theorists. In this approach, meaning is actively produced not only within the sphere of language and representations, but also in the materiality of events and practices that constitute everyday life. In this case, what Sullivan does for educators is provide the basis for investigating human agency within the interlocking dynamics of language and social practice. That is, Sullivan is concerned with how the representation of action is constructed and rooted in particular practices which then take hold at the level of subjectivity and self-representation. Finally, in his willingness to chart out theoretically and politically the move from sociality to subjectivity, from the constitutive force of cultural representations and social practices to the reconstruction of human histories through forms of self-representation and analysis, Sullivan begins to articulate a notion of critical pedagogy largely ignored by radical educators. He begins to map out the theoretical groundwork for a critical pedagogy that links knowledge, power, and desire on the one hand, to the construction of the personal and the wider society as a dialectical process open to forms of self- and social intervention on the other. In doing so, Sullivan offers educators a critical psychology that challenges existing notions of self and human agency. Moreover, he points to alternative ways of finding in the practices of daily life sources of power, resistance, and affirmation that dignify human struggle while recovering the primacy of the political as the basis for understanding the development of the individual as a historical and social construction. It is in this interrelationship between the personal and society that Sullivan situates the basis for a critical psychology that advances the meaning of pedagogy as an emancipatory process of self- and social formation. At its best, this book breaks new ground in developing a critical psychology and pedagogy as part of a broader politics of identity that reconstructs the personal as a social and historical process in order to rewrite the possibility for educators to undertake their own pedagogical practices as part of a wider struggle to change existing relations of power, lived experience, and oppression. In more general terms, Sullivan provides educators with a theoretical and political service by informing his notion of psychology and critical pedagogy with a utopian project grounded in the broad task of deepening and enriching democratic discourse and struggle. This is an important book, one of the few that reconstructs the relationship between psychology, subjectivity, and social struggle in terms that have direct application for parents, students, teachers, and others who want to deepen their understanding of schooling as a process that involves both the production of knowledge and the construction of human experience.

Henry A. Giroux
Paulo Freire

PREFACE

The title of this book when elaborated gives the reader the full import of this work. The use of the notion of the interpretive world alerts the reader that this text will involve itself with ideas coming from hermeneutics, better known as the science of interpretation. The personal world denotes that the psychological world of actors has great import in what this book will bring to the reader. The notion of a "critical psychology" gives the reader a sense that this book will be developing a psychology of the personal world that is critical in nature. I am aware that for many readers of this text, the notion of a critical psychology will have no meaning to start with *per se*. It will be my task to thoroughly elaborate my meaning of "critical psychology" and how it relates to the personal world. Finally, this book will attempt to relate "critical psychology" to pedagogical questions. Because the pedagogical issues that I will deal with are fundamentally informed by a "critical psychology" based on a critical theory of society it follows that the pedagogical questions that are dealt with go naturally under the name "critical pedagogy." As I have already said, all of this elaboration constitutes the work of this book. My own bottom line on the role of psychology in relation to societal work is that it cannot be ignored by social theory and the social sciences. Those making the assumption that psychology lacks relevance in the current workings of society do so at their own peril.

When one is making an assessment of the social sciences, it cannot be ignored that the discipline of psychology plays an extremely important role in the organization and maintenance of institutions in our society. The world of business, government, the military, schooling, and so on, have as part of their endemic practices the use of psychology as an intricate part of their workings. As a discipline, psychology has played a highly significant role in the maintenance of the social order. By *social order maintenance*, I mean here a concerted attempt, both at a conscious and unconscious level to sustain the ongoing life of institutions in their present form and with their present power dynamics. Traditional psychology, as I historically understand it, in its myriad practices has operated as a rationalization for the maintenance of social order and, in the context of which I will be writing, the social order of capitalism affectionately referred to as "Western Democracy."

It would be misleading to have the reader consider that psychology as a discipline within the social sciences is the sole discipline involved in the task of institutional social maintenance. All of the social sciences in their conventional formulations serve a similar task. But psychology as a discipline has certain unique characteristics. First, it is the only discipline within the social sciences that has a virtual absence of critical reflection on its inner workings. It is unique in this by its unreflective insistence that it is a value-free and nonnormative discipline. It is not that the other social science disciplines are that different from psychology on this account. The major difference, however, is that all other disciplines appear to have what one would call a minority position within their ranks that would be called *critical*. Here I am using the word *critical* to indicate that there is some understanding that social inquiry is not value–neutral and is involved in the power dynamics within the society in which it is operating. Psychology, at the level of its paradigms, seems to be unique from the other social disciplines by a total absence of critical discourse and reflective understanding of the power dynamics operating within societal institutions.

Second, psychology has a uniqueness because of its hegemony over the discourse on the notion of the *individuals*. Psychology with its notion of the isolated, developing individual allows for the interpretation that all societal problems can be ultimately located at the door of the individual actor. This allows for an interpretation of society as an aggregate of individuals rather than a totality that is much greater than its individual parts. This fragmented view allows for a way of thinking about society that sidesteps social relationships that go beyond the unit of the individual. To focus on individuals allows one to ignore the complex social dynamics of power that cannot be encapsulated within an individual. It will be one of the tasks of this book to carry out a whole-scale critique of the notion of the individual and present a more relational concept as indicated in the title of this book, which I label as the *personal*.

Third, psychology is unique in the way its breeds out of its considerations the dynamics of power that are embedded in the dynamics of class, gender, and race. It is not that these words do not appear in psychology texts. The problem, however, as I see it, is that it turns these areas of power dynamics that are operating in society into isolated social units rather than problematic and contentious areas of power struggle that are presently operating in our society. Class, race, and gender when they do appear are seen as areas for study in a neutral manner and where issues of social power, domination, and oppression are masked over and concealed. Class conflict, racism and patriarchy are not concepts that are generated within the discipline of psychology.

Finally, psychology, in a majority of instances, has taken as its historical task the manipulation and control of behavior. Thus it is first and foremost a science of prediction and control of human behavior, rather than one of understanding. Since, as a discipline, its mission is nonnormative at the level of discourse, the possibility that it could serve a role in human emancipation and freedom escapes its world view. It is, therefore, amoral and apolitical at the level of its intent. Thus the psychologist Jensen can regard his position on "genetics and racial equality" as a value–neutral and apolitical psychological position. As I will attempt to show in this book, this intention of value neutrality does not operate at the level of its role in society. It is my contention that psychology is for the most part an administrative *formative science* serving the function of legitimation of power for the social order in which it is embedded. In short, it serves the needs of the social order of capitalism where it legitimates this social order by masking its social and political intentions with its diversion into individualism. Here I am only highlighting this historical role. It will be the task of this book to spell out some of these prefatory salvos directed at this discipline.

This book is a counter-position to the traditional psychology that I have just portrayed. I first came to the idea of writing this book when I was reading liberation theology coming out of Latin America, especially the work of Gustavo Gutierrez entitled A *Theology of Liberation.* Basically, Gutierrez attempted to recast theology for the purposes of social transformation rather than for its traditional role as a societal apologist for the maintenance of the social order. Thus, the underlying interest of this approach was an interest in human freedom rather than the control and maintenance of peoples. As the reader will see shortly, this work has as its basis a pedagogy within the context of psychology that formulates what Freire calls "cultural action for freedom." At this point these words are, at their best, some indication of what is to come if I succeed to convince the reader of my task, or, if I fail, they can be relegated to rhetorical flourish. I will work very hard to keep the reader from arriving at the latter position. With that in mind let me attempt to give the reader a capsule summary of what this book will be attempting to accomplish.

First, the book will attempt to hold the individual and society in dynamic tension. Because of the way the notion of the individual has been socially constructed within psychology, it will be necessary initially to embark upon a fundamental critique of individualism. In the course of this critique the notion of the individual will be abandoned and the development of a conception that I am labeling the *personal* will be articulated. The notion of the personal that I am venturing within a critical perspective is no mere substitution for the notion of the individual. It will literally take the first three chapters to clear the ground for my notion of the *personal.* There is also an assumption that the personal world and the larger society in which it is embedded are dialectically related to one another, and that any attempt to collapse that tension would end up by concealing the power dynamics that are operating within a society. Traditionally, the separation of these concepts followed from the specialization and isolation of theory and method within disciplines and subdisciplines. The reader is alerted in advance that she or he will be embarked on a truly interdisciplinary venture that will put a strain on the well-traveled road of discipline separation. Discipline separation has been traditionally embraced because of the belief that a division of labor within the social sciences would have a beneficial explanatory value on one's understanding of the workings of society. Thus, in order to achieve clarity and explanatory power, it was necessary to operate within a continually decreasing "circle of interpretation." The historical would be separated from the political, the psychological from the sociological, and so on, to the point where some would say that what was ultimately achieved by this enterprise of disciplinary boundaries was a crisis of imagination produced by the myopia of specialization. Ignoring, for the moment, the possibility that methodology in the social sciences replicates the social nature of production in the marketplace, it seems appropriate here to focus on this vacuum in imagination and how it affects social inquiry. Here I would like to quote at some length from C. Wright Mills's *Sociological Imagination* (1959). Speaking of the general populace, Mills says:

> It is not only information that they need—in this age of fact, information often dominates their attention and overwhelms their capacities to assimilate it. It is not only the skills of reason that they need—although their struggles to acquire these often exhaust their limited moral energy.
>
> What they need, and what they feel they need, is a quality of mind that will help them to use information and to develop reason in order to achieve lucid summations of what is going on in the world and what may be happening within themselves. (p. 5)

Second, in a broader interdisciplinary effort with an emancipating intent (i.e., the intention to broaden the scope of personal freedom) one would hope that a psychology with a critical emancipating intent would provide a type of interpretation of personal human action that would enable actors to understand what is happening in their world in the context of wider social structures. For example, the worker who is experiencing stress in the workplace will not fall into the trap that his stress in working is simply the result of interpsychic factors. Examination of the workplace proper would also be fair game when tackling the problem of stress. My assumption clearly is that the "personal world" exists, is influenced by, and influences the wider social context and cannot be considered apart from it. It is therefore necessary to be dialectical in order to pursue the approach I am advocating. Mills refers to it as a "sociological imagination," and for all intents and purposes we may consider psychology as critical interpretation of the development of a "psychological imagination" with a critical intention. As Mills puts it:

for that imagination is the capacity to shift from one perspective to another—from the political; to the psychological; from the examination of a single family to comparative assessment of the national, budgets of the world; from the theological school to the military; from the considerations of a national oil industry to studies of contemporary poetry. It is the capacity to range from the most impersonal and remote transformations to the most intimate features of the human self—and see the relations between the two. Back of its use there is always the urge to know the social and historical meaning of the individual in the society and in the period in which he has his quality and his being. (1959, p. 7)

Taking some inspiration from Mills it is my express intention to broaden psychological discourse in order to deal with the intricacies of the personal world as it is dynamically linked to the complexity of institutions in the society where it is embedded. I will also systematically examine the issues of power dynamics that weave themselves into this complex matrix. When we will talk about social power, the personal world will not collapse in on itself as it does when one has resort to the notion of the "individual." The personal world will always be contextualized with an "imagination" that Mills refers to in the above quote.

Third, there is an assumption that is central to the notion of a critical psychology and that is the mode of inquiry that is being pursued here in a normative and therefore value-full rather than value-free way. In the tradition of Durkheim, all of the social sciences are ethical and normative in nature. It is, therefore, the case that a "critical psychology" is in no way an exception to mainstream psychological inquiry in its normativity. Its uniqueness lies in the fact that it makes no pretensions of being value-free and, in addition, it self-reflectively pursues values pertaining to human liberation. Since it is my position that a value-free, assumed social science is an impossibility, it is therefore necessary to tackle up front all of the problems and issues that follow from a normative position. In order to do this, there must be a radical shift in ground from the primacy and preemptiveness of the theoretical (episteme) to an orientation of action within the context of cultural practices (normative). I label this a *praxis* orientation because it starts from the point of view of *human action* and sees theory a moment in the ongoing nature of human activity. This point of entry should not be taken as a reverse dichotomy, that is, the primacy of practice over theory. The idea of praxis assumes that human action is *intentional* in nature and, therefore, that reflection is embedded in human action. Theory is, then, the moments of reflection in action.

Fourth, the radical orientation that I am proposing for a disciplined psychological inquiry involves a shift in the "interest nature" of the definitional structure of the discipline as it is conventionally defined as a predictive science with control of human behavior as an outcome to that of an emancipatory interest in human freedom based on the *intentional action of persons*. This emancipatory concern needs unpacking, which is the reason for this book. At this point, one can say that an emancipatory interest in human freedom rests on the assumption that part of all human action is *creative* and that the personal world of the human creates the world that it inhabits while, at the same time, is determined by it. I will therefore not make what I consider to be a serious error: the dichotomization of human freedom from determinism. Thus a critical psychology looks at the intentions that motivate human actions as *history-making*. We call this latter process *culture*. Since this personal world will be seen to develop out of the intentions of human agency, Freire's notion of *cultural action for freedom* flows very easily from the position developed herein.

Finally, the development of a critical pedagogy for the interpretation of the personal world demands a considerable level of discourse, which, for the practically oriented reader, may be ponderous if it has no concrete payoff at an applied level. I am very sympathetic to this reader and I take it as my task of the closing of this book to give some concrete examples of how a critical psychology might address some applied problems. Because of my own background in education, the examples that I will supply will come from some of my own unique interests. My educational examples are by no means exhaustive; they are simply meant to be exemplary. I would also caution the reader that as a pedagogy for an interpretive critical psychology the idea of a pedagogy is given a generic meaning; that is, by pedagogy I want the reader to know that this work is in no sense a cookbook. In addition, the fact that I use examples from education at the end by no means should the reader believe that this work only applies to educational issues. It would be my position that this pedagogy can be utilized productively in any area or discipline where psychology may constitute part of the discourse.

ACKNOWLEDGMENTS

There are many persons and groups that have influenced my thinking and thus helped in the writing of this book.

I would like to acknowledge a collective dealing with psychology and political economy that I participated in in New York City for several years; its members included John Broughton, Harry Garfinkle, Howard Gruber, Adrienne Harris, Arnold Kaufmann, Joel Kovel, and Ricardo Zuniga.

At my Institute I would like to acknowledge the Critical Psychology and Cultural Studies Working Group: Madan Handa, Mal Levin, David Livingstone, Paul Olsen, Roger Simon, and Gord West.

Thanks to Gregory Baum and Lee Cormie, theologians at St. Michael's College who encouraged my efforts at important stages of this book.

Thanks to colleagues on the OISE-Chile Project: Sergio Martinique, Paul Olsen, Horacio Walker, and Ricardo Zuniga whose joint work with me appears in the final chapter on Critical Pedagogy.

My deep appreciation goes to John Broughton and Henry Giroux who have been extremely supportive in my effort to formulate a critical psychology, specifically in their editorial work for publication. To Hugh Oliver at OISE Press for his encouragement of this work for a Canadian context.

To Morry Ulrich, Donaleen Hawes, Diana Postletwaite, Rikki Hortian, and Yvonne Girdwood, thanks for judicious proofreading of the final manuscript.

Thanks to Larry Rooney of Centre for Training in Psychotherapy whose generous support made this book possible.

Finally, thanks to my wife and children who keep me grounded in the world where social justice has flesh and blood.

I depart from the usual "I do not hold all of those listed above responsible for my ideas." I hold them all responsible. My ideas are formed by the company I keep.

CONTENTS

1

Metaphors of Understanding
A Critical Introduction

> *The history of thought is the history of its models. Classical mechanics, the organism, natural selection, the atomic nucleus or electronics field, the computer: such are some of the objects or systems which first used to organize our understanding of the natural world and have been called upon to illuminate human reality.*
>
> —Jameson, 1972, p. v

The title of this book is *A Critical Psychology: Interpretation of the Personal World*. This chapter attempts to develop an outline and elucidation of the parameters of that definition. Part of the definition of something is to indicate what it is not or what it should not be. Thus, there will be some critical discussion of what one might term "mainstream psychology." I commence this treatment under the assumption that psychological perspectives (e.g., behaviorism, structuralism) are conveniently thought of as metaphors. Ultimately, my intent is to develop a definition of psychology based on a personal metaphor (cf. MacMurray, 1957, 1961). At the level of commonsense language, it seems likely that no psychologist would deny that he or she is attempting to understand people (i.e., persons). However, much of what constitutes psychological theory and research is not couched at the level of ordinary language. In fact, most of the language of psychological theory quickly embraces a formalization of symbols that is oriented away from ordinary language. As we shall point out, formal language is, in part, an attempt to go beyond the vicissitudes of history, which are clearly embedded in our ordinary use of language. In all this, it should be noted that, whatever way we turn, we are embedded in some kind of linguistic system, a "prison house of language" (Jameson, 1972).

Metaphors of Understanding

The world itself and people within it are relational. By this we mean that to know or identify persons, things, or events, we have to identify or contrast them

1

with other persons, things, or events. In order to come to know and understand something, we usually attempt to identify and contrast it with something that we already find familiar. Piaget calls this "assimilation," which means that we attempt to come to an understanding of the unfamiliar by use of the familiar. This process can be identified as metaphorical; that is, we use metaphors in order to say something that we know little about (Te Selle, 1975). The dictionary defines a metaphor as a figure of speech denoting a word phrase, usually one kind of object or idea in place of another, in order to suggest a likeness or analogy between them. A metaphor is, at the very least, an interaction between symbols. Black sees this interaction as a relational event where the conventional wisdom associated with one context serves as the screen or grid through which we see the other context:

> Suppose I look at the night sky through a piece of heavily smoked glass on which certain lines have been left clear. Then I shall see only the stars that can be made to be on the lines previously prepared upon the screen and the stars I do see will be seen as organized by the screen's structure. We can think of a metaphor as such a screen and the system of associated commonplaces of the focal word as the network of lines upon the screen. We can say that the principal subject is "seen through the metaphor expression" or if we prefer that the principal subject is projected upon "the field of the subsidiary subject." (Black, 1962, p. 41)

Another term that is a species of metaphor is *paradigm*, introduced by Kuhn in his *Structure of Scientific Revolutions* (Kuhn, 1962). I am reluctant to use this term in our present context since it tends to convey the feeling of a fully developed and conscious theoretical perspective. Though there are many attempts at systematic formalization of theory in psychology, none of these adds up to or commands the allegiance of the paradigm in the Kuhnian sense. We are, therefore, restricting ourselves to the use of the term *metaphor*. Our use of this term alerts the reader to the fact that we are using language as a "lens" for understanding. To conceive of psychological perspectives as metaphors for understanding means that the problems presented by language affect all theoretical perspectives of whatever variety. Therefore, all theoretical perspectives structure perception and practice as a prism filters light. As metaphor, theoretical language both reveals and conceals different aspects of human reality (Ricoeur, 1970). All language is embedded in certain tacit prerequisites that are often unknown to those utilizing it (Gadamer, 1975a; Polanyi, 1968). For example, language is embedded in sociohistorical realities and it reflects those realities (cf. Marx & Engels, 1960). When those sociohistorical realities are denied, the theory language is said to be "ideological," that is, it supresses some of its own intentions (Habermas, 1970, 1972, 1974; Marx & Engels, 1960). Therefore, in treating theories as metaphors, we are assuming that the prism of language is embedded in sociohistorical realities and not independent of them. Thus, behaviorism is not only a metaphorical language but also a social practice embedded in sociohistorical realities. The praxeology of a metaphor is often denied in the development of the metaphor. For example, psychometric psychologists have, in the past, denied that their perspective on the nature–nurture question was influenced by and influenced immigration policy (see Kamin, 1974). This example is used simply to alert the reader to the fact that all language, including theory language, is embedded in sociohistorical events. This, at any rate, is the perspective out of which I am operating. With this understood, I would now like to discuss psychological theory and practice under the aegis of three root metaphors: the mechanical, the organic, and the personal. This particular breakdown is suggested by John MacMurray (1957, 1961), and it must be understood at the outset that this particular breakdown is, to some extent, arbitrary in character. I choose this particular constellation in the belief that it will be helpful to a person trained as a psychologist. I am saying, in essence, that these three root metaphors conveniently encompass psychological theories that serve or have served as screening devices in our understanding of the human world.

THE MECHANICAL METAPHOR

Machines serving as analogues for the understanding of human behavior have probably always attracted human attention. The attraction became systematic when machines came to the forefront of consciousness at the time of the industrial revolution. During the 16th and 17th centuries we were confronted with a new view of the universe that is both mechanistic and materialistic. Mechanical materialism arose out of the developments achieved in the physical sciences, particularly physics. Mechanism, that is, seeing the physical world in terms of machine analogues, came to be seen as the most important explanatory language in the development of what are now the physical sciences. From the point of view of mechanistic materialism, the world consists of particles of matter in interaction. Each particle has its own existence and becomes a large totality by addition. The totality of interactions between particles forms the totality of everything that happens in the world, and these interactions are mechanical in nature; that is to say, they consist of external influences of one particle upon another. As such, mechanistic materialism saw the whole world as nothing but a complex piece of machinery, a mechanism (Cornforth, 1971). Although originally designed as a metaphor for reflection on phenomena in the physical world, mechanistic materialism historically, during the latter part of the 19th century, became a controlling image for reflection on social phenomena. In the 20th century, the discipline of psychology appropriated mechanism from the physical sciences and used it like a "borrowed tool box" (Hampden-Turner, 1971). The appropriation of "mechanical tools" opened the door to looking at human events as mechanisms not unlike complex machines. Hull (1943), the famous behaviorist theory builder, refers to humans as "complex robots."

Instrumental Rationality and Technical Control

The appropriation of the metaphorical language of mechanistic materialism involves a complex synthesis of several interrelated notions. For example, the pervasive *rationality* exemplified in mechanical metaphors is a combination of logic and empiricism (i.e., logical empiricism). Logical empiricism is a complex amalgam of the historical traditions of rationalism and empiricism with empiricism at the forefront; as we shall see later, structuralism reverses these priorities. Logical empiricism exists within a given societal matrix, so that any form of understanding of, and orientation to, a scientific and technical power needs to elucidate this reference to the investigator's membership in society (Gadamer, 1975a, 1975b; Habermas, 1970). The matrix or metascience of early American psychology was essentially logical empiricism. Radnitzki (1973) ventures that the typical human scientist of the Anglo-American world appears to be programmed by logical empiricism. The dominant image within this matrix places human "behavior" at the center, and it is studied in relation to its component parts (i.e., analysis). At the level of ideas, the philosophy of science concomitant with this image of the human is characterized as "reductionistic," methodological "individualism," and so on. Psychology in its essential defining characteristics becomes a behavioral science, typically behavioristic, physiological, or psychometric in nature (Radnitzki, 1973). Methodological individualism means that the ideal person is considered as a self-contained individualistic system rather than an interdependent system (Sampson, 1977). At the order of events, it may be contemplated that the methodological individualism reflects the historical individual of the surrounding culture (Sampson, 1977). Within the context of the American ethos at the beginning of this century, the budding and neophyte psychological establishment attempted to establish an experimental psychology (i.e., empirical) which would supply the fundamental laws governing all human activity, irrespective of context (Danziger, 1978). Psychology, either knowingly or unknowingly, was entrenched in the American socioeconomic order, and its most articulate spokespersons would express themselves as creating a science that would help us to understand the motives that control the actions of labor and capital. Watson, an early president of the American Psychological Association, suggested that psychology accept the premise that its discipline was to produce data in a practical way to be easily utilized by businesspersons (Ewen, 1976). American psychology was to be an *administrative* science: a technology to be willed by society's managers to direct the actions of those in their charge into desired channels (Danziger, 1978). Although there would be other reasons, it is not farfetched to conceive that for management reasons, psychology would take as its primary definition the prediction and control of behavior.

Analysis. The whole is the sum of its parts; that, in essence, is the principle of analysis. It is an epistemological principle assumed in many areas of inquiry.

It is contrasted with the synthetic principle that the whole is more than the sum of its parts. The *principle of analysis* is clearly accented when mechanical metaphors are used in inquiry. One can easily assent to the idea that the construction of a machine is based on the sum of its parts and that the finished product can be decomposed back into its component parts. As I will discuss shortly, the mode of observation called the *experiment* represents a decomposition process with the intent of finding explanations of and for events. When the principle of analysis is accented, it is assumed that manipulation, prediction, and control of supposedly decomposed conditions are explanations of events. *Explanation* of a phenomenon involves an attempt to manipulate, control, and predict antecedent–consequent conditions with a view to defining linear causality. Causality is a relationship between antecedent conditions and consequences. Manipulation and control assume the ability to control some conditions in nature, to vary these conditions while holding other conditions constant, and then to observe differential consequences in this controlled setting. The stress is on the ability to control the consequences through the systematic variation of antecedent conditions. If antecedent conditions are related to predictable consequences (e.g., if a, then b); a causal relationships between these events is assumed. When these component parts are human events, complete psychological determinism is assumed. *Prediction* follows from manipulation and control of conditions. Prediction assumes determinism, and the aim of prediction is to achieve *causal explanations* of a set of events or phenomena. Explanation is, therefore, said to be a result of the predictive validity of the manipulation and control of the experimenter. A good explanation of an event should have a high predictive component.

It is believed by those who foster it that the psychological experiment achieves some kind of disinterested rationality and, as a technique, is independent of its historical surroundings. My own contention is that the experiment is a reflection of a culture whose reference point is a rationality based on technical control (cf. Habermas, 1970, 1972). In other words, the knowledge is based on a particular *interest* reflected in modern scientific society, and this knowledge-constitutive interest (i.e., technical–control rationality) shapes what counts as knowledge. Thus, technical interest aids in the formulation of the categories relevant to what one takes to be knowledge claims. A rationality formulated as technique is, of necessity, a particular type of rationality governed by technical rules (e.g., the experiment proper).[1] Technical control rationality is connected to Habermas's (1972) description of conventional empirical–analytic sciences. Behaviorism is one psychological variant of what Habermas calls "conventional

[1]It should be clearly understood that the psychological experiment is only one instance of a technical control rationality. Test construction and the statistical techniques used in assessment are another specific example. The experimental method, for some historical reasons, appears to have eclipsed all other techniques as the most substantial technique for the acquisition of knowledge.

empirical–analytical science." It is a family of theoretical and research thrusts that includes several different points of view of how one arrives at true statements of facts about events (i.e., explanation). Hull's (1943) behavior theory was a rather elaborate molecular theoretical system (i.e., hypothetical–deductive) combined with a rigorous tying together of the theoretical system and the empirical data. Hull's system is a combination of deductive theoretical statements (i.e., rationalism) interlocked and intertwined with empirical statements (i.e., empiricism). This is logical empiricism in its clearest formulation. Skinner (1950) eschewed the elaborate theoretical formulations of Hull and others and preferred formulating his behaviorism with a rigorous inductive empiricism. His article entitled "Are Theories of Learning Necessary?" allows one to label him a radical empiricist. We are not using the term *radical* here in a political sense. Skinner is radical because his conception of learning rejected the elaborate theoretical construction characteristic of Hull and Tolman (e.g., Hull's elaborate hypothetico-deductivism).

At the level of practice, all behaviorists of whatever theoretical persuasion agree that the experiment is the preferred mode of verification. Even though there are important practical differences between the ways in which classical and operant conditioning are researched through experiment, all the various experimental formats are alike in their preoccupation with control over what is being studied. All experiments in their pure state are mechanical procedures for the purpose of explanation.

Objective Knowledge. The experiment as a sound practice unreflectively collapses an important epistemological dimension, which I think is important not to overlook. The dimension I am referring to is the dialectic of subjective and objective meaning. The experiment, in practice, is a denial of the importance of subjective meaning. If the mind or consciousness is simply a mechanism in nature, subjectivity assumes minor importance within this perspective or is totally ignored. This is behavioral psychology's classical attitude toward consciousness and subjectivity; for the sake of truth, it should be noted that this attitude has eroded in more recent years.

Fact–Value Dimension. Another dimension that collapsed within the experimental praxis is the normative element (i.e., values). The assumption is that the experiment is an enterprise that is value-neutral. As a methodological ideal borrowed from the natural sciences, it is said to be a method of establishing "true facts." This type of restriction allows some real ethical problems to go unacknowledged (e.g., the Milgram experiment).

The principle of analysis assumed in the experiment systematizes an ignorance toward larger "totalities" in which the experiment is contextualized (i.e., institutional–power relationships). This model has recently come under serious challenge as a result of its epistemological horizon and its value-neutral stance (Gadlin & Ingle, 1975). Experimental self-reflection is a one-way mirror that reflects the technical control rationality of the experimenter, while ignoring the subject's or animal's point of view. Particularly where human subjects are involved, there is a systematic sundering of communication between the experimenter and the subjects. The use of the term *subject* is quite telling in this respect.

It is now becoming apparent that the "detached observer" role of the social scientist possibly masks a situation of domination and control of one group of persons over others. Essentially, the experimental method as a mode of reflection illustrates the condition where there is a minimum of reciprocity between those being studied and the person (i.e., social scientist) who is carrying out the inquiry. As a reflective process, it is seen by Gadlin and Ingle (1975) as a one-way mirror. The mode of reflection generates a process that bends the social reality of communication in one direction (i.e., unilateral), the relationship of communication being one of monologue rather than dialogue. Thus, in the attempt to adopt the viewpoint of a *detached observer*, the experimenter fragments the relationship further by not allowing himself or herself to be influenced by the social reality of those being studied. Upon challenge, a hidden dimension of control is revealed which, under normal circumstances, is taken for granted. The viewpoint of the detached observer masks a power relationship that appears to be hidden from the researcher. The experimenter (i.e., social scientist) is unaware of the fact that he or she is in a power relationship with those who are being studied. From the point of view that we will be developing, the absence of reciprocal communication represents a type of oppression. The communicative position of the experimenter is like that of the Producer in Pirandello's (1952) *Six Characters in Search of an Author:*

> Producer: That's the idea! And if you want my opinion you ought to be grateful for all the attention they are paying you.
>
> Son: Indeed! Thank you! But hasn't it dawned on you yet that you aren't going to be able to stage this play? Not even the thinnest vestige of us is to be found in you—. And all the time your actors are studying us from the outside. Do you think it's possible for us to live confronted by a mirror which, not merely content to freeze us in that particular picture which is fixing our expression, has to draw an image back to us which we can no longer recognize? Our own features, yes—. But twisted in a horrible grimace. (Act 3, p. 274)

A reflexive psychology reveals the value arrogance involved in experimental communication. When the communicative values implied in this perspective are shown to be reflecting wider sociopolitical realities of a repressive nature, they are vigorously denied (see Zuniga, 1975). Denial does not, however, detract from the reality that this type of social science praxis masks political intentions. The technical control rationality is clearly sympathetic to identifiable political intentions (Habermas, 1970). Thus value neutrality cannot, in the end, be retained as a viable concept for inquiry.

Computer Simulation

That psychological theory is culture-contextual is evident with the development of computer systems. With a shift toward complex machine technologies, as witnessed by computer simulation, we see a shift in theory and practice where mechanical metaphors are concerned. The computer is seen to hold out the possibility that the simulation of complex mental processes is now possible (e.g., Newell & Simon, 1961). Neisser (1967) exemplifies the machine-metaphorical use of the computer as a guide to human understanding, as follows:

> The task of the psychologist trying to understand human cognition is analogous to that of a man trying to discover how a computer is programmed. In particular, if the program seems to store and reuse information, he would like to know by what "routines" or "procedures" that it is done. . . . By the same token, it would not help the psychologist to know that memory is carried by RNA as opposed to some other medium. He wants to understand its utilization, not its incarnation. (p. 6)

Recently Neisser (1976) has become disenchanted with his earlier views, and he probably reflects a growing skepticism of the long-term possibilities of the computer analogue as an adequate reflection of human capabilities. At the same time, it should be acknowledged that there is still substantial attraction for computer simulation research, and this will continue to increase with the new communications technologies. I am not here embarked on an elaborate analysis or critique of computer simulation and its currency in contemporary psychological theory and research. It is briefly discussed here to show how mechanical metaphors are transformed by the development of machine technology.

It is, however, important to question the extensive use of the machine metaphor for the full range and diversity of human functioning. As a metaphorical lens or prism, I am cautiously observant of developments in this area.

THE ORGANIC METAPHOR

If mechanical metaphors are premised on physical systems, the metaphoric prism of organic metaphors is premised on biological systems (i.e., life sciences). The term *organic* refers to the processes or products of life—in human beings, animals, or plants (Williams, 1976). Concurrent with the development of the life sciences, there is the development of the distinction between organic and mechanical systems. The fundamental difference between the mechanical and the organic metaphor is essentially that an *organism* is a living, adaptive unity that *transforms* itself while relating dynamically to its environment. Probably the most important single theory that exemplifies the organic metaphor in contemporary times is Darwin's theory of evolution.

By the 20th century, a broad distinction between biological evolution and social evolution had been articulated in diverse areas of the budding social sciences. The early 1900s witnessed a marked interest in social evolutionary theory in sociology and anthropology (Campbell, 1975). This interest has waxed and waned in 20th-century psychology, but it is on the ascendant again with a new social science concern labeled sociobiology (Wilson, 1975).

For the purposes of exposition, we will restrict our discussion of the organic metaphor to two major contemporary movements of importance: structuralism and functionalism as specific exemplars.[2]

Structuralism[3]

In the late 1950s and early 1960s there appeared a rather interesting transitional period in American psychology. There was a crack in the wall of the hegemony of logical empiricism. Behaviorism was becoming much more complicated and there was a movement toward a behavior theory that could deal with the complexities of the human organism. For the first time, we see an attempt to address complex linguistic processes by incorporating the term *meaning* (Osgood, Suci, & Tannenbaum, 1957). The logical empiricism formerly presented by behaviorism was being stretched to its limits. New theoretical shifts were taking place at this time, which would eventually lead to the decade of structuralism in American psychology. Structuralism, as specifically presented to the psychological scene, was to be an essential challenge to the prevalent mechanistic theories. When the Swiss genetic epistemologist Piaget entered the American psychology scene in the 1960s, there had already been a movement toward centralist or mediated behaviorist formulations. The psycholinguist Charles Osgood was suggesting complex mediational processes to explain linguistic meaning. Behaviorism at this time was attempting to come to terms with complex mental processes, and we also saw information processing models spinning off from computer simulation research (Hilgard & Bower, 1966). Behaviorists (e.g.,

[2]Our treatment here of just two examples of organic metaphors is in no sense exhaustive. Our selection is made simply for illustrative purposes. For example, under organic metaphors one could include humanistic psychologists such as Maslow and Perls. The distinction between structualism and functionalism is fraught with ambiguity. Piaget is called a structuralist, but his theory is also embedded in functional definitions (e.g., intelligence). Parsons is considered a functionalist, yet his perspective is informed by structural dimensions. Our distinction here between structuralism and functionalism is simply on the basis of accent. Some theories emphasize and articulate structural dimensions over function (e.g., Piaget, Chomsky). Thus our appellation of the term *structural* does not preclude functions and vice versa.

[3]To give structuralism the appellation of an organic metaphor demands some reservations on my part. I am aware that other authors might not follow me on this point (see Jameson, 1972). The truth is that I am simplifying issues for the purpose of illustration. Specifically, I am accenting those aspects of structural theories which clearly exemplify aspects of what I am calling "organic metaphors."

Berlyne, 1966; Gagné, 1968) and computer-simulation theorists attempted a rapprochement with Piaget's and Chomsky's structuralism. For the most part, these attempted marriages had ill-fated results (e.g., Newell & Simon, 1961; Hunt, 1961). The reason is that, on a fundamental level, structuralism deviates radically from mechanistic theories, even in its complex guises, because there is a synthetic rather than an analytic conception of knowledge. By *synthetic* we mean a preoccupation with structural totalities (i.e., the whole is more than the sum of its parts).

Structuralism is one of several attempts to go beyond some of the dilemmas presented by the methods of logical empiricism (Sullivan, 1980a, 1981; Unger, 1976). A structural conception assumes that a structure (in whatever form it takes) is a *totality*; that is, the whole (i.e., structure) is more than the sum of its parts. In contrast to mechanistic explanation, which is fundamentally an analytic process, all forms of structuralism are based on a principle of synthesis (Unger, 1975). The structure, called "stages" in the work of Piaget, is a holistic entity in which the whole is more than the sum of its parts (Sullivan, 1966, 1980a). As already mentioned, structure as a synthetic principle is diametrically opposite to analysis, as exemplified by even the most complex behavior theories (e.g., Berlyne, 1966). A structure is a holistic entity characterized by *internal* dependencies. This is explicated by Piaget, for example, in his definition of a structure as a system of transformations which, as system, implies a lawfulness of organization independent of the elements that compose it (Dagenais, 1972). This system is characterized as a totality. In other words, whatever the composing elements in the system, they are subordinated to the laws defining the system as a system. In addition, a system is characterized by multiple transformations that are interdependent with each other and with the totality, that is, they are dependent on the structure itself. Finally, a structure is self-regulating and tends toward the conservation and enhancement of the system itself (Dagenais, 1972). Similarly, in linguistics, Chomsky and his followers deny that linguistics can be built on the analysis of elementary particles of meaning (e.g., analytic assumptions). Transformational grammarians share the fact that the speakers of every language are able to construct an infinite number of formally correct and meaningful sentences. Linguistic structuralism has, therefore, been highly critical of behaviorist interpretations of how language is acquired. Consider Chomsky's observation:

> I believe that the study of human psychology has been diverted into side channels by unwillingness to pass the problem of how experience is related to knowledge and belief, a problem which of course presupposes a logically though not necessarily temporally prior investigation of the structure of systems of knowledge and belief. No matter how successfully the study of stimulus-response connections, habit structures, and so on is pursued, it will always fail to touch these central questions. The systems of knowledge and belief that underlie normal human behavior simply cannot be described in terms of networks of association, fabrics of dispositions to respond, habit structures, and the like. At least this seems to be true in the case of language and other known examples of human "cognitive processes." (Chomsky, 1971, pp. 47–48)

It is safe to say that the structuralism of Piaget and Chomsky deviates substantially from all types of neobehaviorism because of its interest in synthetic totalities (e.g., generative grammars, stages of cognitive and moral development, etc.).

Just why structuralism should gain such power is a matter for some complex historical speculation; but it is clear that it is not just the result of the explanatory power of the theories proposed. It was surprising that within a few short years, Piaget's study of cognitive development (in its nascent stages), Chomsky's conceptions about language development, and Kohlberg's articulation of moral development were to become the popular psychological metaphors on the American psychological scene. Wilden (1975) has characterized structuralism, among several psychological currents, as a veritable epistemological shift in the way of conceiving living and social systems. He links this to a progressive transformation of the large socioeconomic structure surrounding psychological speculation:

> The increasing size and complexity of business corporations, as well as their organization in tiers, trees, pyramids, and more intricate topological structures would naturally lead to the systematization of a body of theory designed to explain and control organization. Similarly, one has only to consider the relatively sudden discovery by the industrialized nations that the pursuit of individual economic independence leads ultimately to increasing degrees of collective inter-dependence to realize that we would necessarily come to live in an era when some form of systems ecology would be applied to any and all complexities of system-environment relations. The shift is both a mirror of contemporary socioeconomic reality and an illumination of it. (p. 91)

There has gradually been a shift away from mechanical metaphors that talked about biological and human relations in terms of aggregates, entities, atoms, individuals, closed systems, linear causality, and so on (Wilden, 1975). The new vocabulary employs such terminology as *wholes, interdependent structures, open systems, feedback, information,* and *communication* (Wilden, 1975). Although this shift in epistemology is a contemporary phenomenon, it has historical roots that go back several centuries (Chomsky, 1968; Taylor, 1971). Even as early as Descartes, there was a belief that mechanical metaphors in their nascent state could not explain the complexities of the mind in terms of quantity—that, rather, a qualitative dimension was necessary in any adequate form of explanation. It has taken well over two centuries to replace a traditional and quantitative epistemology with a multidimensional viewpoint of levels and complexity that necessarily involves a comprehension of qualitative considerations as a prerequisite for any quantitative analysis (Wilden, 1975). Dagenais (1972) notes that structuralism rose out of the amalgam of psychology, anthropology, and sociology, passed through the science of linguistics, and has passed back into psychology, psychoanalysis, anthropology, and sociology.

To summarize, structuralism in its psychological and linguistic manifestations represents a substantial change in orientation from classical logical empiricism. In contrast to the methods of behavioral psychology, for example, it does not attempt to order phenomena at the level of empirical events with the objective of demonstrating causality between events. Instead, the method of structuralism seeks, through a process of interpretive abstraction, to tease out the underlying structure of phenomena. Its controlling metaphor is *organism* rather than *physical systems*. It therefore draws its interpretive language from *biology* rather than *physics*, freely utilizing global evolutionary concepts as part of its interpretive system.[4] Structuralism deviates markedly from mechanism at the level of epistemology. The "structures" that are articulated by structuralists are "wholes" or "totalities." A structure is, therefore, more than the sum of its parts. Historically, it is an offshoot of Cartesian rationalism and Kantian *a priorism*. By postulating the existence of *a priori* categories (i.e., structures), which are *active* organizing principles for knowledge acquisition and so on, this method at least concedes something to the notion that meaning is constituted by actors. This is achieved, unfortunately, by severing the link between the ideas of subjectivity and of consciousness (Sullivan, 1980a). In fact, around the issue of the importance of the subjective intentions of actors (i.e., agents), structuralists are anti-phenomenological (Petit, 1975; Piaget, 1971). Structuralists, by and large, reject the standpoint of a psychology based on *intention* of *agents*. The articulation of the structures is from the viewpoint of the social scientist articulating the structure and is not the point of view of those who are studied. As we shall see shortly, this is one of the dimensions in which structuralism differs from a personal metaphor that incorporates the conscious intentions of agents as part of its interpretative practice.

Functionalism

A functionalist position, as I understand it in a psychological context, considers mental processes of sense perception, emotion, volition, and thought as functions of the biological organism in its adaptational effort to influence and to control its environment. Specifically, where psychology has been concerned, this orientation has been involved with the articulation of "traits" that are considered to be adaptive or maladaptive for individual and societal survival. Human traits *per se*, within this perspective, are considered to be adaptive organs.

Intelligence Testing. Although many human traits have been of interest to psychological research (e.g., intelligence, altruism, competitiveness, agression, etc.), by far the most important trait to have been studied is that of intelligence. A broad definition of *intelligence* is "a trait of cognitive judgment that is present in degrees in individuals and groups and is said to have adaptive significance."

---

[4]It must be pointed out that behaviorists have also been introduced to evolutionary theories. Nevertheless, in contrast to organic metaphors, the use of evolutionary concepts is mostly tacit rather than explicit.

The emphasis on degrees expresses the fact that intelligence may be considered a quantitative trait that can be measured and assessed. The testing movement also assumed that individuals and groups had more or less of that trait. Proponents of the testing movement and the testers proper assumed themselves to be in a value-neutral position when making assessments and comparisons between different groups of people. It is within the context of this movement that the nature–nurture controversy was carried out in the past and is still active in the present (e.g., Jensen's 1969 position). The assessment of traits was accomplished through a set of standardized tests based on large-sample statistical comparisons. Because of the pretense of value neutrality, the testers could legitimate broad social policy questions from a position of dispassionate interest. IQ testers assumed themselves to be generating "objective evidence about different population norms." Kamin (1974) has demonstrated the bias of the testing movement and its essentially conservative political functions. It helped to justify essentially repressive policies about different groups and races. Kamin's (1974) historical treatment of the early tester reveals them as essentially racist and sexist by today's standards (e.g., Jews were considered by some testers as an inferior race, thus justifying specific immigration policies).

The assumptions of the testing movement were that certain traits, and their presence or absence in different populations, were socially adaptive to this movement, essentially wedding a functionalist biological perspective to important social questions (e.g., immigration policy, school placement, work placement, etc.). What is important to note here is the position that the testers took vis-à-vis the individuals or groups they were testing. The "objective test" was designed by the tester and usually defined what was adaptive or maladaptive in advance of any conception of adaptation that those tested might have had. The assumptions of what was adaptive or maladaptive were defined in an ethnocentric manner unknown to the testers, since they assumed a certain world view as superior (i.e., white Anglo-Saxon). This nonreflexive approach is still very much apparent in current objective testing. The ethnocentrism of the testing movement has also seriously underestimated the diversity of the linguistic world of cultural groups.

Another variant of psychological functionalism is the whole area of trait differences that has developed around differences between men and women. Of recent popularity is the work of Horner (1972) on the study of women, which explores what she postulates as a motive to "avoid success." Thus, achievement in a social setting is reduced to a social/psychological trait, presumably, more ascendant in women and accounting for their reputed lack of success in achievement settings. The argument for the "fear of success" motive follows a form common to biological functional metaphors. Eichler (1979) captures this form succinctly:

> One biological difference between the sexes, presumed or real, is seized upon and universally applied to all human interactions, be it a metabolic difference between the

> sexes, a hormonal difference, or a general inferiority of development in women.
> (Eichler, 1979, p. 336)

In continuing this position, Eichler (1979) maintains that it is not possible, in principle, to explain social relations in raw biological terms. Conceding that biological factors can play a role in determining social relations (e.g., longevity, infant mortality rates, etc), she nevertheless stresses that these biological conditions in humans are mediated through culture. This is the position I will develop in further detail when gender is discussed more thoroughly in a later chapter.

Sociobiology. The most recent discussion of an interdisciplinary inquiry called "sociobiology" has redirected the focus on cognitive traits such as intelligence to those personality traits that enhance the cohesion of human groups (e.g., altruism) or detract from group cohesiveness (e.g., aggression, competitiveness). This emphasis is partly in response to a perceived crisis in cultural solidity that has accrued historically from the traits encouraging an unrestricted and overriding individualism (Campbell, 1975). Here it is necessary to give to the reader a provisional definition of *sociobiology* so that there is a context for our discussion of it as an organic metaphor. Caplan (1978) defines it as follows:

> Sociobiology is the latest and most strident of a series of efforts in the biological sciences to direct scientific and humanistic attention toward the question of what is, fundamentally, the nature of human nature. Sociobiologists believe that evolutionary inquiry into the origins and developments of social behavior in organisms will shed great light on traditional philosophical puzzles concerning the ability of humans to be both influenced by and freed from the limits set by their biological constitutions. (p. 2)

The recent publication of Wilson's (1975) Pulitzer Prize-winning book *Sociobiology* represents an attempt to establish the social sciences as a branch of evolutionary biology. The potential relevance of this field for psychologists can be seen from a recent presidential address given to the American Psychological Association (Campbell, 1975). In this address, Campbell encourages every psychologist to own this volume, whether she or he agrees with it or not. Campbell (1975) takes from sociobiology the broad evolutionary framework that it offers and the desire to interpret human social processes within a biological rather than mechanical framework. Critics of sociobiology see important and vexing questions arising when biological, organic, evolutionary metaphors move into the areas that distinctly characterize the human (i.e., rationality, morality, culture, mentality, linguistic ability, and intentionality). Caplan (1978) asks whether it is possible to explain priorities such as these by means of purely biological parameters. Campbell, responding in the affirmative, encourages psychologists to pursue the broad outlines of a sociobiology in their own specific work. Campbell (1975) ventures a dialectical treatment of biological and social evolutionary perspectives and tries to assess the significance of social norms and institutions for individuals, with special emphasis on altruistic traits. He assumes, as does Wilson, that our behavior is a product of evolutionary adaptation and is probably designed to maintain a stabilizing effect in a society. He also assumes, with Wilson, that humans have achieved a very high level of cooperation with little sacrifice of personal survival. Cooperation, it is assumed, may well confer a "selective advantage." Two conclusions about humans stem from the "genetics of altruism":

> (1) Human Urban social complexity has been made possible by social evolution rather than biological evolution. (2) This social evolution has had to counter individual selfish tendencies which biological evolution has continued to select as a result of genetic competition among cooperators. (Campbell, 1975, p. 115)

Campbell (1975) assumes that humans have selfish tendencies because biological evolution would select these as a result of interindividual genetic competition. Social order is achieved through norms for altruism derived from social evolutionary processes, as contrasted to biological evolution. These altruistic norms function to override or limit genetic selfishness.

I am not here developing an extensive critique of sociobiology, since it would divert us from our primary purpose. I mention Campbell's suggestions because he is attempting to show the relevance of a sociobiological perspective to psychologists. I do, however, question the ultimate utility of the superordinate use of organic metaphors, such as are used in the superorganic perspectives suggested by sociobiological orientations. My eventual discussion of a personal metaphor suggests that the reductionism implied by mechanical and organic metaphors is ultimately shortsighted for an integrated conception of the human. My own contention in developing a metaphor of the personal is the assumption that human language is an essential and irreducible constitutive element in our understanding of humans. In criticizing sociobiology, Sahlens (1976) brings out the point I am making here:

> If we were to disregard language, culture would differ from animal tradition only in degree. But precisely because [of] this "involvement with language"—a phrase hardly befitting serious scientific discourse—cultural social life differs from the animal in kind. It is not just the expression of an animal of another kind. The reason why human social behavior is not organized by the individual maximization of genetic interest is that human beings are not socially defined by *organic qualities* [my italics] but in terms of symbolic attributes; and a symbol is precisely a meaningful value— such as "close kinship" or "shared blood"—which cannot be determined by the physical properties of that to which it refers. (p. 61)

My treatment of sociobiology in its possible psychological manifestations is all too brief, largely because this is an emergent rather than realized format of theory and research for psychologists. Because of some of its inviting features, I thought it appropriate to at least mention its potential relevance as a new type of organic orientation. It is not an orientation that this book shares, and I see in it problems common to all organic metaphors. In summary, let me elucidate some of the problems.

The use of the term *organic metaphor* in understanding human development has its source in the thinking of Aristotle (MacMurray, 1961). Aristotle's conception of the infant human was that it is an animal organism which becomes rational and acquires a human personality in the process of growing up (MacMurray, 1961). Our own cultural way of thinking has been deeply influenced by the Aristotelian way of thinking, and this use of biological analogies and organic categories has been strongly reinforced by the organic philosophies of the 19th century and the consequent development of evolutionary biology, of which sociobiology is its latest exemplar. Because of the large sweep of evolutionary conceptions and categories, they at first appear as appealing alternative outlooks to metaphors that are more mechanical in nature. Evolutionary conceptions are usually more synthetic than the traditionally analytic mode of thinking characteristic of mechanical metaphors. As a central ordering principle, the organic metaphor is peculiarly reticent on where ethics and the practical life are to be placed within its framework. In the end, it usually becomes an ethics of survival based on the assumption that all organisms adapt in order to survive. Although very sophisticated systems of ethics have been built on this premise, it nevertheless presents some serious problems for the guidance of our practical life. MacMurray (1961), in asserting the primacy of the personal as a central ordering metaphor for our understanding of the human world, has this to say of all conceptions that place superordinate emphasis on the organic conception of adaptation:

> We are not organisms, but persons. The nexus of relations which unites us in a human society is not organic but personal. Human behavior cannot be understood, but only caricatured, if it is represented as an adaptation to environment; and there is no such process as social evolution but, instead, a history which reveals a precarious development and possibilities both of progress and of retrogression . . . the personal necessarily includes an organic aspect . . . and this organic aspect is continuously qualified by its conclusion, so that it cannot even by properly abstracted, except through a prior understanding of the personal structure in which it is an essential, though subordinate component. A descent from the personal is possible, in theory, and indeed in practice; but there is no way to ascend from the organic to the personal. The organic conception of man excludes, by its very nature, all the characteristics in virtue of which we are human beings. To include them we must change our categories afresh from the beginning. (MacMurray, 1961, pp. 46–47)

When we speak here of the inadequacies of the mechanical and the organic as metaphors for our understanding of the human, we do not mean, therefore, that they are totally inappropriate and lacking in merit. No doubt, there are certain aspects of human behavior which can be understood within the prisms of mechanism or organism. As symbolic animals, human beings partly become the symbols they behold. For example, in serious psychopathological occurrences, people have been known to conceive of themselves as machines. I am saying that there is something about the human world which defies that characterization, and we are thus allowed to consider this type of psychopathological process as aberrant. I would contend with MacMurray (1961) that the use of mechanical and organic metaphors is, and should be, restricted in a very real sense. Where useful, they must be embedded in a more complex dialectical metaphor that treats the communicative process in humans as a unique and singular kind of human activity which should subordinate and never be subordinated to organic and mechanical language.

It must be understood that our choice of metaphors is first and foremost a moral rather than intellectual choice. In saying this, one does not preclude intelligence but rather includes cognitional activity as part of moral choice. Our moral choices assume that humans are not only made but also make themselves. In the absence of anything else, mechanical and organic metaphorical devices mask out important human ethical concerns. They are, as I have briefly demonstrated, lacking in critical intent and reflexivity. Until now, my own critical stance on various psychological metaphors leaves the reader with a vacuum. As such, critique does not fill the vacuum it creates. It is, therefore, incumbent upon critics to propose a positive program or alternative. At least, this is the position taken in this work. Accordingly, we move on to a thumbnail sketch of a metaphor we are calling the "personal."

THE PERSONAL METAPHOR

How can one call the personal a metaphor in distinction to the analogues of mechanism and organism? I will develop the idea that the personal metaphor is exemplified in the very process of human communication itself (i.e., language). Since language assumes reciprocity (i.e., communications are always between people), one can say that the unit of analysis is not an individual actor or monad but rather a relationship of *dialogue*. In other words, the "unit of analysis" is a totality (I–thou) that cannot be broken down further without losing the core metaphor of communication. For conventional psychology, this is a radical departure. This will be made clear as I go on. For now, let me offer a provisional definition for the position I am developing as that of a critical interpretation of the personal world that will demand a further explication of the personal world and an *emergent* role for the psychologist as critical interpreter.

The Personal World

The conception of personal world that I am developing must be clearly distinguished from a conception of the personal which is oriented toward the exploration of subjectivity. Much of phenomenological and humanistic perspectives are oriented toward the exploration of subjectivity. My contention is that this is a reaction, in the extreme, to objectivistic psychology (e.g., behaviorism). Without denying the importance of the subject and his or her consciousness, the position developed here is primarily and superordinately focused on language and its cultural functions. Emphasis on language reveals the importance of the relational quality of the personal world that I am attempting to develop. Some preliminary distinctions are therefore in order to prevent unnecessary confusion.

First of all, let me distance myself from what I will call the "politics of subjectivity." For psychology, this politic represents a countercultural vein in conventional psychology identified broadly as humanistic psychology. I situate it as a neoromantic revolt in the 1960s against the technical control rationality so prevalent in behaivorism. The politics of subjectivity issuing from this romantic impulse are well known in humanistic circles:

> Subjective feelings and states have become the only aspects of experience that can be trusted and that really matter. As the world around us appears increasingly remote and inaccessible, we seek refuge in self-absorption, contacted by an ideology that claims this to be the only route to self-fulfillment. This era of radical subjectivity is at once the logical extension of an unbridled individualism and a response to the hollowness of the social relations which a society based upon such individualism has brought about. (Cagan, 1978, p. 232)

The political impulse, generated by this neoromantic revolt against objectivity and its corresponding technologism, was a deliberate emphasis on private consciousness. This privatization of consciousness has been severely criticized as an inadequate alternative to technological rationality (see Cagan, 1978; Jacoby, 1975; Sennett, 1976). This preoccupation with the self lacks a historical dimension that I will attempt to develop as the cultural. Jacoby's (1975) critique of subjective politics is that it identifies the person as existing in a no man's land of free-floating interpersonal relations. I would agree that the critical path to the personal world lies elsewhere, penetrating the categories of individual and society, not merely juggling them. "The individual, before it can determine itself, is determined by the relations in which it is enmeshed. It is a fellow-being before it's a being" (Jacoby, 1975, p. 34).

That, in a nutshell, is the conception of the personal I will be attempting to develop. Our entry point will be language rather than subjectivity. With language preeminent, communication becomes an essential feature of this metaphor, and it reveals the fundamental *relational* quality of a metaphor based on "persons in relation" (MacMurray, 1957):

> Speech is public. It is at once thought and action, or rather a unity of which "mental" and "physical" activity are distinguishable but inseperable aspects; and as a result it establishes communication, and introduces the you as a correlative of the "I." For if

this "I think" logically excludes the second person, the "I say" is logically incomplete. To complete it we must formulate it as follows: I say to you, and I await your response. Thus the problem of the form of the personal emerges as the problem of the form of communication. (p. 74)

The peculiar task of a psychological discipline in this regard would be in the development of some form of systematic interpretation of these communicative expressions or human acts. We are, therefore, talking about an interpretative psychology (see Gauld & Shotter, 1977; Shotter, 1975). The whole issue of an interpretative psychology needs elucidation, and I will commence upon this essential task shortly.

The focus on language as opposed to subjectivity also calls for a shift in thinking as to what is to be the primary unit of analysis for our theoretical and research efforts. The conception of a personal world herein assumes that the primary unit of analysis is the person or the individual. At the same time the individual is not considered as an isolated monad. Our emphasis on the personal does not preclude larger structural entities (e.g., class structure, gender, etc.).

It serves notice that the personal expression is a fundamental entity within this framework and cannot be excluded for any research or theoretical experiences (e.g., Skinner and much of behaviorism). At the same time, this interpretation of individual expressions is not individualistic or egocentric in nature (see MacMurray, 1957; Sampson, 1977, 1981). We are assuming that the individual expressions or symbols are for purposes of communication; therefore, the unit of analysis must be a "you and I" rather than an isolated "I." Our assumption is that individuals use expressions because they intend meanings for others. Expressions are *ambiguous* because the meaning or significance of expressions is contingent upon multiple actors communicating with one another. Humans, it would appear, are peculiar animals involved in webs of significance that they themselves have spun (Geertz, 1973). "Webs of significance" is another way of saying that meaning is multiple or ambiguous, inviting interpretation. A human culture may be defined as a web of significance. Because of the intricate nature of human cultural expressions, it is accepted that the analysis of meaning within an interpretive perspective will not be adequately characterized with an experimental science in search of laws, but rather with a self-consciously interpretive search for meaning (Geertz, 1973). One of the persistent problems of interpretative approaches is their tendency to resist, or be permitted to resist, conceptual articulation and thus to escape systematic modes of assessment (Geertz, 1973). It is crucially important in the development of a self-reflexively interpretive psychology to resist that type of ambiguity which tends to obscure meaning. It is, therefore, necessary to attempt to spell out some of the parameters for an interpretive psychology so that it can be evaluated alongside other suggested approaches.

Interpretation. It has been suggested that psychologists consider themselves "hermeneuts" (Hudson, 1972), after the Greek god Hermes, the "interpreter." Interpretation is an activity that deals with the relational quality of communication. It is an attempt to understand the meaning of symbols. Interpretation attempts to make clear or give the sense of an object of study (Taylor, 1971). Normally it is considered a process that clarifies or renders the meaning of a text; but it can be extended to "text analogues" (e.g., a human person or community or culture) which, in some way at first sight, appears unclear, perplexing, confused, incomplete, cloudy, seemingly contradictory in one way or another. Interpretation aims to bring to light an underlying coherence or sense (Taylor, 1971).

Descartes. The *Discourse on Method* (1637/1960) is the most systematic attempt to eliminate interpretation. Paradoxically, it is an interpretative system nevertheless. In it, Descartes outlines four rules for achieving certainty and eliminating ambiguity:

> The first rule was to accept as true nothing that I did know to be evidently so; that is to say, to avoid carefully precipitancy and prejudice, and to apply my judgments to nothing but that which showed itself so clearly and distinctly to my mind that I should never have occasion to doubt it.
>
> The second was to divide each difficulty I should examine into as many parts as possible, and as would be required the better to solve it.
>
> The third was to conduct my thoughts in an orderly fashion, starting with what was simplest and easiest to know, and rising little by little to the knowledge of the most complex, even supposing an order where there is no natural precedence among the objects of knowledge.
>
> The last rule was to make so complete an enumeration of the links in an argument, and to pass them all so thoroughly under review, that I could be sure I missed nothing. (p. 47)

The first rule establishes methodological *agnosticism* or doubt as a principle for the acquisition of knowledge. Its contemporary counterpart would be the null hypothesis in statistics. The second rule establishes *atomism* as an ordering principle. The third rule establishes *hierarchy* as a principle of composition. And finally, the last rule establishes *induction* and *deduction* as superordinate logical procedures (for example, in distinction to some form of "dialectical logic").

Descartes' methodic doubt was to reflect a demand for certainty which accepted as true only those expressions or ideas that could be said to have achieved *clarity* and *distinction*. Ultimately, Descartes, the mathematician, found clarity and certainty in mathematical expressions. Clear and distinct ideas had no need of interpretation; their coherence or meaning would be self-evident. Descartes wanted assurance and a firm footing for knowledge. For the problem of interpretation is, basically, how we gain assurance that our interpretation of a situation is true or verifiable. By accepting interpretation as a real problem rather than denying it, as Descartes ultimately did, we are left with the fact that we understand expressions or ideas by referring to other expressions or ideas. In other words, we are left with what Descartes tried to eliminate: that is, the "hermeneutical or interpretive circle":

> The circle can be put in part–whole relations; we are trying to establish a reading for
> the whole text and for this we appeal to readings of its partial expressions and yet
> because we are dealing with meaning, with making sense, where expressions only
> make sense or not in relation to others the reading of partial expression depends on
> those of others, and ultimately of the whole. (Taylor, 1971, p. 6)

The circularity of this process has been a sore point where certainty has been the legacy of the Cartesian methodological synthesis. In this methodological world outlook, the method that led to truth and certainty was the one that was allied to propositions or events which were "clear and distinct."

As this method has developed over the centuries in all its guises, it has usually been allied with all methodological outlooks that eschew *ambiguity of expressions* and has attempted to relieve the embarrassment of conflict of interpretations by supplying a method which believes that it can achieve certainty (truth) over interpretation. In the context of our present discussion, this ideal of *certainty* demands that the "hermeneutical circle" must be broken out of because it is a vicious circle (Unger, 1976).

Empiricism and rationalism are two historical ways of attempting to break out of the hermeneutical or interpretative circle. Both these methods are descendants of the Cartesian mind–body dualism. Thus, Western thought may be said to be limited to a fund of basic schemes of explanations; ultimately they can, with all their variations, be boiled down to two ideal types—logical analysis (i.e., rationalism), and causal explanation (i.e., empiricism) (Unger, 1976). Both schemes provide an interpretation of what it means to account for something both in the sense of telling what a phenomenon or event is like, which is description, and in the sense of establishing why it had to follow from something else, which is *explanation* in the strict sense. Both these schemes appear historically in order to deal with the *interpretation* of physical and social events (Unger, 1976). The position being developed in this chapter proceeds under the assumption that psychology is, whether it likes to be or not, an interpretative science. Taylor contends that historically these two *schemes of interpretation* came to be what they were because of the problems presented by *conflicts in interpretation*. Rationalism is essentially the use of deduction. In deduction, certainty is achieved by grasping the inner certainty of propositions. The method of deduction is logical analysis, which is a linear development of arguments. Objectivity or certainty is gained by retreating to a "truth" that is formal and abstracted from concrete historical events. The conclusion in a deductive sequence is, therefore, a formal truth. The methodological thrust of rationalism is to bring understanding (i.e., clear and true interpretation) to an inner clarity that is absolute (i.e., logical argument). Rationalism provides an ordering principle that exists at the level of ideas (Taylor, 1971). It is essentially an ahistorical method of arriving at certainty. Empiricism is a method for arriving at truth at the level of events in history. In contrast to strict rationalism, its truths are time-bound and concrete. It argues linearly at the level of cause and effect, the cause in a time sequence being antecedent to the effect.

Empiricism attempts to break out of the circle of interpretation by attempting to move beyond the problem presented by human subjectivity. Empiricism as a method systematically attempts to reconstruct knowledge in such a way that there is no need to appeal to readings or judgments. For this reason the basic building block of empiricism is the sensory impression or sense datum that psychologists have come to know as the stimulus. At the level of perception, the stimulus is a unit of information that is supposedly not mediated by judgment (Peirce, 1934). Subjectivity is played down within this formulation by alluding to the organism as a *tabula rasa* (Ausubel & Sullivan, 1970; Ausubel, Sullivan, & Ives, 1980). At the sensory level of *brute datum*, it is therefore perceived to be unnecessary to utilize subjective interpretation or judgment. Empiricism as a methodological ideal wants certainty anchored beyond subjective intuition.

One other important feature in the quest for certainty is that its ultimate test is to be found in the individual consciousness. In Descartes' time, this was tantamount to a rejection of scholasticism, which saw truth as resting on the testimony of sages and of the Catholic Church (Gadamer, 1975a). In its more generic form, this was the rejection of historical tradition for an ahistorical alignment of truth within a contemporaneous individualist consciousness. In retrospect, one can see the Cartesian legacy as the beginning of the methods of modern natural science. This was a historical circumstance, which is too often forgotten. The legacy of Descartes represents a bridge into modern consciousness that is exemplified in the qualification of the scientific world view. Gadamer articulates the historical movement of a scientific empiricism. The importance of scientific method consists in the fact that, by its own definition, it investigates only by elaborating questions accessible for mathematical abstraction and mea-surement or its equivalents (Hodges, 1969). One could say, then, that this is the Cartesian legacy.

Vico. In spite of the momentum of a world view wedded to methods from the natural sciences, Descartes had a contemporary, Vico, who was to propose an alternative, based on historical methods, to the natural science methods in the study of the human. In his treatise *The New Science* (1725/1970), Vico attempted to outline a "science of the human" based on *history* rather than *nature.* The "new science" was to be peculiar to human nature: a science of humanity whose dominant framework was to contrast in some crucial ways with the Cartesian synthesis (Belaval, 1969). He concluded that an approach to human studies could not be made by methods of detached observation but only by *understanding* and *interpretation.* Thus, events in the human sciences would be understood *sympathetically* rather than from a position of *detached observa-*

tion (Berlin, 1976). Vico criticized the Cartesian synthesis because it, in its methodological outlook, systematically obliterates the importance of personal and cultural history which is, in essence, cultural memory. The role of the image (i.e., imagination) is also curtailed by the Cartesian critical spirit (Gadamer, 1975b). It was Vico's conviction that Descartes' criteria of "clear and distinct" ideas could not be properly applied outside the fields of mathematics and natural science (Rickman, 1969). Systematic use of historical methods would clearly be needed to explore the full range of human capabilities and the institutional life that ensued from these capabilities. Sympathy as identification was contrasted with the Cartesian method of doubt. We are able to know and identify with persons and institutions because we are part of their makeup. To interpret and come to understand human institutions, it would, therefore, demand a more anthropological perspective at an institutional level and a use of biographical and ethnographic methods at the level of the personal.

The legacy of Vico from a historical perspective follows a different historical line from the Cartesian one. Gadamer has traced these polar tensions into the latter part of the 20th century from a historical perspective while at the same time providing a strong rationale for use of interpretive (hermeneutical) methods. He essentially resurrects the issue of a "human science" in his attempt to understand historical texts. He draws his impetus from the 19th-century German version of the Descartes–Vico tension, which was directed toward the issue of how there could be a truly human science. These issues are discussed in much greater detail and acumen in his masterwork, *Truth and Method* (Gadamer, 1975b). Suffice to say, he picks up on the tradition in German thought, pioneered by German 18th-century historians, which advocated a science of humanity based on sociohistorical reality made meaningful because it consists of expression of human thoughts, intentions, feelings, and valuations. In the tradition of Vico, this line of thinking provided a rationale for studying phenomena as autobiography and biography, where methods used by historians are most appropriate (Gadamer, 1975b). In short, we see here the contrast of the classical world view with that of the hermeneutical or interpretive.

Although these polar tensions have been experienced in continential European thought, especially German thought at the turn of the century, the development of the discipline of American psychology appeared to have sidestepped this antinomy. American psychology brushed over this controversy because of its easy embrace of the scientific and technological perspective.

Normative Science. The antinomy between Descartes and Vico represents real historical moments that are conflictual in nature, concerning conceptions of truth, objectivity, and rationality and the superordinate method of arriving at what is true (is) and what is good (ought). The Cartesian synthesis operates out of an epistemological horizon: How do I know that I know? Vico represents the opposing horizon of starting from the horizon of normative categories: How do I know what to do? Here the philosophical horizon is viewed from the stand point of the practical. In using the term *practical* here, we do not mean to convey the sense of a technological pragmatism. How I know what to do is not simply a pragmatic consideration. Using the question of "what to do" signifies a priority given to the normative (ought) over, but not excluding, the epistemological concern (regarding what is).

The shift to a psychology ventured from a normative standpoint is no mere conceptual shift. It involves substantial changes in practice which, at present, are unfamiliar territory for psychologists trained in the "mainstream." Shotter (1975) dramatizes this point:

> The new psychology of action we propose requires, thus, not just a change of content compared with old, but a radical new form of thought and mode in investigatory activity. It aims at producing not publicly shared objective knowledge, but intersubjectively shared understandings, not discovered by individuals searching in the world above, but made and agreed upon by people working in dialogue together. (p. 135)

It is clear that the dominant interest of psychology as a discipline, up to this point in its short history, has been weighted toward the epistemological horizon. The position I will ultimately articulate in this book will reflect a shift to the normative; that is, the overriding initial concerns will be seen from the standpoint of action. In order to clear the ground for this, it will be necessary here to figure that we are shifting horizon or standpoint (Lonergan, 1957). The type of inquiry I am suggesting is, in a sense, a different kind of science. Habermas (1972) characterizes part of the shift I am taking as historical-hermeneutic:

> The historical hermeneutic sciences view knowledge in a different methodological framework. Here the meaning of the validity of propositions is not constituted in the frame of reference of technical control. The levels of formalized language and objectified experience have not yet been divorced. For theories are not constructed deductively and experience is not organized with regard to the success of operations. Access to the facts is provided by the understanding of meaning, not observation. The verification of lawlike hypotheses in the empirical–analytic sciences has its counterpart here in the interpretation of texts. Thus the rules of hermeneutics determine the possible meaning of the validity of statements of the cultural sciences. (Habermas, 1972, p. 309)

Cultural Science and the Personal World. Habermas (1972) above uses the appellation "cultural sciences." This is most appropriate in the conception of the personal world as will be developed in this work. From the perspective that I will be developing, the personal world is the cultural world; culture is the womb in which personhood grows and transforms. When I say grows and transforms, I am not speaking from the point of view of an organic metaphor. When one speaks of personal growth, that is saying that the personal world is cultivated within cultural forms. By cultural forms, I mean specified lived histories which constitute the relational totality of the personal world. Thus, the relational totality of the "you and I" confirms that the personal world is cultural from the ground up. For me the notion of the personal world as cultural means that personhood is not an abstract entity. My personality expresses my cultural history. To know me, it will be necessary to know a certain species called "male Irish-American Catholic." That appellation alone covers a multitude of evils and many strengths. I'll speak no more of either, but the reader can take the liberty of reading between the lines as my position develops.

   Critical Interpretation. The cultural world of the personal is the world of the stuff which makes for biography and ethnography. It is the world of the lived experience that phenomenologists speak of in their writings. To stop at this point is a radical departure from mainstream psychology. Much of what constitutes phenomenological psychology remains here. We must go further. Culture always exists in dynamic social relations of power. To ignore power relations means that such structural concepts as class structure, gender structures, and so on can be sidestepped in our study of the personal world. A psychological inquiry will be critical if its interpretative system encompasses relationships of power. To deal with power relations, one must introduce structure concepts (e.g., class structure) which are dialectically related to the cultural dimensions specific to distinct but related cultural worlds (e.g., Irish and English). Specifically, the reader will be engaged in a dialectical synergy of the principles of *analysis* and *synthesis.* The analysis of culture, which is the pole of the personal world, is set off and polarized with the structural dimensions of class structure, gender structures, race, and so on. In other words, it is understood at the outset that the personal phenomenological world of actors within cultures is embedded in larger structural totalities of class, gender, race, and so forth which involve relationships of power. The role of critical interpretation is to draw attention to these power relations and bring to light inequities of power. The interest of critical interpretation is *emancipatory*; that is, it challenges the stases of social relations where there are gross inequities in power. The task of critical interpretation, although epistemological, is first and foremost normative. When Marx (1844/1963) said that the role of philosophy is not simply to interpret the world but to change it ("11th Thesis on Feuerbach"), he was, in essence, saying that philosophy should be a normative enterprise. The same can be said for psychology as a social science endeavor. For most of its short history, it has hidden behind the concept of "value-neutral" inquiry in sidestepping the normative dimension. Value neutrality can no longer be sustained as a value position since it has become increasingly clear that it is an ideology sustaining a technical–control rationality (Habermas, 1970). Here, *ideology* means a suppressed interest that is either denied or not seen. Technical–control rationality activity sunders the distinction between the practical and the technical and represses the ethical dimension within it (Habermas, 1970). Depoliticized at the level of theory and theory language, the effectively neutral position masks political intentions. A critical look at behaviorism (Danziger, 1978), structuralism (Buck-Morse, 1975; Gardner, 1972; Sullivan, 1977a, 1977b, 1980a, 1981; Venn & Walkerdine, 1978; Wilden, 1975), psychometric psychology (Hunt & Sullivan, 1974; Kamin, 1974) and sociobiology (Caplan, 1978) gives ample evidence that social science theories are intricately involved in value issues and have broad social policy implications. At the level of superstructure, social science theories are "legitimators" of the status quo, that is, they render interpretations which back up or legitimate a certain sociopolitical constellation of power (Habermas, 1970). The position developed here makes no claims for being value-neutral. We hope that it systematically serves an emancipatory interest by the development of what we are calling "a critical interpretative science of the personal." The question now arises, how does criticism relate to interpretation? Bernstein (1971) locates the line of thinking for a critically interpretative social science in Marx and Hegel:

> It has the power not of delineating some utopian ideal which is to be striven for, but revealing to men a critical understanding of what they were suffering. Unless criticism does this, it becomes idle speculation; the test of the correctness of a radical critique is its ability to bring genuine human problems suffered by man to a self-conscious human form. (Bernstein, 1971, p. 54)

Although my own treatment of critical interpretation does not eschew the utopian, I nevertheless agree that one important aspect of critical interpretation is to bring to awareness (i.e., interpretation) systems of power relations under which people suffer. This makes critical interpretation a *normative* endeavor. The primacy of the *normative* over the *epistemological* is a radical shift in thinking from Descartes and Kant (Bernstein, 1971):

> It is not by any superficial or careless reasoning that most modern thinkers have been led to maintain dichotomies between the is and the ought, the descriptive and the prescriptive, fact and value. In a variety of ways, philosophers have argued that whatever status we assign values, norms, and ideals, they are not objective phenomena to be discovered in nature. Science, our most powerful and successful means for exploring nature, can tell us only what is, it can describe, explain, predict, but cannot tell us in any categorical sense what ought to be. If we want to find the philosophical arguments in support of such a position, we need only study the works of most of the major figures or movements in philosophy since Descartes. Hume (in some of his moods), Kant, classical materialism, logical positivism and empiricism are all agreed about this "dogma." But it is precisely this dogma that is the focal point of Marx (and Hegel's) attack. (p. 71)

From the Greeks to Descartes, we have clearly witnessed a historical shift moving from the Greek preoccupation with the ethical to a preoccupation with epistemological categories. By the time we reach the 18th century, these categories or dimensions of human existence (i.e., the true and the good) have developed an almost separate status from one another. By the time that Kant comes to deal with these dimensions of human life, he is able to treat them under three separate critiques. His *Critique of Pure Reason* essentially deals with epistemological categories and their truth status. His *Critique of Practical Reason* treats separately the category of the ethical. His other critique, which we will not discuss here, deals with the "esthetic." The important point we wish to note about this great thinker is that by the time we have reached his synthesis, one sees the almost complete separation of ethics from epistemology. This is not to say that, in the case of Kant, the ethical is bypassed. For this great thinker, the practical was close to his heart, so much so that he would write a whole critique on the importance of ethical questions. By the 20th century, the nascent field of psychology can abandon the ethical category and claim, as with other social sciences, that its task is value-neutral.

Modern psychology, for the most part, completely sidesteps the ethical dimension in its quest for epistemological certainty. This quest unites very strange bedfellows indeed. Hull, Piaget, and Chomsky can all fall under the same umbrella if one considers that all of their theories are preoccupied with the primacy of the epistemological dimension. Even though theories in contemporary psychology differ in some essential ways, they are brought together under one roof by their relative exclusion of the normative dimension. With the primacy of the epistemological category, we also see the relative emphasis of theory over practice. By the time we reach the 19th century, all these are dichotomized in thought and institutionalized in the buregoning social science disciplines. For the social sciences, the development of good theory becomes a raison d'être. They will proudly stand aside and leave the practical life to the philosopher and the lay person.

It may be said without hesitation that psychology, as a disciplined social science in the 20th century, is pre-Hegelian and pre-Marxian in its philosophical predispositions (Sève, 1978). This does not deny that psychology has conflictual elements within this pre-Hegelian synthesis. One of these conflictual elements can be seen in the distinction between mechanical and organic metaphors already discussed in this chapter. In fact, psychology in the 20th century has been caught philosophically between Hume and Kant. To put it another way, it has been caught between mechanistic empiricism and some form of constructive organicism. The noise created by this conflict has masked its pre-Hegelian origins. My proposed orientation to the practical, in effect, shifts the ground to a different level of argumentation and thus to a different level of practice in the discipline. The metaphor of the personal, which we are developing, self-consciously appropriates the dimension of history as an essential ingredient in psychological inquiry. Philosophically, the metaphor of the personal is therefore indebted to both Hegel and Marx. The centrality of history cannot be underestimated when making this change in perspective. In comparing Kant to Marx, Bernstein (1971) emphasizes some crucial differences that make their perspectives tantamount to different points of departure:

Marx would agree that all observation is "theory laden" and that the reality we know
and encounter is conditioned by the "forms of life" that have evolved in human social
institutions. . . . The central motif here can be traced back to Kant who emphasized
the constructive, categorical aspect of judgment. But unlike Kant, Marx does not
believe there is any Ding-an-sich that stands apart from human knowing, and furthermore, Marx would maintain that our basic categories change and develop in history.
Nor is Marx sympathetic with those thinkers who interpret man's cognitive perspective
as an act of individual will or arbitrary convention. What is distinctive about Marx's
reflections on human cognition is the way in which he relates it to the evolution of
man's practical needs as manifested in his social life. It is praxis that turns out to be the
key for understanding the full range of man's developing cognitive activities. (Bernstein, 1971, p. 73)

This shift in horizon initiated by Hegel and Marx is developed in contemporary form by Habermas, working within the broad tradition called the Frank-
furt school. In *Knowledge and Human Interests* (Habermas, 1972), the traditional conception of rationality as "value neutrality" is challenged and put in
historical context.

In this field of inquiry, which is so close to practice, the concept of value-freedom (or
ethical neutrality) has simply reaffirmed the ethos that modern science owes to the
beginnings of theoretical thought in Greek Philosophy. Psychologically an uncondi-
tional commitment to theory and epistemologically the severance of knowledge from
interest. This is represented in the logic by the distinction between descriptive and
prescriptive statements, which makes grammatically obligatory the filtering out of
merely emotive from cognitive content. (Habermas, 1972, p. 303)

Habermas (1972, 1974) introduces the conception of "knowledge constitutive interests," which are by definition shapes of what counts as the objects and
types of knowledge. As a Marxist, Habermas claims that these interests are basic
because they are rooted in specific fundamental conditions of possible reproduction and self-constitution of the human species (Habermas, 1972). Although the
epistemological status of these interests is open to question (see Bernstein, 1978;
McCarthy, 1978), I nevertheless introduce them here because they are suggestive for the development of my present work. Three primary cognitive interests are articulated by Habermas (1972): the technical, the practical, and the
emancipatory. Three types of sciences are articulated corresponding to these
interests:

1. Empirical–analytic sciences
2. Historical hermeneutic sciences
3. Critical emancipatory social sciences

The empirical–analytic sciences, with their emphasis on technical control,
are evident in most examples of mechanical metaphors that we have given. The
conception of the personal I am attempting to develop incorporates a her-

meneutical dimension but at the same time attempts to be emancipatory and critical in nature. It is hermeneutical in nature because it systematically takes as its task the problems posed by the interpretation of symbols. The peculiar task of a psychological discipline in this regard would be in the development of some forms of interpretation to deal with individual life histories embedded in cultural forms. The position that I have been developing as an interpretive psychology starts out with the assumption that individual selves are agents whose actions intend meaning. In contrast to an American ideal that has treated the self as a self-contained individualistic system (Sampson, 1977), I am proposing a unit of analysis that assumes persons in relation (MacMurray, 1957). The unit is a collective, the you-and-I.[5] Meaning is a constitutive element in a relation of I–thou. Therefore, meaning is not simply that of individual actors but is part of the *expressive* relationship between actors.

This is an important shift in perspective and should be noted, since the ontology of most of mainstream social science in the psychological domain lacks this minimal communal perspective (Taylor, 1971). The considerations we are discussing here are currently being pursued by a network of researchers who conceive of their work as a phenomenological approach to psychology (Giorgi, 1970; Giorgi, Fisher, & Murray, 1975). There is much in this phenomenological line of attack with which we are in broad sympathy. Giorgi's (1970) work, for example, is most helpful in shifting the ground away from mechanism. There is, however, a significant omission in this phenomenological emphasis; this is discussed under Habermas's (1972) third cognitive interest—the critical emancipatory interest. This third interest is fundamental to our development of the "personal" and, I believe, allows me to distinguish my position from straightforward phenomenological viewpoints. This accounts for our use of the term *critical* as one of the terms in the title of this book.

A psychology that is "critically interpretative" rests on several assumptions about the whole process of interpretation. First, a critically interpretative psychology is reflexive or self-reflective in nature. It is understood that psychological interpretation is embedded in history and, therefore, that the psychological interpreter must appropriate the responsibility of operating from a biased viewpoint. She or he is prejudiced. My understanding of bias and prejudice does not assume that this situation should be eliminated. A self-reflexive psychology simply takes the responsibility for having a viewpoint or a set of preunderstandings (regarding prejudice). Self-reflexivity in interpretation is simply accepting the reality of viewpoint, bias, and so on, and dealing with the problematic nature of same.

[5]The unit you-and-I is the most primitive term and cannot be reduced. In saying this is a minimum we are saying that the you-and-I can encompass more than simply two people but never less. As a primitive term, the you-and-I indicates that persons are persons in relation. For me, *persons in relation* is another way of saying *culture*. This will be developed in greater detail in Chapter 3.

One assumes that psychological interpretation is embedded in a societal history and not beyond it. Whatever universality that interpretation achieves, it is a universality that is bound by time and space and, therefore, exists to be transcended. Thus, the conception of truth within this context is dynamic rather than static. Second, a psychology based on a critical interpretation of the personal world is fundamentally interested in the concept of freedom and free acts of individuals and groups. In fact, our very definition of the personal world assumes a relational freedom. Thus, instead of considering interpretation to be disinterested, our own conception embodies an emancipatory interest (cf. Habermas, 1972). This conception of psychology is a part of an emancipatory social science. Its uniqueness in contradistinction to conventional social science is its expressed cognitive interest in *emancipation*. The self-reflection of a critical inquiry brings to light social relationships within society based on power and sustained by inequities of power (regarding domination). The emancipatory cognitive interest brings to light these inequities of power (e.g., between men and women) and attempts to provide a system of self-reflection that will end in a transformation of these relationships of domination. (Fowler, 1974)

Psychology, like most social science disciplines, is derivative of social and economic structures in a society. For the most part, what is considered mainstream psychology is a symbolic legitimation of the economic structures in the society (i.e., the social relations embedded in late capitalism). In a nonreflexive way, it has been the apologist for relations in late capitalism (i.e., ideological). In many instances it helps to defuse emancipatory impulses by "blaming the victims" of a particular economic order (Ryan, 1971). Relating an emancipatory interest to a critical conception of the personal, one sees the ascendance of a set of relations between persons and groups that are based on a communication which is not premised on domination and oppression. A practical emancipatory interest "extends to the maintenance of intersubjectivity of mutual understanding as well as to the creation of communication without domination" (Habermas, 1972, p. 113). Of this we will say more. Briefly, a critically interpretative psychology announces social structures which build up a personal world and human projects and denounces, through its interpretations, social structures that destroy the personal as we conceive it.

Prospectus

The discussion of psychological theories as metaphors was intended to locate, in a critical manner, the point of view of a critical interpretative psychology that I am about to develop. Although critical of other psychological positions as metaphors (e.g., mechanical and organic metaphors), I am nevertheless completely aware that my position is not a replacement for these endeavors. No amount of criticism will make a theory or practice go away when it serves certain societal interests. In addition, these positions are embedded in historical intellectual traditions which give them solidity and longevity. The precariousness of my position is that it has no historical roots in the broad discipline of psychology as it is presently understood. In fact, psychology as a discipline is unique from all other social science disciplines in that it completely lacks a critical perspective. Sociology, anthropology, political science, theology, and so on have substantial scholarly interests that support what I would label "critically interpretative" inquiry. Because of this vacuum in the psychological disciplines, I risk the possibility of being written out of most of the discipline's consensus. Many will say I am doing anthropology, sociology, political science, and so forth. I would contend that psychology needs the presence of a critical emancipatory interest and that it must, of necessity, be interdisciplinary in nature. I can only hope that there will be a significant number of psychologists who see the necessity of the point of view I am trying to develop under critical interpretation. If this happens, I will be satisfied.

The following chapters build on one another dialectically. Therefore, consecutive reading of the chapters is in order. The sketch of the personal metaphor in this chapter was thumbnail. By the end of this work, I hope to have developed an in-depth discussion of the personal world and a need for a critically reflexive psychological interpretation to understand it and to help transform it.

2

HUMAN EXPRESSION
A Relational Act

PROLOGUE

A psychology that is self-consciously interpretive and critical will follow the form of what I am calling the personal metaphor. One of the fundamental assumptions of this point of view is that human behavior is understandable only in terms of a dynamic social reference, the purely isolated self being a social fiction (MacMurray, 1957). The peculiar task of a psychological discipline, in this regard, is in the development of some form of systematic interpretation of communicative expressions, which I hold as synonymous with the term *human act*. I am assuming that individual or collective expressions are symbols for purposes of communication. Therefore, the fundamental unit of analysis must be a dyad (you and I) rather than an isolated individual or monad. The contention here is that individuals use expressions because they intend meaning for others.

EXPRESSION

The dictionary defines the term *expression* as an action of pressing out, to press out an act, process, or instance of representing or conveying in words or some other medium. It also notes that expressions are "signs or tokens." Here the term *human expression* in the chapter title indicates the sign quality of human action. This, of course, is in keeping with our emphasis that human expression is essentially and superordinately linguistic in nature. *Relational act* signifies that human expressions are espressions for others. They are communicative acts. The case can be made that all animals are expressive, and we would not argue against that notion here. From an evolutionary perspective, one can say that, in the broadest sense, animal expression is a particular coordinated set of movements that in some way manifests an interior being externally (Merleau-Ponty, 1963).

Tropisms, or certain stylized actions of animals, can be said to be animal expressions peculiar to different species of animals. One thing that will be argued in this chapter is that human expression cannot be subordinated to general biological expressions or mechanical acts. The emphasis in this chapter is to focus on the peculiar characteristics of the human act from the point of view of the actor or agent. This, of course, is a partial perspective. Since human actions are being treated as communicative expressions, our treatment is, of necessity at the outset, limited and incomplete. The following chapter will complete our conception of the human act as relational. We start our treatment by making some crucial distinctions that have already had important consequences in the short history of psychology as a discipline.

The Intelligibility of Human Expressions

Let us return to the distinction we made in our introductory chapter; that is, the distinction between the mechanical, organic, and personal orders. We will be calling these orders *modes of intelligibility* in this chapter.[1] We use the term *intelligible* to mean that human action forms meaningful complexes that are interpretable. An action or set of actions is interpretable if it can be said to fall under some meaningful schema of interpretation. An action is said to lack intelligibility if it cannot be said to fall under some schema or mode of interpretation. An action in an instance of this kind is judged meaningless. It is important here to emphasize the relational quality of intelligibility. An action, in the end, is not intelligible only from the point of view of the agent but is also dependent upon the interpretive schema of those who receive the expression to interpret.

Mechanical Mode. The mechanical mode of intelligibility rests on the assumption of the causality of physical systems. This assumption is that the *cause* of something *precedes the effect* in a process understood to be in temporal contiguity. What I have called "mainstream experimental psychology" rests on the possibility of explaining human behavior within the parameters of a causal process. The mechanical mode of intelligibility, therefore, assumes that human action or behavior can be made intelligible by the attribution of causality between a behavior and a set of antecedent conditions. The independent variable is the antecedent stimulating condition for the dependent variable or response. Usually, the attribution of causality was carried out under highly controlled conditions that specified in advance the antecedent conditions to be manipulated and the *response* to be evaluated or assessed. Within this mode, the response (R)

---

[1]The distinction we are using is made by John MacMurray in *The Self as Agent* and *Persons in Relation*. This distinction is not exclusive to him. Using different terms (i.e., physical, vital, and human orders), Merleau-Ponty presents a similar trilogy in his *Structure of Behavior* and *Phenomenology of Perception*.

was the behavior being assessed as a result of the experimentally controlled manipulation of antecedent stimulus conditions (S). Thus the appellation "S–R psychology." All this rests on several assumptions about the nature of the human act. The first is that human action is a mechanism like other mechanical processes in nature. To see human action as a mechanism in nature is, in essence, to say that human action has no unique status in the natural world. The second assumption rests on the principle of analysis already discussed in the first chapter, and that is that human action can be understood in terms of its more simple components. Following from the preceding assumption is a third, ancilliary assumption, that of reductionism. One assumes here that human behavior can be reduced to biology, biology can be reduced to physiology, and physiology can be reduced to inorganic physical systems. This accounts for the easy embrace of machines as an analogy for making human behavior intelligible. It also explains why animals could easily be substituted for humans for experimental convenience. The fourth major assumption is that all organisms are *patients* as opposed to *agents* in nature. It must be understood that this assumption is one of degree, with considerable variation between psychologists who endorse causal determinism in human behavior.[2] Nevertheless, it may be said that the organism or subject within the experimental setup is a "patient" in the whole process; that is, he or she or it undergoes the program of the experimental procedure. Here we are making the distinction between a patient who undergoes or receives a treatment and the agent who initiates or transforms his or her (or its) conditions. This distinction is important as we consider the ultimate *possibility and feasibility* of understanding human behavior as causally determined. Within the purview of mechanical intelligibility, the free act based on the intention of an agent is considered as irrelevant or as a fiction.

Historically, considering the prominence of experimental psychology, these assumptions have profoundly influenced the brief history of psychology as a discipline. This can easily be seen in the vast majority of what are called "learning theories" (cf. Hilgard & Bower, 1966). Although most early learning theorists of the behaviorist variety recognized different species capacities, their main emphasis remained on the mechanical and repetitive nature of most human as well as animal acts. This can easily be seen by looking at the way these theorists

---

[2]This is clearly seen in the extremes in behavioral psychology as exemplified in the work of Skinner as opposed to the work of, say, Hull and Tolman. The latter, with their intervening variables (e.g., habit, drive, etc.), attempted to deal systematically with some dispositional properties of the organism in the production of behavior. Skinner eschews the necessity of this way of theorizing in his essay "Are Theories of Learning Necessary?" Focusing on Hull for the moment, one can easily see that his intervening variables do not approach the concept of agency that we will be developing. Hull and Tolman always see these intervening variables as linked to the manipulated conditions of the stimulus. The intervening variable is behavioral psychology's closest concept to what might be called "a history."

treated such concepts as insight and understanding. For the moment we are treating these concepts from the point of view of ordinary language. In Thorndike's early work, we see the role of insight present but minimized. In Thorndike's system, insight simply grows out of earlier habits. In contrast, Pavlov finds no use for the term in his system, but one would have to say that his "second-signal system" is an attempt to come to terms with some of the factors related to insightful behavior. Guthrie is only derisive toward the use of any concept that approaches conscious understanding and insight; in Skinner, the term does not occur (Hilgard & Bower, 1966). Hull, Spence, and Osgood attempt to deal with these concepts in terms of "mediational processes" or intervening variables. The process is always linked to previously formed habits. Tolman is the only major behavioral learning theorist to employ the term *insight,* and he can be considered an isolated case, an exception to the rule (Hilgard & Bower, 1966).

The inability to see the organism and the human person proper as an active organizing power limits the scope of our understanding of human behavior. I would not be so foolish as to venture that we are developing a full conception of human nature and its action possibilities, but I nevertheless contend that the mechanical mode of intelligibility is too restrictive in its scope of what constitutes human powers, to the point of denigration. I am not here disagreeing with the fact that much of human behavior is habitual and therefore determined. I am saying, however, that mechanistic accounts of human behavior seriously underestimate some important and unique characteristics of human functioning by their failure to countenance such concepts as conscious human intentions, insight, intuition, and also unconscious intentions. These are only examples. The implicit fear here is that if such concepts as these were allowed their appropriate hearing, the ultimate possibility of explaining human behavior in terms of causally determined processes would be seriously challenged. The proponents of mechanistic intelligibility rightfully assume that by seriously entertaining these processes they would be abandoning a natural science of human behavior. I would venture that a natural scientific account of human behavior must be abandoned for a more complete understanding of the scope and variety of human functioning—a view that is readily obvious at a commonsense level of observation. If traditional learning theory has laughed at commonsense notions of human understanding as active conscious agents, the "man on the street" has returned the compliment by treating accounts of traditional learning theory as unbelievable.

The Organic Mode. To talk about organic intelligibility is to attempt to understand human behavior at the level of biological systems versus simple physical systems in nature, such as the mechanism. Hence a shift in emphasis from physics to biology. This does not necessarily detract from an interest in habitual behavior patterns as seen in the mechanical mode. To the contrary, biological interpretations see the production of habitual behavior patterns as species-specific adaptation. One, therefore, looks for different habit patterns between species. For this reason, in contrast to the mechanical mode, organic intelligibility is not reductive in nature.

Second, from the point of view of organic biological systems, the organism is seen in an *active* interchange with its environment, in contrast to the reactive position of mechanism. The conception of an active organism as a living system interacting with its environment brings the notion of teleology into consideration. *Teleology* is a term that captures the possibility that organic actions are goal-oriented and directed toward end states. Explanation in terms of a teleological framework substantially shifts the ground from the causal mechanisms exemplified in the mechanical mode to explanatory frameworks that have goal-directedness as part of the explanatory system. Taylor (1964) sees this as a crucial difference between teleological explanations and mechanical explanations, because the former require the use of a premise that violates the formal requirements for mechanical explanations. Teleological explanations assume the fundamental adaptive importance of ecological relationships in end states.

The most important characteristic of organic adaptability is that the teleology involved in adaptation is a habitual pattern that does not constitute consciousness and human intention. This distinction is important when we later consider conscious intentions. The various manifestations of structural conceptions in cognition (Piaget), linguistics (Chomsky), and morality (Kohlberg) are paradigm cases of organic modes of interpretation. The important point to be made about all these cases is that the understanding of a phenomenon is not primarily in terms of the demonstration of a causal sequence, but in the articulation of the *form* or *structure* that generates phenomena (content). This is called "the form/content distinction." All these theorists have criticized mechanistic explanatory systems as essentially involved with surface phenomena. The uniqueness of these systems of interpretation is that they seek "intelligible forms" through a process of abstraction from the phenomena that they are studying (i.e., language samples, moral judgment protocols) and then attribute explanatory power to the forms that are articulated. For example, Chomsky talks of a "generative grammar" that is capable of producing an infinite sequence of linguistic phenomena.

Our intention here is not to issue an elaborate critique of these systems of interpretation but to establish clearly how they differ in some essential ways from the position I am developing. For all their merit (and I say this with a sense of admiration), these systems of interpretation or intelligibility systematically sublate the importance of the role of conscious intentions of the human agents. By this I mean that these systems avoid this dimension as essential in their explanatory frameworks. All these systems ultimately subordinate the importance of *self-consciousness* into larger biological systems.

Finally, emphasis on *active structures* attributed to the organism proper as a historical, universal, abstract form seriously underplays the role of the relational quality of human action. The active forms or structures attributed to the organism are ultimately individualistic in nature. It is not that these theories lack a relational historical element. Rather, the element is so totally subordinated to the emphasis on finding structures inherent to the organism that the historical resistance factor (i.e., the environmental order in which the organism operates) is a stage prop that is the background for action. Our attribution of individualism is a judgment of degree. We say these theories are individualistic because they clearly articulate the structure of the individual while the structure of the environment is left unspecified in the background. At the level of theory, all the structural theories are relational and interactive. At the level of practical consequence, these theories fall far short of the mark of clearly and systematically coordinating organism and environment as correlatives in an adaptive biological process.[3]

We are now about to enter into a discussion of the personal mode of intelligibility. A word of caution is in order. We have not discussed the previous modes of intelligibility simply to dismiss them and, like Dante's Beatrice, bring the reader into Paradise. The reader would simply be misled about my intent. To move to a human order of intelligibility is not to abandon the previous orders. Humans are more than physical mechanisms or biological entities, but at the same time they are that all the same. For example, the nerve impulse is clearly understood at one level of interpretation as a biochemical mechanism (i.e., synaptic transmission). At the same time, we are saying that you cannot move from this level of interpretation and fully comprehend factors that we call characteristically human. In fact, these biological and physiochemical orders may be better known when they are understood and subordinated to a "human level of interpretation" (Merleau-Ponty, 1963). One hopes that the position being developed will make this clear. For now the reader will have to take a promissory note that clarity will ensue.

The Personal Mode. The unique quality of the personal mode of interpretation is that the system of interpretation systematically tries to understand the person as an active agent whose expressions are for others. The unit of analysis, as MacMurray (1957) sees it, is not the I but the you-and-I. This is not a trite distinction. Most personality theories as I understand them are egocentric; that is, they exclusively focus on the I and collapse the dialectic of the you-and-I. When I speak of the personal, I am not just speaking of dyadic relationships. The

[3]Our own treatment will eventually differ from the analytic tradition's discussion of reasons as teleological explanation. We will follow MacMurray's (1957) distinction between teleological mechanism and the concept of intention. We will try to demonstrate the importance of this distinction as an essential differentiating characteristic between organic and human orders of intelligibility.

unit of the you-and-I expresses the fact that all human expressions are *conrelative* expressions between persons. Therefore all human acts are *communicative acts*. All this needs now to be elaborated systematically in this section and the subsequent chapter. In this chapter, we will start out by discussing the *human act*. In the next chapter, we will start out by discussing the human action by discussing it under the appellation *personal world*.

Let us start out by examining how we are going to use the expression "the human act." I am assuming that "the human act" is a significant expression that is directed beyond itself to other selves. Biological acts such as defecation are not considered human acts because they are shared by humans with other species and are not typically directed toward other selves as signals. I call a human act an act—rather than a movement as a behavior—because of the intentional quality of human action. This will be expalined shortly. Further, the human act is bipolar or dialectical in nature; that is, the forward movement of dynamism of action has a negative moment (i.e., dialectical negation) where the act folds back on itself (i.e., reflection). This is why humans have always been referred to as "thinking animals." My assumption is that reflection is embedded in the forward movement of human action, which I will refer to as *agency*. I am assuming the primacy of the self as agent according to MacMurray (1957); that is, the reflective self (self as subject) is embedded in the agency of significant activity for other selves. The position being developed here, therefore, denies the possibility of a psychology based solely on the epistemological subject. The self as knower or the self as subject is not the focal point of our concern. It is here that I part company with much of the recent research on metacognition (e.g., Brown, 1978). To say this is not to deny the importance of the epistemological subject and *cognitional activity*. I am simply saying that the self as knower (epistemological subject) must be subordinated to the wider action context of human action. Several characteristics must be assumed of the *self as agent*.

CONSCIOUSNESS. The *human agent* is a conscious agent; that is, the essence of its activity is a dialectical process of *standing over against* while standing out from the *other*. *Other* here refers to all that is not. At the primordial pre-reflective level, this consciousness from the point of view (this is stretching the point) of the actor is an *I am*, since we are postulating the necessity of a human mode of intelligibility in order to interpret adequately what we are calling human action.[4] We have already hinted that this species-specific characteristic is the

---

[4]We are not saying that organic modes of intelligibility deny the phenomenon of consciousness. We are saying, however, that the self-conscious intentions of human agents are not incorporated systematically into the system of interpretation. Piaget is a case in point. Although he explores and describes conscious processes in elaborate detail, he ends up by articulating structures that are not related to the self-conscious intentions of the subjects studied. Intentions are there in many of his descriptions, and the perceptive reader can use this material with much gain for his or her own purposes.

peculiar propensity in humans for using language. Human consciousness, as one can see in the detailed observations of Piaget and in infant development, moves toward language and is significantly altered and regulated by language thereafter. The capacity for language, and the orientation toward a linguistic community for socialization into that language, makes humans a peculiar species, with a consciousness demanding a different level of intelligibility that cannot be reduced to organic adaptive processes or mechanisms.[5] This will become clearer as we elaborate the other characteristics of human action.

INTENTIONALITY. This characteristic of human action is not independent of consciousness and, in a certain sense, it is an alternate definition of consciousness that amplifies the *objective* rather than *subjective* concerns of conscious activity. To say that consciousness is consciousness of an object or other is to define the *intentionality* of consciousness. Consciousness is, therefore, not a noun but rather a verb. In short it is a process.

> The reflexive monitoring of conduct refers to the intentional or purposive character of human behavior: it emphasizes intentionality as process. Such intentionality is a routine feature of human conduct, and does not imply that actors have definite goals consciously held in mind during the course of their activities. (Giddens, 1979, p. 56)

To be is by definition to "stand out"—over against. Because we are assuming an "action self or subject," we postulate that the verb *to be* is embedded in a wider action context. In other words, the primordial sense of *existence* ensues from an active contact with the other (i.e., all that is not the self). Consciousness is the result of the multidimensional contact with the environment. In the broadest sense, consciousness is at least a property of all animals. We are using *consciousness* here as a prereflective sense; that is, it is not synonymous with intellectual activity but at the same time not totally independent of it where human actors are concerned. Merleau-Ponty (1963) clarifies the distinction we are making:

> Rather, consciousness is a network of significative intentions which are sometimes, on the contrary, lived rather than known. Such a conception will permit us to link consciousness with action by enlarging our idea of action. Human action can be reduced to vital action only if one considers the intellectual analysis by which it passes for a more ingenious means of achieving animal ends. (p. 173)

The last sentence in the quote above opens up the distinction between organic (vital) and human orders of consciousness. So far, our discussion of consciousness makes no clear distinction between organic and human modes of consciousness.[6] To make this distinction is not to deny organic biological modes.

---

[5]This collapse of the organism/environment dialectic can have serious consequences in the interpretation of phenomena. For example, McNeil (1966) can attribute an incredible power of the generative structures of language to the organism to the point where the environment, for all practical purposes, is ignored.

[6]Our position is not as drastic as Shotter's (1975), who believes that from the point of view of this discipline, it is not necessary for psychologists to have extensive knowledge of the nervous system. On the other hand, a complete knowledge of our reasons for acting is incumbent.

It assumes that animals other than humans are capable of conscious activity but also that human consciousness differs from consciousness in general in the same specifiable ways. This is a crucial distinction. If *action* is intentional, it must be directed outward to an alter-self or other. By introducing the concept of consciousness, one should not be accused of subjective idealism. Reflection or thought is the reflective mode of intentionality. It is by definition human action turned in on itself (i.e., reflect or mirror). This again is not to downgrade human reflective activity but to see it in terms of a wider intentional activity. Some of the most dramatic examples of this distinction can be seen in Piaget's observations of the infant's sensorimotor activity. These observations can give the reader a "bird's-eye view" of what we mean by intentional action if the reader does not have children of his or her own. Piaget gives astute examples of what I mean by the intentionality of reflection. (See, for example, his observations under secondary–circular reactions.) Consider one of Piaget's observations made on his child Laurent at the age of 19 months:

> Laurent, from 0;4 (19) as has been seen (Obs. 103) knows how to strike hanging objects intentionally with his hand. At 0;4 (22) he holds a stick; he does not know what to do with it and slowly passes it from hand to hand. The stick then happens to strike a toy hanging from the bassinet hood. Laurent, immediately interested by this unexpected result, keeps the stick raised in the same position, then brings it noticeable nearer to the toy. He strikes it a second time. Then he draws the stick back but moving it as little as possible as though trying to conserve the favorable position, then he brings it nearer to the toy, and so on, more and more rapidly. The dual character of this accommodation may be seen. On the one hand, the new phenomenon makes its appearance by simple fortuitous insertion in an already formed schema and hence differentiates it. But, on the other hand, the child, intentionally and systematically, applies himself to rediscovering the conditions which led him to this unexpected result. (Piaget, 1963, p. 103)

This observation is from a host of examples which exemplify a contention made by Gauld and Shotter (1977) that the infant, if observed astutely, possesses the rudiments of intention, action, conception, and communication.

INTENTION. Human action is not only intentional in the broader sense already described but also more specifically governed by *intentions*. Many of the activities of the human organism are not intended, they are *movements* or *events* in the broader biological sense (e.g., digestion, elimination, reflex activity, etc.). We can never think of synaptic transmission as a biophysical mechanism. We are calling the above *movements* or *events*, which in humans are coordinated and subordinated increasingly as the human develops to higher mental processes. In short, human intentions under normal conditions of psychosocial development increasingly come to coordinate and integrate biological adaptations. This is always a matter of degree, so we do not hold the individual or agent responsible for all his movements. For example, you do not blame a person for a knee-jerk reflex that causes injury. A human act is an *intentional* act if we refer to an *agent* as its source (MacMurray, 1957). I distinguish here human agency from a computer program in that the sources of goal-directed activities of humans are consciously regulated processes. I would call the work of a computer program an event. To call some activity an event or movement is to refer to a nonagent or process. A simple distinction that MacMurray (1957) makes here helps to make a further point. He says: "We express the distinction between acts and events; therefore, if we say: for an event there is a cause; for an act there is a reason" (p. 148). In other words, for an event or movement we ask the question "What caused it?" For an *act* we ask the question "Who did it?" "Why did he or she do it?" "What are his or her reasons for doing it?"

Harré and Secord (1972) see the role of psychology as a discipline as trying to understand the *reasons* for human action. They, in essence, reject mechanism as a mode of intelligibility for psychologists to pursue in the understanding of human action. They distinguish between causes and reasons. They maintain that reasons, which are related in some logical manner to what they explain, and causes, which are related to some physical mechanism, can appear in the explanation of happenings (events, movemnts, etc.), whether these happenings are actions of people or movements of animals. For Harré and Secord (1972) *reasons* and, in our terms, *intentions*, are usually offered in human affairs in the course of providing "justification or excuse for some action" (p. 11). In rejecting mechanism, Harré and Secord (1972) maintain that "Social behavior must be conceived of as actions mediated by *meanings* not responses caused by *stimula*" (my italics; p. 29). Therefore, in adapting the concept of action rather than movement, Harré and Secord (1972) maintain that a *person* as opposed to other species of animals does things for *reasons*. Harré and Secord (1972) project a certain uniqueness to what we are calling "human intentions." They comment:

> We share with animals the power to initiate action; that is, it is not only people who are agents, but our special powers enable us not only to monitor our performances, but because we are aware of our monitoring and have the power of speech we can provide commentaries upon and accounts of our performances and plan ahead of them as well. It is the existence of this (plans) while they are going on (commentaries) and in retrospect derivative capacity to comment upon our actions in anticipation (accounts), that is our most characteristic feature, and around which the science of psychology must turn. (pp. 90–91)

Harré and Secord (1972) refer to the unique character of human intentions as "teleological." They, with other theorists within the more recent tradition of language analysis, make a crucial distinction between causal and teleological explanation (see Bernstein, 1971; Gauld & Shotter, 1977; Harré & Secord, 1972). We feel that this distinction is not sufficiently subtle and serves to obliterate the important distinction between the "organic" and "personal" modes of intelligibility. It is true that psychological inquiry conducted at the mechanical mode of intelligibility eschewed teleological explanation. It is also true that genuine organic interpretations of events easily adopt teleological mechanisms as part of their explanatory apparatus. For example, a species-specific goal-directed activity such as imprinting can and should be called a teleological act. To leave human intentions at the level of organic intelligibility (a teleological explanation) is, in our opinion, deficient. If an *event* (i.e., mechanical mode of interpretation) is conceived of as different from an *act* (i.e., personal mode of interpretation), we would also wish to say that human intentions or plans are not teleological processes. In the stricter sense, one understands the behavior of organisms teleologically in terms of adaptation (MacMurray, 1957). In the above sense, we do not assign a *reason* but rather a motive force. For example, certain animal tropisms (nesting, flock movement, the "dance of the bees," etc.) which can clearly be interpreted as teleological mechanisms (i.e., goal-directed and adaptive) cannot, at the same time, be considered an *intention*. We feel that it is necessary to say with MacMurray (1957) that human action as distinguished from other animal action is not teleological but *intentional* (see also Taylor, 1964). For us, then, the human action based on human intentions provides a crucial distinction between the organic and personal modes of intelligibility. The almost infinite adaptability of human beings makes action based on human intentions an *open-ended process* rather than a teleological adaptation. By *open-ended*, I mean that human action has a "projectual" character that goes beyond adaptation into construction. This constructive aspect will be elaborated in greater detail in the next chapter, where I introduce the notion of "project." Human action is not fully determinate. The end or goal of an intention cannot be specified because human action is to a very great extent limited and supported by the "other" (i.e., resistance). Since human intentions must be coordinated with the intentions of other selves, intentions must be modified in the process of interpersonal interaction. Where this is not possible, one refers to a person as "rigid," stylized, overdetermined, or, in my case, bullheaded. So, the essence of human intentions is their relational and open-ended quality. This relational quality of human intentions, which we will have further occasion to discuss, is summarized by Shotter (1975) when he says:

> The person's own self and the selves of others are both then discovered together in relation to one another; they are reciprocally determined within the same categories as one another. In other words, to be me I need you: I need you to respond to my movements for me to appreciate that my movements have consequences in you. I need you to respond to the meaning in my action for me to appreciate that my action does in fact have a meaning. (p. 110)

Shotter's (1975) position is helpful for now in hinting at the relational quality of human action. We will have to expand it in order to deal with larger structural totalities such as class and gender when we deal with these concepts in Chapter 4. For now, let us provisionally treat human intentions as coordinated and open-ended acts. To speak of them as teleological is to restrict their human quality, which demands a personal mode of interpretation.

This brings me to a final point before we move on. I would agree with others (e.g., Harré & Secord, 1972) that human intentions are the essential ingredients for psychological inquiry. This does not mean that humans cannot be studied under more general characteristics (i.e., mechanical or organic modes). Our position is that this is not psychological inquiry. For us, psychological inquiry involves a movement into the "personal mode of interpretation," tackling human intentions head on, rather than as derivatives from the mechanical and organic orders.

RESPONSIBLE. To speak of *human action* as we are developing this term is to demand a discussion of an ancillary concept, responsible action. Everything I will say on this concept has illustrious forebears. (Book III of Aristotle's *Nicomachean Ethics* is a case in point.) Responsibility is one of the characteristics of a human act insofar as we are accounting for the actions of a person in terms of their desires, intentions, and purpose. This in humans, of necessity, involves the negative pole of action; that is, reflection. Responsible action, has therefore, as part of its ongoing process, a reflective component which in ordinary language we call "deliberation." The attribution of responsibility for an action is canceled out altogether if it can be shown that the behavior concerned was not governed, at least in some of its aspects, by intentions (Taylor, 1964). The deliberation involved in the reflective component of human action raises the thorny issue of the autonomy and freedom of human action.

> Being able to deliberate before one acts (or in the course of a complex action), and as a result make clear to oneself one's own reason for action, is part of what it is to be an autonomous responsible person, not reliant like a child upon others to complete and give meaning to one's acts. (Shotter, 1975, p. 96)

I understand, as do most western systems of jurisprudence, that part of the capacity for responsible action emerges in the psychosocial development. This is not a foregone conclusion, however, since we find extreme cases of adult individuals who, for all intents and purposes, are irresponsible (i.e., lack the capacity for deliberation). One talks sometimes of individuals being creatures of their surroundings. Another way of talking about the lack of responsiblity is to say that a person is ruled by his desires. Desires, here, are seen as potent motives that lack a component of reflection or deliberation. The notion of a deliberate action assumes, after the process of deliberation, that there is a motive force for that process which has consequences that are unique to that process. In short, a responsible act must, in some sense, make a difference in some outcome. This raises the question of whether responsible action is free. Chein (1972) maintains that the notion of freedom rests on three premises: (1) that there are such things as volitional desires, motivations, and so on; (2) that volitions have behavioral consequences; and (3) that volitions are not reducible to variables of the physical environment or to variables of physiological processes. I am using the term *intentions* in the same way that he uses *volitions*. I would add one more premise to Chein's in order to call a free act responsible, and that is that volitions must be capable of undergoing reflective scrutiny (deliberation). To say that a person is *free* is to say that motives or intentions are a constitutive part of human action. Chein (1972) would say that conditions for an action are, therefore, of three kinds: (1) constitutional, (2) environmental, and (3) motivational. His understanding of freedom, from which we draw, should not be understood only in these schematic terms. There is a great deal of subtlety in the crevices and interrelations of these components. The subtlety is seen in the following reflection:

> Behavior is free to the extent that the environment and the consitution do not dictate or preclude a particular action, the greater the degree of freedom that exists within the limits of the imposed constraints. Within the limits of these constraints the behavior that actually occurs is determined by the motivation of the actor. No behavior is ever completely free, some degree of freedom being lost as a consequence of the constraints of constitution and environment but degrees of freedom are also gained from the dependabilities of constitution and environment. The gains and losses, however, do not cancel each other out because they are different in kind. In addition, with respect to any particular behavior, some degree of freedom is lost to the constraints imposed by competing behaviors. A person may be free to the maximum degree that environment and constitution permit if and to the extent that, he does not lose degrees of freedom from constraints imposed by motivational conflicts, sacrifices relatively trivial motives, and effectively sequences or integrates the others. (Chein, 1972, pp. 33–34)

To talk of the free, responsible action must, therefore, be seen within a structure of freedom.[7] We will later consider this as the "intentional intervention of the project." For now, I am not talking about some isolated act free of resistance. The structure of freedom is an agon. The free human action, however graceful it may appear, is the outcome of a tension between all of the factors that Chein (1972) elucidates. This agon or tension, as we are calling it, should not be seen simply in a pejorative light. A person is said to have character when her or his actions are said to be reflectively motivated. This is a complex blend of motivational factors, environment, and constitution. A person is said to be responsible when it can be assumed that his or her actions are under the control of his or her motivational powers. To be a responsible agent is to have personal powers that make a difference to the outcome of actions. This brings up an important distinction which can be called the "agent–patient dialectic" (see Harré & Secord, 1972). The concept of the responsible agent is a one-sided understanding of human action if we do not acknowledge that the agent not only acts but also undergoes or suffers action that is partly out of her or his control.

---

[7]We are raising the question of a free act in this chapter from an egocentric point of view; that is, from the point of view of the agent. As our treatment develops in the subsequent chapters, we will be able to talk about a relational freedom or "our freedom."

We call this "patienthood." To deny the phenomenon of patienthood in human experience would fly in the face of much of human experience that we all have access to in our personal world. This "patient experience" is not only a result of external (i.e., environmental) factors, it may also be a result of our constitutional makeup as competing motivational factors that impede the possibility of human action. We also become slaves to our own habits. The free, responsible act must be seen within this dialectic of agency and patienthood. This dialectic is quite complex and subtle, as we know from our own personal experience. To think of ourselves as only agents is pretentious. To think of ourselves as patients is to attempt to excuse all our actions as beyond our personal powers. Responsible freedom is a limited freedom worked out within the dialectic of agency–patienthood. The prayer, "God grant me the serenity to accept the things I cannot change, courage to change the things I can, and the wisdom to know the difference" expresses this complex balance. To talk of "human freedom" and "responsible action," though, in the end assumes that the self as agent incorporates its own patienthood (i.e., self as subject). A critical ethical assumption pervades this book, and it should not go unacknowledged; that is, that individual persons and the wider community proper have the responsibility of creating institutions that enhance the use of personal powers. I call this, in the next chapter, the "human project." At the individual personal level, to relinquish the possibility of using one's personal powers is irresponsible action—you might say, "playing the patient." At the larger social level, the creation of societal institutions that rob humans of their personal powers, that is, their capacity for responsible action, is by definition an alienating society: I–we share the responsibility to transcend situations that help to create alienated individuals (i.e., patients) and alienating societies. This is a complex issue and a dialectic itself (i.e., alienated individuals create alienating socieities, and vice versa). We will develop this further in subsequent chapters.

SIGNIFICANT. At first blush, it would seem like rhetorical flourish to say that human action is significant. To characterize human action as significant within the perspective we are developing is to emphasize its *sign* or linguistic quality. We will move on in the next chapter to develop the notion of human actions as expressions of a personal world. To say here that human action is significant is simply to anticipate, from the point of view of the actor, that his or her actions are expressions for others. To say that a human act has significance is to say that it has a meaning for others. It is not always easy for agents to find an audience for their expressions, but in the end there must be some audience, however sparse, to make the judgment of the significance of a human act. There is no such thing as a significant act in itself. The meaning or significance of a human act is the place that it occupies in a network of *relationships* (Chein, 1972). Therefore, there is no such a thing outside a relational context. This is not to say that human action is not misunderstood or ignored for either benign or malicious reasons. We will later be critical of social structures that systematically ignore the significant action of certain groups of actors. Under these conditions, these social institutions rob particular agents or groups of agents of their personal powers. Part of the task of a critical psychology will be to elucidate and condemn these types of social structures and demonstrate their deleterious effects on human agency. To do this, we must move out of the egocentric movement we have just developed and consider human action in its wider relational context under the term *personal world*. Before doing this, let me briefly tie up some loose ends and summarize where we have come thus far with this chapter.

Loose Ends: Habits and the Unconscious

Habits and Intentions

This chapter has focused on the intentional base of human action from the point of view of an agent. In this light, we are all creatures of human intentions. Our western legal structure assumes this in attributing responsibility for human actions based on our intentions. A crime has to be *intended* to warrant culpability.

At the same time, our common sense tells us that we are creatures of *habit*. We do many things in a consistent pattern, which is not governed by intentions. Yet, we do not call these *reflexes* because they were acquired through learning. Some of these habits have been learned by unconscious associations, others through our intentions to acquire habits. The whole process of intending to acquire habits we call *discipline*. What must be seen here is that habits and intentions are not separate from one another; rather, they are dialectically related. It is, as we shall see later, the dialectic of freedom and determinism. Much of what constitutes psychology in this century is a solar emphasis on determinism. For example, all behavioral learning theories have made *habit* a core concept. We are now seeing a renaissance of the intentional nature of humans in the recent emphasis on metacognition (Brown, 1978). Here, however, human intentions are seen in a vacuum from the habitual. What is beneficial in the recent emphasis on metacognition is the regulative effect of intentions on human actions. This emphasis is laudable. Intentions can create habits and can transform those that have been learned through unconscious association and are no longer functional. The latter function is what I understand by the process called "working through" in Freudian psychology.

The problem here is that all points of view in this chapter concerned with intentional action are partial and egocentric. By egocentric, I mean from the viewpoint of the single agent. I intend to introduce a corrective in the next chapter, where habits and intentions will be broadened by what I will be calling the *habitus* and *project* of the personal world. In other words, I will attempt to bring the notions of intentions and habits to a broader cultural and sociological horizon. This corrective will be seen when I critique the notion of individualism in the next chapter.

Intentions and the Unconscious

Habitual actions are unintended. This does not mean that the original action that went into making the habit was not intended. Habits do indicate that a pattern of behavior is no longer governed by intentions. In this sense, one can speak of the state of a habit as passive. There are other unconscious actions that do not fall into the category of habit. I am referring to a process, illuminated by Freud, called "repressed intentions." Freud called repressed intentions the "unconscious." For Freud, the unconscious is an *active, dynamic* process whose intention is to *deny* the presence of unacceptable intentions (i.e., the dynamics of superego). Freud has stood the test of time, and it would be difficult to bypass this Freudian contribution. In the Freudian paradigm, the mechanisms of the unconscious operate within the microcosmic world of family dynamics. Psychologists of the psychodynamic variety believe that this is their territorial imperative and boundary. Marx introduced a similar concept from a more macrosocial level by introducing the notion of false consciousness. For our purposes, false consciousness is a set of repressed intentions about the true nature of societal dynamics. Specifically, Marx located the repression in the denial of the economic motive, which pervades capitalism. Many modern social theorists would contend that these two different repressions should be seen dialectically. What is suggested is a merger of Marx and Freud (see Becker, 1975). I do not intend to engage this literature, but my treatment will take into account its concerns. What is at issue when speaking of repressed intentions is the presence of "unfreedom." A critical psychology attempts to open up repressive mechanisms in the micro- and macrocosms and will therefore challenge the very nature of these repressions while advancing the cause of freedom. At this point, my statements are simply rhetoric. We must put flesh on these bones.

SUMMARY

We have developed the notion that human beings are actors whose actions are communicative expressions. This brought home the notion that human action is communication, which makes it a phenomenon of language broadly conceived. Expressions are made to be interpreted and, therefore, the interpretation of expressions is a desire to make them intelligible (i.e., meaningful). Psychology as a profession has no exclusive role in the interpretation of human expressions, although we will argue later for the possibility of a unique role. Nevertheless, we have argued in this chapter that psychology in all its manifestations is in the business of the interpretation of human expressions. From there, we go into the adequacy of the interpretative system being utilized in the interpretation. We have distinguished three broad systems of interpretation and called them modes (i.e., mechanical, organic, and personal). Each of these modes has broad characteristic features that allow us to distinguish them from one another and also to locate them in the history of psychological research and theory. It is obvious from our treatment that we do not treat them as equal in merit. This book will emphasize the mode of the personal as we have developed it in this chapter. All these modes of interpretation are sensitive in their own peculiar ways to the problems that language presents. The mechanical mode of interpretation systematically tries to deal with ambiguity of interpretation by eliminating the ambiguity with operational definitions. We question whether any system of intelligibility can go beyond interpretation (i.e., totally eliminate ambiguity). Mechanism as a mode of interpretation frequently used the machine as an analogue for the understanding of human expressions. This mode also rests on the assumption that humans are physical systems, just like all other systems in nature, and can be best understood in terms of causal mechanisms. There is no apparent need in this system to conceive of human beings as *actors*.

To speak of an organic mode of intelligibility or system of interpretation is to move from physical to biological systems. The organic metaphor acknowledges that *living biological systems* have their own unique status in nature and need to be systematically interpreted in this light. Humans are seen as one organic system in an adaptive evolutionary process. To understand a biological system is to come to terms with the structure and functions of that system in nature. Organic modes in all their variety are holistic in nature and acknowledge that human complexity cannot be simply broken down (analysis) for purposes of understanding. Thus the system of interpretation is usually constructive. The human being as a biological system is seen as an *active system* that transforms and is transformed by its environment. With all their complexity, organic systems of interpretation do not deem it essential to understand the phenomena of consciousness and humans as conscious agents *per se*. This does not necessarily mean in all cases that consciousness and its role is denied. It does mean, however, that it does not, in most cases, play a prominent role. In Chapter 2, our rudimentary presentation of a personal world focused on the unique characteristics of human activity, implying that it is necessary to go beyond the mechanical and organic modes in order to characterize human expression. Our system of interpretation or mode of intelligibility for a personal order is premised on the unique characteristics of the personal world which, in its most basic way, is seen as an interrelation of human actions involved in communicative acts. There, we elucidated that a human act has characteristic features: consciousness, intentionality, intention, responsibility, and significance. We must now see these features in their interpersonal context in the linguistic world we are calling the "personal."

3

THE PERSONAL WORLD
A Relational Event, a Cultural Reality

The title of this chapter is rather wordy. Nevertheless, it does try to say what the work of the chapter will be. The conclusion will be that the personal world is a cultural form. To arrive there, we must take a winding road. Let me help at the outset with some guideposts in the form of an outline.

The last chapter developed the notion of human agency as expression in an egocentric manner—that is, from the point of view of an individual agent. We must now complete this expression by embedding it in the larger structural totality of a personal world (i.e., the world of the you-and-I). To do this, we must clear away an impediment; that of the phenomenon of individualism. Traditional psychology operates from the viewpoint of individualism and therefore is biased toward egocentricism (the solar I) in its interpretation of human action. I will try to show how the egocentric viewpoint is reflective of what I would call a "liberal" sociopolitical synthesis. In addition, an example and set of contrasts are discussed to show how the egocentric viewpoint works out in psychological research. After this ground is cleared, we will go on to explicate the framework of a personal world and a dialectical framework that characterizes the personal world as order, change, and meaning. Finally, we will go on to consider how the personal world as *meaning* is, in essence, a cultural form.

INDIVIDUALISM: AN IMPEDIMENT

Our conception of a personal world must now be considered distinct from a conception of the individual. In fact, the whole historical thrust of liberal individualism makes it difficult to consider the relational totality of a personal world. Some important distinctions and the history behind them must now be made, for reasons of clarity and exposition. This is done to clearly distinguish a personal world from the liberal conception of the individual. To talk about a term is at once to talk of its history. The term *individual* is a case in point. Williams (1976b) in his *Key Words* gives a capsule history, reaching back to medieval times, of this term. In the medieval world, the term *individual* meant "inseparable," and the term was used mainly in theological argument about the Holy Trinity. In premodern times, the term was always used as an identity differentiation within a larger structural totality (e.g., one God and three divine persons). For Williams (1976b), there is a crucial change in emphasis that enabled us to think of the individual as a kind of absolute, divorcing it from any other group membership beyond itself. Subsequent social thinking has depended heavily on the latter definition of the individual as an absolute unto itself. I would call this change in emphasis "egocentric" where the ground is shifted from a you-and-I to an I. The sociopolitical consensus around this term in its modern definition is almost a counterposition of our definition of the personal world as relational. As Williams points out:

> In England, from Hobbes to the Utilitarians, a variety of systems share a common starting point of psychology, ethics, and politics. It is rare, in this tradition, to start from the fact that man is born into relationships. The abstraction of the bare human being, as a separate substance, is ordinarily taken for granted. (p. 77)

The modern definition of the individual as an autonomous social unit is a product of a consensus achieved by liberal social thought. In liberal social theory, individuals are seen as separate, autonomous monads that are unique unto themselves. The primary position of the "state of nature" is characterized by Hobbes as solitary, where the individual contracts ("social contract") out of fear for survival. The creation of a world (i.e., society) is based on a contractual arrangement of separate individual entities. Liberal ideology refers to a style of thought developed at the time of the French Revolution (Mannheim, 1953a). Three pervasive ideas characterize the synthesis of "classical liberalism" (De Lone, 1979). The first idea is that the universe is governed by natural rational laws. This is the core belief for the integrity of natural scientific inquiry. Second, that this natural law could be deciphered or interpreted by the operations of human reason. Finally, the individual's well-being is the ultimate point of societal synthesis. This represents a revolutionary departure from the medieval synthesis—where the stress was on community synthesis while individual integrity was regarded as heresy. The preliberal synthesis was communitarian in nature but with a blunting of the individual for the purposes of community consensus. Therefore, liberalism marks the accent of the individual over and against the community.

The development of thought on natural law at the time of the French Revolution was truly a revolutionary event, which marks the ascent of what is today called "individualism." A central characteristic of the liberal synthesis is the claim, at an abstract level, of universal validity for every individual (Mannheim, 1953a). This was achieved through a metaphor of atomism and mechanism; collecting units into larger totalities additively (e.g., the state, etc.) (Mannheim, 1953a). Here, it is important to point out the close relationship between liberal social and political theory and the historical development of psychological theory. The interweaving of psychology and social theory generated an *atomistic* view of political economy. The conception of the individual as separate (i.e., a social atom) fed into the atomistic view of political economy, society becoming the sum of individual actions and decisions (De Lone, 1979). Here, the psychological tradition of Locke combines with the economic and social theory of Adam Smith, suggesting that psychological attitudes (i.e., abilities, personality, moral traits, etc.) prepare individuals to become signatories to the social contract (De Lone, 1979). Rationality, in the liberal tradition, will be allied to autonomy, reason being the compensating mechanism against unruly desires that threaten the viability of contractual relationships. In the liberal tradition, *reason* is expressed as the universal, formal, abstract, thoughtful, and so on, in contrast to the irrational, which is particularistic, content-laden, concrete, and emotional (Unger, 1976).

The wisdom of hindsight allows us to lay bare some of the distortions of the conception of the human as a conglomeration of autonomous social actors. A more communitarian perspective takes issue with the liberal contractarian view by interjecting a historical perspective. A radical communitarian formulation assumes that a conception of society should be sensitized to historical occurrences (Sullivan, 1977a, 1977b). The person within a communitarian conception is embedded in real historical relations. She or he comes into a world that is already a momentum and where there is a solid, weighty, and dense social structure in which the person is influenced and which he or she operates upon. The personal world I am developing here is embedded in larger structural totalities that are impersonal in nature but nevertheless affect the viability of the personal world. The world of monopoly capitalism and concentrated economic conglomerates (e.g., multinationals) seems remote from what psychologists would call a personal world. This type of isolating is essentially the basic problem to which atomistic theorizing falls prey. Psychologists study individuals and groups as if they were independent of larger social structures. Economists proceed to theorize as if economics were independent from the personal psychological world. When a major multinational relocates to another region for economic gain, no one holds this type of conglomerate responsible for the enormous personal costs on community lives which are affected by sudden and possibly chronic unemployment. Nevertheless, we know that high sudden unemployment is correlated with deviance, alcoholism, depression, and suicide. This brief excursion is intended simply to illustrate a point that I will develop more fully in the next chapter: that an adequate treatment of a personal world cannot be simply psychologistic in nature. The personal world must be embedded in social and political conditions which *situate* the interpretation.

The Impediment

The possibilities for developing this line of social analysis have historical realities which are weighted against it; we now turn to these. Psychology as a discipline is one of the embodiments of individualism. To conceive of a discipline that could carve out for itself the study of the microcosm called the individual is truly a western historical creation. Disciplinary boundaries are in actuality permeable, but they nevertheless express some clear divisions of labor among social inquiries. Psychology, as a discipline, represents the overarching belief that the study of individual and microsocial units is possible and desirable. To be able to demarcate sociology from psychology represents the belief that the individual can be studied as relatively independent from a wider social setting (i.e., social structure). A distinct discipline called psychology is truly a symbol of the liberal tradition, since it is the professional embodiment of the individual as a totality or unit. Psychology as a discipline is truly an expression of liberal individualism.

The fragmentation produced by rigid disciplinary boundaries has had consequences, as to how we are able to think about the person. The person as individual is a conception of the person conceived of as independent from social and historical conditions. Sève (1978) delineates some of the consequences of this type of fragmentation:

> One may at first detach the personality from the social conditions in which it is formed but in doing so one deprives oneself of any way of accounting for its deep-seated *sociality*, and encloses oneself in a hopelessly abstract, non-historical conception of individuality whether in the form of a spiritualism of the person or a biologism of temperament. In either case, the essential historicity of personality escapes. (p. 31)

Riegel (1978) conjectures some of the reasons why a dialectical conception of personality has eluded the discipline of psychology systematically. In his review of diverse attempts to formulate personality theories, he notes that these theories have by and large (despite their differences) been theories which have primarily dealt with individual psychological conditions. For the most part, cultural–sociological considerations entered the discussion only secondarily; presumably they are the task of the sociologist. Lewin broke some new ground by proposing a "field theory" of personality, but it was clear that his formulation was safely within the horizon of individualism. His emphasis on the unique experience of the individual in unique situations committed him in the direction of an individualistic perspective (Riegel, 1978). Riegel (1978), in reviewing this situation, contends that it is only with the development of social and psychological theories (e.g., George Herbert Mead), which concerned themselves with social roles and the social self, that we see a preparation for an alternative away from traditional personality theory, which failed to consider the codetermination of self and the other in the developmental historical context.

The Personal World as a Relational Totality

The viewpoint we are developing is that the person is person only as I-and-you. We are clearly departing from the liberal tradition (see also Sampson, 1977, 1981; Unger, 1975, 1976). There is, therefore, the clear acknowledgement of the existence of collective subjects, which clearly violates the principle of individualism as exemplified in the liberal tradition (Unger, 1975). At a later point, we will refer to this notion of collective subjects as culture. Initially, I would like to explore several reasons why it is desirable to shift to the viewpoint of the I-and-you as suggested by MacMurray (1961). In doing this, one must shift the ground by acknowledging the existence of collective subjects in violation of the principle of individualism. One must countenance the notion of a person as a reciprocal relation. A person is at once subject and object, encompassing both modes simultaneously. The personal world is a unity (I–thou); the person as *subject* is an I and an *object* is a you, since the you is always the other (MacMurray, 1961). Historically, the child development literature has assumed that the child's interaction with objects (nature or I–it relationships) is an adequate analogue for understanding interpersonal interaction (I-you) (see Richards, 1974). A conception of the "unit of the personal" assumes that there is a special class of objects from which the conscious self must also be separate; it is the class of objects who are also subjects (i.e., other selves; Unger, 1975). The child development literature is now developing a corpus of research which indicates that even newborn infants employ different modes of response when relating to people as opposed to things (see Lock, 1978; Richards, 1974). For instance, the vocal responses of 3-month-olds can be much more effectively conditioned with a social than a nonsocial reinforcement (see Richards, 1974). As early as 3 weeks, the young baby expects the human voice to appear in the same orientation as the human face (Ausubel *et al.*, 1980).

Much of the earlier literature on early child development neglects the effective environment in which the child develops; no description is given to the reciprocal interaction of the child with other persons (Ausubel *et al.*, 1980; Ryan, 1974). There is no characterization of the speech of others to the child, and thus the child's speech is treated as an isolated phenomenon (Ryan, 1974). This is illustrative of the individualistic orientation we have just dealt with under liberalism. There is considerable evidence, in contrast, that very early babbling is not random and reflects features of the language spoken around the child. For example, as early as 4 to 6 months, the babbling of infants could be distinguished between Chinese and American parents. Systematic selectivity can be seen in the very production of sounds before speech appears (Ausubel *et al.*, 1980). Ryan (1974) makes the point from her own research that any analysis of human communication must include a description of the structure of intersubjectivity between participants in a dialogue (i.e. I–you–you–I, etc.). In following the lines of analysis as suggested above, Trevarthen (1980) concludes from his studies on infants that within the first few months of life the caretaking interaction indicates powerful evidence of new forms of "joint intentionality." The child, from birth, must be seen as an active participant (agent) in a jointly reciprocal relationship with his or her caretakers (i.e., I–them), rather than a passive object of socialization practices. Communication expresses the cognitive aspects of this reciprocity. The development of individuation within this larger totality is what one calls consciousness. Consciousness is the experience of separation and limitation (i.e., over and against others and nature; Unger, 1975). Consciousness as we are defining it must be seen in a relational totality.

> Consciousness implies autonomous identity, the experience of division from other objects and from other selves. But the medium through which consciousness expresses itself is made up of the symbols of culture, and these, according to the principle of totality, are irreducibly social. When you speak of language or make a gesture, you perceive and communicate meaning in categories that are the common patrimony of many men. By what power can you and they speak to one another? It must be possible for each to view the other's statements and acts as the signs of certain intentions. These intentions can, in turn, be understood because they are intentions you too might have. It follows that consciousness always presupposes the possibility of viewing other persons as selves that could, under favourable enough circumstances, see what one sees and believe what one believes. That is the cognitive aspect of sociability. (Unger, 1975, p. 215)

The cognitive aspect of sociability assumes that some of the above features must be present as early as infancy in order for the child to build up communicative skill (Ausubel et al., 1980).

There is also a moral aspect to sociability, and it would appear to be a requirement for the persons that he or she be recognized by others as a person (Unger, 1975). The absence of this aspect of sociability can have most deleterious effects on the development of the person. The importance of this relational reciprocity cannot be underestimated and ignored. Ausubel et al. (1980) indicate that if these schemes are not securely built, either through misfortune or mismanagement or some endogenous defect in the developing child, the whole system of social skills and affective understandings is put in jeopardy. The constant message in the new work on caretaker–child interaction is the centrality of the interpersonal relationship in the transmission of meaning.

It would seem that humans are possessed of a compulsion to share their conscious understanding and wants as intimately as possible (i.e., dialogue; Trevarthen, 1980). When this dialogical relationship is fragmented or broken, as seen in maternal deprivation, serious consequences ensue (Ausubel & Sullivan, 1970; Ausubel et al., 1980). The early studies on maternal deprivation report findings indicating that after 6 to 9 months of age, prolonged or severe deprivation of maternal care or abrupt separation from the accustomed mother figure during the first 3 years of life often (but not necessarily) leads to extremely serious developmental consequences. Although there are reservations and subtleties to this picture (see Ausubel & Sullivan, 1970), I quote them here to score the importance of the necessity of the relational components (i.e., intersubjective and interpersonal) of the personal world from its origins in infancy. This litera- ture, from both its positive and negative aspects, makes it impossible to think of individuals in terms of isolated units (individualism). The core unit is relational and must be characterized as a *dialogue* (I–thou). From our analysis, it can be stated that the fundamental motives for developing cultural forms are already manifest in prevocative form in infancy (Trevarthen, 1980). From these early infant developments an elaborate sequence of progressively more powerful stages of individual motives and awareness ensues (Trevarthen, 1980).

It is not my task to develop the child-rearing literature in a relational form. Our exploration into this literature was to make the point that the personal world as a relational totality is a given rather than an achievement of human culture and a total necessity or prerequisite for human development.

THE PERSONAL WORLD AS A METAPHOR OF COMMUNICATION

In the first chapter we hinted at the metaphor of the personal world as being that of the communication process itself, which assumes the primacy of the notion of human action as expression. With the assumption of language as fundamental to human existence, it follows that the human sphere (i.e, the field of the personal) cannot be understood adequately through organic or mechanical categories (MacMurray, 1961). The core unit of a communication is dialogical in nature. Human expression, as we have outlined in the previous chapter, must be understood in a dialogical context. In other words, the unit of analysis is not an I but an I-and-thou. Winter (1966) outlines the core features of a dialogical model in Table 1. His model presupposes two tensions: (1) the tension of a *self* coming to sociality through gesture, sign, and symbol or what we are calling "human expression" and (2) the balance of the gesturing self (dynamic) with the meaning-receiving and meaning-giving interpretative response of others. Table 1 identifies three basic elements which he draws from the pioneering work of George Herbert Mead. These elements are (1) dynamic, (2) form, and (3) uni- fication. The *dynamics of a gesture* is an attempt at eliciting attention, the gesture being seen as standing one against the other and reaching toward the other. This is one element of a polar tension. The *formative* element is an interpretative response and constitutes the other side of the polar tension. The interpretative response as *form* is a meaning-giving act (i.e., form receiving as in listening and form giving as in speaking). Unification is the crucial element in this analysis (Winter, 1966). The preeminence of *unification* becomes manifest in the reciprocity of perspectives, which is presupposed in seeing the gesture from

TABLE 1.   A Dialogical Model

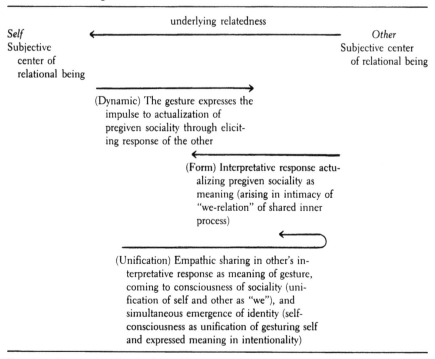

Note. From *Elements for a Social Ethic* by Gibson Winter. Copyright 1966 by Gibson Winter. Reprinted by
   permission of the author and the publisher.

the other's perspective; at the same time, this empathic seeing from the stance of
the other involves a distancing from onself which is accomplished by the mediation of the other's giving of form to the gesture. This makes it possible to share in
a common world of form. Later we will consider it cultural form. For now, the
unification of the polar tensions of *dynamics* and *form* reveals some fundamental
and essential human prerequisites. As Winter (1966) put it:

> The unity of self and other is actualized as a social world through the sharing of
> gestures, signs and language; the unity of the self is actualized simultaneously, as
> personal identity of the intentionality of the self with the responses of the social world
> and particularly of the world of significant others. The structure of dynamics and form
> in their unity as self-consciousness reveals man's essential tendencies as 1) care for
> response 2) reflective awareness and openess to form 3) thrust to integrity and unity.
> (Winter, 1966, pp. 102–103)

This "thrust to integrity and unity" (i.e., unification) should be understood as an
ontological (i.e., essential) and ethical (i.e., oughtness) category. In other words,

it should be seen as an essential characteristic for the achievement of humanness and the solidification of personhood (i.e., individuation) in a personal world (i.e., unification).

Winter (1966) contends that the problem of a human science is to be able to formulate the parameters of the intersubjective world in such a way that the self-transcendence of the intentional consciousness (i.e., dynamic polarity) is held in tension with the structures of the social and cultural world. By and large, psychology as a human science has collapsed this polarity in the historical development of psychological theories. In a very gross way, one could say that theories of psychology have been either *voluntaristic–intentional*, expressing some form of dynamics of an individual self, or conformist, expressing some form of dynamics of a social self. The theory of Piaget, Maslow, and Chomsky would collapse the tension to the side of a *dynamic intentional* self with active personal, cognitive, and linguistic structures. Behavioristic social learning theories in some very essential ways collapse and negate the importance of an active intentional self in order to stress the importance of social conformity (conformist perspectives). The former theories seem to express a form of limitless freedom because of the activities of the intentional organism; the latter seem to stress determinism as a result of being molded (i.e., conformed) to external social structures.

The Pioneering Work of G. H. Mead

George Herbert Mead (1964) would have to be considered a pioneer in the development of a social–relational view of self in his "symbolic interaction" theory of the development of the self. He was able to contrast the difference between an individualistic and a social theory of the self. From the perspective that we are attempting to develop, one would consider his social viewpoint as organic in nature. Nevertheless he, early on, was able to discuss the difference between a type of psychology which assumes a social process or social order as a logical and biological prerequisite for the appearance of selves and a psychology where individual selves are presupposed or prior to social processes (i.e., individualistic). Mead (1964) identified these different perspectives with different historical views of the state:

> The difference between the social and the individual theories of the development of mind, self, and the social processes of experience or behavior is analogous to the difference between evolutionary and the contract theories of the state as held in the past by both rationalists and empiricists. The latter theory takes individuals and their individual experiencing—individual minds and selves—as logically prior to the social process in which they are involved, and explains the existence of that social process in terms of them; whereas the former takes the social process of experience as behaviour as logically prior to the individuals and their individual experiencing which are involved in it, and explains their existence in terms of that social process. (Mead, 1964, p. 242)

Mead (1964), by taking the position of a social self, contended that the mind, self, and so on could never find expression or even come into existence except in terms of a social environment and that an organized set or pattern of social relations and interactions is necessarily presupposed by it and involved in its nature. For Mead, the personal world was a *relational totality*. He perceived personality as an internalization of roles and these roles as patterns of attitudes and actions. He recognized the indetermination of inner and outer conditions by the contrastive comparison of the I and the me's. The I represented the inner biological core of the organism, whereas the me's are achieved by the perceptions and enactments of social roles. Mead never adequately developed a clear conception of the I, and it appears as a creative but mysterious inner force. The major thrust of his work was in the development of the person through role enactments (me's). Mead's conception was a symbolic behaviorism and his work was a daring effort to anchor personal consciousness itself in the social process (Gerth & Mills, 1964). His notion of a "generalized other" (me) consolidated the possibility of linking the private and the public—that is, the innermost acts of the individual with the widest kinds of social–historical phenomena (Gerth & Mills, 1964). Mead's conception of a relational totality essentially accounts for the individual's adoption and confomity to social roles (i.e., social formations). His inability to formulate a clear conception for the I leaves his overall view most incomplete. His "generalized other" accounts for social determinisms (i.e., the reproduction of the social world in new individuals), but there is very little in his position that accounts for social change (i.e., social transformations). His conception of the I as a creative, organic entity hints at the possibility of new creations (i.e., transformation in social roles), but this element of his theoretical formulation was left undeveloped in his thinking. I will return to this issue later in another context, where it will elucidate a conception I wish to develop on human freedom. Despite the shortcomings of Mead's perspective, he nevertheless laid the groundwork for the view of the person as a relational totality with other social selves. I intend to use his core concepts to develop integrative components of a personal world.

INTEGRATIVE COMPONENTS OF A PERSONAL WORLD

The accent at this point is on *personal* and *world*. A concept of the person is always related to a world. At this point it is necessary to say that the world is all that is not I. It is that resistance or counterpoint to the person. When that world constitutes other I's (persons), they are from one person's point of view "you" or "they." Obviously this relationship is reciprocal. We have already indicated the impossibility of considering persons as separate from a world. Thus, to talk about a person is to talk about a personal world. *World* emphasizes the situated character of intentional action. Thus, human action (discussed in the previous chapter as conscious, intentional, intending, responsible, and significant) must be clearly seen as existing in a world (i.e., *we* relation) if action is going to be considered communicative (i.e., expressive). Recall from the first chapter that the argument is to construe the personal world in a metaphor of communication in distinction to the metaphors of organism and mechanism.

At the beginning of this chapter (see Winter's diagram in Table 1), we have talked about the integrative components of a personal world as dynamics—form and unification. What I would like to do now is to hint at how this unification takes place within the context of a schematic model of personality integration. I will express this integration in terms of polarities which must be in tension with one another rather than as discrete categories. My treatment here is dynamic and process-oriented, so readers will be deluding themselves if these polarities are reified into static categories. Let me now outline in Table 2 the polarities as dialectical components of the personal world.

Socialization (Habitus) in Tension with Social Transformation (Project)

By and large, socialization theories of personality are considered discrete from transformational theories. Since most of what constitutes mainstream psychology is "social maintenance" in nature, most theories are conservative in nature; that is, they express an overriding interest in what I will be calling identity, the social self, order, habit (i.e., preconsciousness), ideology, and determinism. A psychology based on prediction and control would naturally move toward this side of the polarity. Transformational theories have been much rarer in psychology. A prediction and control mentality probability finds difficulty in dealing with change; therefore this lacuna ensues. The classical works on person-

TABLE 2. Integrative Polarities of a Personal World

Socialization		Transformation
(Habitus)	←——→	(Project)
1. Social self (me)	←——→	Intentional self (I)
2. Identity	←——→	Individuation
3. Order (reproduction)	←——→	Change (transformation)
4. Preconscious	←——→	Conscious
5. Past (history)	←——→	Future
6. Ideological symbols	←——→	Utopian symbols
7. Determinism	←——→	Freedom
	Dialectical Integration	

al transformational theories have been theories of "conversion." The classic work in this genre would have to be William James' *Varieties of Religious Experience* (1902/1936). In this book, James attempts to come to terms with the reality of radical personality transformation through religious experience. The brilliance of this work has never been truly appreciated in American psychology, although the work was created by an American. Robert Lifton's (1974) studies on thought reform in extreme social situations seems to capture the spirit of this earlier work, but for the most part this genre has been more of interest to theologians than to professional psychologists. In elucidating the components of a personal world, I will attempt to hold the socialization and transformation aspects in dialectical tension. The focus throughout the exposition will be on the tension of what I will be calling "habitus and project." I am using the term *habitus* after Bourdieu and Passeron (1977), whose work complements my own. The notion of project is shared by several authors that I will shortly allude to. Table 3 poses in capsule form the questions posed in the tension of habitus and project.

Let me now explore the polar tensions of what I am calling "habitus" and "project" under the six polarities presented in Table 2.

1. *Social self (Me)—intentional self (I)*. One aspect of the development of a person in a personal world is the development of the social self (me) which Mead characterizes as the mirror image of the culture. Although the appropriation of the social self has frequently been characterized in a passive way (e.g. traditional social learning theory), I am departing from this tradition by emphasizing the agency of the self in the appropriation of a social self. In other words, the habitus of a culture is transmitted in a dynamic and reciprocal interchange between culture and person.

The intentional self is that aspect of selfhood which constitutes the possibility of human creativity (Winter, 1966). The social self, (the Median "me"), with its emphasis on reproduction, must be counterposed with an intentional self (the Median "I") if a legitimate understanding of human freedom is to be sustained as a viable concept in the interpretation of human action. It is clear

TABLE 3.   The Habitus–Project Distinction

Habitus	Project
How does culture reproduce itself?	How does culture transform or change itself?
Another way of putting the question is to ask: How does the personal world become integrated into a larger cultural world so as to reproduce (socialize) that world in the new generation?	Another way of putting the question is to ask: How is the personal world changed by new interactions that move away from the past so as to change the culture (transform) in some essential characteristics?

that human action must be seen in relation to real factors which condition its reproduction (i.e., continuity). Most of what constitutes "mainstream psychology" is geared to capture the habitus in a microcosm. The personal world is not only governed by the past but also projected into a future (Winter, 1966). The notion of "project" expresses the importance of the intentional futurity of human action. The notion of project is more than simply the goal-directedness of human action in the limited sense of purpose. In its broadest and richest sense, the project is the *constitutive* role of the self in action (Winter, 1966). We have outlined this constitutive role in rudimentary form in Chapter 2, in our discussion of human expression. In that sense, the project is characterized as a *conscious* expression, intentional in nature and embodying intentions, responsibility, and significance. Humans define themselves by their projects (Sartre, 1968). If this assumption is accepted, then it has important consequences for any interpretation of human actions. Laing and Cooper (1964) bring this to the forefront in their discussion of the notion of project:

> Any simple observation of the social field should make us realize that the relation to ends is a universal structure of human enterprises and that it is on the basis of this relation that men understand actions and institutions. Comprehension of the other is achieved only through a realization of the ends of his acts and projects. One may watch a man working from a distance and feel that one does not comprehend what he is doing, until one realizes the end at which he is aiming in his labour so that all his different movements become unified in the light of the end. Ends are not mysterious entities or some sort of appendages to acts. They simply represent the depassment of the given in an act which passes from the present to the future. (p. 64)

Human action, as a constitutive act, looks forward in its projects (Winter, 1966). Sartre (1968) maintains that a simple inspection of the social field leads one to discover that the relation to ends (i.e., projects) is a permanent structure of human enterprises. If this is true, then to ignore the projective character of human action is to ignore something essential in human activity. The intentional self or I, therefore, represents the voluntaristic and creative aspects of human action. Mead and Dewey spoke of the intentional self in organic and biological terms. They likened it to impulse. It is impulsive within this interpretation because the action of the intentional self (or I) was seen as transcending or going beyond social norms (the me). Freud would talk about this as the dialectic of the id with the superego. This formulation puts the creative aspects of human actions as an asocial endeavor. This is accomplished in an unreflective manner, since most social theory treats the social order as it is presently constituted as normative. Thus any human action which goes beyond a presently formulated consensus (social order) can be considered impulsive in this light. In order to legitimate the notion of project as constitutive of human action, it is necessary to contrast our discussion of order and reproduction with a conception that gives credence to the possibility of social transformation.

The dialectic between habitus and project is essential to human development. The order that culture conveys provides the basis for a sense of identity. The sense that this order is not an absolute provides the basis for a sense of individuation and uniqueness. These aspects must be seen as polar tensions rather than distinctive categories. Therefore, identity and individuation are two faces of human development. We turn now to that polarity.

2. *Identity—individuation.* Erikson (1959) defines "identity" as a sense of self-sameness in the process of change. The active and generative quality of one's history (i.e., habitus) allows a sense of "self-sameness" to be built up. If this is absent, an individual is said to be "identity diffused." Most psychological discussions of identity are formulated within the framework of individualism. In shifting the ground away from an individualistic framework, we will discuss identity in dialectical terms. Our discussion of identity will be in terms of class, gender, and ethnic identity. Because this is a departure from conventional psychological categories, it is necessary to elaborate. Let me give an example relating to class identity.

The habitus is a generative concept which attempts to account for the effects of collective history. Bourdieu (1977) elaborates on the class nature of habitus as follows:

> Since the history of the individual is never anything other than a certain specification of the collective history of his group or class, each individual system of dispositions may be seen as a structural variant of all the other group or class habitus, expressing the difference between trajectories and positions inside or outside of the class. (p. 86)

To talk about class identity, one must think in dialectical terms. Confrontation between agents of different classes is an interaction defined by the *objective structure* of the relation between the groups involved (Bourdieu, 1977)—for example, a superior giving orders to a subordinate or a professor discussing the relative merits of students in program planning. Confrontation between classes also brings out "systems of dispositions" within and between classes (Bourdieu, 1977). These systems of dispositions as generated by a class habitus can be seen in such areas as linguistic and cultural competence, which are embodied actively in a competence acquired by a particular history (Bourdieu, 1977).

Let me give a few examples of what these differential dispositions might be in a class society. First, let us look at a possible motivational dimension in class terms. The habitus here helps us to understand why a class society can remain somewhat stable through the history of its individual agents. Coles (1977), in a study of children who are born in families of privilege, detects in these children a pervasive feeling of "entitlement." Entitlement signifies that these children expect that things will happen for them and in their favor. Entitlement is a dispositional expression of those familiar with class, prerogatives, money, and power (Coles, 1977). An instance of this can be seen in an interview with a 6-year-old who knew that at 21 she would inherit half a million dollars. Looking at a working-class population of adults, one sees a different dispositional set that nevertheless solidifies and complements the entitlement of the privileged. Sennett and Cobb (1973), in an in-depth study of male working-class adults, indicate that they have a pervasive "feeling of not getting anywhere despite their efforts." There is also a feeling of vulnerability rather than entitlement in contrasting and comparing themselves to others at a higher social and economic level. This is not to say that working-class children do not *resist* the vulnerability discussed above (see Willis, 1977). The problem is that in many instances this resistance eventually is a rebellion that entraps them further in a rigid class identity. Lower-class children in a class-structured society come to see themselves as having "small futures"—the converse of the entitlement of the privileged. This dialectical dispositional movement between classes tends to solidify a class habitus.

The personal world must be seen within the development of a class-structured society. As Bernstein (1975) aptly points out:

> The class structure influences work and educational roles and brings families into a special relationship with each other and deeply penetrates the structure of life experiences within the family. The class structure has deeply marked the distribution of knowledge within society. It has given differential access to the sense that the world is permeable. It has sealed off communities from each other and has ranked these communities on a scale of invidious worth. (pp. 198–199)

Part of this scaling which is based on class identity is seen in the accumulation of "cultural capital" (Bourdieu, 1977). Here we are switching our focus from motivational to cognitive dispositions, which may be characteristic of different class identities. Bernstein (1975) gives one example of what I am trying to get at here in his study of "speech codes" between different social classes. The dominant speech mode of middle-class children is one that is characterized as an "elaborated code." The elaborated code is a speech pattern that reveals subjective intent of the speakers, shows a sensitivity to the implications of separateness and difference, and, finally, involves an orientation to a complex hierarchy for the organization of experience. By contrast, lower-class children reveal a code that Bernstein (1975) labels "restricted." In the restricted code, there is a speech form that discourages the speaker from verbally elaborating subjective intent; it progressively orients the user to descriptive rather than abstract concepts. It is necessary here to make clear the nature of these sociolinguistic patterns. Bernstein (1975) makes it clear that these patterns are independent of nonverbal intelligence measures. The issue here between these class patterns is not fundamentally that of intelligence. From the perspective that is being developed in this book, one should not conclude that these differences are organically related to class placement. Seeing these results within a personal metaphor, we would contend that these code differences are a function of different social-structure and class constraints. They reveal just as much about the class structure as they do about the members of these individual classes. We would contend that these codes could be changed if the class structure (i.e., class habitus) that buttresses these differences actively were changed. Under present class conditions, the codes are illustrative of one group naming the world (i.e., middle-class elaborated code) and another group having their world named for them (see Freire, 1974).

To talk about personal identity in class terms is to accent the relational quality of identity formation. Here I would like to stress that the notion of class identity should not be turned into an absolute. Ethnicity, race, sex, and so on must also be coordinated and integrated into a conception of social identity if this concept is to be productive. Class being equal, there are considerable differences between blacks and Puerto Ricans that demand a subtlety in any class analysis of character structure. Gender identity is another important dimension to be explored even when class identity is equivalent. In the past, however, class differences were mostly ignored in the study of these other differences (e.g., race). The identity of the self is therefore accomplished in historical situations. The consolidation of a personal identity is therefore carried out within real historical conditions that operate in class gender and ethnic structures. To interpret personal identity with these dimensions in mind will demand a considerable amount of theoretical and research sophistication.

The polar dimension to *identity* is the development of *individuation*. Individuation expresses the fact that the process of personal development expresses the possibility of some *uniqueness* and *resistance* to a dominant culture. If culture only reproduced itself in new members, then there would be no creativity in human institutions. This, of course, is not true. The *intentional self* is not only the receiver of cultural constraints; it is also a transformer of the institutions that mold it. A "new generation" always challenges its elders to be different from the past (i.e., habitus). When the balance is weighted toward cultural identity, then cultural conformity predominates. When the balance is weighted toward individuation (i.e., projection) then a condition of radical social change is in operation. The balance of identity and individuation is always delicate. Some epochs are characterized by one or the other of these polar aspects. The 1960s in North America, for example, represented an epoch weighted toward individuation. There was serious challenge to the status quo in class, race, and gender relations. The 1980s appear to have swung toward a more conservative orientation. If an orientation or movement that challenges the status quo is operating, then "individuation" becomes easier to interpret.

Individuation expresses the possibility of the transformation of cultural patterns. The notion of *project* indicates the real possibility for individuation that enhances the possibility of cultural transformation. The project means, in essence, that the past can be transcended. The intentional self is, therefore, an individuating aspect of the self. What we mean here is simply that the self is not only molded by culture (i.e., habitus) but also molds and transforms culture (i.e., project). In talking about individuation, I do not want this concept to be confused with the notion of individualism which I have already critiqued. Individuation, like its polar opposite, identity, is worked out and projected within a culture. It is expressed in the *resistance* and *transcendence* to the status quo. This individuation can be expressed differently across class lines. For example, Keniston's *Young Radicals* (1968) were middle-class students who rejected the normal entitlements of their middle-class background. In the opposite direction, Chicano farm workers made demands for an "entitlement" of the American pie, which was not part of their traditional pattern of interaction. What we are trying to indicate here is that these aspects must be seen dialectically and within historical conditions. The polarity of identity and individuation, in essence, is part of our larger developmental dialectic that I am calling the "polarity of order and change" (transformation).

3. *Order (reproduction)—change (transformation)*. The habitus is the dynamic process of becoming a "me." It is dynamic because it is a generative rather than a passive process. Looking at it in dialectical terms, it is the dialectics of the internalization of externality (the other) into the self or incorporation and the externalization of internality (self-projection or objectification; Bourdieu, 1977). The habitus is, therefore, the product of cultural appropriation and incorporation necessary for these products of collective history (i.e., culture), the objective structures (e.g., language, economy, etc.) succeeding, more or less completely, in reproducing themselves in the form of durable dispositions (i.e., social self or me; Bourdieu, 1977). This social self (me), as we are calling it, is both a product and a producer of a social environment. The social self or habitus must be seen in dynamic structural terms. The structural dialectic is developed by Bourdieu (1977) as follows:

> The structures constitutive of a particular type of environment (e.g., the material conditions of existence characteristic of a class condition) produce *habitus*, systems of durable, transposable dispositions, structured structures predisposed to function as structuring structures, that is, as principles of the generation and structuring of practices and representations which can be objectively "regulated" and "regular" without in any way being the product of obedience to rules, objectively adapted to their goals without presupposing a conscious aiming at ends or an express mastery of the operations necessary to attain them and, being all this, collectively orchestrated without being the product of the orchestrativy action of a conductor. (p. 72)

The structured ordering that is generative in nature has its eye on the past; one could call it the active production (i.e., reproduction) of cultural memory. The social science literature, such as it is, attempts to account for social order and maintenance (Touraine, 1974). In fact, the mainstream definition of psychology as "prediction and control of human behavior" is, of its very nature, a social maintenance (order) endeavor. Within this definition, change must be predictable and orderly in nature in order to have a science that espouses social determinism. The idea of an intentional self (I) sets clear limits to a social science based on social determinism (Winter, 1966). When the "intelligibility of human action" is interpreted in a social–deterministic framework, human creativity becomes anarchic and impulsive. It is considered as disorder rather than some attempt at social transformation. A critical interpretative framework must embrace personal and social change (i.e., transformation) as a legitimate aspect of human action. Sartre (1968) maintains that the most rudimentary action must be determined both in relation to real and present factors that condition it (i.e., order and reproduction) but also in relation to certain objects or purposes still to come that action is trying to bring into being. The idea of the surpassing of the past and present by human action, therefore, establishes transformation and change as a legitimate rather than disordered aspect of human action.

4. *Preconscious—conscious.* The habitus is unconscious as a generative structure. The structures of the habitus are therefore tacit in the sense of what Polyanyi calls the "tacit dimension." The unconscious structures mean the forgetting of history. Like tying one's shoelaces, one assumes from facility that we must have been born with that ability. In reality, by watching a child in his or her nascent movements at this task, we realize that shoe tying is a learned process that has become second nature. Bourdieu (1977) sees the habitus as a generative structure that is made by a history and, in turn, makes history.

> The unconscious is never anything other than the forgetting of history which history itself produces by incorporating the objective structures it produces in the second natures of habitus. . . . in each of us, in varying proportions, there is a part of yesterday's man; it is yesterday's man who inevitably predominates in us, since the present amounts to little compared with the long past in the cause of which we were formed and from which we result. (pp. 78–79)

Personal histories, then, will mirror some aspects of a larger cultural history, and history, instead of being called "dead weight," will be seen as dynamically generative, reproducing itself in predictable cultural ways (i.e., mores and customs). The habitus, then, can be said to be a mediating process generating social practices by individual agents which is culturally reproductive. This is done without explicit reason or signifying intent, making a particular social practice coming from a particular individual appear "sensible" and "reasonable" (Bourdieu, 1977).

The intentional aspect of the self is the conscious producer of human expressions. Consciousness implies the deliberative and reflective actions of an intentional agent. Intentions should therefore be understood as that dimension of human action which is consciously held in mind as orientation toward a goal. The project as a conscious act is, therefore, purposive in nature. Intentional or purposive acts are those which the agent knows or believes can be expected to manifest a particular quality or outcome and in which this knowledge is utilized by the actor to produce the quality or outcome (Giddens, 1977). We have discussed this aspect of the project in Chapter 2 at some length. What I would like to stress here is the dialectic of unconscious and conscious aspects of human agency. Conscious intentions are built on the sediment of past intentions, which are now preconscious. Habit allows for a greater economy in human intentions. Habit allows one to free oneself from constant deliberation in order to project new intentions. In projecting new intentions, old habits may be confirmed or rejected. The building upon habits (preconscious) and the transforming of habits (projects) expresses the dialectic of the conscious and unconscious. It is the *present* embedded in the dialectic of the past and future.

5. *Past (history)—future.* In one sense, the habitus is the rehearsal of what has been in order to keep it happening. It is, therefore, the *past* being reproduced in the *present.* It is history turned into nature (Bourdieu, 1977). Culture is, by definition, second nature. What is natural for humans is that they are, by definition, second natures (i.e., cultural animals). In no other species is the rehearsal of social history so necessary for basic survival. Reproduction of culture is part of the makeup of humans.

The human being is not only a past or a present (a history made) but is a history in the making through his or her projects. Merleau-Ponty (1963) puts this in the following way:

> What defines man is not the capacity to create a second nature—economic, social or cultural—beyond biological nature, it is rather the capacity to go beyond created structures in order to create others. (p. 175)

The intentional futurity of human action should not be seen in a futuristic vacuum. Humans create their futures in history and create it while being weighed down by a past which is, in some very important way, determining. The reproduction of the past in human action serves the maintenance of a specific social order. The projection of human action into the future allows one to, consider the possibility for the transformation of social orders.

6. *Ideological symbols—utopian symbols.* Mannheim (1953b) gave a specific definition to the concept of "ideology" by noting the discovery that emerged from political conflict, namely, that ruling groups can, in their thinking, become intensively involved in reproducing (i.e., maintaining) a particular social order so as to become totally unconscious to certain facts which would undermine their sense of domination. There is an insight implicit in the concept of ideology which alerts one to the collective distortions of habitus; that is, in certain situations the collective unconscious of certain groups obscures the real condition of society both to itself and to others and thereby stabilizes it (Mannheim, 1953b). The work of Marx is an extensive excursus on how class relations and domination produce a collective ideology which is distorted by the unconscious nature of class domination. The habitus is not simply the "collective unconscious of history"; it is the reflection of the power relations productive of a

particular social system. One can, therefore, speak of a "habitus of capitalism," of which we shall say more later. The habitus is, therefore, a generative unconscious production of symbols and linguistic systems that extol the nature of the present social order, actively seeking to maintain it. Ideological symbols are, therefore, symbols of loyalty to the present order, extrolling the worth of that order. Maintenance of these symbols is first projected in the family unit, but in complex societies they are solidified by more impersonal institutions such as the school, mass media, and the state. Ideological symbols (e.g., pledge of allegiance to the flag, etc.) extol the past and help in the production of social maintenance by indicating that the "present order" is the best of all possible worlds. These symbols are the "cultural capital" of ruling classes, where ideological symbols tend to buttress their domination (Bourdieu, 1977). The project, by contrast, moves toward the future and has the potential to challenge the total legitimacy of the past. The first indication of an alternative ordering can be seen in the child's use of negation. Two-year-old children, as a result of their great "no," are felt to be going through the "terrible twos" by parents and psychologists alike. What is implicit in this negation is a challenge to the powers that be (i.e., habitus). Resistance is the first indication that things could or should be otherwise than they are. Negation is a core element in the development of utopian symbols. Utopian symbols are symbolic images of the future that challenge the ultimacy and total legitimacy of the present order. Utopian imagination has a sensitivity to the breaking points of the present system and nourishes a longing for a new kind of social ordering (transformation); thus it exercises a significant role in social change (Baum, 1975). The absence of utopian symbols allows the present order to go unchallenged and results in a static state of affairs in which people become molded to what appear to be the fixed laws of the social system. The project, if it is to be authentic, incorporates utopian symbols that concretize alternative futures:

> Concrete utopians are images of the future that are grounded in athentic intuitions of the ills and contradictions of the present society. Concrete utopias negate the most oppressive elements of this society and present a vision of human life that, even if as such unrealizable, summon forth new ways of thinking and acting that could lead to social change. (Baum, 1975, p. 171)

The notion of project therefore accents the protensive movement of human action set in terms of a posited or fantasied state of affairs in the future perfect tense (Winter, 1968).

7. *The dialectic of determinism—freedom.* In commonsense terms, determinism says "what has happened before will happen again." Determinism is, in essence, the past ordering the present. The habitus is a generative structure that allows some predictability in the social order as well as one's individual personal life. If you know a person or a group history, you will have some orderly sense of

what may happen in new situations. We are not using *determinism* here in terms of mechanical human causality. As we will see when we discuss the notion of project, humans are formed by history (i.e., determinism), but they also alter the course of their histories (i.e., freedom). Humans, as cultural animals, are determined (i.e., made by history) and determining (i.e., make new history). Determinism produced by accumulated history (habitus) allows for the possibility of a sense of identity. Change opens the door to individuation and therefore freedom.

If the commonsense notion of determinism is "what has happened before will happen again," the commonsense version of freedom is that "what has happened before need not happen again." It is not necessary to hold a conception of freedom by throwing away a conception of determinism. A conception of freedom can mean simply that the past does not have absolute power over the present and future. Freedom means a certain openness to the future, where alternatives to the past may operate and possibly be brought to fruition. Sartre (1968) is more lucid in relating a structure of freedom with the notion of project:

> Man defines himself by his project. This material being perpetually goes beyond the condition which is made for him; he reveals and determines his situation by transcending it in order to objectify himself—by work, action, or gesture. The project must not be confused with the will, which is an abstract entity, although the project can assume a voluntary form under certain circumstances. This immediate relation with the Other than oneself, beyond the given and constituted elements, this perpetual production of oneself by work and "praxis," is our peculiar structure. It is neither a will nor a need nor a passion, but our needs—like our passions or like the most abstract of our thoughts—participate in this structure. They are always "outside of themselves toward. . . ." This is what we call existence, and by this we do not mean a stable substance which rests in itself, but rather a perpetual disequilibrium, a wrenching away from itself with all its body. As this impulse toward objectification assumes various forms according to the individual, as it projects us across a field of possibilities, some of which we realize to the exclusion of others, we call it also choice or freedom. . . . (pp. 150–151)

The notion of project or any semblance to it has been absent from the vast corpus of psychological research. This is partly due to the fact that psychology as an institution has been mostly involved in the maintenance of the social order (i.e., socialization). In declaring itself a deterministic science, it eclipsed the notion of freedom. In venturing a conception of freedom as an essential component of critical interpretation, we do not exclude determinisms. Rather, it is necessary to incorporate freedom within a dialectic of freedom and determinism. I would contend that there is no possibility of freedom without a solidified past (i.e., habitus). At the same time, there is an absence of freedom when the past is made an absolute. The transformation of the past (habitus) into possibilities for alternative futures (i.e., projects) is the very essence of human freedom. Humans are certainly made by their past, but, by their projects, they are not condemned to it.

The Personal World as a Located Cultural Form

We have just treated the personal world as a set of dialectical polarities that hold in tension the concepts of socialization and social transformation. Under the tension I have discussed two core notions, the habitus and project, and outlined in dialectical fashion seven polar dimensions that characterize these notions. I would contend that these polarities are the dynamics of culture. The metaphor of the personal assumes a concept of culture within its formulation. The personal world is a cultural world. This is why interpretation is important, since the cultural world creates symbols that need deciphering. A conception of the human as a cultural animal cannot be formulated within a paradigm of mechanism or organism. Shotter (1975) maintains that:

> Man is not just man in nature, he is man in a culture in nature. And a man's culture is not to be characterized in terms of objective properties like all the other things that he sees in nature from within his culture. The culture from within which a man views the world and deliberates upon how to act in it structures his consciousness, and can only be characterized in terms of his beliefs. . . . Thus, if there is a key to the contemporary phase in the development of the human sciences, it is this: there is a third term to the relationship between man and nature, *culture*, which is not genetically inherited but communicated to man after birth as a "second nature." It is this third term that psychology, in its attempts to be scientific, has ignored. (p. 136)

I would like to extend the notion of the personal world to that of a located cultural form. In doing this, we move away from any facile idealization of the personal metaphor. The contention is that the personal world and all its relationships are embedded in a specific history with all of the idiocyncrasies and limitations entailed therein. The personal world is, therefore, a real historical event rather than some abstract formulation of an ideal person. Therefore, when we speak of a personal world, we are essentially talking about an identifiable located cultural form (see Willis, 1977). The essence of that form is constitutive relationships—that is, the particular way a social group is connected to the objects, artifacts, institutions, and systematic practices of others that surround it (Willis, 1977). The individual of a personal world exists as much through similarity as through difference. The paradox here is that individuation is partly achieved by becoming similar to persons in one's group and different from those outside one's group. These constitutive relationships need not imply conscious purpose or intention on the part of the social group (Willis, 1977). In other words, people may share a common world (cultural forms) but do so habitually, unconsciously, and unintentionally. At the same time, parts of that world may be coconstituted intentionally by members. In other words, we are saying that a personal world is a located cultural form created out of habit and intention (i.e., the dialectic of habitus–project). The dialectics of habit and intention allow a personal world the possibility of identity and change at the same time. To talk of the personal world as a located cultural form is, therefore, to talk of a dynamic totality. The personal world as a cultural form implies real exchanges and material dialectics between the structure of human subjectivity, its characterization sensibilities, and its context (Willis, 1977). It is, therefore, a set of relations embedded in material–historical realities. Thus, the personal world is not an abstract idealistic concept; rather, it is the world of groups such as Poles and Irish, blacks, workers, bankers, women, and so on.

What constitutes the boundaries of a personal world? For our purposes, a personal world is an identifiable group of individuals whose relations with one another can be characterized as a reciprocity of equals (relatively speaking) and who center their relations within themselves both materially and symbolically. It is important to distinguish the personal world from larger structural totalities in which it is enmeshed. For example, the commercial system, productive relations, ideological and political formations constitute these larger structural totalities which can and are studied as independent events by other disciplines (e.g., political science, history, economics, sociology, etc.). It is understood in our treatment that these larger structural totalities are not independent of a personal world and cannot be studied as if they were totally discrete facts. This is the topic of the next chapter. In relationship to a personal world, these larger structural totalities can be understood to intervene, redirect, or block the possibility of intent, pure expression, or unity of the personal world. The personal world must be studied dialectically in relation to larger structural totalities. The role of a psychological interpretation of the personal world is simply to accept the microsocial world of the personal without making an individualistic fetish of it as does traditional psychological theorizing. We do not talk about persons in the abstract. Rather, we talk about black persons who are black Americans, French people who are French Canadians. Persons are persons only within a cultural world. There is no person if there is no cultural form. I am, therefore, talking about a concept of the person which is historical in nature. Considering biography as history, I would propose that a critical interpretation of the personal world is an excursion into biography. A psychology of this vintage enables us to focus on the life span (i.e., biography) of the individual as a site of psychological explanation (Hudson, 1972). To do biography is to do an interpretation of a personal world. Critical interpretation is the ability to identify dialectically those factors in a personal world that accent the development of human freedom or detract from that endeavor (i.e., domination). Critical biographical work involves locating biographical material within larger structural totalities. We will introduce these totalities in the next chapter in discussing the notions of class, gender, and ethnicity.

SUMMARY

We have now made the turn out of egocentricity and into culture. This was achieved in a series of steps. Our first task was to distance ourselves from the impediment of individualism, which leads into egocentrism at the level of theory and practice. The next step was to indicate that *intentional expression* at an egocentric level of analysis (see Chapter 2) is the *project* in the personal world. This notion of project was one of the two major components of the personal world in our introduction of the notions of habitus–project. From our treatment of the dialectics of habitus–project in the personal world, we were able to make the transition to the notion of the cultural form. We can now say that the personal world is a cultural form. This equation prevents us from slipping back into egocentric analysis. Willis (1977) makes my point explicit:

> The group is the smallest unit of cultural existence. It is the smallest unit of resistance against the dominant culture, and the immediate form of protection of, and influence on, *particular* subjectivities. It is the pivotal site for the development of wider social and cultural practices. Though the *material* of experience is necessarily often collected (as a research act) from the individual, and though the expression and form of this experience may be personal, the real generator of this experience is the interaction of the group within a specific social and material matrix of symbols, expectations and conditions. Though subjective, then, the focus of my interest is on the *subjectivity* of symbolic systems, actions and values, *not* on the individual person; or more correctly it is only on the individual as he lives out personalized versions of collective strategies. (Willis, 1977, p. 178)

I have given this long quote because of the clarity of focus it gives for the direction I am taking in this book. It is now time to explicate in much greater detail the dialectical relationship between the personal world as cultural form and the larger structural totalities class, race, and gender.

Personal World, Cultural Forms, and the Structures of Class, Gender, Ethnicity, and Age

Introduction

We have just completed a linkage between the personal world of human action and that of the cultural form in that we have built a bridge between the personal world of human intentions and cultural action, an expressive action governed by a dialectical tension identified as habitus–project. In this chapter, I will attempt to sensitize the reader to structural relationships of power and their impact on the personal world. By structural relationships of power, I mean power between agents rather than a specific set of powers supposedly located within agents. These relationships of power will link the personal world of cultural forms to the structures of class, gender, ethnicity, and age.

Power, Agency, and Domination

In English, the word *power* is derived from the Latin word *potere*, of which the root meaning is "to be able to." As a verb, it cannot stand alone and needs completion. Thus, one does not say "I am able to" but "I am able to jump 3 feet high." Strictly speaking, at the level of personal agency one could say that power is a condition where one is "enabled." I would contend that this is a condition of personal agency. From the point of view of individual agency, for the moment one can say that personal powers are present when a human act is identified. In Chapter 2, I identified a human act as having the characteristics of consciousness, intentionality, intentions, responsibility, and significance. What was clear from my treatment in Chapter 2 was that personal agency, in my definition, did not locate agency within agents but rather between agents. This was the reason for my rejection of mechanical and biological metaphors. Therefore, under the personal metaphor I would locate power as a condition between agents. I have maintained that the personal world is a world of mutual reciprocity and equality between agents (I–thou). Thus, there exists a mutual enhancement of personal powers when the personal world and its agents are operating cointentionally. By this, I mean that the world of an agent (I) has its conscious, intentional goals (intentions) that are responsibly significant, enhanced by the other (thou) and vice versa. This type of cointentionality is called cooperation. So mutual agency implies cooperation. When a condition of cooperation is vitiated or absent, one calls this an impersonal relationship. This is a condition where one agent (or agents) treats another agent (or agents) as an object (I–it relationship). We call this relationship inhuman or oppressive. It is a structural condition that will be referred to as *domination*. A condition of domination is operating when the agency of one person or group eclipses or masks the agency of another person or group. Thus, the power of one is at the expense of the other. If the personal relationship could be referred to as *cooperative*, the appellation of *oppression* characterizes a condition of domination. Oppression operates in the following manner: the agency of one person or group (i.e., consciousness, intentionality, intentions, responsibility, and significance) denies the possibility of the other person's or group's consciousness, intentionality, intentions, responsibility, and significance. This situation for those dominated turns agent conditions listed above into their opposite. Thus, for consciousness we have repression, for intentionality we have withdrawal, for intentions we have an absence of goal orientation or rootlessness, for responsibility we have dependency, and for significance we have meaninglessness or anomie. A relationship of domination creates *powerlessness* in the dominated person or group. The most extreme form of this condition is depersonalization, where one person or group treats another person or group as a total object (I–it). This asymmetry in power was described by Hegel as the "master–slave relationship."

Structures of Domination

From my own experience, it is clear that some groups dominate others: men dominate women, adults dominate children, and capital dominates labor. This is not a "fact" *per se*, but I believe that what I am saying is reasonable to assume and can be demonstrated by argument. For example, Wilden (1980) would say these relationships of domination are "real." In other words, they have stability and "social integrity." They are conditions of inequality in social relationships. Wilden (1980) conjectures that there are two ways to camouflage these relationships of inequality. The first one is "imaginary symmetrization." To symmetrize is to venture that capital is equal to labor, women to men, blacks to white, children to adults. Thus, differences between these oppositions are considered accidental and temporary. The apparent unequal relationships can be altered through education, incentives, and so on. I call this liberal ideology (see Chapter 3). The second camouflage is "imaginary inversion" (Wilden, 1980). This inversion is a paranoid set that indulges in stereotypes and agitation. Thus, labor has gotten too big, women are now dominating men, and so on (Wilden, 1980). This is the camouflage of fascist ideology. Both liberal camouflage or ideology and the fascist deny the relationships of inequality to which we have originally alluded. By and large, conventional social science and, for our purposes, conventional psychology indulge in some version of the liberal ideological camouflage (see Sullivan, 1977a, 1977b, 1980a). Specifically, psychologists take structural relationships of power such as capital over labor, men over women, and change them into intrapsychic phenomena. Thus, women's inequality in relation to men can be seen as precipitated by a motive called "fear of success" (Horner, 1970). Black children's inequality to whites can be seen as cultural deprivation. As we shall see later, a critical–interpretative psychology will attempt to deal with these structural inequalities without liberal or fascist camouflage. What we must attempt at the outset is to indicate how these structural inequalities relate to one another and to the specific cultural forms that constitute the fabric and underpinning of any social order.

Domination in the Context of Cultural Forms

In Chapter 3, I indicated how the cultural world is embedded in a dialectic of order and change called the habitus–project tension. It is now necessary to link these concepts to the structures of domination and the dimension of power. Within the dynamic of habitus–project, domination can operate in two distinct but by no means separate ways. The first way is through the destruction and destabilizing of an ordered cultural form (i.e., habitus). Habitus or stabilized social relationships are the firm footings for cultural projects. The second way is through the direct repression of the projective character of a specific cultural form (i.e., project). Repression within this context destroys the dynamic forward movement of a cultural project (i.e., creative project). Domination is achieved by operating simultaneously on both stabilizing and dynamic core of specific cultural forms. Its end product is disabling (i.e., powerlessness).

CLASS AS A STRUCTURE OF DOMINATION

I now enter an area that conventional psychology ignores but that is essential to my treatment of the personal world of specific cultural forms. This is "class analysis" in the tradition of Marxism. I have already alluded to a dominance relationship of capital over labor. This is the category of dominance in which traditional Marxism discusses class analysis. The notion of class, as a result of the profound thinking of Karl Marx, has been identified in its modern coinage with economic categories. It is reasonable to assume that economics would be pre-emptive in a trade society like our own where class relations have a clearly identifiable economic dimension (Touraine, 1979). The complexity of class relations in modern societies makes it difficult to recognize clearly identifiable and recognizable social classes (Touraine, 1979). This does not detract from the importance of considering "class relations" as an important tool for social analy-sis, not only for economic categories but also for social and political categories as well (see Bourdieu & Passeron, 1977; Edwards, 1979; Piore, 1973; Touraine, 1979; Wright, 1976). Touraine (1979) reasons that social class is not defined simply by its relations of production, for this class also has the capacity to manage the state, to improve its ideology, and to repress or alienate its adversaries.

To make "class" a preemptive category for the analysis of dominance rela-tionship is questionable and suspect. Feminists are quick to point out that there are two evils that predate capitalism, namely, racism and sexism, in a criticism of male-dominated socialist revolution (Morgan, 1970).

It is clear that sexism is a more universal category of dominance than class, since it is present in the gender relationships of both dominant and subordinate classes. Racism is also not restricted to the dominant class and is clearly visible in virulent forms in subordinate groups. Frequently racism is a characteristic of relationships between cultural groups in the subordinate classes (e.g. blacks and Puerto Ricans). Just how these relationships of dominance are related is not clear, and no social theory has been successful thus far in explicating their interaction. This makes a case for caution for anyone, like myself, who ventures into this complex area. Thus, a viable class analysis demands a considerable amount of sublety (see Braverman, 1974; Piore, 1973; Wright, 1976). It would be pretentious to attempt to develop the complexity of contemporary class analy-sis in brief. What is being attempted here is to embed our conception of a personal world and its cultural forms in class structural terms. There is no simple class called laborers, for example; rather, there are Chicanos, blacks, Italians, Irish, and so on. It is not important or useful to pinpoint a "class" in contempo-rary class analysis. What is important is to emphasize the hierarchical nature of social relations, which is part and parcel of our contemporary productive and consumptive apparatus. It is here that I wish to locate a critical interpretation of the personal world and its cultural forms. A critical interpretation of that world will be sensitive to the relations of power and domination that prevent and jeopardize the development of human projects for some groups of people be-cause of the projects of others. In short, we are talking of relationships of exploitation. This constitutes a radical departure from most traditional person-ality theory, which has heretofore existed behind the imperatives of class and power, curiously independent and separate from the economic forces operating in society. In a society like our own, one can venture that the economic order of monopoly capitalism is stabilized through the dominance of capital over labor. This is done in numerous ways; the two most prominent are the control that the dominant group has over the means of production and also through incentives that come from consumption of products. Consider the possibility of two classes or groups interacting with one another. Rather than be prematurely specific, let us say one class or group is dominant and the other class is nondominant. The dominant group is characterized as having a clear ideological solidifcation (i.e., habitus) and a consciously operating project. The dominant class has control over the ideology of production, the cultural realm, political and state apparatus, as well as educational institutions (see Kellner, 1978). The dominant class has the capacity to manage the state, to impose its ideologies, and to repress and alienate its adversaries (Touraine, 1979). The nondominant class has a diffused ideology (habitus) or one that conforms in essential features to the habitus of the dominant ideological group. The difference between these groups as regards class habitus is that the dominant ideology is perceived as solidified (a condition of solidarity) in the dominant groups and diffuse (nonsolidarity and division) in the nondominant group. The project of the dominant class is perceived as the cultural project. The dominant group is in hegemonic control of the cultural project. The nondominant groups experience the lack of an authentic cultural project. This is a condition of alienation or oppression for this class, because of the overriding character of the dominant class's project. The first inclination of a project of the nondominant class is the presence of a resistance to the project of the dominant class. A second solidification of resistance is attempting a solidarity and class habitus that is independent of the habitus of the dominant group.

Let me take specific instances now to solidify the position I am attempting to develop. In doing this, I am assuming that class relations in a capitalist society can, after Wright (1976), be analyzed in terms of three processes underlying the social relations of production: (1) control of labor power, (2) control of the physical means of production, and (3) control of investment and resources. Wright (1976) contends that the central class forces in a capitalist society—that is, the bourgeoisie and the proletariat—represent polar class positions within each of these processes. Moreover, the polarities are maintained and legitimated in the ideological sectors such as family, school, and churches (Althusser, 1971; Bourdieu & Passeron, 1977).

Dominant Class

Members of the dominant class experience life as agents. They have a "solidified habitus," which is congruent with the prevalent cultural consensus. Because of the prevalence of sexism across all classes, males are more likely to perceive of themselves as agents than are females. In dominant classes, women solidify male dominance by supporting male agency without participating in it.

The dominant class controls the productive sector and, in essence, the cultural project of capitalism is defined within this class. Capitalism shrinks the scope of the human project by restricting utopian images to profit and consumer images and also lessening the possible range of free acts. Specifically, this can be seen by an examination of some of the empirical work on the phenomenology of the class structure. Maccoby (1976), in a book called *The Gamesmen*, did an intensive study of the upper echelons of the executive world. The "gamesmen," as he calls them, have to compete. They thrive on competition and the solving of problems. They accept, in my view, the dominant ideology of capitalism and enhance themselves on the upward mobility that is there for those who compete and succeed. They have a sense of a project and feel that they are in control of things. At this level of corporate life, the gamesman is a man rather than a woman, which is indicative of the implicit sexism in capitalism. The women of the gamesmen stand behind their men, supporting their projects by raising the children and by moving themselves and their families wherever the "games" have to be played. The gamesman supports "meritocracy" and sees his own success as based on his ability to compete and win. This project is the wider cultural project of capitalism, with competition at the apex.

Does the gamesman learn his project, as it were, "on the job"? By and large, he is probably raised in a "culture of affluence"; the "cultural form" of the gamesman's personal world has some unique characteristics that begin to be nurtured in childhood. It is here that the family and school develop a character which will meld with the expectations of future occupational status (Bourdieau & Passeron, 1977; Connell, 1977). Connell (1977), interviewing children from upper-status suburbs in Australia, gives a taste of this forming of character by early expectations for university education:

> Boy 12: Well, I'd like to—my mother wants me to go to university, and I want to go myself, and I want to say be an engineer kind of—my mother thinks it too hard, but my mother wants me to be a doctor, and I'm not keen on that. I'd like to do something more exciting—my mother said an engineer gets one of the most salaries in the world. (p. 153)

And even in the next instance, where a girl from a dominant class thinks she is not clever enough, a confidence and family support is still perceived:

> Girl 15: I'd like to be a teacher, I think they do a lot better than some people do. I'd like to teach either primary or infants. I'm not sure at the moment, I'd only have to go to teachers' college. Dad wants me to go to university and get a Bachelor of Arts degree but I don't think I'm clever enough for that. . . . I'm going in for a test on Firday to the Guidance Department for an interview about occupations and you have to name the three that you'd like to do. (Which ones did you?) I put teaching first, and then if I couldn't do that I wouldn't mind being a child welfare officer or a social worker, cause I like children. . . . (p. 153)

Compare this statement with that of a lower-class girl of 13:

Girl 13: Well, myself I'd like to be a kindergarten teacher—I've got four brothers and sisters younger than me and I get along with them real good, play games with them on weekends and I get along with children. I'm very patient with them, not like my sister she goes off her rocker (laughs) bashes into them or screams or something. That's what I'd like to be or if I couldn't do that, which I don't think I've got the brains really, the intelligence, you know you've got to go all through school and the university and college and such, then I think I'd like to work either in some sort of shop, or then I'd go in for a factory. . . . (Connell, 1977, p. 152)

It is clear from Connell's examples and others (e.g., Coles, 1977; Willis, 1977) that the class-structure expectations reveal themselves in cultural forms in childhood expectations of students and parents. Let us now look at this outcome in more specific detail in the nondominant class.

Nondominant Class

The experience of a sense of agency is a difficult endeavor for members of nondominant classes. This is not to say that a sense of agency is totally lacking, but, by and large, it is experienced in what might be called the private sector of the family. Here, it is usually the male head of the family who experiences some semblance of power. Outside of the family, in the larger structural realities of work and politics, the member of the nondominant class experiences social reality as arbitrary or clearly within the control of the dominant class, however that is perceived. Members of the nondominant class generally sense the feeling of being a pawn rather than an "origin" of their social reality (De Charms, 1976). This position is operant when the nondominant class concedes the viability and legitimation of the social power of the dominant class. Nascent resistance to the dominant social reality of the dominant class is the kernel of agency that, if organized and consolidated, can challenge the power of the dominant class. Resistance, if politicized, can be the beginning of a project that is emergent and transformative. Resistance in itself is precarious and—when not challenging the structural totality of the dominant class—is short-lived and destructive of solidarity (Willis, 1977). It is not only agency that is lacking in the nondominant class; the "ordered stability" (i.e., habitus) which is integrated into the lives of members of the dominant class is experienced as vicarious and arbitrary by the nondominant class, since there is the absence of true participation in the structure of the dominant social reality. Thus, when a large corporation develops a community, the community can thrive on the economic windfall, but that reality can be decimated by a shift of that corporation out of the area. The absence of decisive control over the corporation in the community's life, a community project, leaves the ordered stability necessary for community life always precarious. It is here that corporate economic decisions have profound psychological consequences (Brenner, 1976). Let me now quote some empirical studies that attempt to elucidate the attempts at integration of the habitus and project of nondominant class members.

Sennett and Cobb (1973), in a book called *The Hidden Injuries of Class*, attempt to construct a quasiphenomenological account of adult working-class males. "Hidden injuries" represent the "personal cost" of the class structure to the psychological lives of these working-class males. What these authors try to demonstrate is how the "victims of a class structure" come to blame themselves for their plight. They are men who are not happy in their jobs, fear upward mobility because of peer rejection, and whose only solace is the fact that their children may be spared the working-class life and the boring jobs that they are required to do. Their major form of transcendence is the family, where consumption of commodities becomes the trade-off for alienating work (Sullivan, 1980a). Sennett and Cobb (1973) demonstrate the total hegemony of the class structure and its power to mute any sense of project in these workers, who blame the absence of project on their own previous educational histories or lack thereof.

There is a depressing tone to this study, and it stems from the apparent total absence of any resistance of these workers which might challenge the nature of their social realities (i.e., dull work) in terms other than that of their own shortcomings. One must question these authors' interpretative horizons, which seem to totally ignore the possible resistance of the working-class males they study. It would be important for a critically interpretative psychology not to miss signs of resistance to class domination, which are potentially transformative in nature. Aronowitz (1973), in a study of automobile workers, would appear to challenge the total passivity of working-class men in highly specialized and boring jobs. The automobile workers in the town plant of General Motors indicate a set of social relationships on the shop floor that are filled with rebellion and acts of resistance. It would be prematurely optimistic to name this kind of resistance a transformative project, but one should not ignore its nascent possibilities. The line workers resist by struggling to organize the production process in their day-to-day life. They do this at various levels of production by attempting to modify and control timing, pacing, and demands made upon them. They also appear to develop a certain camaraderie in their social relationships, creating rituals to break the monotony of their work routines. In general, this is accomplished through humor, small acts of resistance, and acts of outright sabotage that challenge the predefined authority of the workplace (Willis, 1977).

Willis (1977) elucidates very clearly the precarious nature of lower-class adolescent resistance in his ethnorgraphic analysis of social reproduction. His methodological technique maps out the reproductive path where working-class boys come to accept the seeming inevitability of working-class jobs. This, interestingly enough, is partially accomplished by the rampant sexism prevalent among these English working-class youths. In working-class youth, the value of manual labor is tied up with these youths' sense of masculinity (Willis, 1977). One interesting aspect of Willis's sample is the boys' active rebellion against the structure of the school system, in its institutional assault on their mode of dress, their language, their life-style, their sensuality. An active resistance to this assault is apparent in these students' rejection and ridiculing of the messages and demands of the school's overt and hidden curricula. Willis (1977) is very cognizant of the nonpolitical nature of this resistance, which is not directed to the structural dimensions of class, and ultimately determines that this type of resistance leads to entrapment rather than the transformation of institutional life.

What is important for an interpretative psychology of critical import is to sense the effect of the class structure on the personal worlds of cultural forms located within that structure. As with the Aronowitz (1973) and Willis (1977) observations, it is necessary to be sensitized to nascent forms of projects in dominated cultures. A critically sensitive psychology will not simply interpret this resistance as deviance, as is the case of most mainstream psychological interpretations of lower-class cultures. At the same time, this sensitivity must countenance the ambiguous nature of resistance in social positions which are lacking in social power, as are members of nondominant classes.

This leads me now to a summary statement on the nature of class structures and its dialectical relationship with the varied cultural forms that constitute to the dynamics of the class structure. We have established that a class structure is based on economic disparities which establish the dominance of one class over another. This domination is not simply economic in nature. It is maintained and legitimated by family, church, educational institutions, and state structures. It is also accomplished through the structures of ethnicity, gender, and age, albeit in a complex dialectical manner. All of these institutions combine to form the basis of a cultural totality, which we have labeled the "hegemony" of a capitalist class structure. The most pervasive and essential (but by no means exclusive) motive in a capitalist class structure is that of profit and capital accumulation. Profits are systematically accumulated more in the dominating class, and the legitimacy of this enterprise is buffered by the ideological structures of education and the state. There is a seeming naturalness and inevitability in this complex process, which usually goes unquestioned (Gramsci, 1971; Williams, 1976a). It is in this situated world of economics and ideological legitimation that the personal world is lived as a cultural form. Our contention in this chapter is that the cultural forms of the personal world are systemically influenced by the dynamics of the class structure. In schematic and summary form, let us look at this class dynamic when the class structure is stabilized and legitimated and when the class structure is being substantially challenged by the nondominant culture sustaining oppositional forms. The former dynamics will be called "formative" and the latter will be called "transformative." In the transformation phase, the oppositional structures of the nondominant class threaten the hegemonic structures of the dominant class. This can either be a condition of what is popularly called "reform" or "revolution." Tables 4 and 5 summarize the dynamics.

Having now set out a summary in tabular form of the dynamics of the class

Cultural Form of the Dominant Class		Cultural Form of the Nondominant Class
Habitus		Habitus
(a) *Social self*—a solidarity is experienced with one's class. This solidarity is buffered by a clear sense of identity . . .	$\longleftrightarrow$	(a) *Social self*—although there is a "solidarity present because of common fate," it is not buffered by a strong sense of identity . . . .
(b) *Identity*—in which one sees a close set of ties with one's parents and peers, which is integrated into an order . . .	$\longleftrightarrow$	(b) *Identity*—is diffused because the cultural dynamics of class and because the inadequacy of social power mutes a strong identification with one's parents and peers (i.e., father wants son to be different from him).
(c) *Order*—which is backed up by the legitimacy engendered for this class in the family ties, educational system, and state apparatuses. The cumulative residual of this ideological order is preconscious . . .	$\longleftrightarrow$	(c) *Order*—the experience of the social order appears arbitrary, and this class form is not legitimated by family ties, the educational system, or the state apparatuses. The school system slots members of the class for less prestigious educational outcomes, and this is done in such a fashion to allow members to be preconscious . . .
(d) *Preconscious*—so as to appear natural and inevitable rather than appropriated or consolidated. This preconscious consolidation is organized in a clearly ideological . . .	$\longleftrightarrow$	(d) *Preconscious*—of the systematic nature of this legitimated exclusion, thus appearing natural or inevitable and probably the best thing for all involved (i.e., complicity in their own oppression).
(e) *Ideological*—manner which justifies this seeming inevitability as eternal and historical and possibly biologically generated. Thus a determinism . . .	$\longleftrightarrow$	(e) *Ideological*—systems operate in this class by the acceptance of their exclusion from power and prestige as external and ahistorical (we always have been this way—we will always be the way we are now).
(f) *Determinism*—is experienced as to the natural location of one's cultural form in the class structure. This is the experience of natural entitlement, which allows no challenge to the present cultural hegemony.	$\longleftrightarrow$	(f) *Determinism*—is experienced as to the natural location of one's cultural form in the class structure. This is the experience of natural disenfranchisement which presents little challenge to the present cultural hegemony.

Project

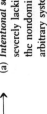

Project

(a) *Intentional self*—a sense of agency and congruence with the larger cultural project is prevalent. Children and adults in dominant social positions perceive themselves as originating their situation or fate. This allows for a sense of individuation . . . .

(b) *Individuation*—which is, in essence, the sense that there is a place in the world for me which I, through my agency, bring about and originate. Change . . . .

(c) *Change*—in a dominant position is experienced as orderly and predictable. The powerful sense of agency stemming from a congruence with the larger cultural hegemony is experienced as possible but systematically in the hands of the agent.

(d) *Conscious*—actions are governed by the directives of the larger cultural project. Under monopoly capitalism, these conscious decisions are governed in a superordinate sense (but not solely) by the profit motive.

(e) *Utopian*—images of change are always governed by reform rather than revolutionary visions. The utopian image in the dominant class is gradualistic and progressive and opposed to revolutionary and system-destabilizing freedom . . . .

(f) *Freedom*—is experienced as the sence of agency, which comes with accomplishing the tasks of the larger cultural projects. It is also the absence of impediments to the agents' sense of agency (i.e., liberal freedom).

(a) *Intentional self*—in the nondominant position is either low or severely lacking in a sense of agency. Children and adults in the nondominant position perceive themselves as pawns in an arbitrary system which is governed by the hegemony of the dominant class's intentions.

(b) *Individuation*—is lacking in any sustained sense. People in the nondominant social position do not experience that they can have a place in the world carved out by their intentions. They have a sense of being pawns in a larger social system.

(c) *Change*—in a nondominant social position is experienced as disorderly, arbitrary, and unpredictable. Since the larger social totalities that this class is embedded in do not respond to its intentions, change is considered luck rather than the predictable outcome of concerted actions governed by one's intentions.

(d) *Conscious*—actions are not integrated into the larger cultural project. In the nondominant formative position, there is a failure in consciousness. Sartre would call this class a class "in itself" but not "for itself."

(e) *Utopian*—images are muted by the failure of this class to believe that consolidated social action can possibly yield to one's intentions. It is a condition of "bad faith," in Sartre's terms.

(f) *Freedom*—if it is perceived at all, is experienced in the microcosm (i.e., family, peers) but absent in a sense of accomplished within the larger cultural project. This absence of freedom is a condition of what Marx called "alienation."

Cultural Form of the Nondominant Class		Cultural Form of the Dominant Class
Habitus		Habitus

(a) *Social self*—a sense of solidarity because of common fate and shared oppression. A "need for roots" and a time when oppression was consolidating is expressed, helping to formulate a sense of identity . . .

(b) *Identity*—is accomplished with retrieval of a past history in order to restore a sense of continuity with the present. The authenticity of ancestors and a shared history allows a sense of order . . .

(c) *Order*—which is countercultural and not centered in the history of the dominant group. The ordered legitimacy of schooling and state institutions is questioned as to its ultimacy and importance for the functioning of one's own particular historical group.

(d) *Preconscious*—trust in the possibility of a social order geared to the authentic needs of one's group is frequently embedded in a religious perspective, which allows groups to trust in a pilgrimage toward new social forms (e.g., Exodus myth).

(e) *Ideological*—order of the dominant group is questioned and rebelled against. The hegemony of the present order is relativized and allows for the rehearsal of emergent social forms.

(f) *Determinism*—as to one's place in the present social order is no longer seen as natural and inevitable. Nondominant group begins to see the present dominance of other social groups as neither inevitable nor desirable.

(a) *Social self*—the solidarity experienced as being part of a dominant class becomes questionable and there are ambiguous areas which lead to a less stable sense of identity . . .

(b) *Identity*—in which the ties with the past are loosened and a certain amount of instability ensues, which challenges the sense of order . . . .

(c) *Order*—which no longer has the uncontested backing and legitimation coming from such ideological sectors as the school, state, and the nondominant class. This lack of an "ordered sense" frequently leads to violence in order to restore the "law and order" of the glorious past.

(d) *Preconscious*—trust in the solidarity and naturalness of the present social order, making unquestionableness of the past questionable and leading to a breakdown in the ideological . . .

(e) *Ideological*—order which either demands a hysterical consistency with the status quo of the past or gradual reforms that allow the integrity of the present order to be retained.

(f) *Determinism*—the natural entitlement no longer is seen as predictable and solidified, which either leads to a consolidation of the past through some power play or some attempts at change or accommodation.

(a) *Intentional self*—the natural sense of agency becomes precarious when a dominant class appears to be losing its dominant footing.

(b) *Individuation*—of dominant members becoms curtailed because the scope of the dominant culture's project is partially walled off by the emerging sense of agency of the nondominant class.

(c) *Change*—occurs when the dominant position is questioned and begins to appear disorderly and unpredictable. The loss of agency within the dominant cultural hegemony makes change appear arbitrary and too much in control of anarchic forces (usually another word for the "emergent opposition of the nondominant class").

(d) *Conscious*—actions become hypervigilant, having lost the absolute sense that the cultural project subscribed to by the dominant class is shared even by those who do not share in the dominant hegemony (i.e., nondominant class).

(e) *Utopian*—images become "negatively transcendent' (how do we get back to the good old days?). The more liberal utopians concede that reform and development of the dominant cultural project is imminent and a sense of gradualism will best accomplish the necessary changes.

(f) *Freedom*—which particularly came from the sense of agency over nondominant classes becomes curtailed. This unlimited freedom is suppressed by the emergent opposition of the nondominant classes presenting alternative projects. "New freedom" is possible if there is an authentic identification with the opposition of the nondominant class.

(a) *Intentional self*—the conception of self in a transformative situation is seen in a dawning sense of agency. The sense that oneself and one's group can create a history rather than being submerged in another's.

(b) *Individuation*—is seen in the experience of a unique sense of identity (i.e., "Black Is Beautiful") with its own unique and idiosyncratic advantages which must be "experienced" and "recognized."

(c) *Change*—in a transformative condition is now seen as a real historical possibility dependent on the ability of one's group to organize (i.e., solidarity) the direction of that change. The hegemony of the dominant group is now seen as systematic rather than arbitrary and, therefore, open to question.

(d) *Conscious*—actions are now organized around the symbols of projected emergent forms. In a transformative situation there is "consciousness raising" and a dawning sense that we are a class—not only a class "in itself" but "for itself."

(e) *Utopian*—images become rich and profusive. When religious symbols are used, the sympols are prophetic in nature. The utopian images ordinarily reject the legitimacy of the present order and project images of emergent forms (e.g., image of the promised land).

(f) *Freedom*—is experienced dialectically. First in the intention of rejecting the absolute ultimacy of the formerly dominant regime and, second, in the sense that by our own agency we can create a new history which is moving away from the oppressive forms of the present.

structure, I must insist that the reader understand the provisional nature of these outlines. Class dynamics must be seen in relational terms of power and legitimation; it would be naive to see my tables as suggesting a simple two-class analysis. In a complex society like our own, it is necessary to comprehend that individuals and groups do not occupy absolute positions and that there are "contested terrains" (Edwards, 1979). This chapter was not meant to exhaust these subtleties but to orient the reader toward the importance of considering the dynamics of class in the development of the personal world of specific cultural forms.

CLASS, CULTURAL FORM, AND ETHNICITY

With the exception of the historic English working class, it is difficult to pinpoint a class per se as a specific "cultural form." I would contend that the personal world as a cultural form is experienced through ethnicity. In other words, people perceive themselves ethnically before there is a consciousness of class location; that is, the premptive experience of the personal world is culture rather than class. One of the most important features of contemporary Marxist analysis is the attempt to relate culture dialectically to class (see Gramsci, 1971; Williams, 1976a). It is here that I take a point of departure. I will try to relate the personal world as a cultural form to the larger structural totality of economic class analysis. Up to now, I have developed the notion of the personal world as a totality, that is, the relational (I and you). I also developed the idea of the personal as a cultural form; that is, we are not persons in relation in the abstract but real histories. Our personal world is a lived history of specific cultural forms or cultures (e.g., Pole, Swede, black, Puerto Rican, Native American, etc.). In this chapter we are embedding the personal world in the larger structural totalities of culture, class, gender, and age. I commence by following Williams (1976a), who emphasizes the "intentional nature" of a class structure analysis. The previous chapters have prepared the way for considering the intentional nature of class. Williams (1976a) sees an emphasis on "intention" as important for the following reasons:

> For while it is true that any society is a complex whole of such practices, it is also true that any society has a specific organization, a specific structure and that the principles of this organization and structure can be seen as directly related to certain social intentions, which in all our experience have been the rule of a particular class. . . . But in many areas of social and political thought, certain kinds of ratifying theory, certain kinds of law, certain kinds of institutions, which after all in Marx's original formulations were very much part of the super-structure—in all that kind of social apparatus and in a decisive area of political and ideological activity and construction if we fail to see a superstructural element we fail to recognize reality at all. These laws, constitutions, theories, ideologies, which are claimed as natural, or as having universal validity and significance, simply have been expressing and ratifying the domination of a particular class. (p. 204)

Williams (1976a) further suggests that the notion of a social totality should be combined with that of the crucial neo-Marxist concept of hegemony. Here the thought of Gramsci (1971) assumes prominent significance (Williams, 1976a). For Gramsci, *hegemony* refers to a form of ideological control in which dominant social practices, beliefs, and values are reproduced and disseminated through a range of institutions such as schools, family, mass media, and so on. Hegemony assumes the existence of a totality that saturates the society to such an extent as even to constitute the limit of common sense for most people under its sway. The important feature that Gramsci puts forward in the concept of hegemony is the emphasis on the reality of *domination*. Williams (1976a) suggests that in any society, in any particular period, there is a central system of practices, meanings, and values that can clearly be seen to be dominant and powerful. Succinctly:

> It is a whole body of practices and expectations; our assignments of energy, our ordinary understanding of the nature of man and of his world. It is a set of meanings and values which as they are experienced as practices appear as reciprocally confirming. It thus constitutes a sense of reality for most people in the society, a sense of the absolute because experienced as reality beyond which it is difficult for most members of the society to move, in most areas of their lives. (p. 205)

Hegemony, because of pervasiveness, relates to all major spheres of social existence; it is convenient here to consider four major ideological realms: (1) the economic realm, which encompasses the ideologies of production, exchanges, distribution, and so on; (2) the cultural realm, encompassing the ideologies of culture, values, mass media, and so on; (3) the political realm, encompassing ideologies of the state, legal–judicial system, police, military, and so on; and (4) the social realm, encompassing ideologies of the private sphere, family, education, social groups, and so on (Kellner, 1978). Psychology and the "personal world as a cultural form" is part of this last realm. One therefore must see this personal sphere as embedded in these larger totalities.

The question that presents itself immediately is: How can this personal world have an integrity if it is totally embedded in the hegemony of the dominant culture? This is an important issue and demands some subtlety in analysis. If the powerful legitimations of modern capitalism exert themselves with such a dominating force in all ideological realms, it would seem that there is no room for any independence from this pervasive consciousness. To say that our personal worlds are not powerfully determined under the hegemony of capitalism would be patently naive. Left at this point, however, we are locked into a total determinism of reproduction ("Whatever has been will be"). Williams (1976a) introduces the notion of oppositional forms to the dominant ethos as a way of handling this problem:

> We have to think again about the sources of that which is not corporate of those practices, experiences, meanings, values, which are not part of the effective dominant

culture. We can express this in two ways. There is clearly something that we can call alternative to the effective dominant culture and there is something we can call oppositional in a true sense. The degree of existence of these alternative and oppositional forms is itself a matter of constant historical variation in real circumstances. (p. 206)

Oppositional Forms as "Residual" or "Emergent"

Williams (1976a) identifies two oppositional forms within the hegemony of the dominant culture. A "residual" is in essence a carryover from a previous historical period. The presence of a residual form is indicative of some experiences, meanings, and values that cannot be expressed or verified in terms of the dominant culture but are, nevertheless, lived on the basis of the residue of some previous social formation. Certain forms of bartering practiced in certain rural areas offer one case in point.

The second is an "emergent" form in opposition to the dominant culture. Emergent forms assume that new meanings and values, new practices, new significances and experiences are continually being created (Williams, 1976a). Williams makes an important distinction between what he calls "alternative" and "oppositional" forms:

> There is a simple theoretical distinction between alternative and oppositional, that is to say, between someone who simply finds a different way to live and wishes to be left alone with it, and someone who finds a different way to live and wants to change society in its light. This is usually the difference between individual and small-group solutions which properly speaking are ultimately revolutionary practices. But it is often a narrow line, in reality, between alternative and oppositional. (pp. 206–207)

Brown (1973) identifies these oppositional forms to the presently constituted "bourgeois hegemony." They are seen in the development of revolutionary movements in both the third world and among the colonized minorities of western metropolitan countries. The oppositional groups to the dominant culture are characterized as "youth culture," "feminist" movements in the west, "black power" and black nationalism (Brown, 1973). As emergent cultural forms, they provide the basis for new identities and, therefore, new cultural projects that challenge the hegemony of the status quo. Combined, these cultural movements are potentially the basis for an alternative cultural identity. There must, therefore, be a sensitivity to emergent cultural forms or countercultural oppositions that are not simply considered as deviant. A sensitivity to all "liberation movements" on their own terms is an important prerequisite. This does not exclude a critical analysis; rather, the critical analysis is based on the ultimate viability of cultural forms that potentially challenge the destructive aspects of cultural forms developed under monopoly capitalism. As social interpreters or hermeneuts, we do not rush in with the view of treating oppositional groups as "deviant." Even when sympathetic, one does not end up by "blaming the victim," which is a common practice of mainstream psychology toward vulnerable cultural groups (Ryan, 1971; Glasgow, 1980). Indeed, it is the task of a critical psychology to identify the hegemonic structural factors in the organization of our society which create systemic oppression for specific cultural groups (e.g. blacks, Native Americans, women, children, etc.). Let me now turn to some *specific* examples of this type of analysis by specifying how they can be related to gender, age, and racial and ethnic inequality.

A Case Study of Ethnicity and Class Dynamics

The study that I am now about to interpret combines class and ethnicity within its overall analysis. The work is Glasgow's (1980) *The Black Underclass*, subtitled *Poverty, Unemployment and the Entrapment of Ghetto Youth*. This is the study of the young blacks in the Watts ghetto and specifically involves the Watts uprising. Glasgow (1980) calls them the "underclass" because they are an identifiable core of black youth that persist from one generation to another in a condition of chronic long-term unemployment and who remain persistently poor and immobile in the economic structure.

Racism, it would appear, is as old as humankind itself. All major social systems in history have suffered from it in one form or another. With this in mind, it may be said that monopoly capitalism does not have a monopoly on aberrant race relations. It does, however, utilize racial differences for its own peculiar designs. Racial differences are a convenient marking for class hierarchies. The mark of the stranger has always been a convenient justification for oppression and exploitation. In a capitalist class-structured society, racial differences allow the possibility of mapping social class differences along racial lines.

No one here is denying that there are differences in cultural forms that proceed along the lines of racial characteristics. This is not an issue here. What will be questioned is (as in the case of gender relations) the pervasive use of organic metaphors that have been used to explain racial differences. In addition, the organic metaphor will be questioned in the case of racial differences, insofar as it seems systematically to legitimate racial exploitation along class lines. Our contention is that racial groups constitute cultural forms that go into the makeup of unique personal worlds. The ambiguity of class boundaries in advanced capitalist society (see Wright, 1976) demands a treatment of race and class of some subtlety. Racial dynamics interact within a class structure in quite an intricate fashion. Even in racial groups whose class origin is similar (i.e., working class), racial division, as with gender division, consolidates the dominant hegemony (Willis, 1977). The divisiveness of cultural forms along racial lines has a considerable amount of psychological dynamics (Willis, 1977). It is here that a more subtle treatment of the relational dynamics of class and race becomes necessary. In an advanced capitalist society one can observe sociological distinctions between middle class, working class, and lower class subcultures (see Piore, 1973). The complex racial dynamics within a class-structured society create different mobility chains (Piore, 1973). Racial dynamics in the lower mobility chains (i.e., working class, lower class) divides and conquers any intimations of solidarity (Willis, 1977):

> It also provides an evident underclass which is more heavily exploited than the white working class, and is therefore indirectly and partially exploited by the working class itself (at least lessening their own exploitation); it also provides an ideological object for feelings about the degeneracy of others and the superiority of the self (thus reinforcing the dominant ideological terms which make the comparison possible). Racism therefore divides the working class both materially and ideologically—Racism must be understood with respect more to the complex social definition of labour power under capitalism than to any pure and inevitable ethnic hostility. (pp. 152–153)

Although there are many important insights in this study, the part that I will accent is the dynamics of the personal world under a formative dynamics, already discussed in Table 4, and the nascent transformation of that world (transformative dynamics, see Tables 5 and 7), which ensued with the initial eruption of the Watts riots in Los Angeles in the late 1960s. The importance of this study here is its exemplifying how the cultural world of a particular racial group transforms itself quite dramatically when the class structure which entraps them is rebelled against. The following is my own interpretation of Glasgow (1980) within the scheme formation–transformation dialectic that has been outlined previously in Tables 4 and 5. Tables 6 and 7 exemplify the structural and personal dynamics of this group of youthful blacks, who are entrapped in the lowest tier of the class system. Table 6 outlines the formative dynamics that were dominant before the Watts riot. Glasgow (1980) indicates that it is necessary to have a radically different approach to social inquiry in order to understand the complex and dramatic alteration of the social world that accompanied and followed the Watts uprising. The first violence is a striking out against the institutions and symbols representing oppression and exploitation.

> The ghetto seethed, tensions mounted, and the police—the hated symbol of black containment in enclaves north and south—finally provided the catalyst that set in motion one of the most ravaging outbursts of blacks in the history of this nation. Their rage was directed at white society's structure, its repressive institutions and their symbols of exploitation in the ghetto: the chain stores, the oligopolies that control the distribution of goods; the lenders, those who hold the indebtedness of the ghetto bound; the absentee landlords; and the agents who control the underclass while safeguarding the rights of those who exploit. The explosion was intended to get even with those whom poor blacks hate and resent, the people who profit from the powerless condition of the poor and the entrapped; it also represented the hope of making some change in their living conditions. (p. 106)

The dramatic shift that occurred after the initial riot cannot be explained in any linear interpretative system. The personal world obviously can change in some quantum fashion when the oppression of the class and racial dynamics are challenged directly.

> A different approach is needed to answer the question of what propelled a young man in 1965 to throw a blazing bottle of gasoline into a store front in the late afternoon when only hours earlier he was with a friend at the beach making love. And it is more important to ascertain what encouraged the same young man to move from violence and destruction to activities for community improvement all within the short period of six months. In the end, we must ask what were the social mechanisms making such dramatic movement possible—from violence to constructive involvement, from gang hooliganism to responsible participation. (Glasgow, 1980, p. 107)

The first attempt at launching an authentic project is through active resistance toward the entrapping social structures. Violence is the initial volley. As one participant put it:

> The brothers got together. I was hollering, "Burn, Baby, Burn." Lou Rawls expressed it well: "Tear it up, blow it up, Tobacco Road, and build it up again." This was the feeling I had. I wanted to destroy and rebuild. (Glasgow, 1980, p. 112)

For the next year this initial resistance consolidated into a sustained community project signaled by the development of a community action group of youth called The Sons of Watts. This community mobilization group were the youth who were formerly "hanging out in the streets." An organization called SWIA (Sons of Watts Improvement Assocation) was started. This community action group was initiated at the grass-roots level and did street cleaning, policing, job training, personal growth programs, and so on. The group was a community expression of black unity: "Everybody was sticking together. Everyone was calling each other 'Brother.' People were more civil and there were no more fights between the brothers. Everyone spoke to each other" (Glasgow, 1980, p. 117).

This sense of solidarity and participation created a sense of agency which issued from the development of a grass-roots community project. The sense of a project moved from initial resistance against the oppressive forces of the ghetto to a belief that with organization and solidarity their lives could possibly change for the better. A positive sense of self-worth followed without the aid of any psychological services.

> The thing that got me was the role I played in maintaining order in our community. I became dedicated as I saw everyone saying "welcome to Watts." No one was ashamed (of the rebellion), they were proud. It made me proud of myself, expecially to my brothers and sisters.
> I saw the power we had during the festival and the people's respect for us. When I decided to come (to the festival), at first I saw it as a good game. Then we talked about the Sons of Watts; it sounded like it could be something. Then I became a Son of

TABLE 6. Schematic Interpretation of Watts Youth before the Ghetto Riot—Formative Dynamics of Underclass Youth Entrapment before Riot

Habitus	Project
(a) *Social self*—in underclass entrapment, the social self accepts the negative identity of the dominant class. Where there is some positive self-conceptions, it is frequently coalesced around the ability to survive in conditions of dire and chronic poverty.	(a) *Intentional self*—is totally occupied with the survival demands of the ghetto life. Although there is resistance and rebellion, it is not directed at the system and is not felt possible to be effective. There is a sense of being a pawn in the larger economic system, which defies attempts at agency.
(b) *Identity*—is achieved by the repetitive quality of survival conditions in chronic unemployment. The repetitive quality of these negative survival conditions engenders a sense of negative self-worth. Survival culture is reactive in origin but not a passive adaptation to encapsulation. Activity sustaining an identity can be extremely resistant, but completely in response to rejection and the destructive aspects of ghetto life.	(b) *Individuation*—is stifled by being locked into a system that hampers movement. A certain cultural style is present, but it is an individuation that has been totally styled by a "history of oppression and exploitation." Within the ghetto a sense of individuation is achieved by proving you can "take a piece out of the system." Thus "conspicuous consumption" becomes one expression of individuation in the ghetto. This consumption usually mimics the consumption patterns of the dominant culture.
(c) *Order*—is achieved by the legitimacy of welfare and state intervention under liberal capitalist hegemony. This minimum order in an otherwise chaotic life is achieved bureaucratically through the facilities of welfare programs, which are permanent when high unemployment is acceptable within the state. There is also a community of survival, which functions at a day-to-day level but at the mercy of police intervention. The presence of the police represents the organized violence of the state maintaining order in ghetto life.	(c) *Change*—in the ghetto is experienced negatively. In the lowest tier of the economic system, change is usually for the worse. You are more likely to be losing a job than finding one, going to prison rather than coming out, losing a friend through self-destruction rather than celebrating his or her good fortune. Change is therefore experienced as a "downward spiral" whose cycle can only be broken by steady employment, "which not only earns money, but also provides opportunities to invest in a future"; this has much to do with building one's sense of self-worth. Thus, "I need a *job*, a job where it's at" (Glasgow, 1980, pp. 71–72).

(d) *Conscious*—actions leading to goal-directed projects are absent. The ethics of survival lead to a hand-to-mouth mentality, which curtails the projection of sustained and long-term problem solving. Glasgow notes that institutionalized racism—characterized as ghetto residence, inner-city educational institutions, police arrests, and so on—does not produce lower motivation; it destroys motivation.

(e) *Utopian*—the downward spiral of chronic unemployment is "negatively utopian." They no longer give a damn. They refuse to search or advertise that they are available. They have lost faith in the social order, in those who had promised some relief; they are skeptical of any change. One such brother clearly states "I haven't been trying—if people come up with something or I hear, I'll go—If it's straight, OK, or I'll leave it alone." Nevertheless the search for a job, for a way to make a living, for some money consumes almost all the energy of ghetto youth (Glasgow, 1980, p. 84). Project in these conditions is limited to survival maneuvers. A large societal project is totally entrapped under conditions of chronic unemployment.

(f) *Freedom*—a condition of bondage is pervasive. The power of the arbitrary nature of a hostile economic system totally limits the possibilities for options toward something different from the present (i.e., alternative futures). It is a condition of limited or "small futures," in which the present exploitation of the economic system is buffered by the oppression produced by institutionalized racism. The dominant class legitimates the presence of the underclass as an unfortunate biological occurrence.

(d) *Preconscious*—solidification of ghetto entrapment is engendered by a generational cycle of chronic unemployment. The situation of a crisis state and its survival measures become "natural" and "everyday" rather than temporary feelings of lack of security that most people feel.

(e) *Ideological*—pursuits of the dominant class are accepted by ghetto youth. Being affected by the mass media, they accept the desirability of consumption and flaunt it when possible. Most of the time, however, they eventually accept that they will not get "a piece of the pie." This is ideologically backed up by the ghetto education, which usually ends in failure. Contrary to popular belief, ghetto youth aspire to graduate from high school; their educational aspirations are dampened as they proceed through a school system that perpetuates a sense of permanent underachievement.

(f) *Determinism*—is felt as the changelessness of chronic unemployment. After these young men learn the educational system, we have the picture of a group of youth who have no educational credentials and little vocational training in the skills necessary for the swiftly changing job market—a group of men totally at the whims of periodic employment.

TABLE 7. Schematic Interpretation of Watts Youth after the Ghetto Riot—Transformative Dynamics of Underclass Youth's Attempts at Transcending Entrapment

Habitus		Project
(a) *Social self*—there is a rejection of the "white man's" definition of their identity. This is initially seen in the resistance to police arrests and rejection of the "law and order" forces as enforcers of the white man's order.	⟷	(a) *Intentional self*—is seen not only in resistance to the projects of "whitey" but also in the "new sense of agency" achieved through the development of grass-roots organizations. There is a dawning sense of the possibility of being an "origin" rather than a pawn in an alien system.
(b) *Identity*—there is a rejection of the negative identity produced by survival tactics of the ghetto. A new community solidarity with the positive sense of self-worth ensuing allows for a feeling of "blackness" that has positive connotations. There is a strong sense of black solidarity.	⟷	(b) *Individuation*—is achieved by a new sense of societal project and a more positive sense of identity. "Black Is Beautiful" means not only a rejection of whites but a sense of uniqueness that there is in being black. This individuation is not individualism, it is a unique "we" consciousness.
(c) *Order*—the hegemony of the "order of the welfare system" is broken by the development of community organizations run by blacks to deal with black needs. There is a rejection of "state order," signified by the attitude toward the police, which is negative; also a sense that the community can provide its own indigenous order through grass-roots organization work.	⟷	(c) *Change*—the sense of altering the downward spiral of ghetto life after the riot is very strong. The belief in change and in that sense upward transcendence unlocks a flurry of activity which exemplifies a sense of exhilaration. "We're going to change things now" is a prominent slogan.

(d) *Preconscious*—solidification of "ghetto entrapment" is questioned with the onset of the riot. The riot, it may be said, is an awakening from the slumber and narcosis of ghetto entrapment. In very specific ways, the spontaneity of the uprising is nevertheless accompanied by a clear sense of what establishments are the exploiters in the ghetto. This preconscious understanding marks out specific establishments for looting and destruction, while others go unharmed.

(e) *Ideological*—rejection of the status quo and the state structures are accompanied by an increasing identification of a larger black consciousness and a longer black history that spans their own individual histories.

(f) *Determinism*—the hegemony of the past can be changed. "Whitey" is going to have to do some moving now. The strong feeling of the weight of an oppressive past is challenged.

(d) *Conscious*—actions became a dominant motif in the post-Watts uprising. A heightened awareness of the possibilities of new problem-solving actions through community organization is present. There is a great deal of planning for a different future where before there was none.

(e) *Utopian symbols*—become extremely important. The possibility of having a different black future is celebrated in symbols, dance, and theater. The new community awareness and solidarity are signified in symbols that appear to challenge the downward spiral of former ghetto life.

(f) *Freedom*—is seen by the belief that the future will not be a repetition of the past. This sense of new project is the very essence of a notion of freedom.

> Watts. It's a good thing. Let me tell you, we are a group of unique people; had a
> chance of being the world's greatest pimps and gangsters. We acted bad; now we can
> be respected. We burned four million dollars worth of property; we have power and
> should be respected. We're trying to do something different now. (Glasgow, 1980, pp.
> 127–128)

The tragedy of all this is seen in the ultimate fragility of small-group movements that challenge the governing hegemony of capital. Watts is a case in point.
Glasgow (1980) brings his sensitive analysis to a sobering conclusion.

> When the real issues of productive functioning are examined, the most obvious fact is
> that these men continued to be jobless, poor, and occupationally obsolescent. Despite
> their efforts at self-help, no stable economic future was in sight. For the most part, the
> income-producing programs did not materialize, and although their job-hunting and
> market-analysis skills became a little more sophisticated, these improvements did not
> pay off in increased employment because the opportunity was not there. The self-help
> community-service-oriented programs, although very few, nevertheless continued to
> be the most lasting functional part of their activity. . . . Much of the early enthusiasm
> for the Sons had worn off by 1975. The equation of oppressive poverty had not been
> broken, and instead increasingly broken was the will of many of the men. Oppor-
> tunities for stable income-producing jobs and the avenues to upward mobility re-
> mained closed. (p. 149)

This indigenous group (Sons of Watts), while it lasted, provided opportunities for underclass men to express themselves and to countenance a sense of
agency and project. This phase is schematically illustrated in Table 7 as the
transformative dynamics.

The Glasgow study on the black underclass is a specific example of the
complex interplay between class dynamics, ethnicity, and the development of a
personal world. It is part of a genre of literature that developed in the wake of the
black movement in the 1960s and an in-depth examination of the black experience, life-styles, community organizing, interpersonal and family relationships,
and so on. I view it as a critical interpretation of the black experience and, at the
same time, a study of the relationship of class and ethnicity. Its critical intent is
expressed in its explicit departure from mainstream social sciences dealing with
ethnicity and more specifically, in this case, black ethnicity.

For example, new importance was given to ethnicity as a factor in black
oppression and to liberation strategies as against class factors; positive ethnocentrism was elevated in contrast with the former deviant subculture thesis. Most
important was the reaffirmation of the black family structure, and one's function
therein, as a prime contributor to blacks' survival. This emphasis replaced the
persistent notion promulgated by mainstream social scientists that the Negro
family was in disarray and that, in fact, it was the primary source of the second-
class position of blacks and the conveyor of a disadvantaged culture.

Instead, this study shows how a specific cultural form develops through a
unique sense of historicity (ethnicity) but embeds that history within the complex

confines of a class analysis. Within this complex dialectic, the personal world and its vicissitudes are explained with a disciplined and critical sensitivity.

The previous example was given to illustrate the relationship between class structure ethnicity and the dynamics of the personal world of specific cultural forms expressed in ethnicity. I would now like to turn to the role that gender plays in a critically interpretative enterprise.

GENDER AND DOMINATION

Changing cultural standards do not alter the fact that sex differentiation constitutes almost a bifurcation in status and roles in almost all cultures from the very beginning of the socialization process. All known human populations appear to honor this dichotomy, and all cultures distinguish males and females on the basis of primary and secondary sex characteristics (Ausubel *et al.*, 1980). By gender, I refer to role attribution between the sexes based on both primary and secondary sex characteristics. The category differentiation based on gender is universal, and this differentiation transcends the category systems of class and ethnicity. In other words, there are women and men in all races and classes.

The notion of gender domination signifies that there are power differences that accrue from the attributions of gender. In most cultures, and in ours specifically, men have historically dominated women in terms of the power relations operating in society. This is referred to as *patriarchy*. Patriarchy signifies that men have premptive power over women at both the economic and cultural symbolic levels. In other words, women occupy an inferior and dependent status that is culturally sanctioned. Historically, this predates capitalism and can also be seen in structures that attempt to transcend capitalism (e.g., eastern European socialism). It appears to be the most universal form of oppression and domination.

I intend to restrict my comments here to a discussion of patriarchy under capitalism. My discussion will suffer from its brevity, but in a critical psychology the issue of gender domination cannot be sidestepped. Let me commence by noting the sustaining power of the gender system and male dominance within it, which has been engendered by the pervasive use of the biological or organic metaphor in the historical explanation of sexual differences. The organic metaphor, as we have already suggested in Chapter 1, is a conservative metaphor for the maintenance of social structures being interpreted. From Aristotle through Jung and Freud, the use of biological metaphors has put woman in the category of "incomplete man" (Whitteck, 1976). At the beginning of the 20th century, biological theories of sex differences were systematically ideological in nature; helping to refute from a so-called scientific perspective the claim of feminists at that time to equal rights for women (Hall, 1976). Even today, biological metaphors of gender differences are used by conservative scholars to sustain the rigid legitimation of fixed roles (Markovic, 1976; Wine, 1980). Now, however, these perspectives are less blatantly sexist and their edges are blunted by technical issues (Hall, 1976). A consideration of women as agents in the appropriation of a personal world is absent from most conceptions of human sexuality where metaphors other than the organic are used (e.g., mechanical metaphors are frequently utilized in obstetrics). Notwithstanding the caveat above, it may be safely said that in terms of gender, biological metaphors predominate (see Chodorow, 1978; Dickason, 1976; Eichler, 1980; Gould, 1976; Hall, 1976; Oakley, 1979; Markovic, 1976; Whitteck, 1976). Chodorow (1978), in criticizing biological metaphors, reiterates the importance of the personal metaphor that this book is being espoused for an understanding and interpretation of the gender system.

> The biological argument for women's mothering is based on facts that derive not from our biological knowledge, but from our definition of the natural situation as this grows out of our participation in certain social arrangements. That women have the extensive and nearly exclusive mothering role they have is a product of a social and cultural translation of their childbearing and lactation capacities. It is not guaranteed or entailed by these capacities themselves. (p. 30)

The personal world, then, molds the contours of capacities and gives them specific use values. In the structural system of capital, the agency of the personal world is stunted and blocked more for women than for men, regardless of class. In that sense the gender system has its own peculiar forms of oppression, which are projected into the larger class system and conversely affected by that system of commodity production. Thus, the oppression produced by the domination existing within the gender system crosses all classes (i.e., male domination) but affects women and men differently in terms of their relations in the larger class structure.

Patriarchy and the Domination of Women's Projects

I have indicated that the focal point of human freedom is in the possibility of experiencing agency in the creation and interpretation of one's world (i.e., project). In this sense, it may be safe to say that women of all classes and races have been denied this sense of agency historically. Patriarchy, as I am using the term, is the systematic masking of the projective character of women's action by men. In most cases, this systematic oppression of men over women is unconscious (i.e., habitual and part of the cultural habitus). This domination of women becomes conscious and intentional historically when women attempt to assert themselves against the dominance of the male project. The domination of women historically takes the form of male condescension or outright violence. Let me briefly schematize structural dimensions of the oppression engendered by gender domination without considering its specific historical contours within class and racial structures. When patriarchy is stabilized, one can say that the structural conditions of oppression are "hegemonic" in the Gramcian sense of this term.

Gender, Class, and the Reproduction of Social Relations under Capitalism

The reader should understand that the schema above (Table 8) should be taken in with a certain cynicism. If left without further comment, this schematization would be ahistorical and would thus defeat the historical sensitivity that I am inviting the reader to consider. This is important, because what I am now about to stress is the historical specificity of patriarchial structures within a capitalist mode of production. This means that male dominance takes historically specific contours within different economic systems. For example, gender domination, until recently, was accomplished through the structure of the nuclear family in modern capitalism. This, as already stated, is done by the separation of the world of work (i.e., production) from the world of the family (i.e., reproduction). In connecting these worlds, Wolff (1976) points out that the most important single act of social production is reproduction, which is not only the conception of children but the caring and raising of them to maturity. But this is done differently in different historical periods. It is only with the beginning of industrialized societies that the separation of work life and family has become prominent and apparently necessary (Kamerman, 1979). The separation of the world of work and family has peculiar consequences for the sexes within capitalist production (Chodorow, 1978; Marcovic, 1976). "Parenting" within the social organization of the nuclear family produces sexual inequality, not simply role differentiation (Chodorow, 1978). This is accomplished by first locating women and men differently within the organization of production (i.e., economic system). Men are, in essence, equated with the public sphere while women are equated with the private (Wolff, 1976). If privacy were the salient characteristic of the personal world, women would be considered more personal and men more impersonal. The position I am venturing rejects a notion of the personal world as private and individual. The differentiation along these lines reflects poorly on both sexes. Hegel was the first modern thinker to systematize the distinction between the public and private spheres (Gould, 1976). He identified the family with the private domain of love and immediacy, whose main function is that of the socialization of children. This was to be contrasted with "civil society," which is based on need and labor rather than sentiment. Gould (1976) sees this distinction as a major mystification, arguing that the family is pervaded throughout by bourgeois or civil society, and that the concrete nature of the family as a social and political institution is concealed under capitalism. In modern monopoly capitalism, the family is a major consuming unit and the target of advertisement unknown in previous historical periods (Ewen, 1976; Gould, 1976; Marcovic, 1976; Sullivan, 1980b).

Male Dominance		Woman Oppression
Habitus		Habitus
(a) *Social self*—a solidarity between men across classes that to be a man is to be identified with a superior gender. Male dominance indicates that the part of one's overall personal identity which is gender-related is conceived of in positive terms.	←——→	(a) *Social self*—the social self is permeated with the sense of inferiority of the women's sex from the cultural surroundings. This is stabilized by the sense that this "inferiority" is biologically based and invariant historically.
(b) *Identity*—male identity is integrated into the wider culture's valuing of the male sex. In extremely macho cultures, this can be seen in the sadness of the family when the first child born is a female.	←——→	(b) *Identity*—a positive sense of the self is not buttressed by the surrounding culture. Identity is achieved in a more derivative manner—females get to perform roles that are respected by male-dominance norms.
(c) *Order*—is achieved by the understanding that cultural structures which make female oppression unconscious (e.g., from the earliest socialization practices, both mothers and fathers treat females as being more dependent and vulnerable in relation to male children).	←——→	(c) *Order*—is achieved within the understanding that females will be dominated by males and thus be protected by the "stronger sex." This notion of the stronger sex concedes that male might makes right.
(d) *Preconscious*—male dominance is achieved by cultural structures that make female oppression unconscious (e.g., from the earliest socialization practices, both mothers and fathers treat females as being more dependent and vulnerable in relation to male children).	←——→	(d) *Preconscious*—a habitual status of dependency and vulnerability for female children allows for an unconscious appropriation of cultural dependency structures that are perceived to be biologically induced rather than culturally learned.
(e) *Ideological*—underpinnings of patriarchy are buttressed by biological metaphors which culturally sanction male dominance because of inherent biological differences where males are superior biologically.	←——→	(e) *Ideological*—underpinnings for female oppression are buttressed by biological metaphors that culturally sanction female inferiority because of inherent biological differences where females are inferior biologically.
(f) *Determinism*—male agency and project are believed to be inevitable and natural consequences of biological superiority.	←——→	(f) *Determinism*—female oppression by male dominant structures are seen as inevitable and natural because of biological inferiority.

Project →   ← Project

(a) *Intentional self*—males perceive themselves to be the focal point of agency in a society under patriarchy. Males perceive that their intentions are preeminent over females because "this is a man's world."

(a) *Intentional self*—under conditions of oppression within patriarchial structures, women are either low or severely lacking in a sense of agency. They perceive their intentions where operating to be subordinate to their male counterparts.

(b) *Individuation*—is the sense that there is a place in the world for me which I, through my agency, bring about. Although class structures make a difference where males are concerned, patriarchy crosses these boundaries in distinct ways.

(b) *Individuation*—under patriarchy is muted and eclipsed because the nondominant social position of women makes it appear inevitable that a world carved out by their intentions is impossible to achieve in an order of male dominance.

(c) *Change*—the ability to reorder the world is understood to be relatively possible for males even where class domination is operating. So, even under conditions of class domination, lower-class males have a greater sense of agency than their female counterparts.

(c) *Change*—for women under patriarchy is sensed to be possible as a result of male agency. Thus, women under stabilized patriarchy see change as possible only as the result of male initiative.

(d) *Conscious*—actions are governed by directives of the larger patriarchial project of men over women. Men see themselves as more goal-oriented than women, exclusive of class structures and class dominance.

(d) *Conscious*—actions for women are habitually oriented to the projects of men under patriarchy. Supposedly behind every male initiation or project is a woman who supports his intentions without reciprocity.

(e) *Utopian*—images of change are imaged as being carried out by solidarity among men within a background of women's support. Male utopian images frequently emphasize control and power over participation and community.

(e) *Utopian*—images are muted and fragmented by the failure of women, under patriarchy, to believe that consolidated social actions could be launched by women as a cultural force. Frequently, this fragmentation of images is exacerbated by competition between women for men's favor.

(f) *Freedom*—is sensed under patriarchy to be the result of male initiative or agency. Even under conditions of class dominance, lower-class males have a greater sense of agency than their female counterparts.

(f) *Freedom*—for women under patriarchy is perceived as coming through the initiation of male agency. One could label this "spurious freedom of alienation," since it is not tied to the direct agency of women.

> Insofar as woman in the family is exploited (by performing unpaid labor) and op-
> pressed (by having to take money from her husband), by being commodified and
> manipulated by advertisements and the media, by being coerced to raise the children
> by herself and in "appropriate" ways, the political emancipation of the woman, as well
> as the assurance of equal opportunity for her, reveals itself to be inadequate. Mini-
> mally, we might say that concrete emancipation requires the overcoming of the
> dependence of the family on capital. (Gould, 1976, p. 36)

The situation reveals its complexity when one understands that gender ideologies are reproduced within the family structure itself. For example, lower-class males enforce the ideology of domesticity on women, which is a virulent sexism. Especially because of the alienating nature of work under capitalism, men reinforce the sexual division of spheres as a defense against powerlessness in the labor market (Chodorow, 1978).

It is important to understand the social construction of the world of the nuclear family for our understanding of the reproduction of the ideology of capital. Chodorow (1978) points out how this is reinforced by mothering in the nuclear family. Mothering in the isolated nuclear family of contemporary capitalist society reproduces specific personality characteristics in men that reinforce and replicate an ideology of male superiority and a concomitant submission to the requirements of production (Chodorow, 1978). Specifically, this is done by preparing men for participation in a male-dominant family life and also for their participation in the capitalist world of work (Chodorow, 1978). When women enter into the public sector of work, which is done increasingly, this does not mean relinquishing their home making responsibilities. In the work force, male domination is seen in economic disparities between men and women and job opportunity. Hutner, an economist, contends that working women are trapped in female "occupational ghettos." They receive low-paying clerical salaries in general, but even in the more prestigious professions (i.e., teaching, liberarianships, nursing, etc.), women are consistently paid lower salaries than men.

The gender system supports the class structure of capital through a complex process mediated by the modern nuclear family. A weak unit for the sustenance of its own designs, it nevertheless functions well carrying out the consumer needs of the corporate system (Sullivan, 1980b). The reproduction of the social relations of production through the reproduction of culture is amplified by the development of a consumer mentality, in which women and now children in our culture are expected to excel (Sullivan, 1980b). This role is not, however, complementary and is only indicative of woman's oppression in the gender system as well as the class system (Marcovic, 1976).

> Private property, in the form of capital, is still everywhere essentially in men's hands.
> There is one economic aspect in which women are relatively powerful: that is con-
> sumption. However, the distinction between private property with respect to the
> means of production and private property with respect to the means of consumption is
> very important from the point of view of the distribution of total social power. Those

who dominate production also control the huge advertising machinery for the creation of artificial needs and the demand desirable at the market. Thus, consumers hardly exert a very significant influence on those who control production; consumers are rather manipulated by them. (Marcovic, 1976, pp. 155–156)

Ethnicity, Culture, and Gender Domination

In a short treatment of such a controversial topic, I feel responsible not to spare the reader some of the complexities which brevity may tend to conceal. One of these complexities is the realization that gender structures and patriarchy are also formed differently within the context of culture and ethnicity. For example, male dominance manifests itself differently in North American culture when compared with the culture of Latin America.

It is informative to make a comparison between North America and Latin America in relation to the hegemonic acceptance of class and gender structures. In North America, the economic order is stabilized and hegemonic; that is, there are no revolutionary upheavals that question the fundamental integrity of the economic order. At the same time, the women's movement, that is, the movement which fundamentally questions patriarchy, is quite vocal and active. The exact opposite prevails in Latin America. There are active revolutionary movements throughout Latin America which fundamentally question the continuing stability of the economic order. Most of these movements do not incorporate within themselves a rejection of oppressions which are gender-related and due to the male dominance of patriarchy. I use this example for one reason only, and that is to sensitize the reader to the complex relationship of patriarchial systems to class and ethnic structures. It will be the task of a more mature critical social inquiry to explore and elucidate the complex relationships between these systems of domination.

Patriarchy Challenged—The Women's Movement

Probably the most steady and insistent movement for cultural change in the last 20 years has been the women's movement, challenging cultural stability based on gender-domination of male over female. This movement is quite complex and varied, takes many complex routes, and has many guises. What is at the bottom line is a challenge made by large numbers and diverse groups of women, with the support of a minority of men, to the accepted habitus that men should dominate women as a cultural project. Part of the challenge of this movement has been in the erosion of sterotypical male and female roles. This erosion is exemplified in challenges to role stereotyping of women by men and also catalyzed by the articulation of atypical male roles that seek wider cultural acceptance (e.g., gay liberation). It is seen in the challenge that the women's movement is currently making on the issue of male dominance and negative discrimination against women in the work force. The challenge is being made by women against male dominance in health and psychological care by professional experts in these areas. What is essential here is the consideration that the preeminence of patriarchy and male dominance is being challenged at diverse levels and sectors of our society. We will explore one area of this challenge in depth in Chapter 6, where critical interpretation and gender domination are discussed at the level of psychological interpretation. For the moment, I understand that my discussion of the gender system is all too schematic. My justification is that it is simply suggestive in trying to map out how gender relations reflect the social relations of the personal world in the class structure of monopoly capitalism. It is my contention that a critical interpretation of the personal world must articulate a place for the gender system in its interpretative horizon. To mask out the gender system in an interpretative social science would simply further contribute to the oppression and exploitation already embedded within this system (see Gould, 1976). It would also serve to hamper attempts at a more personal world based on reciprocity and participation by ignoring the oppressive dominance which presently permeates that system and contributes to the present hegemony of a capitalist social structure. The value judgment here is that when the constraints of capital are overriding, there is a vitiation of the personal world which governs the relations between men and women in all social classes.

AGE AND CLASS DYNAMICS

Psychology's major contribution to a discipline dealing with orderly developments with age is predominantly seen in its subdiscipline, developmental psychology (Ausubel & Sullivan, 1970; Ausubel et al., 1980). Age-related phenomena easily lend themselves to biological metaphors, and developmental psychology's history shows strong currents along this line (Ausubel & Sullivan, 1970; Ausubel, et al., 1980). Developmental psychology in the 20th century has waxed and waned in salience, but is clear that since the 1960s it has been considered a discipline at the forefront by psychological practitioners. The Piagetian system of developmental psychology has been a prime mover of this contemporary interest in a concept of development (Sullivan, 1966; 1981).

One of the most pervasive phenomena seen in developmental psychologies of different persuasions is the systematic isolation of developmental phenomena from sociohistorical contexts (Ingleby, 1974). This is done systematically to relieve the conceptual formulation from the ambiguity of all historical phenomena. This leads to a systematic depoliticization of developmental phenomena which masks the ideological nature of the discipline (Ingleby, 1974). In achieving this systematic isolation of developmental phenomena from historical contexts, developmental theories have fallen prey to unconscious ideological problems (Broughton, 1979; Ingleby, 1974; Sullivan, 1977a,b; Wilden, 1975).

Most recently, mainstream developmental psychologists have begun to explore the contextual and political nature of developmental theory (Bronfenbrenner, 1979; Kessen, 1975). There is now a development literature on the psychohistory of children (Aries, 1962; Davis, 1976; De Mause, 1976). There is also an increasing awareness of the influence of economics on the development of psychohistory. The importance of the development of a psychohistory to accord with age-developmental phenomena is that it embeds age phenomena in social history. Age then becomes one factor in historical interpretations and is influenced by the individual and social history that bounds it. Therefore, to talk about childhood is not to raise it to a universal and invariant phenomenon. For example, prior to the Renaissance, children were simply envisioned as miniature adults, childhood *per se* having no special status (Aries, 1962). Childhood became a special status within a particular cultural history. Childhood is also clearly linked to the economic structure of the society (Aries, 1962). Historically, as fathers moved away from domestic settings, childhood as a unique historical period in the life-cycle became more apparent. The relationship between economics and child psychohistory is just starting to be explored with some precision (see Davis, 1976; De Mause, 1974). Since what is being developed here is an interpretative psychology, the development of the discipline of psychohistory is welcomed. This pertains not only to childhood but to all segments of the life-cycle (see Fowler, 1974).

In this final section, we are attempting to relate age-related phenomena to the economic structures involved in class analysis. Not to attempt this linkage would leave these important developmental considerations outside of the purview of a critically interpretative psychology. It is our contention that age-related developmental phenomena must be linked to the larger structural economic totalities. At present, one major social theorist is attempting to link developmental psychological phenomena to the complex class totalities of late capitalism (see Habermas, 1979). In this work, he considers Piaget, Kohlberg, and Loevinger within the context of larger structural totalities perceived to be operant dialectically within individual psychological development. This accents the importance of linking age-related institutions (like childhood, adolescence, and middle age) to the historical structures of the economy as well as such ideological structures as the family and school. A critical interpretation of the personal world would attempt to understand how an age-related institution (for example, childhood) establishes a social legitimacy in the complexity of modern institutions.

In the development of the liberal state, gradualistic social and economic reforms have been focalized on children (Wisby, 1968). Here social reform is achieved by attempting to make the new generation the focal point for societal change. This has not proven to be an effective place for large structural economic changes and, in many instances, acts as a defuser of larger structural changes (De Lone, 1979). The current interest of the state in the child is clearly a way of saying that reform must come gradually and with the next generation. In contemporary life, formal schooling has assumed the role of preparing the child for tomorrow's reforms. This phenomenon has been developing since the turn of the 20th century (Takanishi, 1978). The development of the modern state through the institution of modern formal schooling becomes an important socializer of the class structure (Bourdieu & Passeron, 1977). Schooling and its age-related phenomena act as a conservative force in the maintenance of the social hegemony of the modern state (Bowles & Gintis, 1976; Bourdieu & Passeron, 1977). Social theorists sensitive to the class nature of the modern state are becoming more sensitized to the role of the school in the maintenance of our modern economy and also its reproductive quality (Bowles & Gintis, 1976; Bourdieu & Passeron, 1977). *Reproduction* signifies that the school prepares different children for their places in the class structure and the eventual world of work. This is done by a complex symbolic enterprise which doles out "cultural capital" along the lines of the society's class structure (Bourdieu & Passeron, 1977). Psychology of a critical import must etch out a place for an in-depth treatment of how the personal world is affected by these complex steering mechanisms. Willis's (1977) *Learning to Labour* is one example of a sophisticated treatment of the world of working-class youth and how they are molded by formal schooling for working-class jobs. This study will be discussed more thoroughly in a later chapter as exemplary of a critically interpretative psychology.

CONCLUSION

What has been attempted in this chapter is ambitious, perhaps too ambitious. The reader should understand the importance of mapping out the features discussed herein for a critical psychology with an emancipatory intent. A critical psychology, like all social inquiry with emancipatory impulses, should embrace the task of searching for the new social relations and the new social conflicts that form themselves in a profoundly transformed cultural field (Touraine, 1979). Psychological inquiry as a particular form of cultural action has the task of both denunciation and annunciation (see Freire, 1974). Denunciation is an examination, with critical attention, of those social structures of class, gender, race, and age that systematically exploit and oppress specific cultural forms. Critical psychology pays specific attention to how the personal world of individual and groups is affected by stabilization of unjust social structures. I have attempted to suggest the direction that this might take in the discussions of the tension of habitus and project under conditions of social maintenance (i.e., formative dynamics or the dynamics of the status quo). Some form of class analysis was considered as essential to this endeavor.

The task of critique should not only sensitize one to the deleterious effects on the personal world produced by unjust social structures. Annunciation, in contrast to denunciation, is the critical attempt to explore new institutional projects that seek to overcome structural injustices by attempting to transform social relations toward more equitable states. In many instances, this is first seen in resistance to the status quo. A critical psychology resists interpretation as social deviance, which is the usual direction that mainstream social science takes. In addition to the above, a critical psychology of the personal world attempts to capture dynamics of habitus and project under conditions of real or possible transformation (i.e., transformative dynamics).

5

INTERPRETATION

Believing . . . that man is an animal suspended in webs of significance he himself has spun, I take culture to be those webs, and the analysis of it to be therefore not an experimental science in search of law but an interpretative one in search of meaning.

—Geertz, 1973, p. 5

THE PERSONAL WORLD AS A TEXT

Ricoeur (1971) has suggested that the model of a text could be most useful in our understanding of human action. In fact, he specifically suggests that meaningful action be considered a text. The understanding of personal human expression that I have developed thus far makes Ricoeur's suggestion quite plausible. Like a text, human action or expression exists to be "interpreted." As I have suggested in Chapter 1, the paradigm of the personal world is communication itself. Consider the possible implications of this in the context of an interpretation of a text. A reader comes to a text to decipher the meaning of the written expressions of an author. Here, the author's expressions are one form of human action: written expression. The text poses a problem to the reader in that she or he must render the author's words meaningful and significant. To consider human actions in the broader sense (written and spoken language, gestures, bodily actions, etc.) as a text to be interpreted means that like a text, human actions are an open work, the meaning of which is in suspense (Ricoeur, 1971). For reasons I have already given in Chapter 1, the shift to a personal metaphor offers certain advantages over mechanical and organic metaphors in the interpretation of human action. However, it is now important to introduce some of the peculiar problems presented to the social inquirer when she or he considers human action as a text to be interpreted. We have already developed the idea of the personal world as a "cultural form" or "form of life." By this, I meant that a cultural form is exemplified in the manner in which a particular social group is connected to the objects, artifacts, institutions, and systematic practices of others that sur-

111

round it. In other words, the *personal world*, as we experience it, is an identifiable cultural form with some unity and coherence of expression. The question
posed now is how an interpreter outside of a particular "cultural form" comes to
an understanding of that form of life. This is the "problem of mediation." Some
social theorists are skeptical that mediation is even possible (see Bauman, 1978).
In essence, they are saying that it is impossible to come to know an alien cultural
form. At the other extreme, there is *imperialistic optimism* about the realities
other than one's own. This is the position of the "expert–interpreter." Mediation
is not necessary here, since all that is demanded is to *assimilate* all alien expressions into one's own system. This form of assimilation presupposes that
social realities other than one's own can be bent totally into one's own system of
expression. The latter position is arrogant, while the former leads to solipsism.
We must avoid these extremes in our attempts to make human actions intelligible. This demands a closer scrutiny of one of the features of human actions
discussed briefly in Chapter 2. That feature or mode was referred to as *significance* or intelligibility (see also Schafer, 1976).

Intelligibility

By significance or intelligibility, I mean that human *action* or *conduct*
presupposes that the human act could be understood by reference to the ends or
intentions an actor is pursuing and also the context or conditions under which
action *pursues* its ends (Unger, 1976). The important assumption is that human
actions (expressions) are meaningful (i.e., have significance) and are, therefore,
not arbitrary. In fact, when an act appears arbitrary, there seems to be a demand
in that situation to make it intelligible. Making an act intelligible is, in essence,
interpretation. Traditional psychological interpretation has historically attempted to couch the explanation of human action within the ideal of causal
explanation. As I indicated in our opening chapter, this type of explanatory
device attempts to state how a given set of actions or facts explains another set of
actions or facts by linking them together in some temporal sequence (i.e., causal
sequence) and attributing one to the other (antecedent–consequent) with more
or less probability (cf. Unger, 1976). An interpretative explanation, by contrast,
explains by showing that an act makes sense against a background of a social code
of rules, practices, or belief. As Unger (1976) puts it, it is a "logic of the
situation" rather than a "logic of cause." Unger (1976) insists that an interpretative explanation be distinguished from causal explanation:

> Thus, if we encounter certain features of an artistic style in a painting, we also expect
> to find other traits of the style in it, though the stylistic attributes cannot be said to
> either cause or logically imply the other. (p. 255)

Therefore, an interpretative account is an illuminative act rather than an
act of causal attribution. It is an illuminative act in that it attempts to uncover the

sense of a given action, practice, or constitutive meaning by uncovering the intentions and desires of particular actors (Fay, 1975). It is illuminative because it attempts to uncover the set of rules that make these social practices intelligible and therefore significant. It is an act of analysis and synthesis, as we will see later, in that the act of interpretation attempts to fit these rule-generated and intentional actions into a more total structure (Fay, 1975). By a more *total structure*, I refer to the relational totality of the personal world as a *cultural form*. In interpretative human action within a more total context of cultural forms, the social scientist is redescribing an act or experience by setting it into progressively larger contexts of purpose and intelligibility (Fay, 1975). More is to be said about this, but let me first reflect on the limits of this undertaking.

To suggest interpretative inquiry as a potent method of social investigation does not necessitate a blindness to its limitations. The study of conscious intentions of agents in relation is not to be considered an exhaustive analysis. There are many events in life that escape explanation in terms of our conscious intentions. The substance of tragedy makes this fact a human reality. All those forces that go beyond the reaches of conscious human intentions humble us to the inherent limitation of interpretative methods. Unger (1976) attributes the inherent limitation of this method to a certain fact about human nature:

> The root of the relatively limited range of the interpretative method lies in the dualism of human nature. Man is consciousness capable of intentionality. But he is also a member of the physical world. Though his intentions permeate some aspects of the situation, they never reach all of them.
> Whenever we set aside the fact of consciousness, we fall into behaviorism. Whenever we disregard the limitations of consciousness, we slide into idealism. Behaviorism and idealism are the two great sins a method of social study can commit, for both distort crucial traits of human existence. (p. 256)

The vulnerability of the present treatment is to err on the side of *idealism*. This, of course, we wish to avoid. Our bottom-line position requires that the interpreter take the agent's purposes seriously, "to grasp his conduct . . . from the actor's own point of view" (Unger, 1976).

THE PROBLEM OF MEDIATION AND THE PARADOXES OF PSYCHOLOGICAL INTERPRETATION

Is it the task of psychological interpretation, and for that matter any form of social scientific interpretation, to simply understand the world from the point of the agent's conscious intentions and actions? Without precluding a profound sensitivity to the actor's point of view, it seems that the answer to the above question must be no (cf. Giddens, 1979). It seems that simply to reflect the reality of agents involved in their own terms would just be a reiteration and repetition of an already achieved common sense. Left at this level, it would seem that psychological interpretation would be an unnecessary repetition of common sense. There would seem to be no point in this redundancy. Historically, psychology as an interpretative system has eschewed common sense and in, the guise of "expertise," treated it as a low-level reality to transcend. In other words, psychology as a natural science systematically attempted to go beyond common sense. This creates its own problem, and we are left with a riddle:

> If we disregard the meanings an act has for its author and for the other members of the society to which he belongs, we run the risk of losing sight of what is peculiarly social in the conduct we are trying to understand. If, however, we insist on sticking close to the reflective understanding of the agent or his fellows, we are deprived of a standard by which to distinguish insight from illusion. (Unger, 1976, p. 15)

What must be involved in interpretative explanation is a dialectic of distance and relation with the phenomena studied. When the dialectic is collapsed on the side of *distance* (i.e., expert viewpoint), there is the possibility of a total *alienation* from what is studied. At the other extreme, when the dialectic collapses on the side of *relation*, there is such a total immersion (if that is possible) that the interpreting observer has difficulty in separating the forest from the trees. In other words, the task of the psychological interpreter is not simply coding expression from the actor's point of view. If the interpreter is to add anything to the situation beyond the actors themselves, there must be some *recoding* or *resymbolization* of the expressions of the actors (Bleich, 1978). The dialectic of distance-and-relation already alluded to becomes important here because:

> Interpretative explanations requires the interpreter to take the agent's purposes seriously, to grasp his conduct, as has often been said, from the actor's own point of view. But for the observer, the social theorist, or historian to understand a subject's behavior meaningfully, he must be able to decipher what the subject is saying and then recode that message into the language of the observer's own culture. In other words, the greater the distance between the observer and the observed, the more important and the more difficult it becomes to translate from one symbol system into another. (Unger, 1976, p. 257)

What Unger is alluding to is what I will be calling the "problem of mediation," to which we now turn.

Psychological Interpretation as a Double Hermeneutic

All interpretations are mediated through language. We are, therefore, dealing with symbol systems that are public or potentially public. In other words, the reality of communication is that it is, by its very nature, public and verifiable. Here we would like to indicate that interpretation is a symbolic expression which attempts to understand the expression of another person or group. This is a symbolic world and we are locked, as was said at the outset, in the "prison house of language." But is psychological interpretation the same as interpretation at the level of common sense? We have already said no to this question, so we must explore how systematic psychological interpretation differs from interpretation at the level of common sense. Here I would like to introduce a notion coined by Giddens (1979) called the *double hermeneutic*. By this notion, we mean that all systematic interpretation is two-tiered. It expresses the dialectic of *distance-and-relation*, as follows. First of all, systematic interpretation must be related to a particular cultural form and its unique expressions so that action may be appreciated from the point of view of the conscious intentions of the actors involved (i.e., relation). Second, systematic interpretation must be done at enough distance from specific cultural expressions to provide critical feedback on these expressions (i.e., distance). We would call this combined process "resymbolization." If there was no necessity for *resymbolization*, then there would be no need for systematic interpretation of the social, scientific kind. Psychologists would simply be like Job's comforters, reiterating the obvious or making things worse.

The reality of multiple interpretations indicates that what we call the "factual world" is an interpretation. The meaning of human expressions is not an inherent feature of objects or persons, nor is it a psychic event in the head of the actor (Bauman, 1978). The ability to *resymbolize* events or expressions is indicative of the reality that interpretation is a constructive act rather than a process of discovery (Bauman, 1978). Our understanding of a normative social science is simply based on the premise that human actions and intentions are performed within the context of *social rules*. Following Hart (1951), we would contend that interpretative explanation is *ascription* rather than *description*. To talk about intentions or to ascribe intention and purpose is not to talk about private evidence. The "intentional explanation" that ascribes intentions and purposes to human expressions is a language act that is *public*. This type of ascription made on the expression of others will now be discussed as *resymbolization*.

Freud as Resymbolizer. At this point, it is fair to give the reader a concrete example of resymbolization. For psychologists, Freud is an opportune example. Psychoanalysis is a paradigmatic example of an interpretative science. In the psychoanalytic relationship of the patient–therapist, it brings out the notion of the double hermeneutic alluded to above. The analysis is an interpretation of the patient's symptoms that are the symbolic expressions of his or her psychological malaise. The symptoms as presented are opaque, incomprehensible, alien, and so on. The therapist takes these symptoms over time and, in the process of the relationship, attempts to *resymbolize* by offering an alternative framework to the symptoms as originally presented. At the beginning, the distance between the patient and therapist is wide and there is little relation. Over time, the chasm of this distance is bridged (relation). At the same time, this bridging does not lend itself to total identity, whereby the therapist would also have to become ill. The dialectic of distance and relation allows the therapist to identify with the patient's history and, at the same time, resymbolize this history from a safe distance. So we see here the notion of systematic interpretation as involving both identification (relation) and detachment (distance). The therapist's interpretations are a resymbolization of the symptoms in a more complete context of their origins, which heretofore was short-circuited by the patient's repression. The adequacy of the interpretation (resymbolization) is assessed by its utility in the patient's life. Therapy helps a patient create a much more conscious means of self-regulation (Bleich, 1978). Thus, an alternative interpretation has an adaptive communal function. Experience is resymbolized into a form with which consciousness may take more initiative (Bleich, 1978). In our terminology, it makes the patient more of an *agent* and less of a *patient*.

THE HERMENEUTIC OR INTERPRETIVE SPIRAL

In talking about the interpretative spiral, two considerations bear mentioning at the outset. First, psychological interpretation is a *relational* act and, second, it is an act that achieves a dialectic between *analysis* and *synthesis*.

Relational Quality of Interpretation

The interpreter enters into a dynamic relationship with the interpreted. To be systematic, psychological interpretation must be disciplined by a certain distance, but this distance is premised on the assumption that in order to understand something one must relate to it with some degree of affinity or sympathy. Therefore, part of the relationship between the interpreter and the interpreted must be personal (I–thou). The bottom line of this is that the psychological interpreter must seriously take into account the world as it is seen from the agent's sense of his or her intentions. In other words, part of the interpretative moment is an attempt to identify the agent's intentions through a sensitizing to his or her *expressions*. Therefore, part of a systematic interpretative process is a compilation of the first-person account of actors. The psychological interpreter enters into relation with those interpreted by becoming sensitive to their expressed intentions. He or she is not there to manipulate, as in experimental psychology (i.e., I–it relation), but to understand and extend the interpretative world of all concerned.

Interpretation as a Dialectic of Analysis and Synthesis

In the first chapter I talked about the principles of analysis and synthesis. I indicated there that mechanical metaphors were premised on the assumption of analysis (i.e., the whole is the sum of its parts). I also indicated that structuralism and other organic metaphors were premised on a principle of synthesis (i.e., the whole is more than the sum of its parts). Finally, I indicated that a personal metaphor involved a system of interpretation that was a dialectical relation of both analysis and synthesis. I will now illustrate this dialectic by discussing the notion of the interpretative *spiral*.

Hermeneutic Spiral. Hermes was "the interpreter"; hence, the science of interpretation was called *hermeneutics*. The notion of a hermeneutic spiral is well known in the area of philology; we will be using here a more colloquial expression, *the interpretive spiral*. Let us consider first the notion of the interpretative spiral when applied to the interpretation of a text:

> The meaning of a text (or anything else) is a complex of sub-meanings or parts which hang together. (Whenever the parts do not cohere, we confront meaninglessness or chaos, not meaning). Thus the complex of parts is not a merely mechanical colloca- tion, but a relational unity in which the relations of the parts to one another and to the whole constitute an essential aspect of their character as parts. That is, the meaning of a part is determined by its relationship to the whole. Thus, the nature of a partial meaning is dependent on the nature of the whole meaning to which it belongs. From the standpoint of knowledge, therefore, we cannot perceive the meaning of a part until after we have grasped the meaning of the whole, since only then can we understand the function of the part within the whole. No matter how much we may emphasize the quasi-independence of certain parts or the priority of our encounter with parts before any sense of the whole arises, still we cannot understand a part as such until we have a sense of the whole. Dilthey called this apparent paradox the hermeneutic circle and observed that it was not vicious because a genuine dialectic always occurs between our idea of the whole and our perception of the parts that constitute it. Once the dialectic has begun, neither side is totally determined by the other. (Hirsch, 1967, pp. 258–259)

This quote is warranted because of its clarity and precision. The dialectical relation of whole to part and vice versa is equally apposite for human expression in general. As I have indicated in Chapters 1 and 2, human action as expression cannot be considered as an isolated unit. Moving from the analogy of the text above to the interpretation of human action as expression, I think one can interpolate from the text to action quite easily. Thus, one could say the follow- ing: The meaning of human action is a complex of submeanings or parts which hang together. This "hanging together" is the fact that human expression is carried out in a personal world of specific cultural forms. Thus, an act can appear meaningless if the interpreter has no sensitivities to the specific cultural form where the action or expression is operating. Thus, a specific human act is meaningful not in itself but in relation to the larger cultural totality in which it operates. A simple analytic attitude obstructs our understanding of human action as expression. As we have indicated in Chapters 2 and 3, the human act must be considered part of larger structural totality that we have identified as the personal world realized in specific located cultural forms.

Resymbolization and the Problems of Horizons

If psychological interpretation or, for that matter, any social science of interpretation simply reiterated and repeated the life world of some particular cultural form, it would be redundant. One could call such interpreters "scribes" rather than interpreters, since nothing new would be added to the situation. It would seem that there would be no pressing necessity for psychological interpretation. Going native, if you will, produced nothing other than what the natives produce themselves. We have already indicated that the function of resymbolizing human action does more than simply catalogue an expression. I would contend that the resymbolization involved in psychological interpretation is similar to the role of a translator of a text. Gadamer's position is that in text translation:

> The interpreter, like the translator, must capture the sense of his material in and through articulating it in a symbolic framework different from that in which it was originally constituted as meaningful. And as the translator must find a common language that presumes the rights of his mother tongue and at the same time respects the foreignness of his text, so too must the interpreter conceptualize his material in such a way that while its foreignness is presumed, it is nevertheless brought into intelligible relation with his own life world. In Gadamer's terms, a successful interpretation entails a fusion of horizons. (McCarthy, 1978, p. 173)

It is clear that there can be no such thing as the *correct interpretation*, because it will vary according to how the horizons meet one another. These meeting points can be considered in the context of what Lonergan (1972) has called *complementary*, *genetic*, and *dialectical* horizons. One can say that a horizon of interpretation is complementary when the interpreter and the interpreted are located within the same or similar cultural forms—for example, a middle-class industrial psychological professional studying middle-management executives. It is likely that these horizons will be complementary and, therefore, the resymbolization produced by the interpreter will not be drastically different from or disconfirming of the interpreted (see Ricoeur, 1973).

The case of genetically different horizons presents a different problem for interpretation. Here it is assumed that the interpreter is developmentally superior to those whom she or he studies. Here one can use the example of adults to children, which developmental psychology presents us with as a given reality. In child development theory and research, it is almost universally assumed that the adult has preemptive status; so in an adequate resymbolization of children, therefore, their world is resymbolized (i.e., interpreted) within the context of some adult normative system. Genetic differences in horizons cannot be restricted, however, to developmental psychology. One can see these assumptions operating in cross-cultural research studies of class differences, gender, and so on. Here again, there is an assumption that may or may not be warranted.

Horizons of interpretation may be dialectical. Here one can anticipate clear conflicts in interpretation between the interpreter's *resymbolization* and the interpreted. Here, for example, a psychologist whose cultural and political horizons are not in synchrony with an industrial business outlook may resymbolize a middle-management executive's world in a way that is conflictual to the latter's world view. Here the resymbolization can be initially abrasive rather than complementary.

Given the possibility of multiple horizons between the *interpreter* and the *interpreted*, it would be foolish to venture that there must be one *correct interpretation*. One must deal with conflict of interpretations due to multiple interpretation and consider their differential adequacy. As we shall say later, this question of adequacy must be carried out in the context of discourse and argument. It is not self-evident. Given this *vulnerability*, the whole process of interpretation must be carried out with a considerable degree of humility and openness. This humility and openness is characterized as a dialogue between the interpreter and the interpreted. It is a dynamic relationship, involving a dialectic of "question and answer" (Gadamer, 1975a).

The Dialectic of "Question and Answer"

The notion of psychological interpretation precludes coming to the situation to predict and control what is being observed and interpreted. The interpreter comes to *dialogue*; the assumption being that there are at least two words spoken in an interpretative situation. In a dialogue there is what one might call a "logic of question and answer" (Gadamer, 1975a). When an interpreter comes to a situation, a certain discourse must be started with those being interpreted which involves a revelation. The discourse is intended to reveal something requiring that the whole sequence be opened up by a question (McCarthy, 1978). Conventional psychology, as I understand it, is not drawn to wonder, which the position of a questioner connotes. To come to a situation with a questioning attitude assumes a certain openness on the part of the interpreter. It is clear that the openness of a questioning attitude is not boundless. As Gadamer (1975a) says, it is limited by the horizon of the interpreter. Thus the asking of the question implies both openness and limitation (McCarthy, 1978). As we indicated earlier, the model here is communication itself as seen in a conversation or discourse. An example from an anthropologist illustrates the dialogical dimensions of questions and answer:

> When I went to Morocco in the summer of 1975 my aims were uncertain. I had been to Morocco as an anthropologist twice before, for two years from 1969–1971, and for two months in the summer of 1973. I had attempted, over that time, to fit these experiences to the demands of academic anthropology and I had found that fit unsatisfactory.
>
> If nothing else, I was determined during the summer of 1975 to confront that dissatisfaction directly. I did not intend to carry out a narrowly defined research

project nor, at the other extreme, would I make the hopeless attempt to "go native." I would simply spend time with people I had come to care about and to enjoy myself with and who seemed to feel similarly towards me, I would try to be sensitive to my needs and theirs, and I would seek to assess my doubts about academic anthropology.

As the summer progressed, the more aware I became that both for myself and for Faqir Mbarek, a 60-year-old Moroccan cultivator whom I had become very close to, our most satisfying project was a series of tape-recorded interviews. These had begun somewhat accidentally. Initially—and I had only one interview in mind—I simply intended to ask him a few general questions about his past and about his attitudes toward his present life. Our second interview was prompted by the unannounced visit from a regional leader of his religious brotherhood. By this time, the form had begun to "take hold": I found myself continuing to single out "events" and Faqir remained more than willing (sometimes suggesting it himself) to sit and talk with me about them. (Dyer, 1979, pp. 216–217)

Recursive Meaning

As with a text, the meaning of human action as expression cannot be established once and for all. This is true because human action expressed in specific cultural forms is dynamic. Horizons, whether from the point of view of the interpreter or the interpreted, are subject to change. Therefore, there are no fixed limits in an interpretation. The limits, at any one time, are fixed by the history of the participants. But history is subject to change by new events. As the anthropological example illustrates, the limits of an interpretative horizon are subject to change when dialogue is present and operating. The interpretative spiral is another way of saying that meaning is recursive. In a text, to say that meaning is recursive means that a text does not establish meaning once and for all; meaning at any one point both depends upon and calls into question what has preceded (Dyer, 1979). The interpretive moment differs markedly from the controlled manipulation to which psychologists are accustomed. The notion of dialogue demands a relational sensitivity as with text interpretation:

> Questions of recursivity can, in principle, be raised at all points in the text. More generally, if we wish to hold to the recursive nature of the fieldwork experience as we pose questions of the text, we must resist irretrievably distorting the text by cutting it into bits and pieces or by playing freely with its actual sequence in time (just as we have tried to resist doing the same to the fieldwork experience by making it into a text). Bearing this in mind, we must ask to what extent this text retains a wholeness, a substantiality, which reflects the recursivity of the experience and yet does not, at the same time, discourage the reader from responding actively to the text. (Dyer, 1979, p. 218)

Reflexive Interpretation

As with text interpretation where the reader assumes an active role in the interpretation of the work, a social scientific interpretation of human action as expression involves the interpreter *actively*. I have already indicated that interpretation is not a passive recording process. In this sense, then, the interpreter is actively involved in a *transaction* with those *interpreted*. The interpreter is not only involved with the actions of others; the interpretation itself must also be considered an act and expression of an agent. Under these conditions the horizon of the interpreter becomes problematic. By problematic, I mean that the horizon of the interpreter must be part of the reflective horizon of the whole interpretative process. Coming to the interpretative situation as an *active agent*, the interpreter must abandon the traditional stance of *expert as distanced rationality*. As an *active agent*, one does not expect mere repetition of the interpretative horizons of the participants. One assumes that a social scientific interpretation of an event will move beyond the point of view of the participants (i.e., resymbolization).

We will consider the adequacy of an interpretation (resymbolization) shortly. For now, let it be understood that one expects the interpretation to be creative in the sense of challenging the common sense. An interpretation is reflexive when the social scientist ponders and reflects on the effects of his or her horizon on the interpretative events. We are not just agents but agents in relation. It is here that the analogy with the text breaks down. In the text, the interpreter speaks to the text by the interpretation of the work. The author, however, does not speak back. When meaning is *recursive*, as in a conversation, we expect that the resymbolization not only challenges the participants but that the resymbolization can also be challenged by the participants. Therefore, some reflection on one's interpretation seems reasonable under the conditions I have just mentioned. It is, in the classical sense, humility (i.e., knowing where one stands). In coming to the situation of attempting to understand the personal world of others (i.e., their project), one must, therefore, reflect on the effects of *bias*. Different problems are presented when the interpretative horizons differ, that is, when the interpretative horizons of the interpreter appear to be complementary, genetic, or dialectical when related to the project of the participants. When the horizon is complementary, is it because the interpreter has not attempted to achieve some creative distance from those interpreted? When the horizon is dialectical, is it because the interpreter is so *distanced* from the project of the interpreted that the oppositional nature of the interpretation is simply gross misunderstanding? When an interpretative horizon is considered genetic, as in developmental psychology, to what extent is the interpretative system of the adult *adultocentric* rather than the system being a reflection of the interpreter's maturity? These are simply some questions that can present themselves when self-reflection (reflexivity) is operating. This and other dimensions must be considered in the next chapter, where the notion of critical interpretation will be developed.

6

CRITICAL INTERPRETATION

What is critical interpretation? Why does psychology need to go beyond interpretation, which, in short, is a study of the constitutive meaning of actors? This chapter will attempt to deal with these questions.[1]

Let it be said initially that a critical psychology does not reject the hermeneutical. By hermeneutical, I mean the interpretation of the meaning of actions from the actor's point of view. If there is such a thing as psychology, then the interpretation of this microcosm cannot be relinquished. It must be understood that critical interpretation does not relinquish the conscious intentions of actors. In fact, a critical interpretation of the personal world is grounded, at the outset, in the "intentional project" of actors or agents. As I will make clear shortly, this is not the whole matter. The presence of the intentional project as part of a critical interpretative system indicates interest in the concept of human freedom. As I have already indicated in Chapters 3 and 4, the projective character of human action has as one of its constituent features the projection of alternatives to the present and past (i.e., freedom). An interpretative psychology commences to be critical when it attempts to elucidate and criticize those features of a human situation that frustrate intentional agency (i.e., the project). This point is emphasized by Fay (1975) as follows:

> The critical model asserts that in order to have a subject matter at all the social scientist must attempt to understand the intentions and desires of actors he is observing, as well as the rules and constitutive meanings of their social order. The reason for this is that—a critical theory is rooted in the *felt* needs and sufferings of a group of people and, therefore, it is absolutely necessary that a critical theorist come to understand these actors from their own point of view, at least as a first step. (pp. 93–94)

If we stopped here we would be guilty of a crass form of idealism. The full scope of institutional living cannot be reduced to conscious intentions of agents.

---

[1]I wish to bring the reader's attention to a new book by Philip Wexler, *Critical Social Psychology*, which covers the social psychology literature in a more detailed manner. It is published by Routledge & Kegan Paul (1982).

A critical interpretative psychology takes cognizance of the fact that much of human action is outside the conscious control of personal agency and is embedded in social conditions outside human consciousness. These are what I will be calling "structural" as opposed to "intentional" conditions for human action. They were referred to in Chapter 4 as structures of domination. These structural determinants are class dynamics, sexism, racism, and adultocentrism. Basically, these structural dynamics are related to intentional action as habitus is to project. Notwithstanding intentional action, human action must also be understood as being caused by social conditions over which the agent exerts no conscious or intentional control. This limits the scope of the project and, therefore, human freedom, since it is important to understand that social structural conditions unconsciously operate as potent determinants of human action. A specific example will elucidate my point. The work of Brenner (1976) concludes that fluctuations in the economy, specifically in the level of unemployment, are the single most important source of changing rates of admission to mental hospitals. This statistic is also related to class structure. For example, the lower one's economic standing, the greater the cumulative impact of economic dislocation and unemployment. Where economic dislocation is present, psychiatric indices go upward. Mental illness drops when employment goes upward, exclusive of therapeutic intervention. Brenner develops a complex line of arguments, but what is important for our purposes is the finding that structural conditions in the economic sphere that are not directly related to intentional control of the actors involved affect mental health.

This finding raises a note of caution which is part of a critical interpretation of human action. The caution is to be careful in a work that fosters an understanding of intentional human action, like the present work, not to weight agents with more agency than they really have at their disposal. This would allow one to treat a complex condition such as unemployment as something under the intentional control of agents. This type of individualistic psychology ends up by "blaming the victim" for a lack of intentional control. We would call this oppressive rather than critical psychology. What is important in a critical psychology is to make some linkages between the structural dynamics of class, race, sexism, and adultocentricism and the projects of human agents embedded in these historically constituted structures. A critical psychology here will suggest a praxis.

> This means that the quasi-causal explanations which are given must be related to the felt needs and sufferings of the social actors in such a way that they show how these feelings can be overcome by the actors coming to understand themselves in their situation as the product of certain inherent contradictions in their social order, contradictions which they can remove by taking an appropriate course of action to change this social order. A critical social theory is meant to inform and guide the activities of a class of dissatisfied actors—revealing how the irrationalities of social life which are causing the dissatisfaction can be eliminated by taking some specific action which the theory calls for. (Fay, 1977, pp. 97–98)

Thus, the constitutive interest of a critical social psychology will be a core interest in human emancipation and liberation. It is, therefore, a liberation psychology.

EMANCIPATORY PSYCHOLOGY AND ITS RELATION TO A CRITICAL THEORY OF SOCIETY

Emancipatory psychology should not be considered a mere buzz word. As I am defining it, it is a psychology with an expressed interest in the possibilities of human freedom and emancipation. Therefore, one of the features of an adequate critical interpretative psychology is the incorporation of this emancipatory intent. Although this intent may seem strange to the ears of many psychological professionals, it is not without precedent in the social sciences outside of psychology. There are critical theoretical efforts in sociology, anthropology, and political theory that have a significant maturity and presence in these disciplines. Theologians also have developed a theological concern called "liberation theology" (Gutierrez, 1973). To talk, then, of an emancipatory psychology is not to talk in a vacuum but to link the intent of a psychology interested in human freedom with a wider critical social theory. This is one of the goals that must be attempted here.

Psychology and Knowledge-Constitutive Interests

In our opening chapter on psychological metaphors, I maintained that a personal metaphor would have to be interpreted in the context of a critical interest. There I discussed the work of Habermas (1972) which bears review at this point. Habermas schematically represents (see Table 9) social theories as expressing three types of knowledge interests and specifies their ontological orientation and the types of inquiry.

In Chapter 1, I have already indicated how these interests map out in psychological concerns. In a certain sense, the last chapter focussed mostly on

TABLE 9.   Knowledge-Constitutive Interests According to Habermas

Ontological elements of self-formative process	Knowledge-constitutive interest	Type of study or inquiry
1. Labor (instrumental action)	Prediction and control	Empirical–analytical sciences
2. Intention	Understanding	Historical–hermeneutic sciences
3. Authority (power)	Emancipation	Critical theory

the second interest, which involved the meaning and rule structure of actors from their own point of view. Thus, the knowledge-constitutive interest was understanding the meaning of intentional action. Habermas (1970) suggests that hermeneutical sciences are limited in scope because they ignore the role of authority and power in meaning constitution. When power is brought into focus, one moves into an emancipatory interest with critical moments. The critical moment simply means that the power is distributed unequally over different societal groupings, and this has a tendency to frustrate the possibility for intentional projects. Without rejecting a hermeneutic–interpretative orientation, it is essential to understand that the notion of human action is tied to power in a logical manner (Giddens, 1977). Giddens develops this idea by venturing that power represents the capacity of human agents to materialize resources for intentional outcomes. These resources constitute the means to achieve outcomes for intentional action (Giddens, 1977). Giddens then goes on to represent power in two senses. In the first sense, power is seen as the transformative capacity of human agency; that is, the capability of the actors to intervene in a series of events so as to alter the course of a situation. In this first sense, I would say that power is the presence of an intentional project.

This notion was introduced by Von Wright (1971) to draw attention to the possibility that the intentions of agents intervene in larger societal processes to affect the course of events. Intentional intervention is, therefore, the agents' capacity or power to alter events in their world. It is important to distinguish between personal powers and liabilities, since the former assume the agents' capacities for intervention (i.e., freedom), whereas the latter connote a state of patienthood as opposed to agency: ". . . 'having the power' involves being in a certain state and in the case of human individuals, being an agent . . ." (Harré & Secord, 1972, pp. 247–248).

In addition to agent concepts, the description of human life requires a full complement of patient concepts. These we shall call, generically, "liabilities." Unlike powers, liabilities may manifest themselves either because of internal changes or because of external influences. One who exercises a power and is an agent must figure as the source of his or her action in his or her or our account of it, while those who succumb to liabilities may either have only themselves to blame, as we say, or it may be that in accounting for the manifesting of the liability we look for the source in circumstances external to the individual.

The notion of intentional intervention, as Von Wright (1971) understands it, is not a naive voluntarism. Intentions are the projective quality of human action. These intentions are not ventured in a vacuum. The sediment of the past (habitus) makes the possibility of intentional interventions limited in scope. Therefore, freedom is at the cutting edge of apparently dynamic repetitive systems. The past has the power to repeat itself. It can change only by the alteration of human intentions. In this context, I see these interventions operating within the dynamics of the dialectics of habitus and project. In this way, one comes up with a paradox. Freedom and determinism are two sides of a coin. Freedom, the capacity of agents to transform the past, operates within the framework of necessity (determinism). Freedom is, therefore, a struggle with the past for an open future. Therefore,

> the notion of intervention puts an end to the intolerable state of opposition between a mentalistic order of understanding and a physicalistic order of explanation. On the one hand, there is no system without initial state, no initial state without intervention, and no intervention without the exercise of capacity. (Ricoeur, 1978, p. 160)

The "exercise of capacity," as Ricoeur (1978) puts it, is the ability to intervene in one's world as an agent. It is here that one can expect to find dialectical differences in interpretative horizons, depending on the scope that one's horizon gives for the understanding of intentional interventions. Horizons of interpretation which speak to that capacity, as I have done throughout this book, may be said to express an interest in the possibility of an emancipatory praxis.

The second sense is more restricted and expresses societal relationships. This *relational sense* expresses the property of interaction and is defined as the capability to secure outcomes, where the realization of these ends depends on the *agency* of *others*. It is in this latter sense that one speaks of men and women having power over others. Giddens (1977) calls this power the "power of domination." I have already given an example of this power of domination in Chapter 4, in my analysis of the black underclass (see Table 6). This sense of power makes plausible our concern in Chapter 4 for the structure of domination in class relations, sexuality, and relations between adults and children (i.e., adultocentrism). What is important for an emancipatory psychology is a critical interpretative system that analyzes those structural conditions in terms of their enabling or disabling the intentional action of agents (i.e., projects). Simple interpretation of the meaning of action does not encompass this task. Fay (1975) faults interpretive social science on this point on four counts. First, "interpretative inquiry" does not examine "structural conditions." It ignores those conditions which give rise to (enable) or deter (disable) action. Second, interpretative models generally neglect in their explanatory system patterns of unintended consequences, for example, the effects of a system as a whole on individual actors without their knowledge that they are sustaining the system (e.g., class structures, etc.). Third, interpretative models alone provide no way to understand structural conflicts within a society (e.g., racial, class, sexual, etc.). Finally, interpretative models neglect explanation of historical change. They are more interested in presently constituted social forms (i.e., forms of life), which accounts for social order, while ignoring social change and personal and societal transformation. To bridge these shortcomings, one needs a way to examine how larger structural totalities can be linked to human agency dialectically. It is to this I will now turn.

Agency and Structure

Giddens (1979) argues that the notions of action and structure presuppose one another and depend on one another in a dialectical relationship. Implicitly, I have argued the same position in Chapters 3 and 4, in my discussion of the dialectical relationship between habitus and project. It is now necessary to extend the ideas on habitus–project by linking it to the agency–structure dialectic. The relation of agency–structure is a structure in itself, which expresses what Giddens (1979) calls a "duality of structure." Giddens (1979) argues that the "structuration" relates to the basic recursive character of mutual social life, expressing the dependence of structure and agency. He explains this duality of structure as follows:

> By duality of structure, I mean that the structural properties of social system are both the medium and the outcome of practices that constitute the system—the identification of structure with constraint is also rejected structure in both enabling and constraining and it is one of the specific tasks of social theory to study the conditions of social systems that govern the interconnections between the two. (Giddens, 1979, pp. 69–70)

Let us now attempt to examine these interconnections within the context of the habitus–project dialectic (see Table 10). In Chapter 3, Table 2, I identified the notion of habitus with socialization and the notion of project with that of social transformation. At both extremes of this polarity, I identified seven key features that were dialectically related to one another.

To speak of dialectical integration, as I did in Chapters 3 and 4, is to say in Giddens's (1979) terms that this is a "dual structure." One presupposes the other. Let us attach to the above polarities the notions of structure and agency. Let us

TABLE 10. Integrative Polarities of the Personal World

Habitus	←——→	Project
1. Social self	←——→	Intentional self (I)
2. Identity	←——→	Individuation
3. Order (reproduction)	←——→	Change (transformation)
4. Preconscious	←——→	Conscious
5. Past (history)	←——→	Future
6. Ideological	←——→	Utopian
7. Determinism	←——→	Freedom

↓
Dialectical
integration
or
duality of
structure

locate structure within the habitus and agency within the project. Yet, let us say that habitus is synonymous with *structure* and *project* is the expression of human agency. These are dual structures because they are mutually dependent on one another for continued life. The problem is that this dual structure and its dialectical relation have been collapsed at one extreme or other in social theorizing, and this has caused a great deal of misunderstanding. Most deterministic theories of human nature collapse their analysis on the habitus–structure side of the polarity. Extreme theories of voluntaristic freedom unencumbered by limits collapse on the project–agency side of the polarity. Following Giddens (1979), I would submit that they must be treated simultaneously and in a more intricate analysis. Let us ponder what is implied here. Our example of infant development in Chapter 3 indicates that the development of a personal world accompanied by a sense of agency is enhanced or debilitated by the structure of the habitus. A disorder induced by chaotic social structures with no stable ideological structures and their accompanying familiarity disables *human agency*. Structures in this sense are ambiguous; that is, they can enable or disable human functioning. An enabling structure enhances human powers and capabilities, whereas a disabling structure detracts from them. Some structures are able to give the agent a sense of personal power that is, in Giddens's (1979) terms, "the capability to make certain accounts count." What a critical social theory must be aware of and take into account is that one person or group's power or project may be another person's or group's bondage. I have already suggested this interrelationship in Chapter 4, in my discussion of class dynamics, gender, ethnicity, and child socialization. Let us now return to these concerns in a discussion of "structures of domination" and "structures of freedom." Let me define a structure of domination as one that hampers human projects and disables the possibility of intentional intervention (i.e., human agency). By contrast, a structure of freedom enhances (i.e., enables) human projects and increases the possibility of intentional intervention. The invariant present in both these structures is power or lack thereof.

Let me now indicate invariant structures and their contribution to the possibilities for human agency. Part of the structure of the habitus is the presence of economic structures. Economic structures are systems of social relations designed for the exploitation of the environment for purposes of human survival. Historically, these structures have varied immensely; the two prominent forms of economic structure today are capitalism and socialism. A second invariant structure is gender. At the basic biological level, this structure of sexuality provides for the replenishment of the human species. The third invariant structure is that of ethnicity. The presence of ethnicity accounts for the universal diversity of the human species. Finally, there is the invariant structure of parenting and adult–child interaction. Because of the sustained dependence of children on adults in the human species, this structure is more characteristic in terms of its impact on the human species than on other animals.

It should be clear by now that these invariant structures are not independent of one another. For example, class relates to ethnicity and they both have implications for child rearing and male–female relations. Although these structures are *invariant*, there are variations in power within these structures that have important implications for the possibility of human agency. An economic structure can be said to be a *structure of domination* when the distribution of power is so skewed to one group that it disables the "projective" character of other groups. This is one of the criticisms of capitalism—that the power is organized so as to enhance or enable one class to the exclusion of others. An economic structure can be said to be a *structure of freedom* when power as enabling is distributed universally and democratically. The same can be said for gender structures. Sexism can be considered a structure of domination within a culture when the projects of one gender (male) are considered more significant than the other (female). Adult–child relations become structures of domination when the dependencies of children are made into invariants (when actually the dependency is variable and will move toward autonomy if encouraged). What is important here is the subtlety of these structures and their interrelation. For example, an economic structure can be considered as liberating (i.e., structure of freedom) at one period and dominating at a later period. The truth of the matter is that we must all live within the ambiguity of social structures. Ambiguity should not lead us into a sterile tolerance which allows us to live with structures of domination because they are intertwined with structures of freedom. The ambiguity of the human condition is that we must all live, as Jesus said, "separating out the cockles and the tares." He said they were intertwined in his parable, but note that he suggests that we must all do the weeding of good from bad. In this sense, an adequate critical psychology must identify and encourage structures of freedom that enhance human agency and correct and help eliminate structures that do not (i.e., structures of domination). Therefore, a critical psychology is in Freire's terms "a joint task of annunciation and denunciation." It is here in the social sphere that value neutrality becomes pernicious. As psychological professionals, we have, it would seem, the moral responsibility to denounce structures of domination that detract from a sense of human agency. Otherwise, we are like Job's comforters, adding insult to injury. This brings us now to a description of how the psychological professional operates within the social order.

PSYCHOLOGY IN THE SOCIAL ORDER

What I am about to discuss is rarely part of the working discussions of psychologists either in theory or practice. It is based on the assumption that psychologists as individuals and institutions are linked to specific "social orders" and that they, therefore, bear the imprint of such an order. Sarason (1981), in the discussion of American social psychology, is quite lucid on this point:

American social psychology has not in any of its major theorizings taken seriously the
psychologist's place in the social arrangements and the bearing that place has on what
happens to him or her as a person as well as on the social consequences of the
psychologist's work. The issue is not in whose domain the problem belongs. It is a
central question for every kind of psychologist because every psychologist's thinking
and work bear the imprint of his or her place in the social arrangements. And the
consequences [of] that work may have to always bear the imprint of those social
arrangements. (p. 72)

When one looks at psychology's brief history in the 20th century, it is clear
that psychologists have born the imprint of existing social arrangements. In the
case of IQ testing in the earlier part of this century, it now can be said, without
rancor, that psychologists helped to sustain the racial and social class steroetypes
of that era (Kamin, 1974; Sarason, 1981). It can also be said that psychology as a
discipline, when following an unreflective course, justifies the existing social
order and its power arrangements (Buss, 1975; Zuniga, 1975). Let me elaborate
on the last point by a critical analysis of what I will call "the horizon of the
expert."

Horizon of the "Expert"

All professionalization assumes as its baseline the existence of expertise.
Expert knowledge assumes specialized knowledge and the ability to exercise
social distance from the phenomena studied. Specialization also assumes a specific focus and, to be "special" this knowledge must possess uniqueness and
identifiable differences from other specialties. American psychology expresses
this uniqueness by emphasizing an intimate knowledge of the individual as the
unit of analysis. As I have already said in Chapter 3, individualism is a *dominant
cultural focus*, and the profession of psychology is a reflection of individualism.
The problem of the "expert's" horizon ensues when that "expertise" is not seen
as a part of existing social arrangements. This is a difficult task, since the
acceptance of this possibility challenges the privileged position of the "expert's
position," bringing its traditional position of dispassionate observation and interpretation under suspicion. Be that as it may, there are sound reasons why
psychologists are influenced by their position in the social order and why they, in
the normal course of events, reflect in their theorizing the existing power arrangements. This is not a static process. The profession of psychology will, in
general, reflect the dynamics of a society over time. In a liberal, expansive era
like the sixties, the theories did reflect that epoch. In a period of financial
retrenchment and conservatism, like the present, one will see theories in psychology that will match the conservatism of the existing social order. These
social currents should not be looked at in simple-minded terms. At any one time
there are conflicting currents. Psychology as a form of social inquiry will reflect
these different currents in its theory and practice. Because psychology seems to

be unique among the social sciences in its inability to reflect on its place in the social order, it will, in this unreflective stance, function as an apologist for the status quo.

Because psychology has not traditionally reflected on its place in the social order, it has tended to act within the present cultural horizon as a *complementary horizon* to other horizons that reflect the power of existing social arrangements (i.e., status quo). It has done this indirectly, though in a complementary fashion, in its theoretical and practical interpretations of class structure, gender differences, and racial differences. With psychology's traditional microsocial focus on "individual psyches," psychological interpretations have attributed only to individuals the reasons why there are different power arrangements (i.e., social order). Let me demonstrate this briefly in the context of social class, gender, and race, since they are the categories where I have developed the idea of structures of domination.

Social Class

The position of "expert professional" of whatever color—be it anthropologist, sociologist, or psychologist—involves the production of a specialized language of interpretation of some phenomena and a social distance from the object being interpreted so as to assume an orientation of detached observation. Although detached observation has been assumed in theory, it has never been clearly demonstrated in practice. This can also be said of other disciplines, that is, that it is part of the dynamics of a social order rather than detached from it. Psychology exists in a particular part of a social order and is embedded in one segment of its social strata. A simpler way of saying the above is that psychological professionals are part of the middle class. By education, training, and income, they are embedded in the dynamics of the middle class. One cannot read any simple formula out of the fact that professionals are part of the middle class. What I want to emphasize here is that "professional expertise" will be affected by the dynamics of the class structure in a society. In general, the class horizon of expert–professionals is rarely considered as part of the self-reflexive process of disciplines. In other words, one could say that it is almost in poor taste to think that professionals would be affected by their origins. *Professional distance*, which is a buzz word for *expertise*, is assumed to be operating in all segments of the professional's life.

Historically, psychology as a form of disciplined inquiry is peculiarly tone deaf to its social class origins. It is the one discipline that I know of that has no well-developed self-reflexivity as to its own place in a larger social structure. As a discipline, psychology negates its own class origins and, in practice, ignores its effects in the psychological phenomena that it attempts to give an account of. Sarason (1974), in speaking of psychologists, notes that by self-selection and training they "naturally" think in terms of motivations, attitudes, personality, and many other interpsychic factors. Because, by background and training, their unit of analysis is the individual, their horizon in general masks or conceals the effects of social structure on personal development. Left to their own devices, you might say that psychologists usually attribute social class dynamics to intrapsychic factors (cf. Ryan, 1974). Although rarely reflected upon in this discipline, psychology usually follows the movements of the larger sociopolitical and economic context. When the temper is liberal and progressive and the economy is expanding, there is a greater emphasis on transformational (change) models and optimism about the effects of the environment for psychological and social change. Thus intelligence, in Piaget's sense, could be considered as a dynamic transformational activity, and intellectual deficit (cultural deprivation) could be ameliorated by education (i.e., environment; Sullivan, 1981). When the social temper became more conservative, conservative biogenetic metaphors (e.g., Jensen) became more popular.

Gender

Traditional psychology and its many persuasions has always dealt with the question of *gender* as derivative. By derivative, I mean that information about sexuality and gender (usually under the rubric of sex differences) is usually derived from a supposedly larger theoretical construction in which sexuality and gender are accidental by-products of the larger theory. Theory in the above context is an attempt to arrive at some *universal truth* that *transcends* the accidental boundaries of *time, space, sexuality,* and so on. Gould (1976) calls this criterion *abstract universality.* She maintains that the traditional philosophical arguments for abstract universality are based on three premises, which she labels essential premises. She frames these premises in the context of philosophy, but I would contend that they are relevant to psychology as a *discipline,* since it is based, as I understand it, on a set of similar premises. Premise 1 states that the appropriate subject matter of philsophy is universal and essential truth that excludes particulars and accidental differences which are, by definition, incompatible with universal norms (i.e., principles or laws). Premise 2 asserts that in the *human domain,* that is the social, one studies what is common to all human beings and all societies in all times, precluding accidental and local parts as aspects of the human or social (i.e., human nature as such). Premise 3 asserts that *gender* "is an accidental and not a universal property of human beings, since one may be human and not female, or human and not male" (Gould, 1976, p. 8). Gould (1976) draws a specific conclusion from these premises as they relate to women. She maintains that these premises allow one to consider femaleness as an accidental property, thus relegating the question of women philosophicallly as a peripheral concern in the acquisition of *universal abstract* truth. The gender domain is not appropriately universal or essential in the sense required from the above premises.

The premises for abstract universality can be considered as part of the interpretative horizon for much of what we would be naming as conventional social science. This horizon, as I understand it, is dialectically opposed to possible horizons of specificty, where such aspects as *gender* and *ethnicity* are considered accidental or nonessential aspects of truth. Gould (1976) maintains that when one is operating out of a horizon of abstract universality, there are certain masked value premises which must be made problematic by critical scrutiny. Critique is necessary, Gould says, because she feels that the interpetative horizon of abstract universality reflects the interests, needs, and prejudices of particular social groups. There are two reasons why this becomes problematic. First, "such essential prejudices may introduce distortions into our very understanding of what is essential" (Gould, 1976, p. 17). Second, "essentialism reflects such interests in a particularly harmful way, because it tends to mask them under the guise of universality and therefore is deceptive" (Gould, 1976, p. 17). There is no claim being made that the criterion of abstract universality is inherently vicious and conscious in its distortions. What Gould (1976) is suggesting, however, is that in actual practice the criterion of universality seems to choose properties as *essential* and *universal* which reflect the interests of a particular gender (i.e., male) and which were associated with roles and functions in which males predominated (Gould, 1976).

Although she is speaking about philosophical discourse and goes on to give specific instances of male dominance in some of the classical philosophers, one can, nevertheless, draw an analogy for the traditional discipline of psychology and cite specific examples of distortions of sexuality that have been masked by the assumptions of abstract essentialism. In the social sciences, and particularly psychology, the issue of gender is usually discussed under the rubric of what we have called in Chapter 1 "organic metaphors." In contemporary thinking since the beginning of this century, gender has been couched within the framework of biological-evolutionary theory (Shields, 1975). Shields (1975) contends that the "interpretative horizon" of evolutionary theory as it came to be applied to the social sciences was male-dominant in that it essentially assumed the biological supremacy of the Caucasian male (Wine *et al.*, 1980). This interpretative horizon was, therefore, skewed from its beginnings to interpret *one gender* and *race* as the apex of evolutionary development.

These turn-of-the-century functionalist–evolutionary perspectives attributed differential functional differences to males and females, always considering males superior. Earlier discussions of differences in brain size between male and female saw men as superior in intellectual capacity because of their larger brain size. Furthermore, a hypothesis of greater male variability, and its relation to social and educational issues, showed males more flexible. Here the Darwinian assumption establishing that variation within a species is a requisite for evolutionary adaptation and progress was buttressed with the belief that men were more variable and, therefore, superior in their potential development (Shields, 1975). Basically, what we are seeing here in a historical perspective is the development of a universalistic norm that just happens to be male-dominant as well as race-dominant. From what one could call a horizon of "feminist psychology," there is the critical understanding that much of our present discussions are similarly afflicted by views of male superiority (Favreau, 1977). Frequently, male and female differences that are considered as descriptive and nonessential are given universality by attributing them to biological origins. In other words, they are considered as universal because of their assumed biological origins. As I have proposed from the outset, a psychology that is a critical interpretation of the personal world will deal with gender as a historically constituted category rather than assuming the preeminence of biological determinants as found in organic metaphors. This does not rule out the presence of biological determinants in both gender similarity and difference. A critical interpretative horizon will, however, resist attributing historically constituted sex differences as if they were biologically given (i.e., attribute sex difference to the same type of organic biological metaphor). There is a universalistic ring to biological metaphors that interpret sex differences as by-products of some "biological universals where males by *nature* rather than *nurture* are superior to females.

In short, then, what must be suggested in our present treatment is an interpretative horizon that deals with gender as historically constituted where sex differences are considered within the context of cultural dominance rather than the by-product of a genetic heritage. To treat sex differences within a cultural horizon that is constituted historically does not solve problems but simply provides a critical lens which can countenance sexual dominance as an offshoot of a male-dominated culture. This involves an alternative notion of *concrete universality* suggested by Gould (1976), which is a counterposition to the position suggested as *abstract universality*. Sexual difference are not mere accidents that are assimilated into biological universals. Gender here is put in the category of a concrete universal. The notion of universality is retained, but it exists in radical transformation:

> Whereas the criterion of abstract universality is concerned only with what is essentially the same and excludes accidental differences, the criterion of concrete universality is concerned also with human and social differences, and includes them not simply as accidents but as aspects which constitute the universal or the essence itself. (Gould, 1976, p. 26)

The universal, however, is not permanently couched in biological or organic categories but, rather, within *historically* constituted categories, which I would maintain as consistent with what I have been calling the personal meta-phor. It is a psychology from the point of view of agents who constitute their worlds by actions in historical time rather than biological time. Therefore:

> Concrete universality thus implies an alternative conception of the nature of history itself. As against the view that historical events are exemplifications of fixed, a priori essences, this view regards essences, as well as history itself, as constituted or created by the actions of individuals. Concrete universality concerns the present as the mo-ment in which individuals create history through their interaction with each other and with the objective world. It sees the past as the set of interactions which provides the circumstances for present action. This action transforms these circumstances in accor-dance with the future envisioned by these agents. (Gould, 1976, p. 27)

Thus, from this interpretative horizon, one can speak of cultural projects that are gender-related and dialectical in their relation to one another, as male and female roles have been historically. Women, for example, could be express-ing a concrete universality (e.g., "women's truth"). Women become a unique category and a "cultural form," as we have indicated, by having a specific role in history unto themselves but also in dialectical tension with cultural roles of a category called men.

What I am about to say is speculative and controversial, and I would beg the reader to treat it as a plausible hypothesis. From a feminist's perspective, one could argue that the psychological horizons, as we understand them, can be considered as arising historically in western culture under the dominance of white males who have taken themselves to be speaking in a universal human voice (Scheman, 1981). As we have already indicated, the tradition is one of abstract universality, so that the issue of gender, as we discuss it here, is masked from the potential awareness of the position of the universalizer. Moreover, it is contended that this specific type of universalization is the reflection of a liberal ideology (Sullivan, 1977a, 1977b, 1981). *Liberal ideology* refers to a style of thought developed at the time of the French Revolution (Mannheim, 1953a). I ventured to suggest earlier that liberal ideology is the philosophical underpinning of the notion of *individualism* and critiqued this idea in Chapter 3. As we said there, the notion of individualism proceeds with the assumption that larger social totalities are the product of the organization of individual units (i.e., principle of analysis). Thus, it is assumed to be a *natural fact* that individuals exist in essence as separate units, so that it can be said that psychological characteristics such as wants, preferences, needs, abilities, and so on are inherent and located "in individuals" (Scheman, 1981). We have already critiqued this from the perspec-tive defined as the personal metaphor (see Chapters 1 and 3).

I will now add that the horizon of individualism as embedded in liberal social theory carries, in addition, the baggage of male dominance and bias. Male dominance means simply that one would expect interpretative horizons to be markedly influenced by points of view that are related to the preemptive status of males historically in our culture and specifically in the profession of psychology. This assumes that women have quite consistently been excluded from the centrally important metaphysical, epistemological, moral, and political conceptions of personhood (Scheman, 1981). The case is made by feminists that men have traditionally held the power to name or define what it is to be human, adult, intelligent, moral, and so on and have done so in response to their own experience of and need for separateness and distinctiveness (Scheman, 1981). By contrast, traditional female roles have emphasized fusion (Bakan, 1966). If this present work simply emphasized the human agent with intentions and meanings that are self-contained, one could say that the bias of individualism was operating. *Individual agency* as a self-contained structure is not, however, the "horizon" under which the perspective being developed here is operating. Personal agency is agency in relation to others, as I have pointed out in Chapter 3. A psychological horizon that is a critical interpretation of the personal world combines feminist critique of male dominance (i.e., self-contained agency) with the relational totality called community (i.e., persons in relation). In this light, I would hope that the perspective anticipates transformed, equitable gender relationships in the wider culture and more specifically at the level of theory and practice of the discipline of psychology.

Ethnicity

Historically, psychology has not used the construct of ethnicity or race in any direct manner at the level of theory. In fact, most of the classical texts on personality do not have a salient place for this construct. Like gender, it is a particularistic construct that contradicts the direction of theorizing attempting to formulate perspectives which are abstract and universal. By and large, the work of treating ethnicity or race has traditionally fallen to sociologists and anthropologists who treat race within the context of culture.

This in no way says that the profession of psychology has not been involved with the phenomena of ethnicity, for the fact of the matter is that, at the level of social policy, its influence in North American psychology has been prepotent. Historically in North America, it was the psychological testing movement that first brought the profession of psychology in contact with *ethnics*. This was through the screening of immigrants through the use of standardized tests of *intelligence*. In general, it was assumed that the standardized test was a way of setting up a universalistic norm for the assessment of intellectual abilities. The assumption was that these standardized tests were "culture-free," that is, that they were not biased in any systematic way against any particular segment of the population. Thus we see here the development of what we have previously called a *universal abstract* norm. At the turn of this century, these tests were considered by the immigration department of the United States as *objective* norms by which to assess the intelligence of new immigrants (Kamin, 1974). By today's standards, the discussion of ethnic groups by some of the major figures of the psychometric testing movement would be considered racist and inflamatory (Kamin, 1974). Yet, this language was considered objective for its time. In addition, the discussion of the determining factors for the presence or absence of intellectual capacity was embedded in the now shopworn (but far from dead) heredity–environment controversy. That controversy was over the relative weight that one should give these assessed psychological traits in relation to genetic factors (heredity) or the environment. In different epochs, psychometricians have come down on one side or the other on this controversy. In general, either side of this interpretive horizon (i.e., genetic or environmental) has been directed pejoratively toward certain cultural and ethnic groups. In fact, the heredity–environment controversy seems to follow economic currents operating in the social order and the values that are precipitated within an expanding and contracting economy. When the economy is *expanding*, there is an optimism that *environmental* factors such as education can improve the lot of disenfranchised minorities. In the 1960s, for example, blacks were considered *culturally deprived*, and this deficit, it was felt, could be alleviated by education and other services. Within the context of what is a universalistic means, it is interesting to note that blacks were perceived to be lacking in culture (i.e., culturally deprived). When the economy went into retrenchment, one finds that environmental theories were eclipsed, since they held out the possibility that environmental factors such as *health* and *education* benefit disenfranchised groups. When this happens, the more conservative genetic theories come to the fore, as witnessed in the Jensen controversy. Here differences in cultures are perceived to be influenced in a major way by genetic dispositions. This justifies a cutback in services, since they supposedly would not be effective in any event (Hunt & Sullivan, 1974).

The Need for Reflexive Interpretation

What we have just tried to document is the conventional bias of psychology within the social order. When this bias is not reflected upon in some critical manner (i.e., nonreflexive), the psychological interpreter has historically ventured interpretations that reflect his or her class origins and the place psychology has in relation to the culture at large. The position of "expert," by definition, leaves the expert as unproblematic. Expertise problematizes all without itself being problematized. Two assumptions tend to mask awareness of problems that expert positions pose. The assumptions are that the expert has distance from extraneous relationships surrounding a phenomenon being studied and that the expert is in a nonnormative or value-free position (i.e., unbiased). As we have hinted in relation to class, gender, and ethnicity, the position of nonbias is difficult to sustain when a historical perspective is taken. The bias of psychology, when left unchecked (i.e., unreflexive), will, in all probability, reflect in sub-stantial ways the biases of the wider culture. In other words, psychological interpretation will normally be a complementary horizon to the status quo, psychological expertise functioning as a form of legitimation or rationalization for the normative order or status quo. Does this mean then that bias of interpreta-tion makes the task of psychological interpretation impossible? We think not. We think that the interpreter must reflect a bias of viewpoint. We would project that a critical psychology would critically reflect in its bias of viewpoint, problematiz-ing itself in relation to the phenomenon studied (i.e., reflexive psychology). The mapping of structure, as I have defined it, onto agency allows us to examine power relations in society and the conflictual nature of power in society. Al-though psychology as a professional discipline has a commitment to even-tem-pered observation and interpretation, it cannot consider itself a neutral umpire in the power dynamics of the society in which it is located. Silence or expressed value neutrality gives consent.

I have just indicated how the value neutrality simply serves the needs of the social order and stabilizes the power dynamics within a society. An "emancipato-ry psychology" with critical intent will serve and help *name the world* (Freire) of oppressed groups and, in essence, serve the cause of freedom. In that sense, order without freedom (domination) will be *criticized* rather than *apologized*. One would, therefore, expect that there would be conflict of interpretations between psychological professionals, depending on their identification with the social order where they are located. For example, *resistance* is almost always considered by social scientists as deviance when it comes from a group that has little social power. If you consider my extended example of the black underclass in Chapter 4, one finds that the author of this book criticizes conventional social science interpretations of resistance because they are always labeled pejoratively (i.e., deviance) when they challenge a dominant economic system. A critical psychol-ogy must examine resistance in a more subtle manner. Resistance can, and many times is, the beginning of an authentic project which is indicative of a developing sense of agency. Resistance becomes an agent process when it fosters the development of community and solidarity. When a personal world appears to be sustained by resistance, one can sense that there is an authentic cultural project, which is not deviance but a community of what one might say is a different order. A critical psychology will judge resistance by its fruits rather than its inconvenience to a particular social order (i.e., deviance). When resistance fosters authentic community, that is, the presence of a personal world (I–thou relations) and in the process challenges an order of domination, it is to be celebrated by a critical psychology. In general, with psychology's focus on the individual (microsocial) while ignoring conditions in a wider social order (mac-rosocial), the structural background conditions for actions are left unanalyzed. I will demonstrate this by example in the next chapter. The fetish of a microsocial focus puts the burden of virtue and vice totally on the *individual* while ignoring the larger social conditions in which human actions are embedded. At the same time, a critical psychology with emancipatory intent must look at resistance critically. Resistance is not a virtue in itself. It must reach a level of community consensus to seriously challenge the dominance of an unjust social order. A focused rebellion and resistance simply encourages counterviolence by the larger social order and, in essence, justifies its continued presence. There must be attractive features in resistance groups which make them real alternatives to some of the destructive features of the present order. When this occurs, one can say that agency transforms the structural conditions rather than being molded by it. Resistance, and the corresponding projects that are suggested by it, must be able to challenge unjust structural conditions to be considered an effective praxis.

In another vein, one can look at the structure–agency interplay in relationship to economic conditions and mental illness (e.g., Brenner, 1973). I have already discussed Brenner's work in several places because it establishes a clearcut relationship between economic conditions and mental problems. What happens when a major economic activity leaves an area suddenly, as is the case with what is now being called "the runaway factory"? Capital, when left unchecked, moves where labor costs are cheapest. Under these constraints, corporate activity (when capital needs are premptive over community needs) tends to leave areas where labor presents problems for profits. What is becoming clear today is that communities with high employment have much lower rates of mental illness when compared to marginal economic communities (Brenner, 1976). This suggests to me a relationship between favorable structural economic conditions and the development of a personal world, where a sense of agency pervades (i.e., agent–structure interplay). The presence of community projects is related to lower mental illness problems in that community. A community economic activity must then be seen as an *enabling structure*, which enhances the agency of community life. What has now become apparent by the "runaway factory" is the whole question of economic (corporate) responsibility. Can the state simply let the corporation serve the needs of capital and have it ignore the needs of the community? When this operates, the state sends in psychologists, psychiatrists, social workers, and so on to pick up the pieces after the corporation has gone on to greener capital pastures. If psychological professionals simply look at the microsocial world of the individual, they end up by treating individuals for mental illness, deviance, and other forms of disabling maneuvers. As I have indicated several times already, this type of attempt ends up "blaming the victim." A critical orientation would take a different tack. Instead of treating individual symptoms and labeling them, it might involve itself in community mobilization to make corporate interests sensitive to the needs of the community. Instead of treating reactive depression, alcoholism, and so on and ameliorating symptoms in a structural vacuum, critical psychological intervention will make the linkages between disabling social structure and personal psychological mal-aise. Psychology's microsocial focus here advocates the personal world of the client over the impersonality of structural decisions. As MacMurray says, the personal world must not be the servant of impersonal structures (MacMurray, 1961). Impersonal structure must serve the personal world and enable viable community.

CAUSE AND INTENTION

The concrete exemplification of an interpretative system which honors the distinction and dialectical relationship of agency and structure raises a final issue of the relationship of cause and intention. I have identified cause with determin-ism and intention with freedom. The dialectical relationship indicates my un-derstanding that freedom is a struggle with necessity. I take this struggle as a given for the human species where the ordered necessity of institutions is created by the free appropriation of a community consensus. Thus, for humans, the determin-istic qualities of institutional structures of order are at their incipient stages, created by a form of free consensus. To talk about human causes is to clearly distinguish them from the mechanical causality of Hume (Von Wright, 1971). To talk about the structural determinism of human institutions which are histor-ically constituted, it is suggested that the term *quasi causal* be used (Von Wright, 1971). Von Wright (1971), in his seminal work *Explanation and Understand-ing*, ventures that when talking about quasicausal factors one is indulging in *explanation*, whereas when one is talking about intentions for action the concept of *understanding* is more apt. In the above sense, explanation is oriented toward *structural* explanations, which attempt to achieve a description of a phe-nomenon in terms of the structures such as class, ethnicity, gender, and so on. Understanding, by contrast, is the interpretative grasp of a lived situation which is supported by *intentions* (Von Wright, 1971). If the duality of the agent–struc-ture dynamics holds, then *understanding* and *explanation* must be dialectically related to one another in a critically interpretative psychology. The proof of the pudding is in the eating. I will close this book with several examples of research that exemplifies this process to a greater or lesser extent. The works are only suggestive and reflect my biases and background. It is with these examples that we will deal with the notion of adequacy of an interpretation.

7

ADEQUACY OF INTERPRETATION

To give an account or interpretation of a situation from the point of view of a systematic social scientific interpretation is to place human action as expression (i.e., the project) in an understandable context (Winter, 1966). As in the logic of text interpretation, the meaning of human action must be understood as *a limited field of possible interpretations or accounts* (Ricoeur 1971). One thing certain can be said when considering accounts: that there are no finalized accounts. Recursive meaning, as I have explained it, means that the demand for final, absolute, unrevisable truth cannot be satisfied. As a text never has one interpretation, so also human action is open to multiple interpretations and is partially contingent on the viewpoint of the interpreter. Conflict of interpretations is the first systematic problem of an interpretative psychology. If one faces the problems of "conflict of interpretations," it gets us into the thorny problem of the "bias of the interpreter," which conventional psychology attempts to ignore. Instead of ignoring bias and treating it as an abberant process in scientific inquiry, an interpretative psychology takes bias as part of its problematic. We are calling bias the "interpretative horizon." The use of the term *bias* in this context is not pejorative. The notion of bias simply is the procedural assumption that the interpreters bring with them a certain horizon of expectations—that is, of beliefs, practices, concepts and norms—that belongs to their own life world. I have already looked at the bias of interpretative horizon in the previous chapter, when I discussed the conventional location of psychology.

We must now consider why the problem of horizon or perspective raises serious problems for most contemporary psychological systems of interpretation. Most contemporary systems act consciously or unconsciously within an absolute viewpoint. A viewpoint is absolute when it is assumed that the limits of bias are not operating. The absolute viewpoint demands that relativity be overcome for the sake of stabilized substantial knowledge. In its most dramatic form, relativism opens a Pandora's box for any perspective that assumes, without question, the priority of its own horizon of interpretation. When this box is opened, it raises the possibility that all limited viewpoints have limited access to an event and are, therefore, equally suspect. This is a severe problem for an interpretative psychology, since it can lead to a total agnosticism or subjectivism. We must leave open the possibility that some interpretations are better than others under certain conditions and in certain situations. As I shall point out later, *deciding on the validity of interpretations must be something that must be argued convincingly by an interpreter.*

The *limits* of the observer's perspective are what I am calling the "horizon." *Horizon* calls forth the notion of *perspective*. "Perspectivism" does not renounce the postulate of objectivity and the possibility of arriving at decisions when there is conflict in interpretations (Lonergan, 1972; Mannheim, 1953b). Objectivity within the perspective of perspectivism is an indirect means for dealing with conflict of interpretations. Therefore, to accept the relational quality of knowledge does not mean that *objectivity* is abandoned. *Relationism* simply asserts that every interpretative statement can be relationally formulated, that is, formulated within the horizon of the interpreter. Relationism need not collapse into relativism:

> It becomes relativism only when it is linked with the older static ideal of eternal, unperspectivistic truths independent of the subjective experience of the observer, and when it is judged by this alien ideal of absolute truth. (Mannheim, 1953b, p. 300)

THE PROBLEM OF MULTIPLE HORIZONS

Multiple horizons open the door to conflicts of interpretation. Conflicts invite resolutions. To resolve a conflict *objectively* is to involve oneself in an adjudication process. But differences in interpretations do not always invite conflict. It is only under certain conditions that horizons of interpretation are in conflict, and it is important to distinguish when these conditions are present or absent.

Lonergan (1972) maintains that horizons of interpretation can be complementary, genetic, or dialectical. First, complementary horizons are different horizons that complement rather than conflict with one another. For example, theories formulated between mechanical metaphors of interpretation, discussed in Chapter 1, are probably complementary even though each separate discipline brings its own separate and idiosyncratic concerns. They are complementary in that they share a similar and complementary horizon on what constitutes evidence, what is adequate theory, and so on. In the sense of a complementary social science perspective, one could also say that the structuralism of Chomsky's linguistic theories, Piaget's genetic epistemology, and Kohlberg's moral stage structure share complementary epistemological horizons.

Second, horizons or perspectives can also differ *genetically*. Here we are talking about how horizons change over time for a given interpreter. A dramatic example is the differences in interpretation one finds in reading Doestoevsky in early college and then again at age 60. Probable differences in interpretation result from different horizons that a person operates out of in two distinct segments of the life cycle. To say that horizons differ genetically means that the differences are related as successive processes of development (Lonergan, 1972). The later stages presuppose earlier stages, partly to include them or possibly transform them. Piaget's stages of intellectual development or Kohlberg's stages of moral reasoning illustrate developmental genetic horizons, which they call stages. Each stage within a developmental context can be considered as an interpretative horizon. The horizons are said to be related *genetically* insofar as all higher stages integrate and transform the horizons of early stages. Since these stages are earlier and later, no two are simultaneous (Lonergan, 1972). Unlike complementary horizons, which are part of a single communal world, genetic horizons are to be seen more in the context of a single biography as a single history (Lonergan, 1972).

Third, horizons can differ *dialectically*. Here, horizons can conflict with one another to a point where they are in *dialectical relation*. This means that the presence of one horizon proposes the negation of another, and vice versa. Here we must face a reality in social inquiry: namely, that the social sciences house interpretative systems which are radically in conflict with one another. To say that a difference is *dialectical* is to understand that differences in some interpretative horizons are not simply linguistic in nature. I have hinted in the first chapter that interpretative horizons based on mechanical metaphors differ radically from those that propose metaphors of the personal. At the level of both theory and research, they differ in a radical sense in epistemological and normative world view. By accepting that interpretative horizons may differ dialectically, one accepts the problematic presented in conflicts of interpretations. One does not totally abandon a desire for truth in this situation; what has to be abandoned is the desire to be in position of the "absolute truth." If truth is relative, it is not necessarily arbitrary. We not only face the problem that interpretations differ over time, since they also differ between interpreters. The latter situation simply illustrates the selectivity of all perspectives when facing one another. Winter (1968) maintains that "the selectivity of perspective does not mean that one view is wrong and another correct; it means only that varying perspectives on a problem illumine different aspects" (p. 168).

It is understood that a social scientific account is different in perspective from the point of view of those interpreted. Given that it differs, one of the first characteristics of an adequate account is its negotiability. This constitutes the first condition for an adequate account.

1. *An adequate account is negotiated.* As Bauman (1978) points out, the epistemology of an interpretative horizon cannot be detached from the sociology

of communication. Here a "horizon of expert" (i.e., nonnegotiated interpretation) is challenged. It is not a foregone conclusion that a social scientific resymbolization is an adequate interpretation; the dictionary says that to negotiate is to
communicate or confer with another so as to arrive at a settlement of some
matter. Since a social scientific account of human action (i.e., the project) is
concerned with delineating the conditions and interests that entered into the
constituting of the project (Winter, 1966), it would simply appear courteous, at
least, to clear the account with those whose project has been interpreted. In other
words, the interpreted must be able to identify themselves in the account given.
If this identification is not possible, it does not necessarily mean that the interpretation is inadequate. It may be that the interpretation reveals something to
the participants that they do not want themselves or others to see. This may not
be conscious. It may be, however, that the interpretation is inadequate; that it
simply is a misunderstanding of the nature of the project interpreted. It could be
a mixture of both. The negotiated account at least gives the reader the knowledge
that the account being given may be problematic and in need of revision. In the
interest of truth, it gives the reader a chance to be part of the judgmental process.

2. *An adequate account presents itself as an argument.* One must accept, at
the outset, the inevitability of conflicts of interpretation. The nature of the
conflicts can vary from situation to situation. One interpretation may be rejected
by the participants. If accepted by the participants, it may be questioned by other
scientific perspectives. For example, throughout this book I have argued that an
adequate account of the personal world as a cultural form cannot be enhanced by
biological metaphors. The fact that biological metaphors have a compelling
attraction for many social scientists means that they cannot be categorically
rejected. Alternatives must be argued and reasoned to be considered plausible.
Nothing, and that includes what is clearest in one's own argument, can be
considered a foregone conclusion. As we have just indicated, all conclusions are
negotiable. All interpretations must labor under the possible handicap of circularity, that is what is proved in the conclusion was assumed in the beginning
(Hirsch, 1967). Therefore, interpretative accounts of necessity must entertain
alternatives. To entertain does not necessarily mean that alternative arguments
must be embraced. Arguments for an interpretation proceed under the assumption that alternative interpretations may be related to one's own in either a
complementary, genetic, or dialectical manner. One argues for an account on
the basis of its validity. Here we are using the term *validity* in a restricted sense.
A valid argument does not connote verification. To speak of verification is to
assume that an account's conclusion is true (Hirsch, 1967). *Validity* connotes a
more humble stance in that one tries to show, in arguing an account, that the
interpretation is plausible. But validation goes beyond mere plausibility. In accepting conflicts of interpretation, one does not have to accept that accounts are
of equal merit. Validation demands adjudication of conflicts:

> The job of validation is to evaluate the disparate constructions which understanding
> has brought forward. Validation is therefore the fundamental task of interpretation as a
> discipline, since whenever agreement already exists there is little practical need for
> validation. (Hirsch, 1967, p. 170)

It is here that it is appropriate to make a distinction, infrequently made, between *understanding* and *explanation*. Ricoeur (1978) contends that understanding and explanation are relative moments in the complex process called interpretation. When interpretative horizons are complementary or identical, there is very little need for explanation. Explanation is warranted only when there is a situation of conflict. Thus, explanation follows because:

> Understanding calls for explanation as soon as there is no longer dialogue, where the
> give and take of questions and answers permit an interpretation to be verified as it
> unfolds. When I do not spontaneously understand, I ask for an explanation and the
> explanation that you offer allows me to understand you better. (Ricoeur, 1978, p. 153)

Here I would agree with both Hirsch (1967) and Ricoeur (1978) that validation is a test of our guesses at interpretation, following a logic of probability rather than a logic of empirical verification. In a certain sense, an interpretation is an argument for, or advocacy of, a point of view or horizon. The idea of advocacy is unknown to psychologists and would probably be considered in a pejorative sense if left unexplained. My contention is that a *valid* argument is a form of advocacy for a particular interpretation. In advocating a particular interpretation, one brings forth factual evidence in favor of a particular interpretation and unfavorable to one's opponents. Validation, in these terms, can be seen as an argumentative discipline comparable to the juridical procedures of legal interpretation (Ricoeur, 1978). Arguments for an interpretation must be seen in a relative light. This does not in itself lead to skepticism. One expects that interpretations can conflict with one another. In arguing for a particular interpretation, one develops evidence to show that an interpretation is *probable* under these circumstances. When an interpretation is in conflict with another interpretation of human action, the better interpretation attempts to show that it is more probable than its adversary under the circumstances. Part of that argumentation is the practical significance of the interpretation. The practical significance of a critical interpretation is in its specification of a praxis of freedom.

    3. *An adequate account expresses an emancipatory praxis.* Our concern over the practical significance must not be identified with "instrumental rationality." I have already expressed my concerns about theories whose practical significance is to manipulate and control others. Our concern is that a critical interpretation have the practical significance of enhancing human freedom. This is basically what I mean by an emancipatory praxis. What is most characteristic about a personal metaphor is its emphasis on the historically constituted nature of the social world. A good social scientific interpretation reveals the nature of the

social world as constituted by *agents* in *relation*. Our assumption has been throughout that we are not organisms or mechanisms but *persons*. The personal world is a world constructed in *history*. An emancipatory account will reveal to the participants the fact that their world is constructed *historically*. To show that a world is built through a history is also to indicate that it can be changed through history. The personal world and its specific expression in diverse cultural forms is, therefore, seen in the light of a constituted history. I have indicated this in Chapter 3 where the dialectis of *habitus* and *project* were considered. This dialectic is important here because it prevents us from giving a facile account of human freedom and human determinism. In considering the dialectic of habitus and project, one does not consider freedom and determinism as operating independently. I would contend that human freedom by free agents happens in an *ordered* (habitus) context, order providing the footing for historical projects. Therefore, one condition for freedom is an ordered environment. Freedom (i.e., projects) is built on the *habitual order* of cultural patterns. Therefore, an arbitrary social order—that is, a cultural situation without habitual patterns (order)— is an enemy to human freedom. This is anarchy in the pejorative sense and the situation invites dictators. Order, when one forgets that it is the historical constitution of human agents (i.e., entrenched patterns), becomes the enemy of human freedom. Here order is seen as some kind of mechanism or the achievement of a biological process (i.e., mechanical and organic metaphors).

This detracts from the human constitution of cultural formation which is the real historical construction of a personal world. To interpret *order* in this manner is to limit the scope of *human projects*. Cultural forms are not just made and repeated (i.e., order), they are also changed and transformed by agents who dream new dreams (i.e., projects). To deny the openness of historical projects is, therefore, a form of *oppression*. I use the term *oppression* here to connote the possibility that some interpretations mask or conceal the scope of human possibilities. An interpretative account, with emancipatory intent, will attempt to express the dialectic of order and change of a specific cultural form. Its practical utility is that it will attempt to portray the resilient nature of habitual patterns, that is, show how history has formed a group through their own agency and continues (i.e., determinism). At the same time, it attempts to express the projective (toward the future) nature of those forms, which is an opening on the future (i.e., transformation). Therefore, the emancipatory account is couched in a language that expresses the possibility for change. The minimum conditions for an account of this nature are that the account show (1) how the immediate social and physical conditions that determine and structure the social world (i.e., habitus) are *mediated* through the agency of actors who have some control over the constitution of that world (i.e., responsibility) and (2) how they take for granted understandings that are also mediated and, therefore, could be otherwise (Corrigan & Willis, 1980). This type of an account is an emancipatory praxis, which, in the words of Marx, not only interprets the world but also suggests how to change it.

4. *An adequate account is critical.* I have already indicated that social scientific accounts are *resymbolizations*. Thus, one does not expect reiteration of the point of view of those interpreted. Resymoblization brings something new to a situation. It characterizes the expressions of others in a new light. As long as accounts are considered negotiable, as in criterion 1, there is no reason for a systematic account of others to be in complete agreement with those interpreted. Consider the example of psychoanalytic interpretation. The patient comes to the analyst and spends a considerable amount of time expressing the understanding he or she has of existing personal problems. In many instances, the symptoms presented appear overdetermined; that is, they repeat themselves insistently and the patient appears to have no control over them. Part of the analytic treatment is to *resymbolize* the patient's symptoms (i.e., analyst's interpretation) by rein-terpreting those symptoms and pointing out their historical origins. The analyst's interpretation frequently meets with resistance and denial by the patient. An analytic interpretation is considered useful if it expands the scope of the patient's horizon, and the eventual acceptance of an analytic interpretation is accompanied by a decrease in overdetermined symptoms. At a microsocial level, one might label a critical interpretation part of the emancipatory praxis of criterion 3.

At the very least, a critical account of the personal world of human actors must accomplish two objectives. First, in resymbolizing the world of others, it should sensitively reflect back to them and others their capacities and powers for *intentional intervention*. This expands the scope of freedom in a positive direction by naming those powers. Second, it also draws attention to the liabilities or impediments to human agency. These liabilities can be psychological factors that are part of a person's makeup and history. They can also be external, that is, persons or institutions that block the agent's intentional interventions. It is here that the bias of horizon (e.g., class, gender, ethnicity) may have deleterious effects. For example, the class nature of a psychological interpretation may find a certain rebellion of lower-class children simply representing personal liabilities. In a more sympathetic light, one could consider rebellion as a resistance (intentional intervention) to arbitrary and unjust social systems. Or the bias produced by gender domination (i.e., male dominance) in psychology may consistently cast women in the role of patient and men as agents. Let us end this chapter with two specific examples of what I would call interpretative studies and conclude by judging them on the four criteria I have just described. I have chosen these two studies in order to help the reader understand how I employ the adequacy criteria. The studies are also suggestive because they lend themselves to comparisons and illustrate the notion of conflict of interpretations. Both studies interpret the actions of working-class boys who could well have been part of a sample of working-class youth. The fact that they are so similar as a population or sample makes the differences in interpretation grounds for asking questions about adequacy in comparative terms.

STUDY 1: THE RULES OF DISORDER

Background

As the authors (Marsh *et al.*, 1978) indicate at the outset, the ostensible subject matter of this book is violence and disorder. Carried out in Great Britain, this is essentially a study of lower-socioeconomic-class males. The settings for this interpretative enquiry are the classroom and the "terraces of football grounds." The authors contend that the systematic interpretative inquiry they offer indicates that the boys in these settings demonstrate none of the anarchy and impulsiveness attributed to them in the popular press. Instead, the interpretation they offer indicates a consistent rule-orientation that belies an attribution of anarchy and impulse. Marsh *et al.* (1978) indicate different interpretative horizons between media interpretations and the interpretations the boys ascribe to their actions. The media interpretation of these youths casts them within a rhetoric of impulse and anarchy, their behavior toward one another appearing to be senseless and opaque. Marsh *et al.* do not propose to repeat either of these rhetorics in their interpretative scheme. Their aim, as they see it, is to discover the content and organization of the social knowledge they believe an individual member has to have in order to be able to perform reasonably well in the social life of his or her group. They make it clear at the outset that they are not proposing a general performance theory based on knowledge of rule structures (i.e., competence). They maintain that in order to accomplish a *performance model* they would have to introduce the *concept of intention* at the level of action. This is important to note here, because what is absent from the outset is the possibility of assessing the possibilities for intentional intervention into the action sequence.

These authors also make a distinction between rules of interpretation and rules of action. Their position is that in order to assert that conduct is orderly, one must demonstrate that it is "rule-governed." Rule governance does not have to be modulated by conscious intentions. In fact, rules are held (often tacitly) by all members of a group or community as representations of legitimacy and acceptability. The rule is a *normative* concept; implicit in the notion is the directive of *ought* and *should*. These authors maintain that rules are not statistical abstractions but are directly discoverable in the accounts that football fans and school troublemakers offer in explaining what they do and why they do it. The strongest test for the existence of a rule is the ability of a member of the group to articulate it. These authors venture that an articulation constitutes a "reason for action." In addition to an articulation, a rule can also be considered present when *breaches* in a rule are articulated (e.g., this is wrong, etc.). The rule is seen in consensus. Consensus connotes social order. Social order presupposed that members of a group have a common knowledge of the rules (Marsh *et al.*, 1978).

Method

Intensive Design. An intensive design is one in which a few members are selected to exemplify a class. This is to be distinguished by a sample (i.e., extensive design) where a sufficiently large number of cases are collected to be statistically representative of a class. Marsh *et al.* (1978) claim that their option for an intensive design is hazardous, but they feel the eventual payoff is worth the risk:

> In the ethogenic approach we follow the example of chemists and anatomists and adopt the intensive design, that is, we undertake a detailed study of a few cases selected as typical. We are sure of the detailed validity of our analyses of our cases. We can only hypothesize that they are typical. Those who would follow the extensive deisgn can be sure their results are typical, but they must hypothesize as to whether the few properties that survive the working of the inverse ratio between extension and intention have an individuality at all. Our football following participants are from one group of fans, supporters of just one local club. With few exceptions, the participants in our study of talk about classroom volume and its accounting are from one school that is graced by some of the fans. We are inclined to think that they are pretty typical, given our less detached work at other football grounds and what we know of other groups of school children. (Marsh *et al.*, 1978, pp. 20–21)

First-Person Accounts. In an earlier work (Harrè and Secord, 1972) one of the authors (Harrè) had a chapter entitled "Why not ask them." There, as well as in this work, a rationale for the importance of first-person accounts is given. The authors feel that in interpreting human action, the best (although not ultimate) authorities as to the action are the actors themselves. Therefore, a sensitivity as to how the actors view their actions is encouraged. They acknowledge the real possibility for personal self-deceit and blindness but nevertheless feel in the long run that a "match emerges gradually between what is seen to happen and what is said to happen" (p. 21). Therefore, they state:

> We take it axiomatic that unless it can be established to the contrary, the best authorities as to what went on are the actors themselves. Their meaning and their rules have priority in the scientific analysis of the phenomena. (p. 22)

A methodological ideal is to combine with the first-person accounts of human action an access to the situation in which the accounts take place (e.g., schools and terraces). One is combining here interview data with some limited form of participant observation.

Concepts Utilized. Four concepts are utilized in this study. They are violence, meaning, aggression, and order. *Violence* connotes an action of physical interference with another, whether or not it is being mediated by the use of a weapon. Examples go from bullying and biting (nonmediated) to a display of a weapon (mediated). Further violence is symbolic when there is a mimicry of interference (e.g., threats). To talk about a notion called "symbolic violence" brings them to a second concept, labeled *meaning*, which is the interpretation of action (either movements or speech) as intelligible because of its relation to the intentions of actors. Meaning, as they interpret it, is achieved by setting up a relational structure between meaningful element of the symbolic system. Thus symbols can stand as the real thing for action in a symbolic system (e.g., clenched fist). Most symbols of violence, if carried out, would lead to death or serious injury. The symbol of violence short-circuits this ultimate outcome and is, therefore, seen as a ritualized aggression that prevents serious injury. The third concept is that of *aggression*. Aggression is distinguished from violence by attributing a biological origin to aggression. The authors maintain that there is a biogenetic origin to aggression. Aggression is, therefore, a biological universal. Aggression as a biological universal takes various historically conditioned forms. Here, a distinction is made between real aggression from another concept called "aggro." Aggro is a ritual manifestation of aggression in symbolic form. The importance of this distinction will be seen later when these authors take a final excursion into sociobiology. Finally, *order* is the concept that highlights the assumption that human action follows rules and is governed by consensus. These authors contend that a test for the presence of order is the degree to which the unexpected does not happen and that expectations are fulfilled.

It should be noted that there is no extensive discussion for the selection of these concepts as part of their interpretation format. I will say more about this later in criticism.

The Schoolroom Setting. There· is no elaborate description of this setting. The authors maintain that they are concerned to explore the interpretation and genesis of disorder and violence in the classroom from the point of view of the pupil. The main shortcoming (the authors acknowledge it) of this part of the investigation is that the researchers had no access to the classroom. They are, therefore, somewhat at a disadvantage in validating the veracity of the pupil's account. The authors indicate a lower-class school, and this is corroborated by student descriptions. The students in the class being investigated are nonacademic by their own descriptions. They perceive the school as a waste of time and not to be taken seriously. They perceive themselves as "written off," since teachers do not place a high value on them.

"Messing About." "Messing about" connotes a consistent classroom interaction between pupils and teacher. The interaction takes the form of an offence–retribution cycle. The basic sequence is as follows: (1) teacher loses control, (2) students made power play, (3) teacher retaliates to restore order. As exemplified in an interview:

> I was in this lesson and two or three of my mates were messing about and I was sat
> across the other side of the classroom and someone chucked a piece of chalk at the
> teacher and then started shouting his mouth off. Straight away the teacher "knew"
> who it was (unjust accusation). He turned round and kicked me out of the classroom
> for doing it. So I hit him. (p. 34)

The authors contend that retaliation, like hitting the teacher, is not blind violence but a maneuver to save a "moral career." The students are very sensitive to offenses to what they consider their dignity and standing (i.e., moral career). Moral career is, therefore, a public reputation that is valued by the participants. A teacher's devaluation is an affront to a moral career. Students maintain that devaluation occurs in three ways. First, there are teachers who are arrogant and distant: "There's a few teachers who you can get on with and talk to. They seem to understand you. But most of the others—it's a nine to four job" (p. 36).

Second, there is anonymity produced by the teachers' not knowing the students' names. Finally, there are offenses of unfairness where a student is compared to other students negatively or a punishment unrelated to the offense is given.

Marsh *et al.* (1978) draw parallels between the order cycle of the school and that which takes place in the home. The students find very little consistent valuing in school or at home. They develop their "moral careers" on the terraces:

> You've got to decide whether it's a freer atmosphere and rowdyism or silence and total
> obedience, because I don't think you have any feelings towards somebody in schools
> where you just have to sit in silence in sort of neat rows. (pp. 52–53)

The Football Grounds (Terraces)

Although many strata of society will watch a football match, this study focuses only on lower-socioeconomic-class youth in this setting. The authors maintain that in this setting there is an order known to the police and the youth which demands that specific locations be adhered to by home- and opposing-team fans. The police place themselves as a wedge between the home-team fans' territory and that of the opposition team.

Method. Besides interviewing, Marsh *et al.* made video recordings at the setting. They maintain that the recordings reveal patterns and groupings in which they were able to attribute a number of salient behavioral and social characteristics to the boys.

The boys looked at in this study ranged from 12 to 17 years of age and a specific grouping wore "aggro outfits," which will be explained shortly. Mainstream vocabulary would put them in the category of "rowdy." The authors feel that this is an excellent setting for the development of what they have called "moral careers." In this setting, a moral career connotes a way of "becoming somebody" and is a highly structured affair. These rowdy events are seen by the authors as intelligible and rule-following rather than anarchic. The moral career in this setting is an available structure in a youth culture for the establishment of a stable self-identity. It seems to enable these boys to achieve kinds of *reputations* and *images* denied them in mainstream society. In other words, it is an attempt to maintain a certain dignity. The data were gathered through videotapes and also biographical materials taken from samples of fans in each group, with special attention to what they have labeled "rowdies" and "town boys."

Rowdies. The authors identify six types of careers: (1) *Chanters* or *chant leaders* who lead in chanting and taunting. (2) *Aggro leaders*, who lead in the expression of aggression that is not seriously injurious. This is a high-status role and the person must be courageous, but not foolishly so. (3) *Nutters*, who number five or six boys. They are individuals whose behavior is considered so outrageous as to fall completely outside the range of rational actions (i.e., goes mad, goes wild). Marsh *et al.* (1978) see the nutter as one who demonstrates to others what they should not do, providing living proof by negative example. (4) *Hooligans* are boys whose actions are generally thought to be worthy of praise. This is contrary to the media's definition of *hooligan*. Usually, their acts cause small damage to property and enrage some members of mainstream culture. Nutters and hooligans have this in common—they provide entertainment. A hooligan is "a jester." (5) An *organizer* is an older boy who does the management work (e.g., gets bases, etc.). (6) A *scapegoat* is an individual who receives negative attributions (i.e., he is someone habitually picked on).

Town Boys. Town boys are boys who have graduated the rowdy group. They are less noisy but clearly tough. They are also seen as heavy drinkers.

The authors suggest that these career structures help to explain social behavior that on the surface appears irrational. In looking at these moral careers, these authors follow a procedure that attempts to discern the rule structure within this subculture at the terraces. They maintain that you can build a picture of what the rules for action might be by extensive interviewing. The terms of reference involve identifying a stable pattern of ascription of meaning to objects and events.

In the 50 interviews done on these boys in groups of three and four, one point seemed to be recurring, and that is, as the authors maintain, that fights, either in the large group or face to face, are not random. Aggression ensues in circumstances where fans are able to *specify* legitimacy for their actions. To summarize the question of rule structure, it may be said that: (1) There is a set of interpretative rules (related to territorial rules and fouls, etc.) indicating when aggression on rival fans is appropriate. (2) Once a fight has commenced, there is a rule structure governing its course. It should be noted that the rules are protective against serious injury, so that no great physical harm normally comes to the participants. (3) Rules indicating the closing off and termination of fights can be isolated. There is a further subtlety within these structures in that rules can be seen as implicit or explicit. These fans, for example, are not conscious of the full range of significance of the rule structure they are following. The authors sometimes purposely alter the accounts of the participants so as to create a discrepancy that may indicate explicitly the presence of an implicit rule. As the authors indicate: "By looking at what they say is wrong with the story we can obtain recognition of the rule-breaches. This, in turn, allows us to specify what the rules themselves are" (p. 111).

Aggro as Ritualized Aggression. The authors contend that up to this point they have simply stood inside the phenomena and have carefully listened to what the fans have to say. I will later challenge this contention. Their claim is that they have attempted a close scrutiny of the events on the terrace and have attempted to outline what they consider to be the social order of shared meaning that exists there. For the participants, their order as outlined is a structural delineation of rule structure. They speculate at the end of this structural interpretation its limitations:

> The existence of order, then, does not, in itself, guarantee Utopia. The only way of deciding the merit or value to society of a particular order is through reference to the function of that order. (p. 117)

In presenting the notion of aggro the authors make an excursion into functional explanation. The shift here, to my mind, is dramatic. They venture that the *rule structure* they interpret is seen as a reason for action. Their excursion into aggro theory assumes that a functional theory can arrive at causal mechanisms. They feel that questions concerning causes might be legitimately posed at a different level of analysis. The level of discourse with aggro is one that is sociobiological in nature. Their functional explanation, therefore, is couched in an organic metaphor. Here, the authors move from a conventional order based on rule structures that are generated in the interpretation of participant accounts to what the authors call a "natural order." In other words, the naturalistic explanation is clearly an account from the outside, an interpretative maneuver that indicates the preoccupations of the researchers rather than the participants.

Marsh *et al.* see that they are now moving into a primary stage of what they call "explanation." The adequacy of this move should be judged in two ways: (1) On the basis of its fit with the commonsense reality of the participants—in other words, it has to "go down" with the fans when it is fed back to them so that they can see themselves in this type of description. (2) On the terms of criteria that are used in the initial interpretation (i.e., moral careers).

The notion of moral careers is the initial framework that also offers prescriptive rules for violence, but the authors believe it is necessary to go beyond this initial framework to the functional sociobiological framework of ritualized aggression (i.e., aggro). Why? Because they feel it necessary to discuss the function that aggro plays in society at large. This theoretical jump is justified because it places football violence in a larger perspective by showing that their aggression is part of a more generalized mode of ritualized aggression that is species generated. Let us look at aggression as a form of ritual (i.e., aggro). The authors define a ritual in terms of four key elements: (1) a pattern of routines of behavior, (2) a system of signs that convey covert messages, (3) the existence of sanctions expressing strong moral approval or disapproval, and (4) a conventional relation between the actions in which the ritual is performed and the social act achieved by its successful completion.

Marsh *et al.* contend that life in the classroom and on the terraces can be functionally catalogued as a form of ritualized aggression (i.e., aggro). They summarize their work as follows:

> In this book we have not sought to excuse the football fan or the classroom trouble-maker. Instead we have simply tried to show that the events which outrage us have a different reality and are capable of being construed in a very different manner. We have tried to reveal social order in events which are traditionally seen as dangerously anarchic. And social order, whether it be in the form of ritual or not, is something that needs to be recognized and seen as having utility and merit. When magistrates and police refer to fans as animals and savages and when teachers are unwittingly engaged in the processes of systematic humiliation and depersonalization of schoolkids, order is threatened. We may never, given our existing social frames of reference, be able to create a system of schooling which kids regard as relevant to their own culture and socialization. And without doubt, we will be able to suppress entirely the aggression and the striving to subdue rivals that has been characteristic of young males in all human societies at all times in history. Given this, we must look to ways of managing hostility and violence rather than naively hoping that they will go away. If we accept that there are, from one significant standpoint at least, *rules* of disorder, we might be able to develop management strategies which have far more purpose and effect than those which have currently emerged from the atmosphere of moral outrage and collective hysteria. (p. 134)

STUDY 2: LEARNING TO LABOUR

Willis's (1977) work is discussed here for several reasons. It deals with a group of working-class boys in England who are roughly comparable to the population of boys in the Marsh *et al.* study just quoted. The treatment of these boys and the interpretation of their world is markedly different and contrasts rather dramatically with the previous study. In my view, this work represents a critical interpretation of the personal world of white working-class youth. It is a critical study because, to my mind, it self-consciously deals with the duality between *agency* and *structure*. For that reason, it provides an excellent example of a critical account. It also brings home to the reader, by contrast, the real possibility of what I have called "conflict of interpretations." Its similarity to *The*

Rules of Disorder lies in its dealing with a comparable population; also, both studies attempt interpretive accounts from the point of view of the actors involved. The studies depart drastically when they move from first-person accounts to causal–structural interpretations. In *The Rules of Disorder*, as we have already seen, the authors move from ethnography to a sociobiological functional metaphor (aggro) in explaining the action of participants. Willis's work also moves beyond interpretation from the point of view of actors and their agency to a *structural–historical* interpretation, which I would deem to be what I have called the personal metaphor. Where structure is biology in *The Rules of Disorder*, it is, by contrast, historically material in *Learning to Labour*. With that in mind, let us now venture a detailed description of this study and then a critical analysis of both these studies as to their adequacy as accounts.

Aim of the Study

The study was designed to explore the transition from school to work of nonacademic working-class boys. The author poses this question in the form of a partial statement: "The difficult thing to explain about how middle class kids get middle class jobs is why others let them. The difficult thing to explain about how working class kids get working class jobs is why they let themselves" (p. 1).

Willis concentrates his efforts on the latter question by focusing on white working-class boys in an industrial town (Hammerstwon) in Great Britain. Concurrently, he does a partial analysis of the role of gender and ethnicity with this type of specified population. Like Marsh *et al.* (1978), Willis (1977) notes that the existence of this culture has been picked up conventionally and pegged by the mass media in sensational modes of violence and, in schools, depicted as lacking in discipline (i.e., deviant).

Method

The study used multiple techniques of data collection. Case-study work, interviewing, group discussions, and participant observation were used over a period of 2 years as the boys proceeded through their last 2 years at school and also into the early months of work. The author justifies his use of qualitative methods for the following reasons:

> The qualitative method and participant observation used in the research, and the ethnographic format of the presentation were dictated by the nature of my interest in the cultural. The techniques are suited to record this level and have a sensibility to meanings and values as well as an ability to represent and interpret symbolic articulations, practices and forms of cultural production. In particular, the ethnographic account without always knowing how, can allow a degree of the activity, creativity and human agency within the object of study to come through into the analysis and the reader's experience. This is vital to my purposes where I view the cultural not simply

as a set of transferred internal structures (as in the usual notions of socialization) nor as the passive result of the action of dominant ideology downwards (as in certain kinds of Marxism) but at least, in part, as the product of collective human praxis. (p. 4)

Let me note parenthetically that Willis's notion of culture shares my assumption that the personal world of culture is both habitus and project. The research carried out involved one main and five comparative studies. The main study was concentrated on 12 nonacademic working-class lads, as Willis calls them, attending a working-class school. This was an all-male school, which was twinned with an all-girls school in the same area. The lads are depicted throughout as "resistant or in rebellion" against the school system. The author also did some comparative work looking at lower-class conformist youth ("ear-oles") and a middle-class population at a residential school. The later groups (i.e., ear-oles and middle class) were selected to give a comparative dimension to the study along the parameters of class, ability, school regime, and orientation to school. The most extensive and intensive work, however, was done with the main group (the lads), who were observed in the school (participant observation), both in class and in the halls, during their leisure activities. In addition, there were regularly recorded group discussions, informal interviews, and diaries. Long taped conservations were also accomplished with parents, teachers, and school officials.

Ethnography: The Study of Culture

Ethnography is the study of the peculiar or typical character of a specific culture. Thus, part of this study is an ethnography of a specific population of white working-class youth. The ethnographic study constitutes one moment in a larger, more total analysis. In my terms, *ethnography*, as Willis uses it, is the study of the personal agency of specific cultural forms, attempting to discern this from first-person accounts. Three chapters are devoted to this enterprise (Chapters 2, 3, and 4), the final chapters being devoted to structural analysis of what I and others have called the agency–structure dialectic. In Willis's terms, it is an analysis of the interrelations between *cultural* and *class-structure* analysis.

Elements of an Oppositional Culture. The *cultural project* of the lads is their opposition or resistance to the larger middle-class norms and values. Some of the salient characteristics of the lads' culture, which Willis discusses from observation and their first-person accounts, are their opposition to authority and rejection of conformity. The lads see themselves in opposition to larger school norms and authority (i.e., countercultural). As they say of the conformists (ear-oles), "It is not so much that they support teachers, rather they support the idea of teachers" (pp. 13, 14). If the school is the "zone of the formal," with its clear structure, school rules, pedagogic practices, and so on, the lads' counterculture is the "zone of the informal." Oppositional culture seeks to go beyond the reach of "the rule." Informal opposition to the school is manifested in the struggle to gain symbolic and physical space and to *defeat* the school's main express purpose to make you *work*.

WILLIS: Do you think you've learnt anything at school, has it changed or moulded your values?

JULY: I don't think the school does fucking anything to you. . . . It never has had much effect on anybody. I don't think (after) you've learnt the basics. I mean school, it's fucking four hours a day. But it ain't the teachers who mould you, it's the fucking kids you meet. You're only with teachers thirty percent of the time in school, the other fucking two-thirds are just talking, fucking pickin' an argument, messing about. (p. 26)

Apropos of work avoidance:

WILLIS: When was the last time you did some writing?

FUZZ: Oh, er, last time was in careers 'cos I writ yes on a piece of paper, that broke me heart.

WILLIS: Why did it break your heart?

FUZZ: I mean to write 'cos I was going to try and go through the term without writing anything. 'Cos since we've cum back, I aint dun nothing (it was half way through term). (p. 27)

Thus, the countercultural infrastructure of the informal group makes possible a distinctive type of class contact for the lads; Willis contends that it is a class culture which is distinct from the dominant one. The main objective of the counterculture is to defeat formality by informal modes of interaction. When the culture becomes fully developed, as in the later years of schooling, it becomes quite adept at managing the formal system and limiting its demands to an absolute minimum.

Part of this resistance is done with humor: "We can make them laff—they can make us laff." Even where there is a violent tone to some forms of interaction, it is seen as an *orderly* process, concurring with the position on violence taken in *The Rules of Disorder*. At the same time, the orderliness of violence is given a different interpretation by Willis:

> It should be noted that despite its destructiveness, anti-social nature and apparent irrationality, violence is not completely random, or in any sense the absolute overthrow of social order. Even when directed at outside groups (and thereby, of course, helping to define an in-group) one of the important aspects of violence is precisely its social meaning within "the lads" own culture. It marks the last move in, and final validation of the informal status system. (p. 35)

Note the different construction of the nature of violence interpreted here with the sociobiological notion of aggro in the previous chapter.

Finally, the group defines itself through what Willis identifies as sexism and racism. Two other groups are set up in opposition and against whom the lads define themselves by opposition by maintaining a clear sense of superiority in relation to girls (women) and ethnic minority groups. Women in this context are seen as sexual objects and comforters. The whore–virgin categorization is marked with these boys. Girl friends or eventual spouses are set in a different category from the "easy lay." A girl friend "must be attractive but not experienced." The lads are very much prone to racial slurring. In Great Britain, such slurs are levied against non-Caucasians—Asians and West Indians.

Racism allows these boys the luxury of looking down on groups more marginal than their own.

Class and Institutional Form of Culture

Willis attempts to make linkages between the counter-school culture and the shop-floor culture. Therefore, the setting for some of his fieldwork is at the factory, where the lads will eventually work, and in the home, to do interviews with the parents. It is here that the author contextualizes the boys as a specific *form of life* that relates school to shop floor to home. A form of life or culture must be seen as partially self-constituted. Although Willis acknowledges the alienating and restrictive conditions of work, he does not reduce the working-class form to simple passive puppeteering:

> They exercise their abilities and seek enjoyment in activity even when most controlled by others. Paradoxically, they thread through the dead experience of work a living culture which is far from a simple reflex of defeat. This is the same fundamental taking hold of an alienating situation that one finds in counter-school culture and its attempt to weave a tapestry of interest and dimension through the dry institutional text. These cultures are not simply layers of padding between human beings and unpleasantness. They are appropriations in their own right, exercises of skill, notions, activities, applied toward particular ends. (p. 52)

Thus, common cultural themes or institutional class forms, as Willis calls them, emerge between counter-school culture and shop-floor culture. (1) Chauvinism, which is masculine toughness exemplified by the lads, is reflected in one of the central themes of the shop floor (male chauvinism). (2) Information control, a main theme of the shop-floor culture, is mirrored in the counter-school culture, where the lads attempt to take control of classes, substitute their own unofficial timetables, and control their own routines. (3) Informal grouping, characterized by the counter-school culture, is also seen as a fundamental organizational unit at the shop. Willis maintains that, at the level of informal groups, there is a zone where there are strategies for wresting control of symbolic and real space from official authority. (4) Idiosyncratic language and humor is highly developed both on the shop floor and in the school. Along with verbal humor, there is a physical humor—the practical joke. At the factory, as in the counter-school culture, many jokes circle around the concept of authority itself. Finally, (5) practice is more important than theory. The rejection of schoolwork in counter-school culture is matched on the shop floor with the massive feeling characteristic of the working class that practice is more important than theory.

Willis is at pains to articulate these themes as part of a salient form of working-class life. The type of resistance embedded in these themes departs drastically from what might be a middle-class theme. As Willis points out:

> When the middle class child is thrown back on his indigenous culture, instead of finding strengthening and confirming oppositional themes there, he finds the same ones. Centripetal forces act to throw him back to the institution. (p. 76)

Willis (1977) maintains that the lads, as a located culture, systematically prepare themselves for a certain kind of work, and this marks them out from the ear-oles (i.e., conformists not only in schoolwork but also in occupation). They (the lads) scoff at the vocational counseling provided by the school. There is a direct link between school and work in the minds of the lads and their parents. Particular job choice does not matter too much to the lads:

SPANKSY: I think that we . . . more or less, we're the ones that do the hard grafting, but not them, they'll be the office workers. . . . I aint got no ambitions, I don't wanna have. . . . I just want to have a nice wage that'd just see me through. (p. 98)

By contrast, conformist working-class youth (ear-oles) have a much greater identification with teachers' authority—career choice, and so on. The ear-oles probably buy into white-collar semiskilled jobs. A resistance to mental work becomes a resistance to white-collar authority for the lads. Here the split between white- and blue-collar worker begins. The split is carried out with some agency, and this must clearly be understood because it is consistent with a choice ideology that is espoused in liberal democracies. So Willis notes:

> It is only in the uncovering of this subjective assent that we will understand their behaviour in a way which properly presents their own full powers, and appreciates the contradictory, half real notion of freedom at stake for them (and others) in a liberal social democracy. (p. 103)

SPIKE: . . . it gets me mad to see these kids working in a fucking office. I just dunno how they do it, honestly. I've got freedom, I've got . . . I can get money, it's hard to explain. (p. 104)

In giving these examples, Willis concludes that the counter-school culture of the lads smooths the way to manual work.

Willis ends his ethnographic section with a paradox and, in my terms, posing the dialectic of agency and structure:

> It is they, not formal schooling, which carry "the lads" over into a certain application to the productive process. In a sense, therefore, there is an element of self-domination in the acceptance of subordinate roles in western capitalism. However, this damnation is experienced paradoxically as a form of true learning, appropriation, and as a kind of resistance. How are we to understand this? (p. 113)

Going beyond Ethnography: Analysis

Part 2 of *Learning to Labour* is entitled "Analysis." Willis claims that it is necessary to go beyond classroom and workplace ethnography to a more structural analysis. The interpretative tools that Willis will utilize draw from a Marxist class analysis. Thus, analysis, for Willis, is a class-structural analysis. Combining class analysis with ethnography makes this study unique and classifies it as a Marxist ethnography. It is here that Willis attempts to embed individual agency (culture) with the larger structural class dynamics of capitalism (structure). In that sense, it honors what Giddens has called "the duality of agency and structure." The interplay between agency and structure is introduced with two structural analytic concepts, *penetration* and *limitation*. These concepts become important when Willis summarizes and projects problems that issue from the ethnography:

> Although we have looked in some detail through case study at the experience and cultural processes of being male, white, working class, unqualified, disaffected and moving into manual work in contemporary capitalism, there are still some mysteries to be explained. . . . We have seen how their genuinely held insights and connections lead finally to an objective work situation which seems to be entrapment rather than liberation. But how does this happen? What are the basic determinants of those cultural forms whose tensions, reversals, continuities and final outcomes we have already explored? (p. 119)

Penetration and limitation are concepts which try to come to grips with the paradox not only of why any unfree conditions could be entered freely but also why social change does not ensue from the counter-school's cultural resistance and opposition to the system. Penetration represents those impulses within a specific cultural form that appear to go beyond the confines of the system. I would call penetration the position of the "self as agent." Given that penetration is not simply a characteristic of a person but of a culture, this agency is expressed as persons in relation (i.e., culture). *Limitation* is meant to designate those blocks or impediments that confuse or impede full development and expression. *Partial penetration* is meant to designate the interaction of these two terms in a concrete culture. Partial penetration is what the ethnography reveals, because it describes the field of play in which impulses and limitations combine but cannot be isolated as shown separately (Willis, 1977, p. 119). At the level of pure theory, one could call penetration the "agency of the project" and limitation the "ideology of the habitus." In concrete cultural expressions, agency is always embedded in ideology, as Willis says, *partially penetrated*. Ideally, penetration is the expression of the agency of the personal world in McMurray's terms. Willis puts it similarly:

> I suggest that the smallest discrete unit which acts as the basis of cultural penetration is the informal group. The group is special and more than the sum of its individual parts. It has, in particular, a social dynamic which is relatively independent of issues and locations, preconceptions and prejudice. (p. 123)

The personal world of specific informal cultural forms is the source of *creativity* that holds out the potential for structural change. For example, the counter-school culture succeeds, in part, in demystifying the school system and the working class's lack of options in a class society. This is a cultural insight and not necessarily held by any one individual in the counterculture. The lads' counterculture is potentially creative through their creative resistance to the larger system's work ideology. For example, the lads see through the over-emphasis on qualifications, the ludicrous nature of sacrifices to obtain worthless recognition, and the remoteness of real opportunities for upward mobility and intrinsic job satisfaction. The problem with creativity and critical acumen at the level of the informal group is that the system is not exposed at the level on which it operates (i.e., formal–structural). The potential for real creative social transformation and creativity is absent because of the severe limitations operating at the level of the informal group.

Limitation. This word refers to or designates those blocks and divisions that impede the full expression of the impulses directed toward cultural penetration. Willis contends that the two most important divisions that disorganize and divert potential penetration are (1) the divisions of mental and manual labor and (2) gender. To a lesser extent, Willis considers *racism* as another division that disorganizes working-class culture from within. Although the lads stand together as an identifiable subculture, they are divided from other sections of the working class. The lads overvalue manual labor and consider the ear-oles effeminate because of their willingness to be part of a white-collar working force. In this manner, the lads disqualify themselves from the possibilities of being involved with mental labor.

Sexism also disorients cultural penentration. The lads' counterculture promotes its own sexism and celebrates it as part of their overall confidence. As it turns out, their sexism reflects attitudes shared by the wider working-class culture. In calling ear-oles effeminate, one detects implicitly the perjorative attitude toward women. As Willis indicates:

> If the currency of femininity were revalued then that of mental work would have to be too. A member of the counter-school culture can only believe in the effeminancy of white collar and office work so long as wives, girlfriends and mothers are regarded as restricted, inferior and incapable of certain things. Despite their greater achievement and conventional hopes for the future, "ear-oles" and their strategies can be ignored because the mode of their success can be discredited as passive, mental and lacking robust masculinity. (pp. 149–150)

Masculinity is seen as both destructive and affirming "labor power." The masculine disdain for qualification, although housing the insight that mental work simply helps in the maintenance of class divisions, also allows members of the middle class to leave the underside of capitalism unquestioned. This lends to the belief that lower classes are where they are because their mental capacities keep them where they are. When one considers the dominant ideology and the value given to different types of labor, it is clear that all classes above the working class do not confound gender and the manual–mental labor distinction. Further they celebrate, justify, and see comparatively their superiority in the mental mode, which is the currency of value in the dominant ideology and culture.

Finally, racism is another division between members of the working class which is a source of division providing an evident underclass to be looked down upon by the white working class. It is a source for projecting by the lads of the degeneracy of others (e.g., West Indian and Pakistani) and the superiority of the self. Thus, racism divides the working class both materially and ideologically.

What is important in the first part of Willis's analysis is that *penetrations* and *limitations* are the moments in the analysis which focus on the culture proper. Penetrations and limitations express the possibilities and limitations for agency at the cultural level. Willis makes it clear that it is impossible in his study to delineate the full complexity at the cultural level with respect to outside deterrents and structure. Nevertheless, he suggests within his own study that it is possible to suggest one important interface between agency and structure or (as he put it) between culture and ideology. This brings him to discuss the role of ideology as part of his analysis, considering the downward impact of structural class conditions on the counterculture.

Ideology and Culture

The notions of penetration and limitation are concepts which can be considered as the problematic of "personal agency". It is the *agent* side of the agent–strucure dialectic. In its pure form (i.e., ideal) it is part of the problem of the projective character of human action. Ideology is the habitus of human action. Willis acknowledges that his emphasis on cultural penetration and the internal cultural limitations, if left at that, would underemphasize the impact of external forces, state institutions, and dominant ideologies acting on the working-class lads. Let it be understood that Willis sees this influence in a dialectical manner; that is, ideology works on and in the cultural. Nevertheless, one must understand that the agent side of the cultural is formed in the backdrop of dominant ideological systems (i.e., habitus). Exclusive of cultural limitations, ideological systems play an important role in the further limitation of cultural penetrations. Where does the ideological exist? Willis maintains that ideological systems arise partly from ruling or central ideas of the age embodied in concrete institutions (e.g., schools, state institutions) and also the more informal media (i.e., TV, radio, etc.). Willis restricts himself to two core concepts in his discussion of ideology (i.e., structure) and its relation to the cultural (i.e., agent). The addition of notions of agency and structure are my interpretations of the meaning of his concepts. At any rate, Willis pinpoints two salient downward vertical impacts of ideology on countercultural penetrations as those of *confirmation* and *dislocation*.

Confirmation is the solidification of those aspects and resolutions of cultural processes which are congruent with the current social organization and interests of production. Within the school, this ideological confirmation of the present system of production comes through career films and vocational guidance. Willis indicates that the clearest example can be seen in the role differentiation between the sexes in careers films. The films do not offer obvious discrimination and sex-role stereotyping, but the sum total of visual images and the implied assumptions remain sexually divided and are picked up by the sexism of the lads' counterculture:

> In a cake factory we see only girls working and the voice-over tells us as we watch a girl icing a cake, "yes, she really is doing it that quickly, the film isn't speeded up. Women are always doing intricate and fiddly things. Their only relation to the more heroic occupations is one of fear and concern for their men-folk. (Willis, 1977, pp. 161–162)

The role of ideological confirmation allows uncertain cultural resolution (e.g., sexual division of labor) to be considered as part of the nature of things (i.e., naturalism). What it does is inform common sense about the "nature of things."

Dislocation is a process whereby something new is brought into a cultural system and has the ability to mute the partial critical insight of that cultural system. For the lads, solidarity with one another is a very important value and has practical significance. This value of solidarity is dislocated and challenged by the dominant ideology of the school. Solidarity is dislocated by the school's stress on and valuing of individualism. A careers teacher is quoted by Willis as follows:

> I've told you before, it's not often I advocate selfishness but in this case I must. Forget your friends sitting around you now you might be together, now having a laugh, and it doesn't matter. But all the friends in the world are no use to you when it comes to finding a job. . . . So, just this time, be selfish; don't worry what your friends are doing, you get out and look after number one, sort out your own jobs and don't wait for your mates. (p. 164)

The confirmation and dislocation of ideological messages surrounds culture with a sense of pervasive naturalism. When blame is ventured, ideology has a message that maintains the integrity of the social structure: "Human nature, not capitalism, is the trap. Ideology has helped to produce that, though not simply from its own resources—it is believed because it is partly self-made" (p. 165).

The Internal Interlocutor. Willis stresses the main impact of what he is calling "ideology," and specifies that his immediate concern is not its direct intervention on cultural penetrations. The implicit work of ideological dislocations works on the cultural world in the following fashion. The lads celebrate their resistance to the formal as an exception to the rule. There is no cumulative impact in the lads resistance. It proceeds blindly to all other's exceptions which, if summated, could overthrow the rule. This lack of awareness of the real possibility of their resistance is a rule unto itself. The suppressed awareness has vulnerability implicit in its silence. Willis contends that it is in this silence that ideology strides. Willis introduces his own version of the devil in what he calls the "internal interlocutor": "Whether right or wrong, whether penetrated or not, it is *the rule,* it is the *voice.* It becomes the internal interlocutor for the weakness of cultural forms" (p. 166).

The voice (internal interlocutor) is the "them" in "us"; the part of the self that accepts the legitimacy of the system even when resisting this has important political implications, which Willis is at pains to emphasize:

> That the them in us survives in us is usually overlooked. This internal division should not be surprising. In a peaceful social democratic society with real class divisions, the "them" and "us" can never be starkly clear. This basic distinction must be a rehearsal and mediated and echoed around from the largest social units to the individual person. . . . It is this which allows the "us" to properly betray itself. Ideology is the "them" in "us." It has been invited. Informality and the strength of personal validation unconnected with a political practice invite it. . . . Once there it confirms partiality and dislocates penetration. It prevents the "us" from becoming a collective assertive "we." (p. 169)

The absence of a personal world, as we have indicated from the outset, has social and political implications, as stated by Willis above. An authentic personal world is necessary for a political praxis. It is the realm of freedom, because it represents the organization of self-in-relation to the future (Willis, 1977):

> Social agents are not passive hearers of ideology, but active appropriators who reproduce existing structures. Capitalist freedoms are potentially real freedoms and capitalism takes the wager, which is the essence of reproduction, that freedom will be used for self-damnation. (p. 175)

ADEQUACY OF THE ACCOUNTS: A COMPARISON

The critique that I will now make of these studies is, in part, a reflection of my own interpretive horizon which by now is known to the reader. Let us consider the issue of adequacy under the four dimensions that I have previously described at the beginning of this chapter.

1. *An adequate account is negotiated.* The authors of *The Rules of Disorder* have a sensitivity for the boys that they are trying to understand and are thus able to part company with media accounts of these youth; they counter in their own interpretative accounts the media definition of these young boys as simply violent. In their account, they attempt to show order where disorder appears at the surface of their actions. Their discussion of "moral careers" as a way of maintaining a sense of dignity indicates that the authors have a feel for the project character of human actions in this instance. In fact, I would say that the notion of moral careers constitutes a partial project for these boys. Although their effort is not systematic or extensive, the authors do attempt to negotiate their accounts with the participants. There is no extensive coverage in this negotiation, so one must be somewhat critical of them here for not carrying out an extensive negotiation with some detailed summaries. This is important, because the authors venture that their account is valid because it does not fly in the face of the actors' interpretive account of their own actions. In other words, they contend that their account is negotiated with the participants. It is our impression that the negotiation is not well documented or discussed and should not be used, on this basis, as a validating mechanism.

Willis's account exemplifies what I deem to be a critical interpretative account of the personal. It is personal in that it captures in ethnographic form (i.e., first-person accounts) a specific cultural world and its strivings (i.e., projects). It is critical because it systematically links the personal world of culture (ethnography) to the structural dimensions of political economy. It is, to my mind, a systematic attempt that explores the duality of structure in what I have previously called the agent–structure dialectic. It is clear that Willis takes a critical perspective toward his own interpretations (i.e., reflexive). Willis indicates that one of the pitfalls of participant observation is its tendency toward the justification of the status quo (conservatism). There is a tendency with participant observation to move in the direction of naturalism. This was indeed the case with the *Rules of Disorder* account, whose naturalism was couched in the sociobiological concept of aggro. Willis is at pains to avoid this naturalistic drift by stressing the historical constitutive character of the cultural life. Another problem with the participant-observation method is its tendency toward condescension in relation to the participants. Even when it takes a sympathetic attitude toward the participants, it is frequently patronizing (Willis, 1977). He sees this as a real problem for social scientific research and ponders at one point whether it is possible to imagine an ethnographic account that challenges the presupposition of the researchers involved. Willis poses for himself the following concern, which he considers must be the concern for the researcher–interpreter of the cultural world of others:

Theories must be judged ultimately for the adequacy they display to the understanding of the phenomenon they purport to explain—not to themselves. This book has attempted . . . to take advantages still offered by a qualitative method to respond descriptively and theoretically to a real and difficult level of social existence whilst resisting tendencies toward empiricism, naturalism and objectification of the subject. (p. 194)

What follows from the above considerations is an edited transcription of a group discussion by some of the lads who were given the opportunity to read early drafts of his books. What clearly indicates the negotiability of this account with the participants involved is the opportunity during this group discussion to critically evaluate his role as researcher and what the results meant to them as particpants. For the most part, the participants were interested only in the ethnographic section and not the analytic section. As one participant said:

Well, I started to read it, I started at the very beginning, y'know, I was gonna read as much as I could, then I just packed it in, just started readin' the parts about us and then little bits in the middle. (p. 195)

The complexity of the analysis section may discourage these boys because the analysis of class structure is couched in language that is foreign to their cultural world. So, negotiation is limited partly by the cognitive world of the participants. Nevertheless, they do speak to the question of veracity of material where the ethnographic accounts are considered. As Chris indicates: "Almost 90 per cent of what I've read in there was, I can actually remember" (p. 196).

In negotiating the account with the participants, one also can sense the importance of establishing the *credibility* of the researcher. With these lads, it is clear that it is not established by professional credentials. As Joey is quick to point out:

When you first started asking questions, something illegal must have come out and we'd told you things we'd done wrong and we never got any backlash off other members of staff which obviously meant you hadn't told anybody. (p. 197)

What is clearly evident from this quote is the trust that must be established if the participants are to reveal themselves. What is clear from this is that there are no "social facts" just there to be collected. They are revealed for interpretation when the researcher is assumed to be credible.

2. *An adequate account is an argument.* By argument, we mean that a particular interpretative account is seen as an advocacy for a particular interpretative horizon with more or less plausibility. In *The Rules of Disorder* the authors understand their account as one that is backed by argument. In fact, their argument attempts to counter media interpretations of youth violence as arbitrary and anarchic. They venture their own argument at two levels. The first is that of a structural articulation of rules interpreting violence at the school and football games of working-class youth. Here the concept of moral careers was introduced

and is ventured as a reason for action. They talk about moral careers as conventional accounts. They then shift to what they say is a causal account embedded in naturalistic explanation. This is their conception of aggro as ritualized aggression. This sociobiological concept is presented as a causal mechanism for violence in these settings. The argument for structural and functional explanation appears to me, however, to be gratuitous. They do not argue in any convincing manner why both must be present as an adequate account. The aggro concept appears as a rabbit out of the hat. Its pretense in the account of human action shows the interpretation in such a way as to prevent this account from being grounds for an emancipatory praxis. The authors do not clearly indicate here their reasons for venturing into sociobiology. Given that they use the concept as a causal mechanism, their thin line of argument for an organic metaphor leaves serious holes in their argument, which I will deal with shortly.

Willis's work, as an account, is seen by the author and revealed to the reader as a particular interpretation of social facts. Recall that the major setting of this study is the institution of the school. Within this work, Willis argues against reproduction theories that ignore the active role of culture in both the maintenance and transformation of a particular society. Specifically, they are in conversation with two major theoretical formulations. The first is the work of Bowles and Gintis, *Schooling in Capitalist America* (1976), and the second is Bourdieu and Passeron's book, *Reproduction in Education, Society and Culture* (1977). It is from this latter work that I have taken the term *habitus*. What is glaringly absent from this work is a notion of *cultural project* which sets up the dialectic of *habitus–project* that I developed in Chapters 3 and 4. With only a notion of habitus, Bourdieu and Passeron (1977) end up by placing sole emphasis on structural factors in the reproduction of cultural learning; the human agent appears hapless before reproductive structural totalities. The power of institutions is conceptualized as "symbolic violence." For them, the school is, par excellence, the structural institution for the reproduction of culture in the young. The educational system inculcates the dominant class position through different cultural constraints. There are different power relations in school according to whether the school caters to elites or groups lower on the status hierarchy. Their argument, as well as that of Bowles and Gintis (1976), accents the pervasive power of economic structures and their linkages to the structure of the school. One could call them structuralists in this light. What is missing is the real or potential role of the agent within culture to reproduce or possibly transform structures that influence their lives. Their structuralism leads a total pessimism toward the resistance or potential projects of the human agent. Their emphasis is on habitus to the exclusion of agency. The school inculcates different classes and the process of inculcation is internalized. Habitus is capable of perpetuating itself after pedagogic action has ceased.

Willis enters here with a concept of culture analyzed through ethnographic first-person accounts. Within this account, the concepts of penetration and limitation are set up to enter into a dialectical relationship with what Bourdieu and Passeron (1977) call "the symbolic violence of structures." The subcultural world of the lads, then, is the focal point not only for the reproduction and continuity of structures but also for their potential transformation. Introducing the agency of subculture in his emphasis on resistance and penetration, Willis opens the door to a realm of freedom which is absent in the other theoretical formulations. He does this without underestimating the powerful determining forces of economic structures which are represented symbolically in the school.

The argument of Willis opens the door to a notion of project and agency where it was heretofore absent. His emphasis on culture and its dialectical relationship to the class structure of modern society under monopoly capitalism would classify him as a cultural Marxist within a Marxist formulation. The argument that he ventures also implicitly critiques formulations that exclude the notions of personal agency. When he argues against naturalism, I take that to include *The Rules of Disorder*. Here, personal agency collapses into a sociobiological formulation called aggro which leaves the economic structures operating in society and selectivity on agents of different social classes unquestioned and uncriticized. Aggro takes what Willis calls "penetration" and casts it in a biological organismic light which I would label "psychologism." Psychologism is where the agency–structure dialectic is collapsed into the psyche. To be sure, it must be understood that it is not a foregone conclusion that one of these interpretations is transparently more adequate than others. The adequacy must be argued because they are conflicts of interpretations in what are apparently similar phenomena. This is why I deem that one criterion of adequacy is that the theory must present itself as an argument to be evaluated rather than a truth that appears to be unassailable.

3. *An adequate account expresses an emancipatory praxis.* In the third criterion of adequacy, I have maintained that an account must express an emancipatory praxis. It makes a case for the freedom of agency. *The Rules of Disorder* contradicts the possibility of freedom in the aggro concept. In interpreting order in this manner, the authors limit the scope of the project exemplified in the development of the moral careers. One must ask here why dignity must fall to a ritual that locks people into institutions that prevent them from transforming their lives. Why does this ritualized aggression seem to exercise itself in a political social situation? The question of the class manifestation of a ritual is never asked. Aggro and its biological gloss explains why things are the way they are. It has no openness to a transformed future where myth has utopian rather than simply ideological elements. If Job were to be confronted in the 20th century, possibly these authors would be one group of his comforters.

It must be understood that the authors of *The Rules of Disorder* would not judge themselves under this norm. In fact, the *value* of emancipation is one that most social psychologists tend to ignore. One chooses it as a norm for adequacy if, in one's theory, there is an interest in human freedom and emancipation. Specifically, I have outlined two minimum conditions: (1) The account must show how the immediate social and material conditions that determine the social world are mediated through the agency of actors who have some control over the constitution of their world. In Willis's study, this is precisely the importance of the ethnographic data and the corresponding concepts of penetration and limitation. The reader senses in the accounts the personal responsibility of actors in the partial creation of their world. (2) The account will show how taken-for-granted self-understandings are socially mediated and could be otherwise (i.e., indicates alternatives). Willis resists a naturalism (e.g., aggro) in his accounts, and his formulation of penetration indicates the possibility for structural change. His critical analysis of limitations in the lads culture (i.e., sexism and racism) indicates that he does not see these inevitable outcomes of class struggle. In other words, he sees the lads as having the capability of intentional intervention into these structures, that is, the capacity of power to change them (i.e., transform). In other words, lower-class boys do not have to be sexist. In introducing the possibility for intentional intervention with his notion of subcultural penetration and resistance, he nevertheless is soberly aware of the limitations that hamper the full impact of personal agency. He outlines and discusses these structurally limiting factors under the terms *racism, sexism,* and *individualism.* All these limiting factors detract from a solidarity potent enough to challenge class structural totalities. Because Willis's interpretative account has a concept of intentional intervention in the duality of penetration and limitation, his account expresses, to my mind, an emancipatory praxis. It should also be noted that he gives some specific suggestions for a different type of vocational guidance and a different type of education for disaffected working-class youth. Part of a long chapter deals with issues he thinks are important for teachers and vocational guidance personnel who have occasion to work with cultures like that of the lads. In recognizing the limitations of the lads' culture, he offsets this with an appreciation of the partial penetration of these youths who criticize the larger culture. He is thus prevented from the all too common drift toward blaming the victim.

4. *An adequate account is critical.* Finally, an adequate account must be a critical interpretation of the world of personal agency. As was said in the previous chapter, critical interpretation as a way of resymbolizing the world of others requires a sensitivity in reflecting back to the participants and other interested parties (e.g., social scientists, social policymakers, etc.), their capacities for *intentional intervention* (i.e., free acts of agents in creating a world). *The Rules of Disorder* clearly lacks this critical moment as an account. As we said earlier, a critical account must resymbolize the world of others and should sensitively reflect back to them their capacities for intentional intervention. We see a class bias in this interpretation, since the aggro ritual simply leaves the actors in their

state with a myth to live by. The account seems to ignore the agent quality of aggression and the possible truth that rebellion is more than a ritual liability. The authors interpret resistance as a biological process rather than one form of intentional intervention, however unsuccessful to arbitrary indignities produced by the class structure in modern societies.

By contrast, *Learning to Labour* presents the idea of intentional intervention by using the concept of partial penetration. The whole idea of partial penetration, as seen in the lads countercultural resistance, is indicative of the possibilities for intentional intervention in the world of these lads. What is different about Willis's account of lower-class rebellion and resistance is its positive value within his interpretive system. In contrast to much social science interpretation of lower-class strata, he does not move to interpret their rebellion as simple deviance. At the same time, he is able to state some real reservations about "resistance" within the context of lower-class penetration. Here a critical interpretation of personal agency also considers the liabilities of a particular cultural form. This is clearly seen in Willis's extensive discussion of what he calls "limitations" and what I am calling "liabilities." What is unique about Willis's account is that he treats liabilities dialectically in relation to agency (i.e., penetration) and embeds the agency–liability dialectic into the agency–structure dialectic. In presenting liabilities within the agency–structure dialectic, he does not fall into blaming the victim for all the liabilities to personal agency. At the same time, this agency–structure dialectic allows him to attribute some personal responsibility to the agents involved, with full knowledge of the powerful effects of social structure on the possibilities for personal agency.

To this point, I have presented the most positive features of the study as I understand it. This I have done for two reasons. First, I think it is an excellent study, barring some reservations that I am about to discuss. Second, the study exemplifies all the significant features and concerns that I have developed throughout this work as a critical interpretation of the personal world. It should be pointed out that Willis does not present himself as a psychologist. So why call this study a psychology that exemplifies a psychology as critical interpretation of the personal world? I do this because psychology has traditionally laid claim to the world of the microcosm, be it individual or person. In that sense, Willis is incorporating—by use of ethnography—the interpersonal world of persons in relation (i.e., culture) within the context of a social structural class analysis of a Marxist variety. One, therefore, sees this study as a nascent form of inquiry which is interdisciplinary in nature. This is exactly what psychology as a critical interpretation is all about. Therefore, psychologists who attempt a critical interpretation of the personal world will need a greater knowledge of cognate disciplines such as anthropology, sociology, political science, and economics. In the past, the socialization of a psychologist into other disciplines was reductionistic in orientation, knowledge of biology and chemistry and physics being the main sister disciplines. This is not to say that psychologists must abandon these latter goals. What is being said is that it must include the former disciplines if the psychology being propagated is to have a critical intent.

Let me now conclude with some caveats on Willis's study, so the reader will understand that no study, critical or uncritical, is above criticism. Some caveats are as follows. Ethnography is labor-intensive work, so it is understandable that samples exemplifying a culture will be small in number. Nevertheless, this study never addresses the problem of its small sample size or the fact that there are a great deal of narrative data on only a few of the lads. Joey seems to be extensively quoted, whereas others are not mentioned. I think Willis has not adequately addressed this problem and the corresponding issue of universality and generality that is drawn from a small sample of a subculture. To what extent does a small sample of this nature represent a subculture? This question is not adequately addressed in this work. One can also say that he makes too much of lower-class resistance and rebellion. Given the apolitical nature of their rebellion, which the author freely acknowledges, one could ponder their rebellion as "alienated" rebellion and opposed to "integrated" rebellion. Here I am continuing a distinction that I made in Chapter 4, when I discussed the Watts uprising. Resistance is easily classified as deviance when rebellion is not centered on a project with *utopian* symbols. The lads have no utopian symbols that project beyond their present state in the class structure. This is evident in the quotes supplied by Willis. Recall that when Watts reached the critical juncture of an integrated black cultural project, rebellion and resistance were coupled with utopian goals which led to cultural projects in the ghetto that even detractors had to acclaim. The lads macho, individualism, sexism, and racism are hardly the stuff of social transformation and utopian striving. All movements of social transformation (violent and nonviolent) have a moral persuasion that not only challenges the enclaves of the status quo but also their moral integrity. This is demonstrated in the utopian and charismatic leaders of all modern movements of social transformation (e.g., Gandhi, Cesar Chavez, Malcolm X, Martin Luther King). I am not convinced by Willis that "cultural resistance," which the lads demonstrate, can effectively transform the class structure by simply being politicized. The power of their project is not only weakened by their own divisiveness but also the total absence of real utopian symbols. Without engaging in victim blaming, one must nevertheless see their rebellion in the present state as alienated in nature (see Table 4). This alienation must not be reduced to a sociobiological concept like aggro. It must be seen as *historical* in nature and capable of being transformed under the right social condition by utopian projects.

METHOD REVISITED

The two stuides just described in their particularity can now be seen in a more generic and historical context. Both studies strike a very different balance on the agency–structure dialectic. Their differences, however, have a long social and political history to explain why they essentially come down on opposite poles of an agency–structure dialectic. Dawe (1978) traces this to a fundamental dualism which has emerged historically from the Enlightenment formulation. He elucidates the dualism as follows:

> There has been a manifest conflict between two types of social analysis, variously labelled as being between the organismic and mechanistic approaches, methodological collectivism and individualism, holism and atomism, the conservative and emancipatory perspectives, and so on. The debate about these issues . . . are all different versions of the fundamental debate about the abiding conflict between the domination of the system and the exertion of human agency. (p. 366)

Dawe contends that the basic contemporary conflicts in the human sciences are around these two opposing views of human potential. Theories that accent the importance of the social system are willy-nilly pessimistic about human actors, envisioning them as manipulable but as also tending on their own initiatives toward destructive actions. The bottom line of the above perspective sees the survival of society in the containment of human agency. The essential emphasis is on social order (i.e., habitus).

The other side of this dualism emphasizes *freedom* over *order*. Here, the recognition of constraints on human actors is seen as coming from the actions of others. I have referred to this as "domination." Within this perspective, society is the outcome of autonomous, creative human actions. The moral focus of this perspective is the idea of human control or direction over the system (Dawe, 1978).

As a dualism, both systems are inadequate and have severe limitations at their extremes. One system sacrifices *freedom* for the sake of social order, the other sacrifices social coherence for the sake of freedom (i.e., anarchy). Most of what constitutes conventional psychology errs on the side of order. Thus, my contention earlier that psychology serves the cause of the social order over the individual. Even where there is a focus on the individual, conventional psychology implicitly brings the individual in line with the social order. At the same time, most reactions to social order maintenance have been libertarian in nature. I count most of the human potential movement of the 1960s under this aegis.

What is needed now in social theory and practice are perspectives which pose the agency–structure issue in dialectical terms. To my mind, the Willis study captures this dialectical spirit, whereas *The Rules of Disorder* collapses agency into a functional sociobiology which is "social order"-maintaining. But it must be understood that the notion of agent freedom located in our agency-structure dialectic must encompass a freedom that goes beyond libertarianism. Berlin (1969), in a discussion of two concepts of liberty, calls the concern for freedom that I am involved with status *freedom. It is not individual liberty* in the traditional liberal sense. Rather:

> It is something no less profoundly needed and passionately fought for by human
> beings—it is something akin to, but not itself freedom: although it entails negative
> freedom for the entire group, it is more closely related to solidarity, fraternity, mutual
> understanding, need for association on equal terms. . . . The desire for recognition is
> a desire for something different: for union, closer understanding, integration of in-
> terests, a life of common dependence and common sacrifice. (Berlin, 1969, p. 158)

I differ with Berlin (1969) that one can associate liberty from solidarity. This disassociation has been characteristic of the liberal concept of freedom. But freedom as allied with *solidarity* is achieved through *totalitarianism*. It must be clearly understood that the sense of freedom achieved under these conditions is a caricature of the human efforts toward creative agency.

To conclude, the belief in personal agency, project, freedom, and emancipation, which I have engaged the reader in through this book, is a *value* rather than a *fact*. As a *value*, these interests must come under *factual* scrutiny. In other words, one can ask: Are these values real? The answer to this question for a professional psychologist such as myself will not come from within my discipline. These concerns, which are moral in nature, one brings to the discipline. I fully understand that to say that psychology is the study of the personal world of human freedom flies in the face of much of what constitutes the discipline of psychology. I can only hope that my ideas have been developed in this book to make the idea of freedom a tolerable idea for some. I am, however, more ambitious than that. I would hope that an interest in *human emancipation* would strike a chord which is cordial rather than barely tolerable.

It seems to me that an interest in human freedom is more vital today than at any other period in history. If one looks at Skinner, one gets the impression that "freedom" has failed: "Now let's try some systematic control." It is not that freedom has failed. In relation to freedom, one can repeat Chesterton's words on Christianity: "It has not been tried and found wanting, it has been found wanting but hasn't been tried." This certainly can be said of psychology in its short history.

8

Critical Pedagogy
Selected Examples

This chapter labeled "critical pedagogy" will attempt to give a number of examples of how the critical approach that I have been advocating in this book can be applied to educational topics. It is not my objective to give an extensive and exhaustive treatment of how critical psychology might apply to educational issues and problems. Rather, what I will be seeking to do here is to give some selected examples from my own work in several educational areas in order to help the reader of this book see how a critical approach can be applied to certain educational problems that I deal with as an educational psychologist. The book you have just read is not a cookbook and ultimately the reader must be left to her or his own devices in applying a critical approach to her or his own work. What I hope to achieve, by the examples that I will offer from my own work in education, is a belief that a critical framework can be profitably applied to important educational problems. The specific examples that I will delineate are from my own peculiar educational interests. These interests include such areas as computers in education, education and the mass media, and popular education in a comparative educational context. I will elaborate on these topic areas with extensive examples from my current work.

EXAMPLE 1: COMPUTERS IN EDUCATION[1]

Background

The past few years in education have witnessed a mania sparked by computers. But the flurry of activity and speculation is everywhere. The January,

[1]The work discussed below comes from a major research project carried out by myself and several other Institute colleagues and students under the title "The Development of Policy and Research Projections for Computers in Education" (1986). Funded by Social Science and Humanities Research Council of Canada, Project number 499–83–0017. Much of the work that is written in this section is with my colleague Paul Olson whom I gratefully acknowledge.

177

1983, cover of *Time* magazine gives a glimpse of the cultural ebullience of the topic. The issue is normally devoted to the "Man of the Year" and features a person on the cover, but in this issue, there is no man on the cover; in its place, there is a plaster model sitting on a chair, looking at a computer. And, instead of the 1983 award going to the "Man" of the year, it is presented to the "computer." The title of the cover story is "The Machine of the Year: The Computer Moves In." The view that the computer is the wave of the future is widely shared in the popular culture. Yankelovich's study of American public opinion, for example, reported in the Time cover issue, showed that 80 percent of Americans expect that in the very near future the computer will be as commonplace in the household as the television. Sixty-eight percent of the same sample believe that the computer will ultimately raise production and improve the quality of their children's education. There are great cultural expectations for the computer. Canadians along with Americans share these great expectations for the computer. By September of 1984, there were approximately 27,000 microcomputers across Canada; in schools, on average, there was one computer for every 200 children (Sharon and Mehler, 1985). While this relatively small ratio currently creates a "politics of scarcity" around the computer, a number of ministries have two- to five-year plans designed to increase dramatically the hardware and software support available to schools in their provinces. In Ontario, for example, the Ministry of Education has agreed to fund 70 percent of the purchase cost of the Ontario-built Icon system. Similar schemes are in existence everywhere across Canada. Boards seem to share in the belief that computers have an inherent capacity to assist in mathematics instruction, to teach word-processing and programming, and in general to enhance the learning environment.

The general interest in educational computing mirrors a wider transformation within the society itself. Canadians seem to share an enthusiasm for computers in many areas of life. In a recent report by the Canadian Department of Labor (In the Chips: Opportunity for People Partnerships), the computer is pictured as a "triggering technology" (1982). A "triggering technology," according to the report, is industry that will improve economic growth by utilizing or developing computers and "high" technology. The report advocates supporting further development of microelectronics because of the supposed benefits of technological innovation. Questions about computer deployment are proposed in this light as essentially technical ones, that is, as a matter of developing adequate hardware and software to get on with the job of delivering the new order. Questions of implementation, of the delivery of the fullest social benefit and the impact of the new millennium, are seen as primarily technical, even if pressing, issues.

There is, however, an underside, or alternative view, of educational computing, which, we believe, relates to a blindness within educational theorizing;

this is the tendency to underplay or to ignore the fundamental issue of power distribution. There is every indication in the history of technological innovation in the 20th century, that innovations become a means of control and have differential results for different classes, racial groups, gender divisions, and so on (Braverman, 1974). There is also sound historical evidence that schooling better serves the needs of dominant groups within the work world (Connell, 1983, 1985). Thus the computer, as well as other information technologies, may possibly accentuate and amplify power inequalities within our society. The whole issue of how "computer literacy" will affect job and status opportunities is an open one at this point, but there is every reason to believe that new status divisions in the labor force created by changes in production facilitated by computers will create power differentials in society itself, acting to "skill" some workers (thereby giving them more power) while "deskilling" others (thereby lessening their power). Michael Apple's (1979, 1984) work on the effects of computer-assisted instruction in the United States shows that standardized computer-based programs often act to deskill teachers by "modularizing" curriculum and thereby effectively limit what an individual teacher may undertake (Apple, 1979). Even more powerful is the potential impact of such standardized curriculums on the presentation of particular points of view. In the Canadian textbook industry, for instance, the selection of texts is frequently influenced by decisions made in a few U.S. states, particularly California and Texas. The decision to follow the standards set by these states is not a pedagogical or educational one but, instead, an economic one. If a text is approved in Texas, or in California, or, better in both (together they have a population far greater than all of Canada), then it is a virtually assured success. If a text fails to make the approval lists in Texas and/ or California it is open to question how successful it will be. Practically, this means that a full range of views, including those held by many Canadians, is not presented. And the reason is that such views may prove offensive to particular constituencies of Americans. The most notorious example of this kind of information control occurred at Ginn Publishing when it summarily fired its entire textbook staff for failing to get Ginn textbooks approved on the Texas state curriculum (Apple, 1984). This incident may seem irrelevant to our concerns about educational computing in Canada, but I would like to suggest that it provides a lesson (Apple, 1984). While computing may seem to be a general, technical skill, the content of computer programs is highly susceptible, in much the same way as textbooks, to social pressures that determine and stratify the educational curriculum. Such seemingly remote social processes have effects ranging from the banal to the profound. Malone's (1981) review of children's preferences and motivations in the use of computer games, for instance, shows that sensationalism and sensory stimulation were chief components in determining children's interest levels (Malone, 1981). From a content level, the most popular games featured hangings and explosion-games that presented the joys of domination. Listed at the bottom of the preference list were programs aimed at being educational. The microchips for many of the "invader" games that were very popular with school-aged, computer-oriented boys were originally developed, not coincidentally, by the U.S. military. While we are not suggesting that computing promotes militarism or antisocial behavior, we are suggesting that there is little evidence indicating that the content or medium of computing has inherently superior pedagogical, never mind moral, properties for teaching children. Innis and McLuhan (1951) were instrumental in pointing out that particular forms of communication convey biases and that changing the form, or power structure, of the media changes how information is processed (Innis, 1951; McLuhan, 1969). The computer itself, while individually operated, "engages" children in a kind of detached "technical" sense; nonetheless, higher and higher levels of sensory input are required to keep them engaged (they are, after all, staring at a dot screen).

In evaluating the possible impact of the computer medium, there is the question of how computer instruction will affect established trends of school performance for various groups. For instance, a number of historical reviews of schooling and the curriculum document how social sorting in schools done on the basis of class, gender, and ethnicity results in a different access to society's opportunity structure (Prentice, 1974; Sullivan, 1983b). Although computers are nominally classless and sexless, their use-patterns are filtered through institutions, like the school, which have, as part of their "de facto" work, the perpetration of dominant systems of thought and language, leading to class, gender, and racial inequalities in schooling. It is not hard to imagine how such divisions will occur again with computers. The reciprocal relationship between schooling and technology is not well established. It thus seems most probable that the level of skill training in high technologies will increase. The pattern for market demand seems to be ill established; for example, the Economic Council of Canada in "Jobs for the Eighties" reports that high technology is a key area of vocational growth in Canada (Economic Council of Canada, 1982). Similarly, the national assessment of education in the U.S. (1982) suggests:

> The gap between the number of highly-skilled workers needed and the number of students prepared for high-level jobs is widening. Clearly we are not cultivating the raw material, our future workers, who will be vital for both economic progress and ultimately for economic survival. (U.S. Department of Education, 1982)

This view has been eagerly taken up by a variety of key Canadian educational leaders. Former Ontario Minister of Education Bette Stephenson, for example, was quoted in the *World of Computers* as saying:

> As this specialized edition of *Education Ontario* will demonstrate, education will have an even more important role in shaping the computer age we are entering.
> Our technological future can be what philosophers have dreamed of for centuries

... or it can be a nightmare of mechanization. Schools will have strong influence in which future awaits us. (Stephenson, 1982)

With the dawning of the "Age of the Chip," the link between the implementation of the microtechnological revolution and the transformation of the economic and educational order is widely postulated (Berg and Bramble, 1983; Canadian Department of Labour, 1982; Papert, 1980; Schiller, 1983; Science Council of Canada, 1982). Anticipation is in the air. Virtually all researchers in this area emphasize that computers will have an impact that will pose special problems for the form and content of schooling. But how all this will transpire (and for whose benefit) is still an open question.

Indeed, the assessments of the exact nature of the computer's impact on schooling are filled with contradictions at this early juncture. We are, for instance, assured by one group of notable scholars that the *medium* of technology will revolutionize the forms of learning (Jamison, Suppes & Wells, 1974; Papert, 1980). But with this bit of hopeful wisdom in hand, we proceed toward our next socioeducational insight. Quickly however, we are greeted with the sobering news from equally eminent researchers that when controls are made for exogenous factors (e.g., Hawthorne effect, variances and the method of instruction, quality of teachers, etc.), there are no long-term benefits provided by computers or other slick-trick educational innovations. First we go east; then we go west. Inconsistent conclusions abound with respect to the most interesting issues raised by the social impact of computers on schooling. Some examples are listed below. Do schools "skill" or "deskill"? (Apple, 1979). Canadian data seem to suggest that they do both. Jane Gaskell's (1981; 1984) work at the University of British Columbia shows how girls' education varies radically depending on whether one is taking computing in the business stream or in the academic stream. The contrasts are revealing. Within the business stream, for instance, there is repeated emphasis upon *mechanical* and *routinized* tasks to *service* the machine. There is very little learning of general skills (e.g., underlying logics, programming skills, symbolic codes, etc.) which might later be translated to another context. The girls interviewed by Gaskell were aware that mechanical skills would not lead to high-level careers. Nonetheless, they felt that in relation to other studies the business stream was "the most practical." For working-class girls, the choice of secretary does indeed reflect a good understanding of real life possibilities, at least in the current situation. Of women working in British Columbia, for instance, a full 50 percent are employed in clerical occupations. Among working-class women, this figure rises to three in four. This pattern contrasts dramatically with programming in the academic stream. Here the emphasis is on *general* and *symbolic* processes which lead to long-term *control*, regardless of the systems that may evolve. The emphasis is on high-level programs and forms of technical knowledge that give this control. What we are the witnessing, in effect, is the use of computers to stratify knowledge, hence establishing a new entrance gate for "achievers" and a new barrier for those destined to less desirable fates.

Do computers reduce or increase differences in class-based learning? In our own studies (Sullivan, Olson, Logan, 1986), we tentatively have found on a limited sample that middle-class children have more frequent access than working-class children to advanced computers in both home and community situations. Since we know that such nonschool settings have a powerful impact on how children perform within schools, there is every reason to believe that this will also influence the level, availability, and ultimate usages of knowledge based along class lines. Since this knowledge, more so than conventional education, is capital intensive (you need an expensive computer, peripherals, software, training books, etc.), it leads to a possible powerful basis for further class division between those who can pay and those who cannot. Campbell (1983) in an overview article of U.S. results found that in 1983, 67 percent of wealthier U.S. boards had computers while only 41 percent of poor schools had microcomputers; that one study of schools in New Jersey found gaps in programming usage between white and black schools by margins of 3 to 1; that richer suburban boards teach programming skills while poorer schools use computer assisted instruction (CAI). Campbell's survey also reviewed learning gaps between poorer and richer, blacks and whites in computer usage such as those found in curricular areas. A study comparing Newark, New Jersey, city children to their suburban counterparts found differences in availability of both hardware and software. The same study also found that even the best Newark inner-city children tended to be two years behind their suburban counterparts in computer use ability.

Will they centralize or decentralize education as a source of knowledge? Again, the speculation in the area is highly divided. In Canada, our colleague, Robert Logan, working from the McLuhan and futurist perspectives, argues the common position that computers offer us unlimited potential for highly individualized instruction and for making knowledge more available (Logan, 1982). However, another colleague of ours, Ted Humphries (1980), argues that computers create powerful databases capable of invading privacy and automating the workplace thus representing a fundamental erosion of individuality (and privacy) (Humphries, 1980).

Does the implementation of computers assist curriculum, and in developing individual autonomy, or does it lead to greater dependence on rigid learning packages and rote form? Our own work in the area suggests that the answer here is highly dependent on how the program itself is *implemented* and that *teaching* is an influential determinant of computing outcomes (Fullan, 1982). How computer use is integrated with the curriculum also appears to be an influential factor in this area. Nonetheless, there is no single, clear answer provided by the literature.

The list saunters on. And, at any turn, if you name your preference, you can readily garner evidence to give you confidence that you are headed in the right direction. It is plain that a new day is upon us. But where we are going is in question.

If the computer has failed to fire us with unified resolve about its effects, it has certainly not failed to spark our passion and our imagination. There is a plethora of technical material about the computer, but there is little that is without bias. Almost none of this material is without an opinion on where computers can (and should) take us. And, again, sharp division exists about effects.

The views, again, tend to be organized around sharp polarities: one extreme is protechnological or *millennialist*, while the other is antitechnologist, or *cataclysmic*, seeing such technological innovations as hyperextensions of the state's bureaucratic and mechanized control (Sullivan, 1983b). Within these conflicting archetypes, there is considerable variability in the form of argumentation and the sophistication of proponents. Nonetheless, there are those favoring such technology (Papert, 1980; Martin, 1981) who argue that computer-based learning will lead to greater individualized freedom and to the breakdown of authoritarianism and standardized classroom forms and mentalities (Papert, 1980). Again, they see the use of computers as resulting in an expansion of literacy, economic opportunity, and generalized decentralization of social control. Various theorists within the protechnological camp draw upon McLuhan's work to argue the decentralizing nature of the medium, comparing its impact to that of the alphabet in extending individual knowledge and control (Logan, 1982). Opponents of the new technologies argue that the use of computers to "deskill" work represents an extension of technical control (Noble, 1977). They link the technology to an increase in the gap of wealth between classes and between nations; for example in industrialized countries, like Canada, and Third World countries. Others in this camp emphasize the disastrous effects on dislocated workers, particularly the historically disadvantaged such as minorities and women (Canada, Canadian Department of Labour, 1982; Bluestone & Harrison, 1982), and/or fundamental civil liberties such as the protection of privacy (Humphries, 1980). What we are witnessing in the research on computers' impact is the emergence of a discourse based less on overt facts about the computer's *technical* effects than on covert treatises about what schools can and should do. In essence, in the guise of a *research* debate is a *moral* debate (Wootton, 1975, Sullivan, 1983b). This discourse is akin to a theological debate between the believers in the computer and the heretics (Sullivan, 1983b).

Now, schooling itself has always been promoted for the sake of a people's future, social, moral, and technical development. That it has, in fact, been a contested terrain for competing ideologies is plain in schooling's history (Prentice, 1977; Archer, 1979; Bernstein, 1971; Apple & Weis, 1983; Whitty and Young, 1977; Harp & Hafley, 1980; Livingstone, 1983). The current debates on computing and schooling also mirror the older ideological debates on schooling. The form of these debates' argument conforms even more closely, however, to futurist debates on the general societal effects of computers. It is within the arena of combative ideologies that we must understand *Time*'s honoring the computer as "Man of the Year" and, conversely, the thesis that the "Third Wave" should be greeted apprehensively (Grant, 1967; Ellul, 1964; Schiller, 1983).

We submit that in order to comprehend both the plurality of effects attributed to the computer and the moral tone of discussion, it is vital that we examine how the so-called consequences of computer implementation affect different individuals and serve different social interests. It is also useful to examine how individual or group intentions, which computers should serve, come to represent explicitly or to establish differential relationships of utility for different persons in critical interactions such as those among schools, technology, and homes. The issues here range from career patterns and marketing strategies to microsocial issues such as teacher–student interactions and the ways in which computers have radically reordered market possibilities. What we are arguing is that a historical and contextual approach is needed. We are not denying that the debate around computing is (and should be) a moral one; but, rather, that assessment of trends needs to be grounded in particular understandings of how different aspects of computer use affect various groups. Our ethnographic work, to be quoted shortly, is a step in this direction.

Again, we suggest the debate suffers from lapses within educational research; the last five decades have been dominated by a liberal or universalist model portraying schooling as equal and occurring by consensus. Whatever may be its other advantages, steadfastly holding to this position tends to downplay or to ignore the existence of very real structural, cultural, and other power-relationship conflicts within schools and society (Giroux, 1983). But this consensus by these oversights also eclipses the role of "intentional agency" as a part of the educational planning process. Such eclipses are tantamount to tunnel vision; but its own unwillingness to engage social struggle gives a form or a style that favors *technical* solutions and efficiency models. These positions, while appearing technical, can become implicit value positions and thus, for instance, lead to a view that technology is good for society (Feinberg and Rosemount, 1975). This is why *Time* can center-stage the "Computer" to the exclusion of all forms of personal agency, be they male or female. This is one reason why we are presently looking to solve problems by the use of machines as if there were no tradeoff. The digital computer, with its incredible capacity for speed and memory, outperforms the computational paces obtainable by humans. Our romance with speed, once vested in the automobile, is enhanced with the advent of the computer. Earlier technologies such as cars are fast, so they must be good. And, by extrapolation, computers must be really good.

In order to understand computers and information technologies, we must understand what they are and what they can do. What they are, very plain and simple, are efficient tools for information processing. This treatment is simple enough on the surface; yet, as we are continuously rediscovering in a host of diverse settings, the full range of the impact of the computer as a tool is complex. Knowledge of how and where computers can be efficiently used will doubtless remain an ongoing discovery. But technical understanding of possible usages is not enough. No tool autonomously organizes and employs itself alone from tabula rasa to the operational program. Tools are used by people for particular ends (good and bad). Understanding who uses them, how, and for whose benefits (the structure of intentional action) is necessary if we are to assess how computers are likely to be actually employed. Now, computers announce a remarkable technical advance because they facilitate the rapid execution of a multiplicity of work processes. The introduction of computer technology alters the parameters (and the cost) for executing work, or in some cases is necessary if work is to be undertaken at all. The level of technology theoretically limits productive capacities (i.e., workloads, etc.). But what work is to be done, by whom, and for whose benefit, questions of distribution and processes of production, cannot be given by technology alone. Understanding how computers affect schools, labor markets, and models of social organization, therefore, requires that we look at the various interests that are served and the organizational as well as purely technical decisions. This is a most appropriate project if we are to adequately evaluate the effects of computer implementations since the computer as a tool *does* fundamentally *reorganize material relationships and organizations of production.*

Because the computer affects directly so many of the most important areas of human activity, the organization of information, processes of production, our psychological sense of the possible, and so on, it also potentially changes relationships of social power. Many of these relationships are structural relationships, for example, changes in how work gets done (essays are now word processed, math drills in schools are computer assisted; tickets are booked by computers globally). Who controls such information very much affects one's level of power within society, one's ability to get a job and even how much of some kinds of knowledge one may obtain. Industrial societies, like Canada, count on computers for the "competitive edge." Yet all these structural changes are ultimately made by people. Not everyone's interest is the same. Understanding this is massively helpful to separating authentic educational benefits of computers from vested claims. When we move beyond the mania of hopes and fears that cloud our perceptions about computers in education to a critical evaluation of how they work in practice, we will best be able to use the potential computers hold for schools.

We must take a hard look at the applied uses of computer technology and ask ourselves if these methods are authentically better ways of doing work. We must calculate the effects of deskilling, the depersonalization of learning, and the areas where computers are pedagogically helpful. We must be practical in our assessment of whether they are more or less expensive (and fashionable) toys. At the same time, we should explore ways to use the computer to assist us in education. If some drill is better done on a computer than at a desk, then we should do the work in this manner. Where computers free us from drudgery or open new avenues of art, science, printing, and the like, we should foster their growth. What is most essential, however, is that we consciously understand what is happening in practice, how it is happening, and whom it serves. Ultimately, it is we as conscious actors who must generate the metaphors about computers, and control the practical uses of computers. The principle of critically evaluating what our education is about is equally applied to computerized and noncomputerized learning. The computer simply reopens old questions about technology, equality, and whose school interests should be served.

It can be concluded for now that the effects of computers are mixed. We must be both empirical and critical in our claims about their impact. Dreams and fears are part of being human. But if we are to use computers as tools, tutors, and machines to serve our students, we must examine the full range of their actual use. Democratic ends, not fashion, not technical analysis, not market forces, should control the use of computers. Knowledge ought to bring us greater flexibility and freedom, not new forms of subordination.

A Comparative Ethnographic Example

The concerns laid out in Chapter 4 around social power and issues of class, race, and gender can be made more concrete for the reader in the area of computer education by describing a very small segment from our ethnographic work (Sullivan, Olson and Logan 1986). At this point we would like to have the reader get the flavor of how computer technology is utilized in two very different schools. These schools are part of the six schools in which our research team has done extensive ethnographic descriptions. Our schools were chosen in order to have a variety of settings in order to make critical comparisons: we observed what might be called an elite-humanistic school, two working-class ethnic schools, a middle-class school where computers were being used for special education, a model school where a very special program was being utilized in its first year that had computers as its distinctive characteristic and, finally, a school in a rural area. We will describe in some detail the rural and model school to give the reader a broad view of computer usage within the school context and also demonstrate how a critical analysis can be utilized in this educational area.

Some Preliminary Considerations on Class, Race, and Gender

Conception of Class. Race, class, and gender are among the most written about subjects within the social and psychological literature. The recent major work of theorists of class as diverse as Althusser (1971), Giddens (1979) and Connell (1982, 1983) makes it abundantly clear that even the definition of class is problematic. Still, it is generally accepted that in terms of life expectations, one's family background and socioeconomic status very much determine economic possibilities, access to power, as well as influence personal values and an array of other human relations (Coleman, 1966; Jencks, 1979; Anyon, 1980, 1981a; Connell, 1983; Apple & Weis, 1983; Olson, 1981).

The approach herein to class is a holistic and cultural one. Specifically, one postulates that class, while rooted in forms of economic and historical inequalities, is also a set of lived experiential relationships that have a life of their own and must be understood in specific historical contexts and not treated as taken for granted structural inequalities. This last claim warrants some explication.

Most of the traditional approaches to class have focused heavily, if not exclusively, upon an economistic or monetary structuralist approach to the topic. This is as true of the traditional stratification literature (Parsons, 1951; Coleman, 1966) as it is of much of the classical radical and standard Marxist discourse (Althusser, 1971; Bourdieu, 1977; Bowles & Gintes, 1976). Within the past two decades this approach has been questioned by a variety of authors who, while accepting the importance of aggregated structural differences, also emphasize the importance of how cultural forms (Williams, 1973; Willis, 1977; Bourdieu, 1977), the status assigned to knowledge in particular contexts (Whitty & Young, 1977; Apple 1979), and the agency that individuals bring to situations affect how class comes into operation (Freire, 1970; Giddens, 1979). In a similar vein, empirical ethnographic work in comparative school settings has emphasized how the technical and pedagogical forms of schooling alter the content and understanding of how and what curriculum is presented in schools (Connell, 1983; Gaskell, 1984) This raises a variety of questions.

First, it suggests that class is a cultural and subjective form as well as an economic one. This has profound psychological and temperamental correlates that frequently parallel but are not mechanically or reductionistically given by socioeconomic status alone. Particular fusions of collective or individual understandings, serendipitous and irregular moments are a part of class action. Further, relations of class, both macrostructurally and at the personal level, are influenced by the time and place in which they are set. This framework was at least in part understood in classical econometric approaches, yet we would like to argue that the point is epistemologically a far more general one. How class comes to be understood as lived experience to individuals is always mediated through the particular configurations of their particular situations, which bear a dynamic relationship between structural forces and those of individual agency. It is not just that people are always (happily) not doing what they are supposed to do, but while abstractions about class relationships help to summarize trends in comparative historical situations, these trends are nonetheless base reflections of relationships, understandings, and practices particular to that situation as it has historically emerged. These practices may (in principle) be altered by shifts in intentional action, in relations of structural power, changes in technology, or quirks of the situation. Class relationships, therefore, while describable as statistical abstractions for prevailing socioeconomic and power relationships never fully determine action since actors (and particular social relations in varying historical times) change what is understood and what is possible.

This realization of the complex and nonreductionist relationships of structural, individual, cultural and historically particular moments, Giddens (1979) described with the somewhat awkward neologism "structuration." In our account of class we implicitly rely upon this conception. Additionally, I would like to argue that the relationships of class and the understanding of their indirect impacts must be understood as an "ecology" or "totality" that sets a backdrop for class relationships. Hence, within any particular situation the dominant class relationships are set. Thus, for instance, the fact that Canada has a particular economic structure that, as argued above, is undergoing complex technological change, dramatically influences how people value the ways in which their children are educated. Yet again, as we shall try to illustrate in our comparison of practice by class base in schools, how this comes to be understood by parents and teachers is very much changed, mediated by their own class background. Class in this conception is the nexus of cultural, psychological, and ideological forms that emerge from the totality of operating one kind of social form versus another. What seems to make sense regarding computers in schools is in part influenced by who you are and how you have come to understand what schools will do for you in that context. Yet the idea of a "totality" and an "ecology" has another, perhaps less obvious, notion. That is, the notion that within any aggregated macroconception there is layered or nested a series of other social and institutional forms with their own histories, agendas, and mandates. Ethnographic work has the potential to bring this to light. Comprehending this is vital for several reasons. First, it suggests that the social structure, while having an overall pattern does not act monolithically. Governmental institutions like schools or various subunits within the school system, cultural groups, ideologies, material circumstances, and so on, may all act in quite varying and even contradictory ways. These variances, we would like to argue, produce as well as reproduce variations in social practice. Again, we are arguing for the importance of the textual documentation of various settings to see how these often quite different interests act and interact. Hence, as in the interpretation of the computer ethnographic work in schools, while the economic structure is changing, and new moral panics about the impacts of shifts wrought by computers are developing, these must also be understood in the ways in which schools have come to work, the roles and pedagogical forms teachers have assumed, the way differing social classes, ethnicities, and genders have come to relate to schools and work, and so on. What impact computers have on schools varies quite dramatically depending on which layer of analysis one is situated. Analyzing relative positions and the importance of these positions, and reintegrating them, we see as part and parcel of seeing how class and computer use interact.

   Concepts of Gender as Forms of Inequality. The past two decades have seen some of the most dramatic shifts in our understanding of how deeply gender and race are both implicated in the maintenance of inequality and the functional operation of a wide variety of societies. The newer insights on the psychological, cultural, and economic impact of gender of the last two decades are possibly the most important revolution in the social sciences since the introduction of class analysis in the last century.

   We believe it is vital to understand that conceptually and as a matter of practice, class and gender are separable. This is interpretively important since there is, especially among those whose major analytical frame is class, a tendency to engage in the "comma, comma, comma" syndrome whereby analysis of class is offered with race and gender thrown in as if they were add-ons of the same dimension (Anyon, 1981; Connell, 1983). This approach is fundamentally flawed in a number of important respects. First, there is the very real issue that the realm of class analysis has focused primarily on divisions promulgated from differentiations deriving from the public sphere of paid labor, social status, varying relations to the state, and the like. While variations in these realms have certainly influenced how women stand in relationship to other women and men, the profound way in which the relations of domestic labor and relations of reproduction have shaped and underpinned how all work can be carried out is left all but unaddressed in class analysis. Second, there is the historical reality that legally and as a matter of practice women were left in subordinate positions that could not easily be explained in class terms. And while authors like Julliet Mitchell and A. Oakley (1976) have forcefully argued that gender constitutes an independent sphere (akin to the way in which Engels had argued that the law functioned inside of varying social forms), there is little in class analysis itself that would readily explain the transcultural pattern of gender inequality in most societies, the historical exclusion of women from positions of power, education, and the like (A. Oakley, 1979).

   Such analysis also does not explain the profound ways in which socialization to gender and the reality of the so-called "double standard" (Eichler, 1980) and "double shift" has changed the consciousness and comparative sensibilities of the respective gender groups (Chodorow, 1978; Gilligan, 1985). These differences are not merely ones of class form but have to do with the ways in which members of one gender or another come probabilistically to see spheres of interest and even the likelihood of seeing an activity as benign or malignant. From issues as diverse as relations of intimacy, and a sense of the efficacy of militarism, there are statistically significant cross-gender differences.

This said, there are similarities in our approaches to class and gender. These again are rooted in the need for historically specific analysis and in the need to understand where typologies break down as well as show consistencies. This bears directly on our approach in relation to debates within the gender itself. In particular, the tendency to reduce gender into class analysis, especially the efforts to merge neo-Marxist approaches to feminism, leads an analyst such as Heidi Hartmann (1979) in her influential article, "The Unhappy Marriage of Marxism and Feminism" to postulate the so-called "dual" approach to class and gender whereby each is seen as an important, but separate avenue of social inequality.

There are a number of strengths to this approach. First, it allows the relations of gender to be put front and center without recourse to reductionism to class. This is more than the important issue of political mobilization and the control of an oppressed group by discourse. It also puts forward the psychodynamic and material ways in which the images of embodiment, issues of pornography, and issues of the family values are profound social forms in themselves. Second, it facilitates the analysis of patriarchy and domestic forms as dynamics coded in familial, institutional, and psychological realms. In short, it performs a uniquely appropriate task: it places the dynamics of gender, sexuality, and patriarchy in their legal, cultural, economic, and psychological manifestations as central topics for analysis.

Nonetheless, we would like to argue that there are other less analytically desirable features to this approach. First is one of ideology. The analysis of gender as a categorical dimension leads readily to a reductionism or conspiratorial analysis of patriarchy. Connell (1983) notes that this may lead to a rhetoric of neobiological determinist approach. The analysis bears a curious inversion of the analysis it rejects: whereas females were historically demeaned for supposed deficiencies in their biologies, males are now the object of biological preordained damnation. We submit that this approach fundamentally misses the socially constructed nature of all forms of power and inequality. Such approaches also miss the real variation in how individuals support or oppose these forms of inequality. As we shall try to illustrate in the analysis of our direct observation of boys and girls learning computers, while there are definite and important trends—some of which bear the background of living in a society where gender differences saturate the family and popular forms of the culture—these trends need to be highly nuanced by counter-examples. Inequalities, we submit, are not innate but are generated in particular places and with particular social and cultural conditions. Inequalities are never absolute, but are worked out in those circumstances. We understand this as a vital analytical and "political" question, in that knowing that historical forms run deeply but are always, in principle, changeable. This directs us to how policies, alliances, and alternative practices may be drawn upon in order to change inequalities. Ultimately, we are arguing for a social constructional and critical approach to forms of inequality. And while the objections raised here to direct or indirect biological and reductionist approaches are hardly limited to the feminist discourse, nor do we mean them to in any way lessen the fundamental seriousness with which the analysis of patriarchy, domestic labor, depth psychology is offered by feminists. Space limitations and the central project of trying to make sense of our direct ethnography dictate that our own theoretical treatment of gender, class, and race is at best superficial and at worst still guilty of the comma, comma, comma reductionism discussed above. Whether one agrees or challenges our approach, we believe that specification of our own assumptions about the constructional nature of social action is vital to understanding how we present action as fitting together.

Race as a Variable. Like gender, the study of the fundamental relationship of race and ethnicity to inequality, identity, status, and the operation of schools has advanced significantly in the past few years. Notably, it has become apparent that beyond the issues of cultural difference and pluralism, in particular situations relations of ethnicity are, as with gender, factors of inequality. Increasingly, the analysis of ethnicity and the relationships of ethnicity to power have come to focus on two related issues. How do dominant groups generate institutions and ideologies to perpetuate such inequalities; and, how does the integration of particular peoples as "ethnics" create forms of identification, state policy, and groupings that did not exist without the context of the unequal status of groups in the labor market, the values afforded their culture, language, and so on. In this respect, the ways that the discourse of "ethnicity" reflects indirect divisions have become an increasing avenue of study.

For example, the fact that peoples from as diverse languages, cultures, and customs as Indians, Chinese, Japanese, Koreans, and Vietnamese are summarily collapsed as "Asian" upon arriving in Canada says much about how the society regards them as outsiders as it does about any unique feature of the group. Similarly, decisions on when and where to offer cultural facilities such as so-called home or "heritage" languages show the relative positions of groups. So that when heritage language is placed as an "after-school" program in Ontario, it signals the value of the language as less (or different from) the regular curriculum.

Like the analysis of gender and class, recent work on race has taken up the analysis of official discourse and media representations and correlation of these with differences in status. For instance, those in economically and structurally subordinated sectors of the ethnic hierarchy are referred to as "minorities" while the ethnic minority groups that disproportionately control a society are referred to as "elites." The bureaucratic institutionalization of these distinctions, various theorists have argued, is more than nominal or coincidental but constitutes processing codes whose own labeling bears a tacit model of why groups are different.

Particularly, the isolation of minorities leads to a code of ritual segregation that leads to what Bernstein (1971) refers to as "compensatory approaches." One refers to the essence of these as "mug and jug" approaches. The underlying postulate is that if minorities "fail" in school or the job market, it is because they are deficient in some commodity: the use of English, motivation, vocational training, and so on. The typical corrective course is to compensate for these deficiencies by compensatory programs. We take from the jug and pour to the mug. Freire (1970) and Giroux (1983) argue in a similar analysis, that this constitutes a "banking" approach toward those deemed deficient.

There are a multiplicity of critiques of this approach. First and foremost is the fact that the compensatory model leaves invisible the structural relations of inequality of society itself, and that if particular groups are underemployed, it may have to do with structural relations and racism in the society and not just alleged individual and collective deficiencies. So-called helping programs, in this way, may become transformed to subtle, sometimes not so subtle, forms of "blaming the victim" and redirecting attention from structural inequalities. Second, compensatory approaches fail to recognize what are often cultural and stylistic differences in patterns of speech, interaction, and understandings of situation. As such, they are prone to substitute psychological explanations where technical ones are required.

Ethnicity and race, are, of course, also powerful centers of cultural and personal identifications of self and a focus for a collective understanding of one's history and a background to family life. In this regard, the relationship of the family, peers, and identity is itself a source of socialization even more influential in a child's development than school. Ethnicity, therefore, shapes much of the child's expectation in school and sets a frame by which schools as institutions and also teachers make sense and relate to their students. Ethnicity, in short, is a central focus for a child's identity, and how the relations of the way the cultural and institutional relations of the family mesh with language patterns, mores, and practice of the home has much to do with how well children will "fit" into particular schools (Bernstein, 1975). Again, ethnicity is a "site" or "habitus" for identity formation (Bourdieu & Passeron, 1977; Sullivan 1983b). The relations of its own structurization, how various groups have come to relate to schooling in their own biographies, or how individual school systems or teachers accommodate, ignore, or thwart these identities may have much to do with both how children relate in schools and how their own accomplishments are rewarded or underplayed.

In the analysis above we have been arguing for the logical separation of race, class, and gender, and the nonreducibility of one form of inequality to another. This separation, however, may be misleading. Race, gender, and class we are specifically arguing are not innately meaningful categories as such, but are made to be dramatically so by processes of social differentiation and inequality in particular histories. Life histories of individuals happen as wholes and not as categorically separate parts. One is never solely a "woman" or solely a "white," but is a constellation of these as fused moments of history. And while functionalist approaches have tended to use an added sum approach to the intersections of categorical property spaces (i.e., "this is the handiwork of white, male, middle-class Canadians) the concept of role artificially rigidifies the emergent complexity of how these become emphasized or submerged in action. This rather statically limited approach also negates by omission the possibilities of change and issues such as morality, the active relations of structured power inequalities, and the possibilities of transcendence (Connell, 1982).

Because the categories we are assessing are areas of contested meaning, in action their interactions also come to have particular status, forms, and identities specific to those combinations. Since these combinations are in practice little more than surrogates or glosses for analyzing the practical conditions people find themselves in, understanding these differences when they come to play as significant variables is also crucial. What is meant by "crucial" may only be reference to specific histories and, like much of ascriptive social science, is incessantly fettered with the nagging problems of the adequacy of interpretation. While this claim may seem abstract, in practical situations its relevance may range from the obvious to the subtle. Perhaps an example will help. Historically only men could vote in preconfederation Canada. Yet, at the same time in which Murray was Canada's first Governor General, black men could not vote (Murray was in fact a slave owner). In the British colonies to the south the situation was worse: only propertied white males could vote. No one factor could explain who had the vote: rich women and rich blacks—few though they were—could not vote. Neither could propertyless white males. The combination gave a relationship not specified fully by any of the parts. And while our example may seem far from the discussion of children using computers, we shall try to illustrate that how the subcultural practices, fashions, and relative status of various ethnic, class, and gender groupings combine with other factors, such as teacher and school support, will have much to do with the childrens' own perceived and real accomplishments on computers.

Selkirk Elementary School, the Model School: Description of the Setting

Selkirk Elementary School is a suburban school located at the northeast end of metropolitan Toronto. It is located in a neighborhood with large sprawling and expensive ranch-style houses. There is every indication that the majority of the children in this school are from well-to-do families. An example of this affluence is illustrated by a brief conversation of two boys on the stairway when the investigators first entered the school. As the boys passed two OISE (Ontario Institute for Studies in Education) researchers on the stairs, one was commenting to the other, "Hey, guess what! I bought a forty-dollar sweater this weekend. Was it okay!" They quickly moved out of earshot. The children in this school, with rare exceptions, were stylishly dressed and very fashion-conscious. When we first met the principal of the school in the teachers' room, he indicated to us that these children come from families whose parents work as dentists, accountants, lawyers, business executives, and so on. He characterized these parents as being "demanding, interested, intelligent, worried and assertive." This school community is about 60 percent Jewish, but it also has a small but steady migrant Japanese community. To explain this migrant phenomenon, some commercial Japanese companies rent units in nearby townhouses, where they house some of their managers and families, for periods of three and four years. These families return to Japan, and are then replaced by new ones; this, then, is an ongoing process. One Indian girl and one black boy attend this school as well. Thus, in this school, the only minority really visible in number are the Japanese students.

The physical location of the Selkirk Elementary School is a residential street completely away from any commercial enterprises. The school itself is a two-story building, small, plain, and artless on the outside. The interior is not much different, with the exception of children's drawings and school work on the walls. It is a small school, having approximately 150 pupils. It has grades kindergarten through sixth. There are double grades, such as grades three and four in one room, and a small accelerated class. The computer lab is the newly added feature to this school's existing program. This year, Selkirk School was designated a model school for computers in the Toronto school system. There is only one other with a designation similar to this one in the Toronto Board of Education.

The description that follows is an attempt to characterize a day at Selkirk School, looking at the way computers are being utilized in both the lab and the individual class. Since a class is divided each time for lab purposes, half of a class stays in homeroom, and the other half goes to the computer lab. The observations that will be described were taken from authentic class episodes of the fifth grade class. They were taken at the latter part of the school year in order to be able to show some of the skills that had developed since the beginning of the year (observation dates were March 25 and May 2, 1984). The observations described cover both computer use in the homeroom class (children who do not go to the lab) and the computer use of the children in the lab proper. We have chosen the fifth grade class because the fifth grade teacher (Bob Pluster) uses the computer in his homeroom routinely, whereas the sixth grade teacher (Derek Brown) does not. The description is, in one sense, constructed, since the lab descriptions and the homeroom class observations do not occur on the same day, but in close time proximity to one another. Unfortunately, we did not have an opportunity to observe both lab and homeroom situations simultaneously. Nevertheless, we are assuming that our constructed description typifies a normal morning of computer use for this fifth grade class, in both the homeroom and the lab.

The Homeroom. The grade five students enter the grade five class. They proceed to group themselves around five large tables. Bob Pluster proceeds to take the class roll very promptly, and when this is completed he says, "I guess this is group two's day to go to the computer lab." When he says this, a group of twelve children get up, walk out of the room, and proceed to the computer lab next door.

Today there is one Commodore Pet that is at the side of the room, to Pluster's left. He says, "Frank and Lisa on the machine." A boy and a girl proceed to the Pet. Having done this, he starts to give other assignments to the rest of the class, who are not using computers. Some get spelling work at the blackboard and others are given math work at their seats. The division of labor within the class seems to be an orderly and well worked-out procedure.

The two children who have gone to the computer have a game of fraction estimations, which was put there at the beginning of the class, by the teacher. They seem to have difficulty starting on their own, and proceed on a trial and error basis. The teacher now goes over to the children at the computer and asks them a question to get them started:

"How do you write a fraction line?"

The boy says, "I don't know."

The teacher asks, "Did you follow the instructions?"

"Yes," says the boy and the teacher says, "OK, try using the slash to make fractions."

The teacher then says to the two children, by way of preparation, "We have been working on equivalent fractions for the last while." He says this to remind them what is likely to be at issue with the computer task that they are working on. He then reviews a lesson where they use mental calculation to estimate fractions. The estimate line is vertical and the teacher shows the children at the computer by a question and a prompt: "You will have to, in this problem, get a fraction between 2/5 and 2/6." He then proceeds to give them a lesson on fraction estimates at the blackboard. To do this, he goes through the process of making a common denominator. He does an example and comes up with a fraction of 11/30, and he tells the two children to try that estimate on the computer. They try it and it works. The teacher, looking satisfied, says to them, "Now you are on your own," and leaves these children to themselves as he moves to another part of the class.[2]

---

[2]As it turns out, this teacher has been dealing with functions by having the children learn a procedure called estimation. Here the computer is being used as an adjunct to this set of lessons.

The two children then proceed in a manner that appears random, and therefore it seems that they are only guessing. For example, they start with an estimate of 2/5, which is close to the desired estimate, and then they jump to 2/9, applying no apparent logic. They do this for a while, and then the boy, frustrated, says to the girl, "I quit, this is too hard." The teacher then comes over and asks what the matter is, and the children say they don't know what they are doing. He invites them over to the blackboard and starts to go over a lesson that he did in class on common denominators. This lasts approximately five minutes and when the teacher thinks they have grasped the concept, he sends them back to the computer.

As it turns out, each pair of children receive approximately fifteen minutes on the computer. Thus, the children who just had the lesson don't go back to the computer, for the teacher calls two other children because it is their turn. Of this new pair, one of the boys catches on quickly, but, as I note later on, it seems that all the children have their own particular style. This second pair of children behave quite like the first pair; it seems that the instructions with this program are absent.

The computer feedback has some aspects that are interesting. For example, to a girl who just made a correct answer, the following response is given: "YOU GET A CIGAR." In another case, after several random attempts by one girl, the following feedback was elicited: "MAY I RECOMMEND A PSYCHIA-TRIST?"

It is clear that when the teacher is in close proximity to the students, some of these children are able to start working the program. Here, however, the teacher's accessibility is limited, given his other responsibilities in class. And furthermore, it happens that he has no backup in the form of adequate instructions to accompany the program.

When the other half of Pluster's fifth grade class comes back to homeroom (not without noise or interruption), he initiates a blackboard lesson on equivalent fractions, with the whole class. At the end of the lesson, he says to me that this is necessary in order for the children to make better use of the computer. He, therefore, felt that the children on the computer needed more math instruction before they could profit from the Pet computer program.

The Lab. The half of Pluster's fifth grade class assigned to the computer lab this morning comes into the lab and gathers on the rug in front of the teacher. They are scuffling and making noise at a moderate level and Liz Blair, the computer lab teacher, says, "When you're ready . . ."; the implication is clear by their behavior that they are not ready, and this statement is designed to bring them into tow. As one looks around the room, there are six Icons, eight Apples, and three Pets. The three Pets are not plugged in, which is what has been observed during other lab visits. The Icons have been out of use previously, too, but today they are ready to go.[3] Although they have a plethora of uses, they will be used for the Logo program, which will be described shortly.

The teacher announces to some children that they may go over to the Icon and she states, "You can gain access to the Icon by using your name." (The name is stored in the Icon's memory.) There are a couple of children talking in low voices. The teacher stops and makes the remark: "Are you going to interrupt constantly? If you are, I would like to see you outside." The boy to whom she was speaking says, "No." She continues, "I would like you all today to test your log-in names to be sure they work. (This is only for the Icons.) Some of you will be working on the Icons, and others on the Apples. By the end of today, save your procedures and move it to this machine over here (she points) and print it. The procedure is to be between two different shapes and moving from one shape to another."

To facilitate the reader's understanding of a Logo task, this program will be briefly described. Logo is a procedural language specifically designed for children's education. Logo programs are created by combining commands into groups called procedures; these procedures are then used as steps in other procedures, and so on, to arbitrary levels of complexity. Each individual step of a Logo procedure may be any primitive Logo command, or any user-defined procedure. Procedures are able to communicate among themselves, via outputs and inputs. An example of a Logo procedure is one of the given Logo assignments for today. These children have been working on the Logo program for the past two months because the Icon has often not been working properly. When the students first began to use the Logo program, Blair let them explore its possibilities on their own. Now, according to her, she sends them to do this program with worksheet assignments. This is because she has more specific expectations regarding this language than she had before.

Let us return, once again, to the task of observing. One of the students now says to Blair, after being told to log in, that he did not save his work from yesterday.[4] The teacher says, "That's no problem for today's assignment." She then says to all the children, "Let's review the differences between Apple Logo and Icon Logo." Since all of the children use both of the machines on a rotary basis, she attempts to eliminate confusion. With some initial confusion, the children seem to gain more clarity with respect to some of the differences in commands between the Apple and the Icon.

At this point, Blair proceeds with the Logo assignment, and begins to explain what they are supposed to be doing today. She gives the assignment quite clearly,

---

[3]The Icon is a computer that was specifically designed for classroom use, through the initiation of the Ministry of Education of Ontario. The Apples and Pets are commercially bought computers.
[4]The children work cumulatively with this program and they are expected to store their work in their own file.

with a very definite expectation that this is their job for the morning. Their task, then, is to write a procedure in Logo, and then save the procedure. The procedure is the following: "Draw a geometric shape and then move to another part of the screen, then draw a different geometric shape, and then stop."

The choices which are given to the children are (a) the type of geometric shape they wish to draw; (b) the manner in which they want to move; and (c) the way in which they want to do the procedure. But, given this leeway, the expectation is that each student will do the same task.

The teacher now intends to send the children off to the machines. Thus, she says to them, "You can work by yourselves or together, whichever you have been doing before today." She points to the children and says when they can get up and go to their machines. Today, the children seem to be able to choose whatever machine they want. Interestingly, most of the children go immediately to the Icons. We say this because we feel it is useful to note selective preferences that children make on the use of computer hardware.

Focusing, for the moment, on one pair of boys who are working side by side with two Icons, in starting their Logo program together, one boy follows the exact procedures of the other boy. Boy A is copying Boy B, command by command. Boy A puts in the command "Forward 16"; Boy B then puts in the same command. Their designs thus turn out to be exact replicas. The first boy then turns around and says to the rest of the class, "Look, Stan is copying me." At the same time, he did not seem to be bothered by this classmate copying his work; it seemed that he just wanted all to know that this was his work.

Now looking across the room at the Apples, one boy is sitting by an Apple, probably working a Logo program. Suddenly he exclaims, to no one in particular and everyone in general, "How big is the box supposed to be? What are we supposed to do? What are we supposed to do for Christ's sake?" The teacher does not respond. He then stares, and sits, and stares, for quite a long time. Finally, he goes back to work. He looks at his procedure sheet. This boy appears to know Basic,[5] and he has become confused because Logo is not programmed in line numbers. He has a procedure named "Box," but it doesn't work, despite trying a few times. He gets an "error" feedback, which tells him what his problem is, but he takes no notice. Again, he starts to exclaim to no one in particular and everyone in general, "What are we supposed to do? Hey, what are we supposed to do?"

A Japanese girl, sitting near him, comes over and says to him, "You're supposed to draw two shapes, one on either side of the screen, and all in one

---

[5]A computer language built into many computers that can be bypassed with another language (e.g., Logo) by the use of a software program. Logo, as opposed to Basic, is a computer language designed for children.

procedure." To illustrate, she points to her screen. Displayed on her screen, in two different parts of it, are a hexagon and a square.

He pays no attention to this information, and says again, "What are you supposed to do?" A boy sitting on the other side of him explains again; his explanation is similar to the girl's description. This same boy has now received the instructions three times. Still, he sits and says yet again, "I don't understand. What are we supposed to do?"

Another boy is struggling with his Logo shape and nothing seems to be working properly for him. He keeps getting feedback that says, "THERE IS NO PROCEDURE NAMED. THERE IS NO PROCEDURE NAMED." His first problem is that he has the "caps lock" off.[6] Since the teacher is busy at the other side of the room, one of the members of our study team, who sees the small snag, tells the boy why he is having difficulty. This student, however, continued to have problems because he typed a square bracket with the "Caps Lock" off, which looked fine on the screen, but the computer did not take this command. He continued to make little progress.

Now we turn our attention to two Japanese girls who have finished their procedures. They are working together, more or less, side by side, on separate computers. Their work is not exactly the same; that is, each girl has different shapes and their procedures are a little different. One of the girls is finished completely. She then starts to command the computer to run the procedure, by typing in the command "Shapes." The procedure proceeds to work like a charm. Thus, she draws a square on one part of the screen, and then the "Turtle" moves across the screen, without leaving a track. In this part of the screen, she draws a hexagon and then stops. Appearing to be very pleased, she turns to her friend and says, "Look, it works!" The other girl is now trying hers, with different shapes. It works too. She then says to her classmate, who completed her assignment first, "How do I save?" The girl who had finished first then came over to the girl requesting help, and told her what to type on her computer. She then stood aside and let her classmate do it herself. She did not do what many other children did in this situation; that is, she did not move in and take over the keyboarding (i.e., jump onto the computer keyboard and type rather than suggest to the other student what she must keyboard to succeed). The computer, however, did not cooperate. A message appeared, "DISK ERROR." The guide or helper student did not seem perplexed by this, but pointed out to her friend, "Oh, you don't have the disk in." The girl who was trying to "save," in a panicky voice, said, "Oh, did I erase Shapes?" The helper said, "Ask Mrs. Blair." The potential "saver" says, "I'll go and get my disk, and then I'll try again." This time, all

---

[6]A computer command "caps lock" is designed for another computer manipulation. Here, it must be disengaged for the children to proceed with this specific program.

works well. She types "Save," the name of her procedure, and smiles as the disk light goes on.

The student helper says, "OK, then check it. Type 'READ SPACE QUOTE SHAPES.' " "OK," says the "saver." She does the command and the components of this procedure are defined on the screen. Both are very pleased. They smile at each other and look fondly at the computer.

Now these same girls attempt to work on the next step. They are trying to work out how to save a picture, quite separately from the "Save" command. The teacher has already given the procedures for "Save" and "Save Pict," and has written the review of it on a sheet. They remember most of it, but not all. They are trying to work this out through their discussion. They are talking to each other about how to save a picture. Each one has some information. They take turns making suggestions and listening to each other and trying to arrive at a solution. Their thinking and their problem-solving of this task are quite impressive. However, they do not arrive at a satisfactory solution. One of them goes to get the teacher, who comes over right away. She then proceeds to explain the instructions in an exacting manner, and, in so doing, she clarifies what they have been confused about. In their case, then, they seemed to be confused about what the difference was between saving a picture and the computer command "Save."

Moving back again to the boy who seemed stuck and kept saying, "What am I supposed to do," one notes that he never specifically asks the teacher for help. He still sits fiddling at the computer, swearing under, and slightly above, his breath. In watching him, you get the impression that he has no real expectation that he is ever going to know what to do. He continues to sit and accomplish nothing of the task.

Returning to the computers where the Japanese girls are located, one notes that they have completed their full procedure. Now they are taking their disk over to the Apple computer that is connected to the printer. They encounter difficulty and they appear mixed up about how to get the printer to print the Logo figures. After floundering for a short time, one of the girls goes over to enlist the aid of their teacher. Blair comes over, looks up on the wall, and then asks them, "Did you follow the steps outlined in the chart on the wall?" One of the girls says, "Not completely, Mrs. Blair."

The teacher tells them to follow them exactly, and she stays with them until they are halfway through the steps. As was indicated earlier, with respect to Pluster's class, giving so much time to these girls is difficult because Blair, too, has so many other responsibilities in the orderly running of her class. At this point, the class ends.

What is clear from the above descriptions is the variation between students in terms of motivation and competence. To be sure, later observations, taken at the end of the school term, will show that some of the children become very competent using the Logo program.

Danberry Elementary School, Rural: Description of the Setting

Danberry is a consolidated public elementary school located in a town of several thousand in a rural area of Ontario. The school is housed in a modern red brick structure juxtaposed to a wooded area. The school was built in the 1960s as part of a program to consolidate "one-room" schools. This shift is reflected in the school's human resources as well; the principal and staff see themselves and are very much a part of contemporary education.

In its work the staff services a range of clientele in terms of their home backgrounds. Demographically, the school services both the town in which it is located and also the outlying agricultural and forested areas. The student population is divided relatively equally between town and surrounding area. This diversity is extended to the range of socioeconomic backgrounds from which the school draws. These predictably reflect the range of employment opportunities accessible to the community. This latter fact of access to urban economic diversification is in part a feature that distinguishes the rural school we observed from some other rural settings.

The town itself is located within 80 miles of a metropolitan service center and is within easy drive of a university community. The target population the school draws from has a distribution that is more cosmopolitan and contains a higher proportion of professionals than is often found in more isolated rural areas. Commuters and professionals are very much a part of the community's mix, as are those in agricultural occupations and those with rural service functions. The town also harbors a variety of persons who value the juncture of the arts and rural life. The community, while rural, is no backwater outpost. It is a mix of classical rural and contemporary-minded individuals who are striving to revive rural values.

Closer examination reveals that the community is not fully cloistered. The surrounding landscape is marked by light manufacturing plants and residents are within easy commuting distance of authentically heavy industrial plants. One of Ontario's major highways is within several miles of the school and truck drivers and mechanics are part of the cohort of parents. Within commuting distance of the community are prisons and other institutions. Modern industrial life is very much at hand for those who look. This is a place where wood, conservation areas, a country boutique, the local little league and school hockey blend with old stone buildings and a potters' kiln to produce a slower, agrarian pace. This is not the hustle or bustle of suburban Ontario. This is the heartland stock of rural Ontario.

Danberry School has a diversity of economic means that segregates the home realities of its students; but there are also factors that unify them. Ethnically, for example, the school is quite homogeneously Anglo-Saxon with a mix of East Europeans, Germans, and others. One finds the occasional Chinese or Pakistani, or black, but overwhelmingly the town and school are white. The emphasis by school and community alike is put on the uniqueness of the community as a "liveable" place of neighbors who get on and are not as divided as found in the social problems of cities. Hence, while class is a de facto division in the school, it is not a source of resistance or open conflict. Largely, it is invisible to most of its school's participants. "Local" issues, or comparisons such as those of "our" school with the local separate schools are more likely to pervade ratepayers' minds than are their relations to other status groups. The economic realities are one of diversity, while the interactional temperament is one of unity.

Many schools, including ours, are organized around time organizational modules that are absolutely obvious to those who work in schools and completely foreign to those who don't. Educationalist Edgar Z. Freidenberg captures this relationship nicely by observing that schools do not work on "clock" time. Neither do they follow the regular calendar organization. Instead, the school's work flow is organized around a rotary period structure, which is organized around "days." Days range from 1 to 5, but not from Monday to Friday. This is because schools are places of incessant interruptions; there are professional development days, numerous holidays, and the like. This is important because Jack[7] teaches computers during selected periods on particular days of the week. One needs, however, to consult one's score card to tell which day of the week this will be.

During these days Jack will typically have a class during a period change marked by the obligatory bell ringing.[8] When the children are assigned to groups to go to the library, this is the point where some of a small group of them will go off to the computer room. The first class we will describe today begins at 12:45 p.m. The class is a mixture of grade five and six levels. One or two of the children are school grade repeaters so that some of those in the same grade may be one year apart. The children are talking as they sit, but the librarian signals for silence and begins to list a compendium of those children with overdue books. One or two try to make excuses for this low-level life of crime, but the librarian lectures them on the virtues of punctual book return. The students in the class are to receive a somewhat didactic lesson on Canada's role in the great wars and why people may be trying to sell them poppies. Jack enters to retrieve those who are supposed to receive computer instruction. The librarian, in a public voice, recites the offences against punctual return, carried out by class members, and laments the state of studentdom. Jack looks sympathetic and half

---

[7]This is the teacher assigned to computer coordination at Danberry.

[8]It should be noted here that computer usage is assigned to a very small room in the school where all of the hardware is located. Jack is in charge of this room.

smiling, shakes his head. The students are noticeably more attentive to Jack. "Did you people do that? I don't know, I'm sure you people know better than that and won't do it again." Jack then takes seven children with him to the computer room. Previously, he had turned on the machines and loaded the disk drives.

The children take a couple of minutes to settle in. One boy, Shawn, sits at the end of the computer near the door to the library. The seat next to him is vacant. Down this row, two girls, Annette and Marie, who seem to be friendly, sit next to each other. Annette is dressed in a navy dress like those worn in older days. Next to them is Donny, who is attired in jeans, and a black and red sweatshirt; he is wearing an arm bracelet. He is physically big and fairly loud. Next to him is Paul, a friend. At the desk next to the printer and opposite the door to the corridor is Jimmy, a friend of Donny and Paul. Around the corner, at the computer next to the board and facing away from the other computers is Fred, a close friend of Donny and Paul, and more verbal than Jimmy. Donny is clearly the male leader of this group.

The time is now 12:57. Shawn asks, "Do we have to do this? I hate this. I can't do this and I hate it." Jack looks at him and with a quiet but sympathetically firm voice says, "Sit down, Shawn, you'll be able to do this." Jack begins by telling them that today he is going to start to teach them about how the computer can be used for wordprocessing. He asks if any of them ever write stories.

Fred asks, "What do we have to write about?" Jack replies, "You can write about what you want; maybe a teacher has given you an assignment and you have to do it. If you use the computer you can just go ahead and write it and change it later. You don't have to worry about spelling or mistakes because you can correct them later." Marie looks slightly incredulous and says, "We don't have to spell right?" Jack replies, smiling, "Well, yes, but it's easier, because you can concentrate on your ideas and correct the paper later, or you can print the story, or save it on a disk." Marie excitedly says, "We can print it!" Jack replies, "Yes you can, and if you get cleared to use the machine you can come in here and you are welcome to sign up to use the machines to work on your assignments."

For some children in this class this is their first attempt at computer use. Jack then asks, "Do you people know how to load your drives?" Several tentatively reply, ". . . sort of . . . " and remind Jack that they had two lessons last year. Jack replies, "OK, we'd better review some things." Jack holds up a floppy disk. He asks, "What's this?" A chorus of " . . . a disk . . . " comes back. Jack acknowledges this and begins a standard lecture: "This is a floppy disk; when it's blank, it's worth maybe two dollars, but when it's loaded with special programs it may be worth a couple of hundred dollars." Jack then goes on to explain a list of potential dangers to touching disks, trying to take disks out of drives when the red light is on, and other potential sources of machine failure. Jack has the children load the disks, and turn machines on and off; he circulates as he observes their activities.

The lesson progresses. Briefly, he reminds the children of the various functions of the Commodore keys and reviews what a wordprocessing system can do. Jack begins to tell the children again about what they can do with wordprocessors. Next, he reviews what types of stories they might want to write. All this takes him until well past 1:15. Based on Jack's suggestions, the children begin to write stories as Jack circulates to help individual children. Several of the children occasionally talk to one another or ask for help. Sometimes one child will reach over and operate another's keys to show him how to operate a particular function. Occasionally, they will read another's story and copy from it or ridicule it. The boys tend to be more boisterous than the girls, except that Marie laughs a lot.

The children slowly complete a series of short stories of about a paragraph in length. Only Jimmy's is longer. After about five minutes of writing, Jack tells them to "wrap it up" so that they can save and print the stories. Jack begins to help various children print their stories. The children get up as this is being done and roam around reading each other's stories with occasional sarcastic criticism or occasional admiration, at what others have thought up. During the printing process, Jack repeatedly asks whose disk is hooked to the printer and also tries to encourage the children in their writing efforts. He reminds them that they are welcome to use the machines when they are cleared if they sign up first. The children seem genuinely excited about getting hard copy of their work, but neither Jimmy nor Shawn wants his printout.

The printout procedure goes on past the time when the bell for the next period rings. In the corridor there is a mild pandemonium that breaks loose as classes change. One boy comes in and exchanges handshakes with Donny in the fashion of urban ghetto gangs. Outside, there are several children waiting. They are waiting to use the computers for the "free" period.

The decision to have Jack teach children in *all* classes was intended to ensure that each student would have a minimal level of exposure to the machine that could then be carried to further levels of expertise by individual students, or in other classes by the regular classroom teacher, or in specialized enriched classes, or outside the regular school structure. This decision had a number of developmental consequences. First, the teaching load, as previously discussed, is mainly borne by Jack. If, as is the case, Jack has eight classes to teach, which must be partitioned into four to five groups, each of which must be given three to six lessons, the amount of attention he can give to each individual is correspondingly limited. Because groups are fractured in this way, the "developmental cycle" that progresses through the year in a regular curricular program is considerably shorter in practice than would be found if computers were a regular, structurally integrated part of the curriculum.

How much students know about computers, how they use them, and where and when such usage takes place is far more dependent in Danberry on extra-curricular circumstances than in some other schools. This relatively short and irregular pattern of computer instruction to any one *individual* student is further exacerbated by the relative nonuse of computers for curricular goals by other teachers.

Conclusion

We have given the reader a flavor of two of the schools that we observed. It is hoped that the reader gets a flavor of the class and gender issues that we have already indicated earlier. The importance of the ethnographic work is that it shows a concrete context wherein these dimensions operate. In addition, the ethnographic work tempers ideological speculations on how such dimensions interact. Although these schools differ markedly as regards computer usage, it nevertheless should be pointed out that the computer in all the schools we observed (including the model schools) is not in the forefront of the average teacher's planning. The computer valuation, at this point, is a valuation in the minds of the corporate and entrepreneurial sectors as a marketing penetration. When this so-called revolution reaches the school, it appears to hit the will of one of the most traditional cultural instruments in all cultures; that is, the school:

> the strategies commonly used by promoters of changes whether they be legislators, administrators, or other teachers, frequently do not work because they are derived from a world or from premises different from the teachers? (Fullan, 1982, p. 115)

In an affluent country such as Canada, one is not on "thin ice" when one conjectures that computer technologies exist, at this point, on the periphery of the school system. From our extensive observations, we see no computer revolution. What we do see is a slowly incremental use of the computer in various ways in the school culture. It is used, in most cases, by a minority of a school's personnel.

EXAMPLE 2: A CRITICAL PEDAGOGY OF MORAL ACTION: TELEVISION AND CULTURAL VALUES[9]

If you ask the average teacher who he or she competes with for the minds and hearts of children (as far as education is concerned), it is not surprising to

[9]Portions of this section are taken from my article on the mass media from the *Critical Pedagogy Reader* edited by David Livingstone with permission of Bergin & Garvey Publishers.

have the answer given: the television. This would not be said of the radio sixty years ago, which prompts a second question: "Why this difference between media?" One tentative answer is that western culture has increasingly come under the influence of commercial interests outside both home and school, and here one observes that both parents and teachers compete with a new constellation of socialization agents in mass media personalities. The transmission of culture through socialization agents is a relational activity where the new generation comes into contact with the older generation's cultural myths, values, and so on. The process is a dynamic interchange and in a sense there can be a reciprocity of roles between the generations. The older generation generally attempts to replicate itself (that is, social formation or socialization) and the newer generation tends to force changes in predominant cultural images (that is, transformation or social change). This process is dialectical and it should not be surprising that the values change. It is safe to say that, in general, the older generation tends to consciously or unconsciously replicate or reproduce some of its dominant accepted myths. The "cultural myths" are the predominant cultural images by which a culture represents itself (Sullivan, 1980).

Culture is mediated; that is, its symbols and images are passed on by institutions. Obviously, the most important mediating institution in the socialization of children was the family structure. In simpler cultures, it has been historically the only mediating device for cultural transmission. The second major mediating institution has been the school. Before the advent of the modern era, schools and family were the two *main* cultural mediators; that is, they carried or mediated the cultural messages to the younger generation. As already indicated, the twentieth century has seen a complete reversal of this process. In our own time, the family has been devastated as a cultural mediating device. Parents essentially relinquish this role to the schools where possible. This cultural transformation is quite complex and I cannot deal with this dramatic change for our present purposes. What I would like to call your attention to is the advent of a new major mediating device for socialization in the twentieth century, that of the "mass media" of communications. We will be focusing upon it here because it carries, in an unequivocal manner, the message of the central myths of "commodity culture." The "mass media" (that is, newsprint, comics, radio, and television), when compared with parents and schools, are more anonymous and more democratic at the same time. As opposed to parents who concentrate their efforts on their own children and possibly their neighbors', mass media are directed to a wider range of people (that is, masses) but with patently more utilitarian motives. In essence, the "mass media" are supported by modern advertising whose main message is to sell products as commodities to people on a large scale (mass production and mass consumption). It can be seen in some of the early advertising journals that the "mass media" were in conflict with the family. The advertising business both welcomed the demise of familial authority and, at the same time, was careful not to demystify all authority:

> Rather it pointed toward the commodity market and its propaganda to replace the father's authority. Business was to provide the source of a lifestyle, where before the father had been the dictator of family spirit. (Ewen, 1976, pp. 131–132)

The decline of direct parental authority can be seen in all of Disney's comics, where there is a total absence of parental figures which, rather interestingly, goes unnoticed (Dorfman & Mattelhart, 1975).

This section will consciously concentrate on the television as a moral educator. Here we will consider the medium of television as a powerful device for cultural transmission. Nevertheless, the average person takes this medium for granted. It is a household expense like a car or a toilet. Yet it is much more important as a moral influence than we care to think because it is a symbol-making medium. As a symbol-making cultural invention, one should not be so snobbish as to discount its influence.

Media and the Moral Act

To speak of the mass media as moral educators is to indicate that a particular type of communication system has the capacity to influence moral actions. To talk of a moral act being influenced, it is necessary to clarify the nature of that act being influenced. I have indicated in Chapter 2 that the defining characteristic of a *human act* has the features of consciousness, intentionality, intention, responsibility, and significance. For my purposes here, I would like to amplify the last two features since they define human action as at once moral and communicative. Responsibility is one characteristic of a "human act" insofar as one is accounting for the actions of a person in terms of her or his desires, intentions, and purposes. This in humans, of necessity, involves the negative pole of action, that is, reflection. "Responsible action" has, therefore, as part of its ongoing process, a reflective component, which in ordinary language we call "deliberation." It follows that a fundamental condition of education is the fostering of moral conduct, which by my definition is responsible action. The attribution of responsibility for an action is canceled out altogether if it can be shown that the behavior conceived was not governed, at least in some of its aspects, by intentions (Taylor, 1964). The "deliberation" involved in the "reflective" component of human action opens up the question of the autonomy or freedom of human action. The notion of a "deliberate action" assumes that after the process of "deliberation" there is a motive force that carries that action to some outcome or completion. Education is, in the best sense, the cultivation of responsible moral agency. One ventures that education in goodness must mean education in value-realization and that authentic moral education must involve the removal of all *inertial obstacles* that tend to block or deflect the positive direction of moral action. One of the issues that we must face here is whether mass media communications systems foster responsible moral action (i.e., are educational) or are *inertial obstacles* (i.e., miseducational) in relation to responsible human action. Before going into this issue, let me turn to the feature of the "human act" as *significant*.

As already indicated, I develop the notion that a "human act" has a *sign* quality that makes it simultaneously an *act* and *an expression*. Therefore, the sign quality of "human act" puts it in the category of a *communicative event*. A "human act" is not an isolated event, but rather, relational. Therefore, there is no such thing as a significant act in itself. The meaning or significance of a human act is the place that it occupies in a network of relationships (Chein, 1972). I assume, after Geertz (1973), that significant human action is cultural action:

> man is an animal suspended in webs of significance he himself spun, I take culture
> to be those webs. (p. 5)

This notion of "cultural action" will take on a deeper meaning later when we consider Freire's notion of "cultural action for freedom" (1974). What is important now is to establish in the mind of the reader that "moral conduct" or "responsible action" exists within the framework of *communications*. My task will be to assess how mass communications influence moral actions.

Mirroring: The Possibility That We Become What We Behold

It is often said that morality is fostered by *good example*. It is also said that "evil" is fostered by *bad example*. There is an intuition here that we are strongly influenced by the company we keep. There is also interjected into this discourse the idea that individuals can rise above their surroundings. This is usually said to someone who cannot avoid bad company, as it were. What is implicit in all of this is the belief that a moral point of view, or lack thereof, is mediated through social influences. Nothing astounding here, except we tend to forget the effects of normative influence. In some families, one of these influences is the television, which will interact more with the children than with their parents (Sullivan, 1980a). Although the school still plays a significant role in the legitimation of culture, it now has a contender in the medium of television. For example, before a child reaches the age of 20 in America, she or he will have seen 350,000 television commercials. The average American child, it is estimated, will have seen 18,000 commercial messages each year or over three hours of television advertising a week (Sullivan, 1980a). One might say that children keep a good deal of company with the ethos of consumption. The television is a mirror of commodity culture (Sullivan, 1980a).

In order to consider the effects of social influences on moral character, one must not fall into the trap of thinking that those being socialized (children) are *passive* and those socializing (parents) are *active*. It is a mixture of both as any parent will attest. What is important to consider from the side of the cultural socialization agents such as parents, teachers, and mass media personnel, is the extent to which they encourage a *sense of agency* in those whom they would try to influence. We should, therefore, judge socialization agents such as parents, schools, and mass media, on their power to influence or detract from the development of moral agency (i.e., capacity for responsible action). It can be said in some instances that parents and schools are frequently impediments to the fostering or impeding of moral agency. The notion of mirror is helpful here because it introduces the idea of images and imaging, which I will pursue in more detail in my treatment of the television medium and its influence as a moral educator or miseducator.

A mirror is a *reflector*. It can give us images of ourselves and our surroundings. When you look in the mirror, you are not seeing you but an image or reflection of you. Depending on the qualities of the mirror, you may appear fatter, thinner, taller, or smaller. You may be flattered or miffed. This "image" may start you on a regimen of eating or not eating. The reflector thus can encourage or discourage certain types of action. Thus, socialization agents are reflectors or mirrors of cultural codes. One part of a cultural code is its *moral code*, which gives signals that actions are good or bad, worthy or unworthy, and so forth. As I said earlier, human action is embedded in *webs of significance*, part of that web being a cultured moral code. Television as it has developed in North America does reflect a moral code, where *consumption* is the major cultural action fostered for the attainment of the good life.

Television as a technological device has been around since 1925. It was not until the 1940s, however, that the advertising industry saw the commercial possibilities that this medium offered (Mander, 1978). Mander goes so far as to say that television is the invention of modern advertising. Of all media mentioned, it is the most active in the creation of "images" while reducing its watchers to a relative state of passivity (Sullivan, 1980a). For example, in radio you must create your own images since only the audio is supplied. Television does both. The television, which works best in a dark room with a viewer sitting, aids in the achievement of a passive state. From there, Mander points out that:

> Every advertiser, for example, knows that before you can convince anyone of anything you shatter their existing mental set and then restructure an awareness along lines which are useful to you. You do this with a few simple techniques like fast-moving images, jumping among attention focuses, and switching moods. There's nothing to it. (p. 197)

The "socially constructed" nature of television makes it more of a "private event" even though the viewer-listener is receiving communications. A morally responsible actor is not a "private actor." As I have already said, a "human act" is an "expression" that has as one of its distinguishing characteristics "significance." Significance implies that moral action has a public nature. It is a premise of commercial television that the viewer is a "consumer" rather than an actor. A responsible actor deliberates. Reflection, however, is the enemy of commercial interests. Modern advertising is designed to short-circuit *reflection* and *deliberation*, because your judgment may arrive at a conclusion different from the product being advertised. There are some research indications that television viewings tend to disengage analytical thinking (Nelson, 1980). This finding does not mean that it is impossible to be analytical while viewing, but it is not a normal outcome of conventional viewing.

> Thus, as viewers, it is possible to watch television in an analytical-critical frame of mind: noticing specific camera angles, camera distances, sound-image and relationships, the use of moving camera, etc., and determining the extent to which such techniques constitute its over-all meaning. This kind of attentive viewing engages both hemispheres rather than putting one on "hold" [the left]. Yet the typical viewing situation is one which discourages this kind of critical attentiveness. (Nelson, 1980, p. 30)

TV and the Decline of Public Life

Moreover, the advent of commercial television as a cultural institution follows a steady development that can be characterized as a decline in "public life." This decline has been building up since the 19th century (Sullivan, 1983a). The paradox here is that the decline in public presence is synonymous with the steady advance of communications technologies which have reached revolutionary proportions in the present. In post–World War II history, what has increasingly occurred since 1945 is the indirect mediation of significant events through the new technologies provided by our mass media of communication systems (radio, TV, newspapers, etc.). Without other forms of public expression, these vicariate events become our public rituals. We depend on them as a means of communication with a wider world than our own immediate surroundings. The turning point for this was the assassination of President Kennedy in 1963 (Sullivan, 1980b). Television was the focal point for a national ritual. It has increasingly taken on this role since that time. With satellite communications, probably more people witnessed the British royal wedding of Charles and Diana than any other event in the history of the human race.

We are now in the midst of what is being called a "communications revolution." It is a revolution because we are said to be moving, in a rather dramatic fashion, from an industrial society to a communications society. There are some indications that something of the nature of a "cultural revolution" is taking place. It must be admitted that increasingly our way of life and our cultural interests are being molded by the new communications technologies. It is no exaggeration to suggest that most North Americans, at least, wake up to early morning programing via TV, commute in a car where a radio gives them traffic reports, news and financial information, and so on. Some members will watch children's programing, soap operas, game shows, health and beauty programs, exercise programs, and the like during day-time programing. In the early evening some will watch the evening news, more will congregate to watch some of the new soaps, such as Dallas or a TV detective-crime program. Some of the less socially sensitive members of the family will tune out from the spuriously public event of night-time TV watching and tune into another world offered by the Sony Walkman. Others will read the newspapers of their choice. Some will leave the room and go to their new pocket computer where they will engage in some of the many versions of Pac-Man or one of its competitors. What I want the reader to be sensitized to, by my examples, is the preemptive dependence that our culture is developing on the technologies of modern communications. It is likely, in a typical North American family, that each individual in that family will have been spoken to by TV figures more than they have been spoken to by one another.

Moreover, what is interesting and important to note about these mass media communications technologies (i.e., radio, TV, newspapers, etc.) is that the programs of these media, and the commercial interests that sponsor them, proceed on the assumption that there is a public to be formed (i.e., passive public) to certain commercial and consumption values. Kavanaugh (1981) refers to these values as the "commodity form." What is very evident in conventional "commercial programing" of whatever variety, be it news, soap, game shows, and so on, is that there is no expectation that you will go out into the streets and do something other than "consume products" as advertised. In fact, the main objective of a network such as CBS, be it radio or television, is to keep the viewer or listener tuned into its channel in order to hear the commercials which pay for the programing. Each program has a hooker advertisement for some of the fare to be seen later that evening. Sennett makes the same point:

> The mass media infinitely heighten the knowledge people have of what transpires in the society, and they infinitely inhibit the capacity of people to convert that knowledge into political action. You cannot talk back to your T.V. set, you can only turn it off. Unless you are something of a crank and immediately telephone your friends to inform them you have tuned out an obnoxious politician and urge them also to turn off their T.V. sets, any gesture of response you make is an invisible act. (Sennett, 1978, p. 283)

In the process of discussing the new technologies of mass communications, we have moved to the opposite of public expression, that of the privatizing of consciousness and human experience. It seems contradictory to say, for example, that a viewer having increased access to world events via the evening news should be privatizing in terms of his or her own consciousness. Nevertheless, there is a paradox here that needs elucidation. The mass media give viewers access to many events outside their immediate awareness, but in a form that leaves her or him as a private spectator to the events seen. He or she is asked to make no public commitments on the basis of the communication. It is a communication done in the privacy of one's own home and is, therefore, at the level of structure, a private experience.

Television, as already indicated, is also monological in form. There are the program communicator and the listener. People are not encouraged to discuss and problematize what they are seeing or hearing. For each viewer or hearer it is a private and intimate event between the program communicator and each individual viewer or hearer. It is for this reason I call this an event of "privatized consciousness." Because of the privatized nature of public mass communications, it avoids public scrutiny. The television is as familiar to the family as the family pet. It's taken for granted. At the same time, it is the reflector or mirror of the most powerful commercial interests of our culture (Smythe, 1980).

Let me now make some summary statements to this point before proceeding to some new issues. I have characterized the "human act" as conscious, intentional, intending, responsible, and significant. I have specifically elaborated the characteristics of responsibility and significance because they amplify the *moral* and *public* nature of human action. A moral act is a responsible act that involves *deliberation* in order to call it a free act. It is public because it is an *expression* that opens on a "world." It is "*significant.*" It seems to me that the task of the moral educator is to foster institutions that encourage human acts that are *responsible* and *significant*. Part of that moral education is to eliminate or, at least, problem-pose those institutions that reduce us to *irresponsibility* and *insignificance* and encourage us to be *patients* rather than *human agents* (see Chapter 3).

Because of the powerful influence of television as an inertial obstacle to "human agency," there is a positive case to be made for the problematizing of this medium as part of a program in moral education. Let me now suggest some parameters for the development of a problem-posing experience with the mass-medium of television.

The Moral Act as Cultural Action

The idea that a moral act is responsible and significant assumes a "culture" that can enhance or deplete one's *responsibility* and *significance* as a moral actor. In other words, moral action is not simply an individual action, it is at the same time, cultural action. Moral action and the development of character must be seen as a gift from one's society or culture. The formation of character takes place within the womb or matrix of one's culture. Every culture produces a set or cluster of images that, in some way, characterizes the important concerns with which society must deal in order to be called a culture. There are images for social maintenance and social change. Sometimes these images are combined, sometimes they are separate. Either way, these images become part of the symbolic system of the child as she or he moves toward adulthood. The television is a medium par excellence of "images" (Sullivan, 1980b). The issue of control over our symbol-making capacities has some important consequences for the cultivation or lack thereof of moral action. Every stable culture has within it dominant symbols that rehearse why a culture is what it is as well as what it ought to be. Thomas Groome refers to these symbol systems as stories and visions. The "story" is the linkage of the past to the present. The "vision" is the linkage of the present into the future. These are not distinct. Rather, the story and the vision are the dynamic interplay of humankind's need for *stability* (story) and *change* (vision). It is in this interplay that cultural values are created, maintained, and altered. In Chapters 3 and 4 I refer to the cultural story as *habitus* or that dynamic within a culture that preserves our cultural memory.

Because of the stabilizing aspects of the cultural story or habitus, individuals are given a continuity with the past. This perception of order and continuity is buttressed by "ideological symbols" that give a sense of stability and inevitability to a particular cultural synthesis. To live is to change, however, and any culture that denies this will eventually die. A culture's "vision" is its ability to continue coherent change. I call this vision the cultural "project." The "project" is that dynamic within a culture that augments a "future"; it is the work we do today for tomorrow. Because of the transformative nature (i.e., challenged form) of the cultural project or vision, members are given a projection into the future. This perception of cultural change is buttressed by "utopian symbols" (i.e., not yet) that give a sense of direction to cultural change. A culture's perspective or value consensus lives ambiguously within this *story* and *vision*. It is important that these symbol systems are not separate at the level of practical life. Any culture is a complex mixture of a dominant story and project and nondominant alternatives. Western culture, in our case North American culture, is the receiver of a dominant story and project that has been developing over several centuries. While I cannot go into the complexity of this history, I would like the reader to attend to the contemporary version of that dominant myth (i.e., cultural story and vision) as it is reflected in the culture's most important medium of communication: television. It is here that one can see rehearsed our culture's habitus and project (i.e., ideological and utopian symbols).

Let us first notice that the communicator addresses us on the TV as individuals, rather than groups, and the individual, for all intents and purposes, is a receiver of information. We are individuals who have a right to own, a duty to consume, and the cultural task of believing that this is the best of all possible worlds. It is the cultural story of "consumer capitalism" and the main cultural memory is that we have consumed yesterday and therefore have a right, indeed an obligation, to consume today. We also come to learn that there are those who know more and those who know less; as viewers, we happen to be the ones who know less. We are never asked to use our judgment. We are to rely on the judgment of "experts." With rare exceptions, they never problem-pose their "expertise," so we, in effect, accept their judgments as absolute. At the level of viewing we come to realize that although all people are equal, some nevertheless are better than others. Thus merit becomes an essential caveat in our notion of equality. Therefore, at the level of media images, men are said to be equal to women. At the same time, the portrayal of men's roles in contrast to women's roles shows males to be more important and significant (i.e., better) than females. The same applies when capital and labor, whites and blacks, First and Third World are considered (Sullivan, 1983a). Further, one of the dominant actors within our culture is not a person but technology. Although it is not a person it is personified and we come to believe that technology accomplishes cultural tasks. For example, a multinational corporation like United Technologies presents advertisements depicting "technology" as a cultural actor and transformer of our world. Here we come to believe that "technology" creates culture rather than being the byproduct of a cultural consensus. What is absent from all of these commercials is the "human agency" and judgment that decide how our technological inventions come to fruition. For example, nuclear reactors don't just happen. They are the outcome of human decisions that are not shown in these commercials (Sullivan, 1983a).

The cultural vision or project of the dominant myth is the idea of "progress." Progress symbols project the vision that we go forward gradually but inevitably. Mass media encourage us to think that we can move forward best by not questioning the integrity of the dominant cultural story. Thus the agents of utopian change remain the same as the agents of the cultural story. They are capitalist white men from the First World. Progress achieves equality by molding all within the confines of the dominant myth. This is done by exploiting nature or manipulation. It is the cultural myth of mastery over stewardship. In addition, the utopian symbol of progress constantly erodes the cultural story by tying it to the "myth of consumption." The products or the effects that we have acquired from products are constantly eroded by new products for consumption. Thus, the car, toothpaste, and stereo that we bought yesterday are no longer adequate given the new line of commodities. The only stability in the story is the process of consumption itself and not the products. Although it is never the center stage of TV programing, it is intimated that lethal armaments, although undesirable, are inevitable necessities for the maintenance of progress. I might add that all of this cultural myth-making can be done in the privacy of your own living room. It is best done when the communication is private and unquestioned. Thus, a public political life in which we make judgments is not encouraged.

The TV frequently eclipses the need for public rituals that go beyond addressing the individual by providing quasipublic events such as the Super Bowl in the United States. It is interesting that a sports event of this kind could assume such prominence. However, upon closer scrutiny, it becomes clear why this is so. The event extols the nation with a flag ceremony, male dominance, technology, competition and merit rewarded in the game's "star" system.

Commercial television, then, if looked at carefully, allows one to codify the dominant cultural story and vision. It is the dominant story and vision because commercial television is the forum for the most powerful commercial interests in our society. They sponsor the programs. It is within this dominant *story* and *vision* that we individually and collectively attempt to make our way as *responsible* and *significant* moral actors.

What I would like to entertain now is the extent to which the dominant cultural *story* and *vision* increase or detract from our capacities to be moral actors within culture.

Consumer Capitalism: The Dominant Cultural Story and Vision

May I say at the outset of this section that it is essential for people to have a sense of order (i.e., habitus) in order to perform responsible action. Freedom is built on an ordered social fabric (Marris, 1974). A sense of order is the matrix for responsible and significant action. Weil dramatizes the need for a stable social fabric as follows:

> The first of the soul's needs, the one which touches most nearly its eternal destiny, is order; that is to say, a texture of social relationships such that no one is compelled to violate imperative obligations in order to carry out other ones. It is only where this, in fact, occurs that external circumstances have any power to inflict spiritual violence on the soul. (Weil, 1971, p. 18)

Weil is saying that a culture's *sense of order* is an antidote to violations of the soul. And "violation of the soul," as she states it, is the capacity to negate one's sense of responsible moral action. I maintain that the dominant story and vision of commercial capitalism have progressively eroded our moral sense in the 20th century. The dominant story and vision of the mass media do not mirror moral action, but rather, consumer action. The intent of a commercial is not to encourage you to be a "moral agent." The object of a commercial is to "penetrate" any sense of order or resistance you might have to its message and thus render you a passive subject with consumption needs.

Media carry the messages of legitimation, and "mass media," as we shall see, help to manipulate public opinion into consumptive patterns of commodity culture. Ewen gives a current history of the "mass media" and their systematic attempts to manipulate public opinion through advertising. In North America, a significant turn of events took place around 1920. Up to that time there was a considerable amount of "labor unrest" that focused upon both working conditions and wages. Concentrations of wealth (for example, Rockefeller and Ford) increased the resentment against these "captains of industry." By 1920, the North American labor movement was receiving better wages and there were significant attempts to bring the workforce in line with industry. One of the carrots was to sell labor on the idea of the necessity of consumption of products. With higher wages, it was found that labor could buy more products and this stimulated industry. The question now was, how could the "mass population" come to accept poor working conditions, which many industrial jobs have as a natural outcome of "mass production?" The consensus was to draw the attention of the public away from the alienating production process and focus upon the attractiveness of the products to be consumed or purchased as the outcome of that process. To this day, it is extremely rare for an advertisement to show a product in the making. This refocusing away from production to the product was to be accomplished through advertising. Legitimacy of the capitalist world order would be achieved not by coercion symbolized by the presence of the "captains of industry." Rather, a more anonymous group of people (the "ad men") would achieve this through the manipulation of the public's consciousness on a mass scale. Ewen calls advertisers the "captains of consciousness." The message would be common to the population at large. In essence, that message would be in all of its guises the advertising "pitch" for the consumption of products. We seem to take all of this for granted, that in advertising we live and move and have our being. But one must realize that this is an invention of the 20th century (Sullivan, 1980b).

Cultural stability is accomplished through the education of our children, yet in a real sense children bring new realities into our world. In one sense, there is a feeling of hope for the new generation in our elders. This occurs partly by accident through a certain slippage in the socialization process. As we have already indicated, parents and schooling are partly responsible for the reproductive process of culture, but in the 20th century a significant new organ of socialization has, in some significant ways, replaced, or at least encircled, these traditional socializers. In 1964 television as a medium created the "child market," which specifically pitches its programing at children from three to eleven years of age (Goldsen, 1975). Television enters almost every home, rich and poor alike, and makes no literacy demands (Mander, 1978). It is, if I may be facetious, a very democratic instrument. In their own distinct way, all of the "mass media" serve the cause of "consumer culture." As Dorfman and Mattelhart (1975) point out about the Disney comics:

> As we have observed, all the relationships in the Disney world are compulsively consumerist; commodities in the marketplace of objects and ideas. The magazine is part of the situation. The Disney industrial empire itself arose to service a society demanding entertainment; it is part of an entertainment whose business it is to feed

> leisure with more leisure disguised as fantasy. The cultural industry is the sole remaining machine which has purged its contents of society's conflicts, and therefore, is the only means of escape into a future which otherwise is implacably blocked by reality. It is a playground to which all children (and adults) can come, and which very few can leave. (pp. 306–307)

At this point, I would like the reader to understand that I do not believe people are inherently passive and pacified by consumer images. We bring to these media a certain complicity with our dominant culture:

> It is obvious that as children, teenagers, and adults, audience members come to the TV tube with rich past experience, with commodities-in-general. They have observed and evaluated old and new models of products on the street, in the homes of friends and peer group members, and on the persons of people they see at the job front; the school, and in all other social relationships (including transportation vehicles). They will also have discussed with family members, friends and strangers the merits and demerits of the old and new models in any of a thousand different social contexts. (Smythe, 1980)

At some level we must assume responsibility for the lives we lead or are prepared to tolerate. It would be educationally dishonest to simply blame the mass media for our passivity before commercial images of the good life. At the same time, we cannot ignore the power of the mass media as an instrument for value formation within our culture today. Moreover, educators must come to terms with the reality that a medium such as television is a moral education into the dominant cultural story and vision of North American culture. It is the bard for the glorification of technological wizardry, consumption, competition, individualism, narcissism, and so forth (Sullivan, 1983c). The anchor persons for the evening news are now assuming the legitimacy of cardinals in times past. Walter Cronkite was revered more than presidents and trusted more than clergy. This new class of experts extol the values of "expertise" and "technology." Technological experts are constantly marched out to explain to the unwashed public the significance of an "event." This is not restricted to the news. A football game is a national ritual for Americans. The Super Bowl pulls out all the stops on the wonders of science and technology. Statistics, experts, bards of the turf all converge on the event, the game proper being a small portion of a larger extravaganza (Sullivan, 1983c). If McDonald's does it all for you and Walter Cronkite says "that's the way it is," where in this discourse is the opening for your own capacities for critical judgment on cultural events? Without a sense of resistance to our present dominant cultural forms, our capacities for moral actions are rendered inert. This is irresponsibility and social anomaly.

Nondominant Cultural Stories and Visions: Cultural Resistance to the Dominant Forms

The general description of the dominant cultural story and vision does not exhaust the stories and visions within a complex culture such as our own. There always exist within a culture oppositional stories and visions. Normally, these currents are contained and do not challenge the dominant myth (Sullivan, 1983c). In the normal course of events, the dominant cultural form is said to be hegemonic (see Gramsci, 1971). Hegemony refers to a form of ideological control in which dominant social practices, beliefs, and values are reproduced and solidified through a range of institutions (e.g., schools, church and, in the present case, television). The hegemonic presence of the dominant cultural story and vision is not restricted to only mass media communications. Hegemony, because of pervasiveness, relates to all major spheres of social existence and it is convenient here to consider what Kellner (1978) identifies as the four major ideological realms: (1) the economic realm, which encompasses the ideologies of production, exchanges, distribution, and so on; (2) the cultural realm, encompassing the ideologies of culture, values, mass media, and so forth; (3) the political realm, encompassing ideologies of the state, legal-judicial system, police, military, and so on; and (4) the social realm encompassing the ideologies of the private sphere, family, education, social groups, and so forth. If the powerful legitimation of modern capitalism exerts itself with such a dominating force (i.e., hegemony) in all ideological realms, it would seem that there is no room for any independence from this pervasive consciousness. To say that our personal worlds are not powerfully determined (i.e., reproduced) under the hegemony of capitalism would be patently naive. Almost all social classes in our society adopt the powerful consumer values of the dominant culture, even if some of those classes are hardly in the position to consume. Nevertheless, we do see breaks in the dominant form. Sartre (1968) in defining his notion of the human project declares that "every man is defined negatively by the sum total of possibles which are impossible for him; that is, by a future more or less blocked off" (p. 95). How could this be if the "hegemony" we have just spoken of is all-pervasive? Left at this point, we are locked into a total determinism of reproduction ("Whatever has been will be"). Williams (1973) introduces the notion of "oppositional forms" to the dominant ethos as a way of handling this problem:

> We have to think again about the sources of that which is not corporate of those practices, experiences, meanings, values, which are not part of the effective dominant culture. We can express this in two ways. There is clearly something that we can call alternative to the effective dominant culture and there is something we can call oppositional in a true sense. The degree of existence of these alternative and oppositional forms is itself a matter of constant historical variation in real circumstances. (p. 206)

In the same work, Williams identifies two oppositional forms to the "hegemony" of the dominant culture. A "residual" is in essence a carryover from a previous historical period. The presence of a "residual form" is indicative that some experiences, meanings, and values which cannot be expressed or verified in terms of the dominant culture, are, nevertheless lived on the basis of the residue of some previous social formation. A certain nostalgia for a past cultural synthesis can be laced with Romantic utopianism or a cultural pessimism. Conservation of values from a previous epoch is remembered and extolled. A sense of history or lost history is intimated in the rejection of the anomaly of the present dominant commercial form. The nostalgia can be held with a sophisticated criticism of present values and, in many cases, a repulsion of the moral outcomes of our present cultural values. To speak of an "emergent form" in opposition to the dominant culture is to assume that new meanings and values, new practices, new significances and experiences are continually being created (Williams, 1973). The "emergent form," like the residual form, questions the dominant cultural images but does not retreat from those images to an earlier cultural synthesis. What we see in "emergent forms" is the culture's development of a new set of moral concerns that have not been on the culture's moral agenda up to now; the concerns of ecologists for the environment, feminists for gender domination, the peace movement, and so on, are some of the new moral agendas that our culture is facing. The stories and visions for these nascent concerns are in the making and are thus emergent.

To be a moral actor within these types of concerns demands new *responsibilities* and *significances*. Part of the problem of realizing new moral responsibilities is the veritable crowding out of these oppositional images within the media organs of the dominant culture (see Cover, 1983; Kavanaugh, 1983; Slinger, 1983). The onslaught of mass media images acts as a veritable eclipse overriding oppositional images. If one thinks that part of what constitutes a moral action is deliberation and critical reflection, then it is necessary to come to terms with factors that discourage deliberation. Why deliberate when there are "experts?" Does not the TV extol the value of "expertise" in its day-to-day programing? The television as medium suggests that "technological expertise" makes unnecessary our need for deliberation and reflection. Technological experts are not only there to sell products in the programing. The "technological experts" are constantly marched out to explain to the audience the "meaning of events." This hermeneutical exercise is what Freire (1974) calls "naming the world." The main function of the larger commercial venture, of which programing is only a part, is to make you a "consumer" rather than an "actor." Advertisers frequently talk about "penetrating" an audience (Ewen, 1976). The image it conveys to me is that of an "invader." At the level of culture it is what Freire (1974) calls "cultural invasion":

> Cultural invasion, which like divisive tactics and manipulation, also serves the end of conquest. In this phenomenon the invaders penetrate the cultural context of another group, in disrespect of the latter's potentialities, they impose their own view of the world upon those they invade and inhibit creativity of the invaded by curbing their expression. (pp. 150–151)

I call the reader's attention to the last sentence in the above quote where it is indicated that *creativity* is linked to *expression*. I have already indicated that moral action is an expression that must have *significance* and *responsibility* (i.e., deliberation). In order for "moral action" to be *significant*, it is necessary to reflect and deliberate on those institutions that culturally act as a narcotic on "moral awareness." This "moral awareness" is what Freire (1974) calls "critical awareness." It is a reflective cultural action (praxis) that poses problems about one's circumstances and is open to new ideas and new ways of looking at "taken for granted" cultural realities. The normal communication framework of TV media is *monological* in nature. Critical awareness through the problem-posing of media programing moves the situation to that of a *dialogue*. Linguistically, education for a critical (deliberation) consciousness has an essential ingredient, *dialogue* with one's world and events, such that the person involved in this dialogue is less prone to media-hyped images to mystify events in the world (McDonald's does not do it all for you).

Why the Need for a Critical Pedagogy of the Mass Media

It is my contention that we are living in a decadent historical period, which is not sustaining further continuity. This is not the remark of a pessimist. People in all ages have had to live through and act within periods of historical decadence, and have had to do so morally. The *Meditations* of Marcus Aurelius is a classic illustration that morality is not to be eschewed while living through decadence. Kipling could not see the decadence of the British Empire and extolled his mother country as the flower of civilization. Yet that Empire would be dismantled within 50 years of his death by numerous liberation movements. It is very convenient in the present political climate (i.e., Reagan and Bush) to cover up our decadence by pointing to the state socialism of Russia. Somehow if the Russians would go away our cultural project could get back on track. But the Russians have not polluted our cities, put acid in our rain, demoralized our minority groups, or caused our once beautiful cities to decline. The Russians have not forced us to speak about the importance of democracy, and to support (in the name of democracy) Ferdinand Marcos, D'Aubuisson, the former Argentine military junta, and the atrocities of Augusto Pinochet in Chile, to name a few. Our astronomical military arsenal may be premised on the need to defend ourselves against the godless Russians, but how are we to account for our total preoccupation with violence when we walk through a video arcade or a toy store for children. How are the Russians to blame for the escalation of the pornography industry, where violence toward women is extolled and justified on the basis that it sells. I want to make clear to the reader that I am sensitive to the many strengths that our cultural history has sustained. Historically, our Western political institutions have cultivated political democracies, eliminated infant mortality, provided an economic system that allowed for economic and social mobility, to name only a few advantages. Thus, in saying that we are living through a period of decadence and decline does not preclude periods of cultural flowering. What I am saying, however, and this may appear to some as pessimism, is that we are now on a permanent path of decline. What is meant by decline here is that the regenerating capacities of our present social and industrial order are depleted. In other words, it is a dying social order. The response to this decline may be provisionally classified into three main categories. The first category is the response of depression, cynicism, and alienation: "Eat, drink and be merry, for tomorrow you die." It is startling to think of how many North Americans indulge in this response. For example, opinion polls carried out in the United States indicate that a significant portion of our youth feel that they will not see the new century because of nuclear holocaust. Symptomatic of this is the recent suicide pact devised by Brown University seniors if a scenario of nuclear holocaust becomes a reality (Sullivan, 1980b).

The second response to cultural decline is that of denial and manic posturing. The presidential campaign of Ronald Reagan represents what I would label denial. In the face of nuclear holocaust, we get the response of arms build-up. In the face of industrial pollution, we have the response of more production and consumption. The religious right, as exemplified by Jerry Falwell, sees all of America's military and industrial endeavors as a continuation of the message of Jesus. A more sophisticated theodicy, harboring the same American cultural mania, can be seen in the Catholic theologian Michael Novak, who writes such texts as the *Spirit of Democratic Capitalism* while employed by the American Free Enterprise Institute.

The third response to cultural decline is to embark on a cultural journey to create new cultural forms. This is an attempt to respond *creatively* to decline by attempting to move out into new cultural directions and horizons. Here one attempts to rethink one's response to production and consumption, the categories of men and women, global and national community, developed and developing nations' relations, one's attitude toward nature and the environment, and so on.

Rather than appear to create a stereotype, it would be my contention that all of us dwell to a greater or lesser extent on all three responses to decline. A biblical example from the Exodus story highlights the conflictual nature of our cultural ambiguity. The Exodus represents a creative journey (the desert experience), but, as the story illustrates, the Israelites when encountering difficulties ask to go back to the addictions of the cultural past ("Let us return to the flesh-pots of Egypt"). What was needed then, as is needed now, is a *resistance* to returning to old haunts and idols. Thus, one does not only have to create the new, one must also resist the addiction of past cultural accomplishments which will no longer give life. It is here that I return to the question of the television as a cultural media. The mass media is the mirroring of our dominant culture and its purpose is to sustain this culture and addict one to its ways. This brings me to the main point of this section, that of the need of a critical pedagogy of

TABLE 1.   Media Constructions from the Point of View of Producers

(a) *Social Self*

The media persona of a social self is one of total integration in a capitalist world view. Producers of media, as well as producers of goods, present the social system as an integrated world view. Production of products, "progress" expertise, and the good life that producers offer consumers is a fundamental assumption.

(a) *Intentional Self*

The movers and shakers within the dominant system are all integrated into the capital system. All heroics do not challenge but extol the cultural thrust of capitalism. Doctors, lawyers, athletes, stars are all social actors who have survived the "meritocracy" of staff competition. Thus, change agents within the capital cultural system extol its ability to alter itself in a gradualistic fashion.

(b) *Identity*

All media personalities, as well as products, are identified as continuous with the system. Deviance from the good life is treated as "criminal." Criminal within this system is blue collar crime, ethnics, labor union strikes. White collar crime is not perceived or depicted within this system, so it is never codified to be made problematic for the viewer.

(b) *Individuation*

People who stand out in the system are those who play ball with the cultural framework. They are usually imaged as middle class, male, and nonethnics, and so on. They are all "individuals" who are making it on their own steam. Therefore, groups of individuals such as "labor unions," "gays" are considered with suspicion since they challenge the system in a collective manner. Challenge to the social system is both "disloyal" and deviant at the same time.

(c) *Order*

The sense of order is that of a "liberal democratic" social consensus. Science, technology, and expertise keep the system on a steady evolutionary path which, in essence, is the myth of "progress." All dissident elements that challenge the integrity of this system of order are depicted as anarchic and deviant. Thus strikers, guerrillas, anticapitalists are portrayed in a demonic light.

(c) *Change*

The dominant system is seen as a mythic structure which is ahistoricized. Progress of a gradual and evolutionary nature is seen as the only road to change in the dominant system. The "change" direction is seen as both conservative and in many instances, reactionary. Thus *change* is seen as bringing back the dominant system to its original integrity. Thus the recent Moral Majority Movement is the bringing of order back into the system and the buffering of its integrity with a religious canopy that is fundamentally conservative in nature.

(d) *Mythic Pre-Consciousness*

As already indicated, the social system is not seen as an historical appropriation; for example, products are never depicted as objects where labor and management have contested. The world of "experts" is seen as a perennial institution that has been with us from the beginning of time.

(d) *Mythic Consciousness*

This is the very consciousness of the world of advertising itself. It is the corporate world's systematic attempt to set the cultural agenda of the general populace (i.e., mass-cultural). It is the development of "consumer-consciousness": a cultural saturation with products to be consumed. From a critical perspective, it is a consciousness that cuts off the history of production. One never sees the "agonies" of production, but rather the wonderland of products.

(e) *Ideological Symbols*

The media itself, as we experience it from day to day, is an extremely honed ideological system of symbols extolling the virtues of products, science, technology, competition, flag, nation, and so on. The "Super Bowl" is a mythic event that utilizes all these symbols within one event for a national celebration of the American way of life.

(e) *Utopian Symbols*

Advertising takes the symbols of human home (i.e., utopian) and links them to products. Human intimacy will be accomplished by Bell Telephone. McDonald's is a place where family will be brought together. Our sense of mysticism, connection, and a sense of wonder in the universe is linked to the drinking of milk. Our sense of *gratitude* for being alive is linked to a product "Thank you very much, milk."

the mass media. A pedagogy of the mass media is only one moment in a larger task of cultural creativity. It is a *moment of resistance* in a larger enterprise. Television is the major addictive lure to the flesh-pots of our culture. It is the place where industrial capitalism is valorized 24 hours a day. It is to this type of pedagogy of resistance that I now turn.

Critical Pedagogy and the Social Structures of Power

A fundamental assumption of a critical pedagogy is that it is a broad educational venture that self-consciously challenges and seeks to transform the dominant values within our culture. A capsule summary of these values appears in Tables 8–1 and 8–2. The general descriptions of the dominant cultural story (habitus) and vision (project), as indicated in Tables 8–1 and 8–2, are not hegemonic in any absolute sense, although the cultural saturation of our dominant mass forms gives one the sense of a pervasive cultural mind-set. One postulates the need of a "critical pedagogy" because the need is experienced by individuals or groups that are not conforming to the dominant value system. There are, within our culture, challenges to the dominant ethos by the peace movement, ecology movement, solidarity movement, connected to the Third World, and so on. Normally, these oppositional currents are constrained and do not fundamentally challenge the dominant myth (Sullivan, 1983b). In the normal course of events, the dominant cultural story and vision are said to be hegemonic (see Gramsci, 1971). For political purposes, this chapter attempts to convey the power of the mass media in the making of the dominant cultural consensus (i.e., liberal democracy and economic capitalism). It is necessary to point out here that the dominant cultural story and vision are not restricted to only mass media communications. The hegemony or mass consensus is related to all major spheres of social existence.

Action versus Consumption

Mass communications, be they radio, television, or newspapers, assume that the hearer, viewer, or reader is a *consumer* rather than a *social actor*. Those

TABLE 2. Media Constructions from the Point of View of Consumers

(a) *Social Self*

While "producers" present a world of total integration to be achieved through consumption, the universe is penetrated with messages of their potential inadequacy if they do not buy their latest product. A sense of "history" is dissipated by a barrage of messages that the past is obsolete. "Yesterday's deodorant will not serve the new you." The consumer, in order to be manipulated into consumption, must be kept in a state of ahistorical suspension.

(b) *Identity*

The social identity of the consumer is an enclosed "individual" (You, you're the one). A collective sense of self is totally denied in mass-media communications. Therefore, a collective understanding of one's social identity is never symbolized. In addition, the viewer has a very restricted sense of what is individually heroic with the proliferation of doctors, lawyers, police, and experts being extolled as key characters within our culture. The "consumer" is characterized as an encapsulated self full of unfulfilled needs.

(c) *Order*

The "consumer" has a very precarious sense of order or roots. The past is obsolete so he or she has no *footing* in history. The present is the time to buy new products to overcome one's obsolescence. Order is recreated for the consumer by science, technology, expertise, and product consumption. Disorder is also projected into alien groups (e.g., communists, French Canadians, blacks, sandanistas). Although the consumer is seen always in a state of "disorder," order is always seen as restored by acceptance of the dominant system (i.e., producer values).

(d) *Mythic Preconsciousness*

An unarticulated belief system that the world is a place of perpetual wants and needs that are not being met. Producers feed on this vague sense and feed it through "advertising." The "need to create" through "cultural action" is turned back on itself as interpreted as a "need to consume." This is what the Ewens label the "channeling."

(a) *Intentional Self*

A self that decides and deliberates is never cultivated by producers in their communications to viewers. Therefore, people's capacity for intentional action and deliberation is constantly trivialized and belittled in a subtle manner. The viewers' capacity for critical judgment or their creative abilities are always sidestepped. There is always some "expert" or "product" to short-circuit the viewer's need for "cultural action" (McDonald's will do it all for you).

(b) *Individuation*

In the mass media, a particular sense of actor individualization is quite truncated. In all instances, individualization is achieved through consumption of some product or merchandise. There is a restricted range of people who are seen as making it. The Bank of America card carrier in some executive organization, doctors, lawyers. Labor leaders are not characterized as individual but as potential catalysts for mass disturbance (e.g., strikes). Thus, for the mass-populace who watch television, there is very little mirrored back to them as to their own cultural worth.

(c) *Change*

Societal change is always orderly and follows the line of *progress*. Thus, the idea of orderly change through *progress* is seen as the fundamental principle by which one accesses social change. All ideologies or social movements that question or undercut the "liberal idea of progress" are seen as anarchic, deviant, and seditious. Thus, the world that challenges the liberal idea of change through progress is seen as "guerrilla activity," which is aligned to this system's major paranoid system, that is, communism and creeping socialism. Right-wing atrocities, which are embarrassingly violent for the liberal-minded set, are seen as unfortunate reactions to left-wing terror.

(d) *Mythic Consciousness*

Tied to the unarticulated need structures created by modern advertising, a product consciousness is timed to this need system. A sense of hope, for example, can be tied to a specific deodorant. The very idea of the progress ideology of liberation can be tied to a company: Ronald Reagan used to be the voice over for General Electric's advertisements when "progress was General Electric's most important product."

(e) *Ideological Symbols*

Ideological symbols of group integrity are, for the most part, media created. In our culture, we celebrate competition over cooperation, individual as opposed to collective heroics, "expertise" over self-taught skills, liberal democracy based on an absolute belief in "the individual" over a collective sense of identity that is perceived as warlike communism. In the mass media, the consumer does not *create* symbols of order, they are ready-made to be consumed of desire.

(e) *Utopian Symbols*

The mass media takes utopian symbols and locates them in the "producer" rather than the "consumer." Thus, the consumer does not create symbols of societal transcendence, rather they are ready-made and given through mass media productions. Thus, symbols of cultural vision and hope are tied to products and industrial and ideological concerns. (We're United Technologies; we are in the business of creating every option for you.)

communicated to in the mass media are receivers and consumers; human action is peripheral to the whole enterprise (see Tables 1 and 2).

This eclipse of *human action* has profound significance because human action is the locus of cultural creation and transformation as I will point out shortly. So if the main motive of, say, advertising is to create consumers, the encouragement of creative critical human action will be an agenda to be short-circuited.

> The power to dominate a culture's symbol producing apparatus is the power to create the ambience that forms consciousness itself. It is a power we see exercised daily by the television business as it penetrates virtually every home with the most massive continuing spectacle human history has ever known. Wittingly and unwittingly, this business and its client industries set the stage for a never ending performance stripping away emotional associations that centuries of cultural experience have linked to patterns of behaviour, institutional forms, attitudes, and values that many cultures and subcultures revere and need to keep vigorous if they are to survive. (Goldsen, 1975, pp. 14–55)

In Chapter 2, by contrast, I have indicated that the defining characteristics of a *human act* have the features of consciousness, intentionality, intention, responsibility, and significance. For my purposes here, I would like to amplify on the above features since they will help me to distinguish the *human act* from a *consumptive act*. (1) *Consciousness*: The human agent is a conscious agent, that is, the essence of its activity is a dialectical process of standing over against while standing out from the other. (2) *Intentionality*: Human action is not only conscious, it is, at the same time, intentionally reflexive. It has a purposive character. (3) *Intentions*: Human action is not only intentioned in the broader sense, it is governed by specific *intentions* which give the act creative direction. (4) *Responsible*: Responsibility is one characteristic of a "human act" insofar as one is accounting for the actions of a person in terms of their desires, intentions, and purposes. This, in humans, of necessity involves the negative pole of action, that is, reflection. (5) *Significant*: A human act as significant indicates the expressive characteristic of human action. Thus, a human act is a *sign* involved in naming and creating a world. The fundamental task of commercial radio or television is not to culture our human creating through human action but to "channel our desire" (Ewen and Ewen, 1982) for purposes of consumption of capital products. Thus, the direction of modern advertising is to eclipse the "human act" by shortcircuiting consciousness, human intentionality, and creative human intentions, which may not be consumer oriented. In addition, responsible deliberation is discouraged because decisions based on *reflection* don't necessarily sell products. Finally, it is contrary to the assumptions of consumer capitalism to encourage the *expressive significance* of human action in the viewers. The only *sign* for the commercial venture is the product logo. The consumer of products is not expected to *name the world*. The world is already made (mythic), it is only necessary that it be consumed as products or information ("and that's the way it is," spake Walter Cronkite).

In summary, I have tried to show in this section that the mass media plays a very significant role in late capitalism. It does so by blunting and domesticating cultural contradictions and by directing *human agents* into consumer patterns; a diversion of profound political significance (see Ewen, 1976).

The Form of a Critical Pedagogy

Within our culture today there are emergent themes that are oppositional to the dominant social mythology of capitalism. Frequently, these oppositional forms are not coordinated into a larger social expression of opposition (i.e., a movement). Thus, many oppositional strains within our culture exist as independent expressions of oppositions (e.g., ecology, labor concerns, Third World solidarity movements, peace movements). At times these oppositional strains converge on a social concern (e.g., recent peace movement activities) but this is the exception rather than the rule. It would be foolish to intimate that mass media programing is totally devoid of oppositional currents. The television movie airing of the "Last Day" in 1982 is one indication that oppositional programs do surface on commercial programing. There are also alternative oppositional programs on some of the Public Broadcasting channels. However, in relation to all of commercial television programing, these attempts are miniscule. In addition, the mass media accent their differences and cover up their similarities as oppositional currents to the dominant social mythology of capitalism. Rather than seeing these oppositional strains as *resistance* to the dominant myth, they are frequently characterized within the mass media as simply *deviance* from the accepted cultural norm (i.e., hegemony). In a very real sense, the pervasive onslaught of mass media images acts as a veritable eclipse trivializing oppositional images. The mass media act as a "cultural invader" (see Freire, 1974) because they rob culturally oppositional forms of their *creative significance*, within the dominant culture. I have emphasized *creative significance* because, as moral agents, our expressions must have (and must be seen to have) the qualities of *significance* and *responsibility* (i.e., deliberation). In order for oppositional expression to be *significant,* it is necessary to reflect and deliberate on those institutions that culturally act as a narcotic to critical oppositional awareness.

Culturing of Resistance

One must accept as a given within present-day popular culture that the mass media are a popular molder of the dominant cultural values of capitalism. It is, therefore, politically obtuse to treat the mass media as a peripheral concern in a liberatory educational praxis. It is now possible to use mass-media programing as a curriculum for a critical pedagogy of our cultural values. With video cassette recorders (VCR) the viewer now has a chance to control and edit dominant images and reflect on their influence to the oppositional currents. Therefore, a critical media pedagogy confronts dominant images (i.e., resistance) rather than withdrawing from them (as if ignorance could detract from their cultural power). With a VCR the viewer assumes a modicum of control so as to gain a footing to problem-pose dominant images (see Freire, 1974). This media-image should be problem-posed in groups where people can dialogue about the cultural realities that form their awareness. The normal viewing of TV, for example, does not allow dialogue and usually the viewers do not converse with one another (i.e., it is monological). Under the "hegemony of the mass media," we have been cultivated as passive *consumers* of information. Therefore, a critical pedagogy of the mass media would be a culture of resistance to the dominant cultural myths of liberal capitalism. The need for a critical pedagogy, of course, will only be experienced when there is a sense that the dominant cultural myths are problematic to human survival and enhancement. What I am saying may first appear contradictory, given that the mass media communications system is a veritable communications eclipse around transformative and oppositional cultural stories (habitus) and visions (project). The cultural domination of the mass media presents a practical problem for oppositional currents within mass culture. Problem-posing a medium such as television has the effects of giving one easy access to the dominant myth making in our culture. Since we are culturally saturated with these stories and visions, it is important to assess the effect they have on us. This is a first step in a problem-posing process (i.e., critical awareness). To explore media images further, one does not have to devise complicated learning processes. For example, a simple way to problem-pose television programing is to ask, "What is left in and what is left out of a program? Who benefits from what is left in and what is left out?" These probes are purposely simple because they tap into what Gramsci (1971) calls the public's *"good sense."* This critical *good sense* is there to be developed and does not have to be constructed. One can see this *good sense* or critical ability when one asks children to do some reflection on TV commercials. You can see this *good sense* when you problem-pose soap operas in a women's reflection group. It is a latent awareness, in the viewers, that mass-media images conceal more than they reveal and that the concealment serves to subjugate the viewers' awareness of social processes.

Developing Societal "Projects"

Developing resistance to mass-media images as a critical pedagogy cannot be an end in itself. The culturing of resistance can only be seen as one aspect of a *deliberative moment* in critical pedagogy. In a manner of speaking, resistance is a *"negative moment"* that has the potential to *reveal* the normally *concealed* condition of domination. As indicated earlier (see Tables 8–1 and 8–2), the condition of domination is operating when the agency of one person or group eclipses or masks the agency of another person or group. Thus, the power of one is at the expense of the other. To reiterate, domination or oppression operates when the agency of one's person or group (i.e., consciousness, intentionality, intentions, responsibility, and significance) denies the possibility of another person's or group's consciousness, intentionality, intentions, responsibility, and significance. This situation for those who are dominated, turns agent conditions listed above into their opposite. Thus, for consciousness we have repression or concealment, for intentionality we have withdrawal or "privatization," for intentions we have an absence of goal orientation or rootlessness, for responsibility we have dependency, and for significance we have meaninglessness, or anomie. This is the condition of the "consumer" within the mass media as I outlined in Table 8–2. The culturing of resistance to "mass media images" simply names the oppression and codes existing power relations. Thus reflection on the mass media cannot be considered as complete unless it opens on and is motivated by the domain of politics in the public sphere (e.g., schooling, state apparatuses, work settings, etc.). The latter cannot be done in front of a "television." It is in the *public sphere* that the world can be *named* and this is where the action of agents (not consumers) becomes "cultural action" that has *significance*, it means something. McDonalds will not do it all for you anymore than Walter Cronkite could have told us, without question, that "that's the way it is." A critical pedagogy serves the educational function of helping actors to "name the world" with their own reflective judgment.

Why Do It? How To

Given the critical perspective I have developed here one can ask, "Why would one attempt to reflect on something that has such ambiguous educational merit? Would it not be better to encourage people not to addict themselves to mass media programing?" My answer to this is that television is so popular in the culture that an injunction to not watch would probably be followed only by a small segment of the population (i.e., the snobs). In addition, I feel that there is some merit to taking popular culture interests and transforming them toward educational ends. Thus my suggestion for a critical pedagogy of the mass media is not to encourage television watching, but to take people's watching habits and transform them into attempts at cultural analysis. It is my conviction that media analysis is only a small part of a curriculum for critical cultural inquiry. I see the analysis of media as a reflective moment where people can examine some powerful influences on their lives, be they children or adults. This is not a substitute for acting in the world to transform it. Therefore, cultural action is not to be short-circuited by cultural analysis (i.e., in this case, media analysis). My own personal experience with television may be helpful for the reader to appreciate its impact.

For most of my adult life I have been a television snob. From the age of 20 to 40 years, I simply did not watch television. During some of those years I was involved in the development of educational curriculum on moral formation. In working in high school classes I became convinced, through discussions with students, of the importance of television on value formation. I decided at about the age of 40 to study the effects of television myself. While this was beginning, I was also struck by how my children were influenced by TV. My concern for children and television watching continues to be a problem for me as they are growing up. I have no easy answer for parents on this matter since I have not arrived at a clear articulated stance on this matter. I have come to realize, from my experience, that you can use television imagery as a way to reflect on your cultural values. It is not the only means to this type of reflection, but it is a powerful entry point to tap into your own (and others') popular beliefs and attitudes. Television is definitely a molder of these cultural beliefs and attitudes. With the advent of the VCR, one can now flexibly monitor programing for educational purposes. Here I am not simply talking about educational television. For example, I teach summer graduates on the subject of mass media and I rely heavily on edited programing of contemporary shows. Thus, in addition to the evening news we watch such programs as *Hill Street Blues*, *Dynasty*, rock videos, the Super Bowl, and so on. As we watch collectively and problem-pose as a group, I am amazed at the discussions on social values that ensue. Even students who consider themselves TV snobs are amazed at how they can be influenced by TV images. Let me conclude this chapter by discussing several areas of cultural values that can be coordinated with the media programing I use in this course.

A Few Examples

I close with a selected set of examples only suggestive of the particular form that a critical pedagogy of mass media might take in specific instances. It seems to me that it is possible to use mass media in an infinite number of ways for cultural reflection. One can raise questions about peace, ecology, health care, sexual stereotyping, corporate images, and labor images, to name a few. I will, at this point, suggest three areas, which the reader must realize are my own idiosyncratic examples.

Children's Values. The case can be made that children's cultural values can be strongly influenced by a mass medium such as television (Sullivan, 1980b; 1983a,b). A teacher who would like to have children reflect critically on their values concerning consumption, sex roles, sports, attitudes toward violence, and so forth, can easily utilize popular programing. One could take the Saturday-morning programing directed toward children and explore values in our culture. Commercials can be reviewed, heroes and heroines can be discussed as a way to having children see the images considered important within our culture. When the mass media are problem-posed in this manner, children can achieve a certain distance from the emphasis on consumption, competition, and violence which is so pervasive on commercial TV's children's programing (Sullivan, 1980b). This is the place where children can explore alternative cultural options to their mass-media images (e.g., peaceful resolution to problems, cooperation versus competition). It is a place where children can explore the limitations of TV's cultural images while watching popular TV programs. This can be done by editing commercials and programs. Since a VCR can freeze frames, one is allowed a modicum of control over images for more conscious deliberation of dominant cultural images (i.e., agency). Surprisingly, children have what Gramsci (1971) calls the "good sense" to critically assess commercial images saturating the programing directed toward them in the mass media.

Women's Issues and the Mass Media. The "women's movement" is one of the emergent oppositional forms dealing with exploitation along gender lines. Careful attention to the mass-media presentation of sex roless indicates the dominant values of commodity culture vis-à-vis women. A judicious editing of advertising can be very revealing when considering the exploitation of women as commodities. The recent film *Killing Us Softly* is a collage of advertisement with the dramatic effect of coding the attitudes of modern advertising toward women. Women are constantly depicted as fickle, as temperamental, and as sexual objects for men's uses. In conventional advertising there is no sense of a "project" for women. Women exist as the "project" of men. They are constantly pictured as adornments to commodities, or adornments to men. A sustained look at modern advertising also reveals the high tolerance that our culture has toward violence to women. The recent documentary film of the National Film Board of Canada, *Not a Love Story*, illustrates the extension of this violence to pornography, where women are perceived as desiring the violence that men visit on them for their sexual pleasure. Advertisements appear to be a very good revelation of the exploitation of women by the male cultural project.

But the exploration of gender relations does not have to be restricted to "advertisements." Soap operas, sit-coms, and detective stories can be equally revealing. For example, even where women are acting as detectives (e.g., *Police Woman, Charlie's Angels, Lobo,* etc.), women, more than men, use sexuality to lure criminals. Men are also seen as the dominant intelligence in the police hierarchy (e.g., Charlie's Angels always calling in to the invisible Charlie). Soaps also show women as either very naive or as vicious schemers.

The exploration of sex roles through the "mass media" can be a critical pedagogical exercise for both men and women who are trying to transform the present gender hegemony. What the media reveal about sex roles is the powerful exploitative images that our culture has toward the sexes. This type of coding helps to name and clarify the oppressive structures of gender that saturate popular awareness and resist transformation.

The Coverage of Labor Issues. In a very interesting study entitled *Television: Corporate America's Game,* rank-and-file workers from three unions examined television programing. They concluded that all major networks treated labor issues in a negative light. Almost all major networks illustrated a favorable bias in reporting management issues. There was also a very marked positive aura for corporate activity. In addition, in regular programing there was a predominance of models who were from a professional class (e.g., doctors, lawyers, psychiatrists, etc.). Crime was invariably blue-collar crime. Law enforcement was usually carried out against working-class people or unemployed marginals. What is important about this type of study is the consciousness-raising that this activity had for rank-and-file union members. It dramatized the uphill battle that labor has in having its agendas presented fairly and accurately by the mass media. It also showed how labor resistance and initiatives are trivialized and made to appear "deviant" by the mass media. Thus, when a "labor union" withholds its labor, it receives the appellation "strike," which has a violent connotation. Thus far, there is no comparable violent symbolism for a "runaway corporation" which structurally affects more people than a "strike."

Again, I have only given the above examples to illustrate how a study of the mass media can be part of a "consciousness-raising" critical pedagogy. The resourceful reader can think of many more examples. My one major conclusion from this long exercise is that mass-media communications must be an essential part of a "critical pedagogy," and if we ignore it, we do so at our political peril.

EXAMPLE 3: CRITICAL ETHNOGRAPHY AND CRITICAL INTERPRETATION[10]

In Chapter 7 I made a comparison between two ethnographic studies in order to deal with issues surrounding evaluation and adequacy of interpretation

---

[10]Portions of this study appear in *Phenomenology + Pedagogy: A Human Science Journal,* vol. 5, No. 1, 1987 and are used with permission. It is written by Edmund Sullivan and Chilean colleagues Sergio Martinic and Horacio Walker.

within a critical framework. The studies that I used in that chapter are not related to pedagogical issues, and what I propose to do in this section is to illustrate issues surrounding program evaluation in education with specific emphasis on my work in the area of popular education in Chile. Although I will again use the Marsh, Rosser and Harré (1978) study for comparative purposes as I did in Chapter 7, the main purpose of my present effort is to show how critical interpretation can make a substantial difference when applied to program evaluation. I will also attempt in this section to illustrate to the reader that "qualitative evaluation" is in no way synonymous with critical interpretation. The reader should be aware that what I will be doing in this section is an exercise in critical interpretation by comparing two ethnographic studies. The reason that we think this is a fruitful exercise in comparison is because it brings out crucial differences in what are frequently called qualitative methods. One can find today in any one of the subdisciplines of the social sciences a controversy labeled "quantitative versus qualitative research." First of all, the controversy assumes that a viable distinction can be made between these approaches. Second, there is an assumption that one of the approaches is better than the other. At present, one sees the quantitative approach as the dominant paradigm with the qualitative approach as the challenging usurper. We find this distinction frequently spurious and unproductive when the argument of one versus the other makes the distinction into an either/or categorization. In this section we will not be dealing with this controversy. We will make some crucial comparisons between two types of ethnographic studies. Ethnography is very often catalogued as qualitative methods. What our comparison will hopefully show is that even studies that are labeled qualitative have crucial differences that can be just as controversial as the quantitative-qualitative distinction. It is our contention that the label "qualitative research" houses a variety of methods that can be at odds with themselves on crucial issues, the nature of which is ideological. My own effort in this section is to show how the ideological element operates in two different ethnographic studies. We start this comparison by reiterating some of the major points made in Chapter 6 on critical interpretation.

Critical Interpretation

In both Chapters 6 and 7 I have identified some core features of critical interpretive inquiry. The first feature is the incorporation of intentions of actors into social inquiry. The second feature, not excluding the above, is to locate the intentions of social actors within concrete structures of social power. What distinguishes "critical interpretation" from other types of qualitative inquiry is its express emphasis in keeping at the forefront the presence or absence of social power. Why the use of the term *interpretation*? It is our position that human action is intentional and that intentional acts have a sign quality that makes them expressive. Thus when we use the term "human expression" it is indicative of the sign quality of human action. The sign quality of human action makes human action expressions for others. The fact that they are expressions means that they are subject to interpretation. Interpretation is open ended and, therefore, human action is subject to multiple interpretations. It is our contention that "critical interpretation" differs from other varieties of social inquiry labeled qualitative, interpretive, phenomenological, and so forth, in an emphasis on the dual nature of human agency (intentionality) and its corresponding dialectical polarity "structure" (Giddens, 1979). Giddens sees the basis of structuration as a recursive action in the development of social life. Thus it is a contention within a "critical interpretive" framework that human agency and intentions must be seen in a structural totality of social life. Within this structural totality of social life, specific aspects of social power are highlighted. The first aspect is the structuration of economic structures. Economic systems are systems of social relations designed for the exploitation of the environment for purposes of survival. Historically, these structures have varied immensely; the two dominant forms today are capitalism and socialism. The second aspect is the invariant structure of gender. Finally, the structure of ethnicity accounts for the diversity of the human species and is the matrix of diverse cultural development within the species. All of the structures that we have listed have within them enclaves of social power, which can enhance or detract from human agency (intention). It is the task of critical interpretive inquiry to illuminate the range of social power embedded in the above structures. One of the problems encountered in interpretive inquiry is the tendency to collapse the agency-structure dialectic (see Chapter 6, pp. 128–130). One extreme is the inflated emphasis on human agency seen in voluntaristic theories where freedom from structure is emphasized. The other extreme can be seen in deterministic theories where voluntarism is downplayed and social structures are emphasized. It is my wish in this section to avoid the pitfalls of the above extremes. In this section we will describe two ethnographic studies. Our intention is to compare them by the yardstick we have labeled "critical interpretation." The first study to be described was carried out by my Chilean co-worker (Walker, 1986). It is an ethnography of the community mobilization by women of a soup kitchen in one of the popular sectors in Santiago, Chile. The second is an ethnography already discussed in Chapter 7: the Marsh, Rosser and Harré study done in England focusing on violence at football games. It will be my task to show how these disparate ethnographies can be fruitfully compared. We proceed to the description of our first study: the soup kitchen. In fairness to the reader, at the outset, he or she should be aware that our own theoretical bias falls within the domain that we have labeled "critical interpretation." It is our intention to briefly describe two ethnographic studies for the purposes of comparison. The study that we are about to describe falls within that rubric and was carried out by the third author (Walker, 1986).

The Soup Kitchen Study

The research is entitled "The Transformation of Practices in Grass-Roots Organizations: A Case Study." Walker (1986) used an ethnographic approach to evaluation in the study of a soup kitchen's organization of social practices in Puento Alto, a county of Metro Santiago. Like many of the soup kitchens of its kind in present day Chile, it constitutes a concrete response to the extreme economic conditions that are currently being endured in popular sectors in Chile under the military regime of Augusto Pinochet. The ethnographic strategy in this study is based on interviews of the participants in the soup kitchen and first-hand observations of the researcher. The soup kitchen is a community project organized by a group of women in a popular sector with the help of a church agency. It's sole purpose is to provide for people living in marginal economic conditions. What is important at the outset is to alert the reader that the inter-pretation of this soup kitchen will be done not only by the professional researcher but also by other groups that are living in a popular sector. The importance of the latter form of interpretation will be discussed later. The original interviews were also supplemented by four months of on-site observations. Our intention here is to give sufficient description of the ethnographic study so as to help the reader follow this comparison with another ethnographic study to be described shortly. The name we will use for this specific soup kitchen is the Maria Goretti Soup Kitchen. The main directional theme of this research project is to begin a type of research that examines in detail the organizational practices of a group of women from their point of view. Martinic, (1984, 1985b) has argued the need for first-person accounts because of important differences that appear to be different types of locations where popular mobilization is operating (e.g., urban-rural differences, gender differences, etc.). Thus the Walker (1986) study high-lights organizational differences made along gender lines, in this case, the or-ganizational practices of women attempting to run a soup kitchen.

In the Chilean context, the soup kitchen work that we are about to describe is a popular education effort. By popular education, we mean the educational practices that are developed when people at the grass-roots levels organize them-selves for survival purposes. These efforts are developed beyond the boundaries of formal schooling. A soup kitchen is just one of myriad forms of these popular educational enterprises. Taken as a totality, the soup kitchen can be considered as part of a social movement (Martinic, 1984). The following is a brief description of the Maria Goretti Soup Kitchen. It is constructed by Walker (1986) but is, at the same time, a story using the participants' own words.

> This *olla común* (soup kitchen) took off several years ago. In those days it was a
> *comedor* (a soup kitchen only for children) for thirty-two children. It was started by
> a Yugoslavian nun. She helped us through a priest. They brought us groceries and
> milk for the children. None of the nuns could continue with us and they appointed

an *encargada* (staff person in charge of the program appointed by church authorities). She was a person who worked for the community. At the time we started working with the Vicariate and Caritas. They gave us lots of groceries. But what happened, things didn't arrive at the *comedor*, but the *encargada*'s home. She left us things measured, the oil, the sugar, everything. The *encargada* took personal advantage of the situation. She would never let us go for the groceries, she always went with her husband, since her husband had a truck. She didn't let us go to meetings either; she went by herself until she was required to attend with an executive. What happened is that the mothers started to get suspicious. So then we elected an executive of three mothers, who started to go with her to the meetings which were held there in the church. For the first time the mothers started realizing that meetings were held, that other things could be done. Then the struggle began to hand over the *comedor* to the mothers. At that time we were not as many as we are now; we were like twenty mothers, but we had about forty children in the *comedor*. When we started with that *encargada* none of the mothers agreed because we were used to working with the nun. The *encargada* was a mother who has a huge house on this same street, a mother who for us was not equal. But because we had to have an *encargada*, and the *encargada* was chosen by the Church, we had to accept her, not very happily.

Then the struggle began for the control of the *comedor* by the mothers. When the church representative resigned, she also gave up the place where the soup kitchen was located. We were left with our hands tied and had to start looking for space and a shack. The parish priest donated half the money to buy the shack and we found a lot where we had to pay rent.

Many mothers withdrew from the group for the simple reason that they thought they were going to be worse off because it was as if the mothers already got used to the *encargada* and thought they would not be able to struggle by themselves to get the *comedor* going.

Then soon, more people started joining once they saw that things were working. The ones who participate here are mostly from the Irarrazaval area. The same señoras that know us are the ones that make contact with us and ask to join the *olla*. We had struggled for a long time as a *comedor*, when we started talking about forming an *olla común*. But we didn't know that the *olla común* had been operating for a long time because all the mothers brought something. We never planned to have the first *olla comúna* in this county, because we, as *comedor*, started becoming an *olla* without knowing that we were already an *olla*.

As we continued our struggle with raffles, with *onces* (gatherings where tea and biscuits are served with the purpose of collecting money), and with dances. We have had problems with bad executives such as when we had a dance, we collected some funds and they were lost. We have collected some 35,000 pesos (35 dollars) with such sacrifice and the President suddenly came up with this story of how she lent the money to a retired woman. She told us that when she got to the retirement allowance she was going to give the money back.

Now we work well, all together. We have a fine executive. The president has been in charge for four years and is very correct. There have been several secretaries and treasurers though. This year we elected a new secretary and treasurer. The three of them work very well together as an executive. Things are collected at the market and some shops give us groceries. Every mother knows she is to bring a daily contribution: carrots, potatoes, onions, whatever. Besides that, the Vicariate gives us three provision allotments every month: milk, flour, and a third, that varies, spaghetti, rice or beans. Alicia from the Vicariate works with us. But she doesn't come all of the time. Sometimes she comes for a while to the meetings. We have to turn in our questionnaires to her with the number of participants so that they can give us the *alimentos* each month. If we have problems we can talk them over with her, but many times we solved them by ourselves.

We function well although at times some of the mothers get mad. There are times when they don't have contributions, because the majority work in POJH and have more than one child; they all have three, four, five, seven children. Then the mothers can't bring a contribution every day, although it is an obligation. We take turns cooking, two mothers for a whole week. Now we are many. At the present time we are thirty-one because now food is given even to the husbands. We meet once a week, every Tuesday. In the meetings we talk just about anything. The executive explains everything straight out. It is an obligation to attend the meetings. A person who misses three times without a good reason gets kicked out of the organization. It is the only way.

We take wagons around on pick-ups. We, the women, do everything, that is, we are alone, we don't have many men. Since we started as a group we have been independent. We don't like men to participate, that is, we are used to struggling alone. If the roof needs to be fixed, we just fix it; just women, we have done it before. We have had storms, roof boards flying off and we have had to fix everything. We climb on the roof and nail them down while someone holds the ladder.

When we started working as an *olla*, it was when the political stuff was starting up again, when the protests began. We didn't have anything to eat, all the señoras sometimes, didn't even have breakfast for the children. We were suffering from everything the government was doing; we started protesting. Because of that we got a bad reputation; we have been called different names and accused of being a political centre and things like that. But now people have awakened more, I mean, we were the first to start to protest in the area. There had never been protest in this area. This group of ours is very hardworking. It participates in quite a few things such as land takeovers, training workshops and other workshops.

Another difficulty we have had is that people are ashamed to participate in *olla*. Sometimes they don't have anything to eat, but they don't approach us. Sometimes our husbands don't like to see us involved in these things and even less in the *olla*. (Walker, 1986, pp. 15–17)

One of the salient features of this study is that it is, in effect, a women's organization. At this point in the community's consciousness women's participation is conscious and intentional on their part as the following exchange illustrates.

INTERVIEWER: "And do men participate?"

SEÑORA MIRTA: "No. We are only women. When there is something to be fixed, then husbands come to help, to hammer nails."

INTERVIEWER: "Would you like them to participate?"

SEÑORA MIRTA: "No because we are used to being by ourselves. It would be, I think, uncomfortable to be with men because we have been alone for many years."

INTERVIEWER: "And why would that have been uncomfortable?"

SEÑORA MIRTA: "Because like this, being among women, there is more trust than with men, I think that would be lost."

On the basis of the participant observations and the interviews, the study moved in a systematic direction of interpretation that we are naming "critical interpretation." First, there is an attempt to identify the main contradictions underlying the soup kitchen's story. Second, there will follow a procedure of multiple interpretation we feel is unique to this critical ethnography. The soup kitchen will be interpreted not only by the researcher, but also will be interpreted by other grass-roots organizations. Finally, the interpretation will be broadened to account for the analysis of class and gender that appears operating uniquely in this setting. Thus, the microanalysis of the organizational practices will be related to the macrostructures in which they are situated. Central to this context is the analysis of popular education as a praxis of transformation of organizational practices (Walker, 1986).

Thus, this study self-consciously goes beyond an ethnographic account to a level of analysis that we are calling "critical interpretation" or, if you will, critical ethnography. This process is referred to in Chapter 5 as a "double hermeneutic." By this notion we mean that all systematic interpretation is two-tiered. It expresses the dialectic of distance and relation, as follows. First of all, systematic interpretation must be related to a particular cultural form and its unique expression so that action may be appreciated from the point of view of the conscious intentions of actors (i.e., relation). Second, systematic interpretation must be done at enough distance from specific cultural expressions to provide critical feedback on these expressions (i.e., distance).

This ethnography about the soup kitchen does exactly the above. There are extensive interviews with the participants and extended descriptions in the words of the participants. Thus, the actors proper are clearly part of the interpretive process. Nevertheless, there are other horizons of interpretations that are utilized in the ethnography. Other popular education groups are consulted for their interpretation and the ethnographer proper in this study (Walker, 1986) also develops lines of interpretation that go well beyond the point of view and language of the participants. Walker (1986) does this in several different ways throughout this thesis, but for our purposes we will only consider four major areas of contradiction that he develops as part of a critical interpretation of this particular popular education effort. These areas of contradiction are developed on the basis of the intensive ethnographic work, but they are not part of the discourse of the participants involved. We will focus here on these contradictions as one way of demonstrating a facet of what we are calling "critical ethnography." The four contradictory areas that Walker (1986) elucidates are as follows: (1) a contradiction called dependence–independence; (2) social versus traditional explanations of women's oppression; (3) politization versus apolitization and, finally; (4) organization versus disorganization.

Dependence/Independence Contradiction. It has been our contention that a critical interpretation goes well beyond the level of first-person accounts and participant observation. What is unique about the idea of a critical interpretive account is that there is a systematic attempt on the part of the investigator to code relationships of domination and also focus on aspects of social organization that impede the agency and freedom of individuals and groups. In this present study, one major aspect of critical interpretation is revealed in an aspect that is labeled the "contradiction" (identified through first-person accounts) of dependence/independence. In the particular instance of this soup kitchen, one finds it a theme that recurs; that is, how agencies and key people are the point of contradiction in the development of authentic communities. This particular community had to deal with a religious community that was extremely helpful in getting this organization started, international agencies of aid, and in particular a solidarity church-related agency labeled the "Vicariate." At the beginning there was a considerable amount of go-between work in the community and those outside organizations. At the outset there was a particular woman called the *encargada* who was initially the liaison and coordinator between the external agencies and the community. She very quickly became the focal point of criticism for the other women in the community when a consensus developed among the women that she acted arbitrarily and in an authoritarian manner and without consultation with the others. Part of the initial quest toward more independent initiatives is seen in the fact that the women in the community confronted the *encargada* and eventually eased her out of this role. This initiative toward a more independent and egalitarian set of relationships took place within the group proper. It should be pointed out that the pressures toward independence were a two-way process in most instances where this particular community related to the Vicariate. These were relational moves between the group and the external agency. Summing up this tension, Walker (1986) notes how the Vicariate gradually took over the *comedor* program, with their own staff replacing the local coordinating role of formal church structures in place at the start. The effect was the gradual winding down of the *comedores* and their transformation into *ollas comúnas.* Alicia tells about this process of transformation in this community:

> We (the solidarity group from east Santiago Vicariate) organized summer camps in 1978 for children. Several women from different groups went to cook at the camps. We had sent them away from Santiago, to the beach, for a week. As a result a sort of intercommunication was formed among groups and experiences. Ideas were exchanged and the groups started realizing how backward they were from an organizational point of view. The women started realizing what they could do by themselves. I believe that there has been a whole process of self-affirmation as persons and as a group as well. They became aware of their abilities to manage an organization, even the most organized have the problems that they have.

In summing up this process of achieving independence from formally dependent situations in this community, Walker (1986) stresses that:

> The struggle for autonomy did not come just from the Vicariate, but also within the group. For this reason I see it as a dialectical process in which the idea of transformation is developed simultaneously within the group and within the Vicariate. When the group rid itself of the *encargada* it organized itself internally, broadening the members' participation. This was a definite step towards more independence. They started bringing their donations and supplying parts of the food on their own. As the women state in the story: "We never thought we were going to become the first *olla* commune in the country, because we as *comedor*, started turning it into an *olla* without knowing that we were already an *olla*." (p. 21)

Social/Traditional Explanations of Women's Oppression: The Gender Dimension. Walker (1986) identifies gender as one of the fundamental interpretive categories of his study of this soup-kitchen project. Gender is identified as central because it relates to why and to what extent women participate and why men do not participate in organizations of community survival such as soup kitchens. Additionally, gender helps in an interpretive understanding of some of the fundamental problems that exist within this organization's life. The interviews as a totality demanded that the researcher view gender as essential to the interpretive understanding of this organization. This dimension of interpretation assumed salience in this research effort, not only because the vast majority of the members of this organization were women, but also because it was felt that being a woman was related to specific practices that gave this group a specific character.

What is telling about all of the interviews with these women is the fact that their relationships with their husbands or *convivientes* had histories of pain and frustration. Although each interview with these women had its unique characteristics, all relationships with men were interpreted as extremely problematic. Thus the participation of women in this organization is seen as a struggle, sometimes because of male opposition, sometimes because of exploitation at home. There are three men that are affiliated with this soup kitchen and their reasons for participation are important but will not be discussed here. Suffice to say that in this group they are not in attendance at social gatherings and are more in that type of assistance relationship to the women organizers already discussed. The absence of men is not accidental. Women in this group self-consciously exclude men on important occasions. This was done when a trip was organized to a beach at Puente Alto, which constituted a few days of vacation. In the preparatory discussions for this trip, it was decided by total agreement among the women, that no adult men were to be allowed to go. This instance is interpreted by Walker (1986) as part of a more generic gender problem that is felt to exist at two levels. The first is in the more private sphere (relations with men and motherhood) and the second is in participation in activities outside of the home. Walker (1986) summarizes this problem as follows:

> Understanding the conflicts experienced in these two types of situations differ from women to women. Some have individual, psychological and even religious explanations of women's oppression. A minority understands the relationship of institutionalized oppression to the social construction of gender relations. These contradictory views bring about conflicts in the group. However, it is interesting to note that sometimes the resolution of conflict satisfies everyone. For example, while the understanding of why men must be kept out of the group differ significantly from group to group, excluding men satisfies all of them, given that all of them experience in one way or another a basic oppression. (p. 24)

Political/Apolitical. The awareness of gender relations, as discussed above, as socially constructed has fundamental political implications for the basic definition of what constitutes the political proper. One is the reconceptualization of being political as entailing the questioning of the dominant power relations in the home. These issues were not unrelated to the survival needs in these homes that have been created by the military junta under which they are presently living. As one of the older participants in this soup kitchen recounts, the political focus started in 1983 when there were the first major public challenges to Pinochet's iron rule since the coup.

> Then politics started too, because the demonstrations began. We hardly had anything to eat. Most of the señoras couldn't give breakfast to their children. We were suffering from all the government was doing. We started protesting. Because we went out protesting we got a bad reputation. We were called different things and some people said that the *olla* was a political centre and things like that. Even sometimes, mothers who really needed us, who didn't have anything would not go into the *olla* centre to put food into their pots for home for the simple reason that the organization was already tainted with the label political. They blamed us for anything that happened in the neighborhood: power blackouts, passing out leaflets and everything. We were the first to start the demonstrations in our neighborhood. A group of women from the soup kitchen went out to protest, no one had protested here before. The first day we went out with pots, but the pots got damaged so we decided to use metal barrels and we beat on it with pieces of steel. Now other people in the area are participating too. The police didn't come for the first demonstrations. But the police and the military came for the last two (Sept. 4–5 and October 27–28, 1984). They started throwing tear bombs at us. We had some molotov cocktails prepared in bottles just in case they decided to come into our houses. We had a centre open but with the doors closed. (Walker, 1986, p. 26)

Here it must be noted that this explicit discussion of this organization's activities as political is not typical. Explicit statements such as the above are made spontaneously by a small number and it was the contention that the researcher should not actively pursue these topics since he felt that talking politics with an outsider is considered dangerous. However interesting questioning might be, the researcher restrained himself from this type of intrusion on community sensibilities. When it is seen to be expressed in the interviews, the political/apolitical contradiction is seen in conflicting views regarding members' participation in the soup-kitchen activities against the dictatorship. There are also conflicting views on the development of group activities such as discussions to raise awareness about government oppression and the need for organized resistance.

The foregoing discussion of the conflicts between political and apolitical reflects a restricted conception of the political. The lack of an articulated discourse or of participation in the traditional political action (e.g., party politics) does not denote a lack of political consciousness or political activity. Walker (1986) contends that for this particular organization and others of its kind, political action can be seen in the everyday struggle of the organization under the present larger political conditions under the dictatorship.

Organization/Disorganization. In the context of present-day Chile, the issue of organization in one's social life is one of suspicion. Under the dictatorship, simply being organized is a struggle because it is repressed frequently by the government. According to the municipal authorities (the local representatives of the state) church-related organizations are seen as a threat. The only formally permitted organizations are those sponsored by the state authorities. No financial or technical support is given to other groups.

Overall, the organizational process is a struggle against apathy. The majority of people in popular sectors do not belong to organizations such as the soup kitchen described. What is important for our purposes is that entering an organization is a decision that implies abandoning the "majority attitude" of passivity. Furthermore, joining a soup kitchen not only requires exchanging passivity for action, but it also requires overcoming social stigma. Within the organization, democratic relations struggle against authoritarianism, and the active participation of some is contrasted to the passivity of others.

The idea of organization for this soup kitchen has as one of its features the idea of strong leadership. The head of this organization, Señora Meche is described by one of the members. Señora Meche has been a leader for the past five years:

> Well, Señora Meche comes in and says "good afternoon to everyone, we are going to start the meeting, I would like you to tell me how the food was this week." And all of the Moms respond, lets say it was good, and in the meeting we make all of the decisions that we need to resolve problems. She (Señora Meche) gives her opinion and we all respond. If anyone has any doubts we get to say that we have doubts and then we reach agreement.

Here, strong leadership is seen in the ability to conduct meetings where the group is able to achieve consensus on a problem being discussed. And, although the greater the agreement, the better the organization is, participation in the process of agreement is highly valued. People are expected to express their opinions and doubts. They are also expected to act on behalf of the organization through concrete activities. Among the main activities involved in being organized are: attending the Tuesday meetings, speaking up at the meetings, and spreading the word when schedules are altered. There are also taking turns at cooking, participating in raffles, occasionally attending Vicariate meetings, and so on. What is important is that these activities seem to be done by all members. Given the hostile response of the authorities to any type of organization, these types of organized participatory responses can be said to exist in atmospheres where organization and apathy are the norm.

At this point we would like to remind the reader that we are only discussing a very specific set of elements in this soup kitchen's ethnography. The full ethnography attempts to address questions that go well beyond issues related to first-person accounts of the participants. In the subsequent example that I will introduce, I will attempt to address further questions of a different nature (e.g., What are the possibilities for grass-roots organizations in the marginal world engaging in broader social movements?). Here we are focusing on first-person accounts and also on a level of interpretation that goes beyond first-person narratives to interpretations of this soup kitchen by other popular education groups and by Walker of some of the tensions and polarities previously discussed. Here we have concentrated on the researcher's interpretation by arguing that the practices of this soup kitchen are socially constructed and that the reasons guiding their construction provide cultural significance that is both needed to provide meaning to participants and to facilitate reproduction of ongoing social practices (Walker, 1986). Thus, we have highlighted the participant's social practices in terms of how they can be interpreted to exist from the point of view of an outside researcher as a cluster of contradictory relations. By focusing on these contradictory relations, there is an attempt to highlight how organizational practices are dynamically developed and not mechanically reproduced. The reproduction of practices has been examined in relation to a structure of domination within which these practices operate. Both social and gender relations are discussed as relationships of domination; thus, it is a critical interpretation. Our discussion here must be seen as limited to the above since the study in its entirety goes well beyond issues of domination to an interpretation of organizational resistances that represents, it is argued, the seeds of attempts at social transformation of some of the contradictions. The character of this process of resistance has fundamental political implications. The question of power is first formulated at the level of everyday life (i.e., participants' accounts), then from these accounts there is formulated by the researcher the "story" of the group. Interpretations of this story beyond the narrative level of the participants are then done by other grass-roots organizations as well as the researcher's interpretive intervention. It was the intention in this study from the beginning that there be other interpretations of the soup kitchen by other grass-roots organizations. Thus the researcher sought other interpretations from grass-roots organizations. It was the researcher's view that he needed other interpretations that were already part of the specific culture of the soup-kitchen people. Four grass-roots organizations were solicited. The advantages of this multiple interpretation were said to be the following. First, the interpretation of organizational practices must be culturally immersed. The fact that other organizations shared the same socioeconomic backgrounds helped ground the researcher's own interpretation. It was felt that the researcher's interpretation could be extended and supplemented by groups that were sympathetic to the soup kitchen's struggle. Second, taking into account the other organizations' interpretations was a way to understand the organizational experience of each of the group-interpreter's influence on the sense each makes of the Maria Goretti story. The construction of meaning is illuminated by their practices. Therefore, contrasting experiences enrich the interpretation. The gender issue, for example, as seen by the different group interpreters, allows the researcher to situate its significance within a cultural perspective that transcends the organizations dominated by women as in the soup kitchen. The multiplicity of organizational experiences and the way they relate to the construction of meaning of someone else's practices was said to aid in situating Maria Goretti in broader terms (e.g., a movement). Third, a multiple interpretation was also related to the idea of process. Taking the story to another group brings up new questions, expanding the researcher's perspective.

In summary, the interpretive process started with the problematic description of the soup kitchen's practices and then went on to discuss in a depth that is not captured in this present treatment, a critical structural analysis that linked those practices to social relations. What we have done in this present treatment is to look at structural features of a specific community project that go beyond the narrative accounts of the participants and at the same time use this narrative base for discussing what are considered important dimensions with contradictory underpinnings for the life of one particular community organization.

Method Revisited: A Comparative Analysis

Up to this point we have concentrated our analysis on a certain type of community analysis presently being carried out in a popular sector in Chile. Our next objective is to summarize a study for the purpose of critical comparison. It now seems appropriate to shift our analysis to look at the idea of a critical social science in a context of comparative analysis. An intricate part of the ethnographic method was the use of first-person accounts. This is certainly one essential component of a qualitative analysis. We must remind ourselves of some pitfalls of simply interviewing participants. Certainly some of the recent phenomenological approaches advocating first-person accounts appear, from our perspective, to drift toward some kind of psychological reductionism. To be sure, the cultural world of the *personal* that can be gleaned from the interviews quoted is the stuff that makes for biography and ethnography. It is the world of the "lived experience" that North American phenomenologists speak of in their writing. As the study that we have quoted in the Chilean context shows, however, a critical perspective must go beyond a mere phenomenological emphasis. That being considered, it is also important to be sensitive to the variety of approaches that appear to be alternatives to maintstream positivism. One important distinction that can now be made is that between research based on, and attempts to develop, theory and a type of research that one can label "action research" (Touraine, 1981; Zuniga, 1986b). Zuniga (1986b) characterizes "action research" as a genre of research that locates itself within some type of social transformation movement and identifies with the broad direction of the values of that movement's direction. The work of the researchers in the "systemization project" clearly falls into the latter category (Zuniga, 1986b). It is very clear from the descriptin of the systemization project that action research is in no way devoid of theoretical interest, the most important of which is a theory based on dynamic social practices with emancipatory intentions (Garcia-Huidobro and Pina, 1984; Habermas, 1972; Martinic, 1984). Here one can now make some interesting comparisons between the North American and Chilean context, which we hope will be of some interest to the reader.

First, in the action research that we have been characterizing in the systemization project and specifically the soup kitchen study, there is clearly an emphasis in studying participants in the project with the idea of "collective action" as the totality within which individual actions receive or are denied significance. This is important as a point of emphasis, because we see the direction of qualitative research in a North American context as underemphasizing the collective when participant accounts are being analyzed. Thus in the soup kitchen study, the categories of contradiction such as dependence/independence, social/traditional explanations of women, political/apolitical, and so forth are not formulated specifically around the simple personal life history of the participants, but are formulated with a view to understand the collective striving of the group as a whole. Therefore, even though the interviews clearly have a personal flavor, they are taken together as an avenue to an understanding of the collective life of a community. By contrast, studies of working-class women in a North American context are more often than not couched in a type of methodological procedure of interviewing that stresses what we label an individualistic orientation. Here we frequently have a set of interviews on individual people that are not in contact with one another in any sense that one could label a community. Their interviews taken together are then analyzed in a class context. *Worlds of Pain* by Lilian Ruben (1976) is illustrative of this type of analysis. It is an intensive study of white lower-working-class families. What is important is that these families are not in personal contact with one another, but the methodology treated them as a group for the purposes of a class analysis of working-class family life. Based on interviews with men and women who make up these working-class families, the study attempts to link the interiority of family life (i.e., the microcosm of a personal world) with the work that these people do. In other words, the study attempts to locate their place in a class structure analysis and attempts to show the effects that this has on their personal lives within their families. As the author states:

> Indeed, while there are hundreds of studies of marriage and the family each year, few ever mention the word "class"—an indication of how invisible the class structure has been to those who conceptualize and carry out those projects. (Rubin, 1976, p. 5)

In contrast to Rubin's work, the soup kitchen ethnography simultaneously emphasizes the importance of collectives as units of analysis even with studies with a phenomenological and ethnographic emphasis. The reason we say this is because we draw from the soup kitchen collective a hope that is absent in the Rubin analysis.

A second example that we would like to bring to the reader's attention for illustration and comparison comes from the work of Harré and associates (Harré & Secord, 1972; Marsh, et al., 1978). Harré and Secord (1972) represents the first major systematic attempt to critique mainstream positivistic research and also to provide a sustained rationale for an alternative set of principles that would serve as an umbrella for attempts to break ground on what we have been previously labeling interpretive and ethnographic. They label their work "ethogeny," and within part of this perspective one sees a place for first-person accounts and participant observation. At the level of critique of mainstream research and theory, it is evident that there is a clear indication that we share much in common with their analysis. Given some of these similarities it is very important to accent differences because it is clear from some of the subsequent work of Harré and colleagues that the pursuit of an ethnographical or phenomenological emphasis does not move one into the emphasis that we have been labeling "critical interpretation." This comparison will be important because it dramatizes important differences between what we consider to be diverse approaches to ethnography even when they share common criticisms to mainstream research. The following example is from the work of Marsh, Rosser, and Harré (1978) because it clearly illustrates that ethnography and phenomenology do not necessarily lead to a research strategy with emancipatory intentions. This is not to say that there is a clear right and wrong direction for ethnographic work, but rather that alternative directions can be taken that must be examined on their own merits and also in comparison. The comparison we wish to make here is to help the reader see that "critical interpretation" is one interpretation amongst other ethnographic approaches, and it must be justified on grounds other than that it provides a different approach to mainstream studies. In addition, it is clear that some of the emancipatory critical interpretation cannot be accomplished in some of the directions taken by groups of researchers that fall under the rubric of an ethnographic emphasis. March, *et al.* (1978), indicate at the outset that the ostensible subject matter of their book is the study of violence and disorder as they relate to problems created at football games in Great Britain. Given the tragedy in Belgium, where a number of Italian football fans died in violent encounters with British fans, this cannot be an inconsequential topic for social inquiry in a British context. This study predates this dramatic event but its social relevance is clearly established as a social problem in Great Britain. This particular study is an intensive ethnography of a group of lower-class males who attend these games. A comparison with Chilean women seeking to organize themselves for survival purposes certainly appears on the surface to be quite remote. We are not seeking to compare two populations but to make some critical comparisons in ethnographic studies given that they can take very different directions after the primary ethnographic work is completed.

The Rules for Disorder

The corpus of this study is already described in Chapter 7, pages 150 to 156. The reader is asked to review these pages before we embark upon a comparative analysis.

A Comparison of Critical Interpretation and Ethogeny in Ethnographic Study and Research

Similarities between Critical Interpretation and Ethogeny at the Brute-data Level. As the reader by now is amply aware, these two studies bear very little resemblance at the phenomenal level. The subjects studied are vastly different along gender and age lines. In addition, there are totally different cultural contexts studied. On first look, there seem very good reasons to be ventured that any comparison made between these populations is in serious risk of being invalid. It is our belief, however, that certain comparisons between these studies can elucidate some controversial issues latent in studies seeing themselves as alternatives to quantitative methodologies. It is our conviction that the recent critiques of quantitative methodologies, with their suggestion that they can be supplanted by qualitative methods, are frequently superficial panaceas with vacuous claims. We would hope the comparisons we are about to make will help the reader to see that what is being labeled "qualitative emphasis" in research has many of the contradictions within it as its quantitative counterparts. In fact, it is our belief that it is not really fruitful to make a cold and hard distinction between quantitative and qualitative methodologies. It is our own position that the direction we have called "critical interpretation" can combine both qualitative and quantitative methods. What we will try to attempt here is to demonstrate that the varieties of research strategies that go under the rubric of postpositivistic alternatives can be very different indeed, even when they are using similar research tools (e.g., personal interviews, participant observation). Our present effort is a limited attempt to show that comparisons of this nature can be fruitful both at the level of theory and of research practices. With this in mind, let us now turn to a comparison of the two studies we have just summarized.

What can easily be seen from both studies is their likeness at the "brute-data" or narrative level. Both studies have a base level that can be labeled commonsense language. By this we mean that the discourse at this level can be understood by professional and nonprofessional alike. Thus we mean that both studies depend on a first level that is narrative in nature. Much of this database is interview material or concrete descriptions of the participants in the study. Here one can see the fundamental similarity in research that labels itself as qualitative in that its basic structure is built on narrative description rather than indexical or quantitative findings. That being said, the similarities stop here and thus make it important to discuss different genres of qualitative research as the two studies exemplify. One of the first points of departure is the implicit or explicit political orientation of the research. We will use the term *intentionality* to classify this dimension.

Intentionality of the Researcher within the Research Effort. In our previous descriptions of the two research efforts we tangentially alluded to the intentionality of the researchers within the research effort. It is now important to bring out some differences in bold relief; they account for different directions and conceptualizations that qualitative research efforts take. First of all, the study of the soup kitchen is carried out by a research group that has an affinity relationship with the group they are studying. By affinity relationship, we mean that the research team, although different than the participants in education and economic status, nevertheless share many common values as to the direction of the society in which they live. This relationship is quite explicit in the soup kitchen study. In contrast, the researchers in the Marsh study are not in any sense whatsoever on the same moral or political trajectory as those that they study. Here we see the difference between research for action's sake (Zuniga, 1986) and research for the development of new theoretical horizons (see Harré and Secord, 1972).

When one considers the soup kitchen study, we see an action-research orientation that brings the research effort into a different professional light. The research is not simply to create new knowledge; rather we see in Schon's words (1983) "a new breed of citizen-professional committed to social justice." There is the assumption that the knowledge arising from this type of effort has the merit of reminding us that knowledge is possible only in as much as popular movements shatter categories of order and thus cause both the social relations and mechanisms of domination to emerge (Touraine, 1981). When one looks at research, it is possible to see the Marsh study as one that has a radically different orientation than the Walker study. If the Walker study (1986) highlights possibilities for societal transformation, the Marsh study is potent in demonstrating societal maintenance. The research direction of the soup kitchen study was definitely sympathetic to the political direction of the participants:

> Information gathering for the study entailed four months of observations and ethnographic interviews. This field work was not my first contact with the reality of the poor in Chile and their organizations. My past involvement through CIDE as an educational worker put me in contact with similar situations. I arrived in the field with an idea of what the popular work was about, with prejudices and beliefs. Overall I brought to the study an expanded sympathy towards the oppressed and a deep belief in that justice has to come. (Walker, 1986)

The Marsh study, by contrast, indicates that the researchers are not belief-bound. In fact, they posit a vantage point that is clearly objective. In making this distinction at this point we do not intend that one is particularly superior to the other. What we will attempt to show is that this difference in orientation has a very marked differential impact on the conceptual constructions that will develop beyond the narrative level of discourse.

From Intentionality of the Research to Differential Categorization. By intentionality of the research we mean the theoretical (epistemological) and normative (ethical) thrust of the research effort. We encounter here a discourse that goes beyond the commonsense or narrative level. It is our belief that this level contains both normative and theoretical directions reflecting the underlying values that the research contains. It is our view that social science is not value free and is, therefore, subject to analysis on both theoretical and normative grounds. On this assumption it is interesting to compare the category system developed in the soup kitchen with the system developed in the study of Marsh. What is to be immediately noted in the soup kitchen study is that the categories beyond brute data are political and dialectical at the same time. Thus we have a system of interpretation that deals in political categories of social power. Independence/dependence, social versus traditional explanations of women's oppression, and organization all deal with social power issues and concrete tensions of a historical nature both within and outside the group. In contrast, the study of Marsh *et al.* moves in a very different direction. Here we see that the researchers are moving from brute data to a grammar on rule structure of group order. Although the rule structure analysis does not preclude social power issues, one can see that the emphasis is on social order rather than social change and moves their analysis to a level of abstraction that is quite different in nature. The study by Marsh *et al.* (1978) develops a theory that is directed at how social maintenance is maintained in what appears to be a chaotic situation. Beyond the narrative discourse in this study, one sees a structuralism and functionalism that are directed at the understanding of how the social order is maintained. The authors, in this study, attempt to show that football violence has a functional significance for the participants and a structural significance for the larger society in which it occurs. The concept of "aggro" is developed in order to place human aggression in a societal understanding that views it as a natural part of being human. This orientation can be classified as sociobiological in form. Nowhere in this study can one see the actions of individuals as transformative in nature. Willis (1977), studying a very similar population of working-class youth, interprets their aggression, by contrast, as a precursor to social change. Thus we see that the normative direction of theoretical concepts can move in quite different directions.

The bias of the soup kitchen is that it is immersed in a formulation that is skewed as potentially transformative in nature. The power of its analysis is its political interest in social transformation. What is lacking in this study is the very powerful influence that the military junta has in maintaining a military and fascist social order. When structural concepts are introduced showing the difficulties of social change, they are then directed at demonstrating that social change is possible. Thus the emphasis here is on social transformation by researchers who believe that there are compelling social injustices that warrant analysis in transformational terms. The converse is the case in the football study. The authors, in this study, never question the social order in which they are living and look at aggression as a simple outgrowth of societal living. They never ponder that the violence they are observing could be a type of protest or resistance to the larger society in which, by their social class, they are rendered marginal. What is clear in the discourse of these researchers is that they do not see it in their theoretical view, the necessity to formulate concepts involving social transformation. The fact that this could be a possible option can be seen in a comparison of this study with the study of Willis of working-class boys. What is to be distilled from the above comparisons is how important the intentional base is in ordering the theoretical direction of the discourse beyond the narrative level.

The Issue of Generalizability in Ethnographic Research. There is an antinomy in the style of research when one takes into consideration how one arrives at more general conclusions. In mainstream social scientific research this is accomplished by going from a sample to a population. The question now arising in ethnographic studies is how does one go from a specific instance to a more general conclusion. Marsh *et al.* (1978) feel that generalization is hazardous, it nevertheless can be possible under the following conditions:

> In the ethnogenic approach we follow the example of chemists and anatomists adopting an intensive design, that is, we undertake a detailed study of a few cases selected as typical. We are sure of the detailed validity of our analysis of our cases. We can only hypothesize that they are typical. Those who would follow the extensive design can be sure their results are typical, but they must hypothesize as to whether the few properties that survive the working of the inverse ratio between extension and intension have an individuality at all. Our football-following participants are from one group of fans, supporters from just one local club. With few exceptions, the participants in our study of talk about classroom volume and its accounting are from one school

that is graced by the fans. We are inclined to think that they are pretty typical, given
our less detached work at other football grounds and what we know of other groups
of school children. (pp. 20–21)

The study of the soup kitchen gets at the question of generalizability in a
different manner. Recall that in this study the researcher did not only give his
interpretive work to the reader. He also solicited other popular groups to make
interpretations on the basis of the group story that he had devised at the outset.
It must be noted that these groups made no direct interpretations. Their interpretive work was made on the group story devised by the researcher. Hence
multiple interpretation here refers not to the ideas of a group of interpreters who
engage collectively in the research, but rather to one interpretation that relies
heavily on the research of others. Walker (1986) delineates several advantages
to this type of multiple interpretation.

> First, the interpretation of organizational practices must be culturally immersed. The
> fact that other organizations which share the socio-economic and cultural background
> of Maria Goretti participate in the interpretation allows me to ground my own ideas
> in the culture. My immersion in the understanding of Maria Goretti's practices is
> facilitated by the involvement–distance dialectic of multiple interpreters. On one
> hand I discuss the story with others (group–interpreters) who are sympathetic to the
> group's struggle. However, their distance and different organizational context illu-
> minates Maria Goretti's practices, enriching their interpretation. My distance is sup-
> plemented by the other's distance (which differs fundamentally from mine). Second,
> taking account of other organizations' interpretations helps me to understand the way
> the organizational experience of each of the group–interpreters influences the sense
> each makes of Maria Goretti's story. The construction and meaning is illuminated
> by their practices. Therefore contrasting experiences enrich the interpretation. . . .
> The multiplicity of organizational experiences and the way they relate to the con-
> struction or meaning of someone else's practices helps situate Maria Goretti in broader
> terms, that is, in terms of a movement, a project. (Walker, 1986, pp. 46–47)

What is essential for the reader to see here is the very different motives that
these two studies have in establishing wider significance. Marsh *et al.* deal with
generalization in the more conventional sense, that is, is the population they
have examined typical? We say conventional here because the researchers are
attuned to the issue of generalization already established by mainstream quantitative research. As in quantitative research, there is the epistemological issue
of the typicalness of the study. In contrast, the soup kitchen study is interested
in questions of generalization on both epistemological and normative (political)
reasons. It is our understanding that the political intent of the research on the
soup kitchen sets it off from other types of ethnographies so as to be labeled
"critical interpretation." Thus questions of generalization are contemplated for
very different motives. The soup kitchen study is couched in questions of generalization relating to social movements. Thus, interpretation plays a fundamental role, epistemologically and methodologically, in bringing people together

to reflect upon their practices, plan new action, evaluate their activities, and engage in an overall process of questioning the everyday world in order to transform it (Walker, 1986). Hence interpretation is not neutral. It provides us with the opportunity to reflect on social and cultural reality from a particular position of interest. Therefore, questions of generalization are not put forward in order to see if a particular group is typical to a larger abstract population. The political intent of critical ethnography, as we see it, is to draw lines differentiating between dominating rich and oppressed poor, whites and blacks, military men and peacemakers, women and men. All these different situations in the world are related to specific ways of understanding our own situation. An interpretation of what happens to a given individual relates to an alternative view coexisting with contradictory views held by other groups. There is a conflict of interests between these views. The task of widening the range of a study of a particular interpretation is to see that group as part of a larger movement in society that has as its intent an interest that challenges oppression. Thus the desire to situate the soup kitchen study in a wider context is motivated by an emancipatory interest in human liberation. That is the normative work of critical interpretation absent in other qualitative alternatives such as the Marsh study.

   Question of Validity within the Context of Qualitative Interpretation. One of the central questions for social scientific research is the issue of validity of interpretation. There are, within this collective belief, both theoretical and practical considerations. For example, on the practical end, the issue of validity has implications for the funding of research efforts. In an otherwise sympathetic review of popular education efforts, Zuniga (1986) raises an important caveat for the qualitative research. He maintains that investigation of action in this area has demonstrated its practical utility, its political significance but not its "epistemological truth." This question of validation of new methodologies is important if these efforts are able to enter the arena of dialogue with mainstream social research. It is our contention that one must, from the outset, accept the inevitability of dealing with questions pertaining to validation. Given this limit, one must see epistemological validity and adequacy as argument (see Chapter 7). In this light we must accept, at the outset, the inevitability of conflict of interpretations. The nature of conflicts can vary from situation to situation. One interpretation may be rejected by the participants. If accepted by the participants, it may be rejected by alternative interpretations. This possibility was built into the soup kitchen study, which involved not only professional researchers but other popular education groups and the participants themselves as well. Thus, alternatives must be seen as arguments rather than conclusions. All conclusions are, therefore, negotiable. Within this context, the issue of validity seems very different than mainstream positivistic research. From the mainstream one might consider that this is, pejoratively, soft validity. It is nevertheless our contention that interpretations must entertain alternative interpretation by necessity. To entertain alternatives does not necessarily mean that all arguments must be embraced. Here, we must point out that we are using the term "validity" in a restricted sense. A valid argument within this perspective does not connote "verification." To speak of verification is to assume that an accounts conclusion is true (Hirsch, 1967a). Validity from our perspective must, of necessity, be more humble in stance, in that one tries to show in arguing an account that the interpretation is plausible. But validation goes beyond mere plausibility. In accepting conflict of interpretations, one does not have to accept that all accounts are of equal merit. Validation demands adjudication of conflicts of interpretation (see Chapter 5). The job of validation is to evaluate the disparate constructions that understanding has brought forward. Validation is therefore the fundamental task of interpretation as a discipline, since whenever agreement already exists there is little practical need for validation (Hirsch, 1967a).

It is here that it is appropriate to make a distinction, infrequently made, between understanding and explanation. Ricoeur (1978) contends that understanding and explanation are relative moments in the complex process called interpretation. When interpretive horizons are complementary or identical, there is very little need for explanation. Explanation is warranted only when there is a situation of conflict. Thus explanation follows because:

> Understanding calls for explanation as soon as there is no longer dialogue, where the give and take of question and answers permit an interpretation to be verified as it unfolds. When I do not spontaneously understand, I ask for explanation and the explanation that you offer allows me to understand you better. (Ricoeur, 1978, p. 153)

Here we would agree with both Hirsch (1967a) and Ricoeur (1978) that validation is a test of our guesses at interpretation following a logic of probability rather than a logic of empirical verification. In a certain sense, an interpretation is an argument for, or advocacy of, a point of view or horizon. Our contention is that a valid argument is a form of advocacy for a particular interpretation. In advocating a particular interpretation, one brings forth factual evidence for that particular interpretation. Validation, in these terms, can be seen as an argumentative discipline, comparable to juridical procedures of legal interpretation (Ricoeur, 1978). Arguments for an interpretation must be seen in a relative light. In arguing for a particular interpretation, one develops evidence that a particular interpretation is "probable" under these circumstances. When an interpretation is in conflict with another interpretation, the better interpretation attempts to show that it is more probable than its adversary under these circumstances.

INTERPRETIVE ARGUMENT AS PUT FORTH IN THE SOUP KITCHEN STUDY. In the soup kitchen study the argument developed for critical interpretation is that everyday practices have contradictory relationships because organizational practices operate within spheres of contradiction. It is a contention, in this study, that the resolution of these contradictions consolidates the development of the organization proper. It is also argued that organizations cannot be understood simply from first-person accounts: it is necessary to see these organizations in their permanent relationship to external institutions that have a significant relationship in the defining of their particular practices. The Church, popular education projects, other local organizations, and political parties belong to a support network in which they interact with one another in a mutual reinforcing process. In the soup kitchen study, the Church (Vicariate) and popular education projects are seen as the most important sources of aid for grass-roots organizations mobilized in the *poblaciónes* after the 1973 military coup.

Looking at organizations as practices in contradictions highlights the group processes in the Maria Goretti Soup Kitchen as simultaneously one of reproduction and transformation. The methodological approach makes visible the ways in which everyday practices are embedded in practices of domination. It also shows how the struggle of the organization is primarily a struggle against the reproduction of these structures. The analysis of social and gender relations, as structures of domination, indicates how organizational practices are socially constructed and deeply rooted in structures that made the researchers take for granted the way in which reality presented itself in their experience.

The transformation of organizational practices is fundamentally related to the development of critical consciousness. Popular education was examined as praxis, which aims at consciousness raising. It was argued that some crucial aspects must be considered in the development of critical consciousness. First, it is important to identify oppression in everyday relations, for everyday life is what fundamentally defines us in the world. Second, it is important to identify forms of resistance. Here, the development of conflictual relations is central to the development of forms of opposition. Political subjects are constituted when they enter into conflictual relationships that challenge structures of domination. Third, there must be a process where experiences and resistance are collectivized. It is important to look at structures of domination as socially constructed. The structural dimension of domination must be understood. The realm of everyday life is transcended by the macrostructures of society. Fourth, there is a development of alternative practices, a process in which the intentionality of transformation comes into focus.

The development of critical consciousness in the Maria Goretti Soup Kitchen and in other grass-roots organizations suggests a reconceptualization of consciousness that makes a distinction between consciousness in discourse and consciousness in action. Those who understand consciousness as the expression of change in a particular kind of discourse identified as political typically ignore the transformative action of those who have not articulated their experience in this discourse. The oversight applies, in particular, to the participants of the organization in the marginal sectors, especially women. In this study, by contrast, action has been taken as a significant indicator of critical consciousness.

The reconceptualization of critical consciousness is linked to a reconceptualization of the political. It is argued that the experience of the Maria Goretti Soup Kitchen reveals the fundamentally political character of their process of development. The reconceptualization of the political has implied a critique of the public/private split and of its consequent identification of the political in the public sphere. It is argued that hegemony is reproduced through everyday practices. Therefore, the question of power is shifted, from the external structures determining our everyday life to everyday in relation to the macrostructure. Within this perspective, those forms of struggle found in the Maria Goretti Soup Kitchen that resist oppression in the private sphere are political struggles. Popular educators, although allied with these forms of struggle, need to deepen their conceptualization of the political, for the development of critical consciousness is crucial to an understanding of how to work politically in education.

The development of a transformative organizational praxis needs to be related to a macrolevel; a relation with the macrolevel must be established. It is argued for local development of an adequate perspective that provides a framework to relate microexperiences to broader instances of coordination. This is especially important in terms of the construction of a popular education project. It is assumed that no microexperiences will be successful if they are not related to higher levels of organization and coordination. This is the level of a social movement. The idea of local development adequately addresses the relation between everyday organizational practices and a concept of decentralized development allowing a higher degree of autonomy for organizations to implement their programs. Central to this study was the development of an interpretation of the Maria Goretti Soup Kitchen in order to understand organizational practices from the viewpoint of the participants by developing an ethnographic case study and multiple interpretations of the case. The decoding of the cultural significance of the organizational practices was an important part of the process of interpretation. This is the reason why the researcher has attempted to use the words of the participants and has used a considerable number of quotations from the soup kitchen members as well as from those other interpreters who shared a similar cultural background. The interpretation attempted to provide an argument as to how and why one understands the soup kitchen as a process of transformation of organizational practices.

INTERPRETIVE ARGUMENT AS PUT FORTH IN THE FOOTBALL STUDY. In the *Rules of Disorder*, Marsh *et al.* (1978) understand their account as one that is backed by argument. In fact, their argument attempts to counter media interpretations of youth violence as arbitrary and anarchic. They venture their own argument at two levels. The first is that of a structural articulation of rules interpreting violence at the schools and football games of working-class youth. Here the concept of moral careers was introduced and was ventured as a central reason for action. They talk about "moral careers" as conventional accounts.

They then shift to what they say is a causal account embedded in naturalistic explanation. The sociobiological concept of "aggro" is presented as a causal mechanism for violence in these settings. Thus, for these authors the ethnographic work is filtered through conventional categories of social science, that is, structural concepts (i.e., moral careers) and functional concepts (i.e., aggro). As was said earlier, critical interpretation as a way of resymbolizing the world of others requires a sensitivity in reflecting back to the participants and other interested parties (i.e., social scientists, social policymakers, etc.) and their capacities for "intentional intervention" (i.e., free acts of agents creating a world). *The Rules of Disorder* clearly lacks this critical moment in its argument. The functional concept of aggro, for example, themetizes the participants' actions within a biological framework and thus ignores the agent's quality of aggression and the possible truth that rebellion is more than ritual liability. Thus, within this frame of reference, the authors interpret resistance and aggression as biological processes rather than forms of intentional intervention in societal processes.

This concludes our comparative analysis of two ethnographic studies. If we have demonstrated that ethnographies embrace different theories and research practices, even when they are seen as replacing mainstream quantitative analysis, then we have succeeded in our task.

EXAMPLE 4: LOCAL DEVELOPMENT[11]

In the previous example I compared two ethnographic evaluations in an attempt to show fruitful differences in ethnographic comparisons that frequently fall under the umbrella of quantitative studies. In the example I am about to give, one of those studies will occupy us here. What we would like to study in more detail in is an evaluation done on a soup kitchen in Santiago, Chile. The present analysis will attempt to locate this soup kitchen project in a larger social context. We will attempt to do this by using dialectical concepts of *habitus* and *project*—discussed extensively in Chapters 3 and 4—and also, in some detail, my previous example on media analysis.

In the previous example, four areas of contradiction were analyzed: dependence-independence, social versus traditional explanation of oppression, politization versus apolitization, and organization versus disorganization. It is not our intent to review these contradictions here. What I will attempt now is to broaden the base of a particular popular education effort in an attempt to show its possible wider significance. In that sense, we are attempting a form of gen-

[11]The Chile-OISE Co-operative Project. Funded by the Canadian International Development Research Corporation (I.D.R.C.), 1984.

eralization. In the present case, we will attempt to answer such questions as: What are the possibilities for grass-roots organizations in the marginal world engaging in a broader movement? How could this involvement be developed? What are the contents of such a project? In answering these questions, we will argue for the significance of these types of organizations in terms of their contribution to a project. Then, the analysis will address the issues of the reproduction and transformation of organizational practices by discussing the tension produced between habitus and project. The theoretical assumptions underlying these concepts help us to develop an understanding of the dynamics of transformation. Finally, we will discuss the idea of local development (LD) as a model that may articulate the construction of a project.

A brief recapitulation will be offered before moving into a discussion on the construction of a project.

We have, in summary form, referred to the organizational practices that conform to the everyday life of the Maria Goretti Soup Kitchen (see Example 3). We have indicated that several practices exist and operate in contradictory relation. By focusing on contradictions, we have attempted to highlight how organizational practices are dynamically developed, not mechanically reproduced. The reproduction of practices has been examined in relation to a structure of domination within which these practices operate. Both social and gender relations have been discussed as relations of domination. On the other hand, the Maria Goretti Soup Kitchen represents a struggle for transformation. The character of this process of resistance has fundamental political implications. The question of power is formulated at the level of everyday life relations, which has important implications for the discussion on hegemonic and counter-hegemonic projects. Central to this process of transformation is the development of critical consciousness. Popular education has been examined as a strategy that raises issues regarding *the political* as a key aspect of the process of consciousness raising. Hence, grass-roots organizations in marginal areas fulfill needs that go beyond mere survival. And this is not only the organization's responsibility. A support network provides financial and educational assistance. The role of the Vicariate of Solidarity, the human rights branch of the Catholic Church, and other Church-related institutions has been central to the improvement of people's needs at the grass-roots level.

Now, it is our desire to address the way in which grass-roots organizations may be linked to the construction of a popular project. Transformation as both an ideal and a praxis must also be examined in relation to the macrostructure of domination. It would be misleading to suggest that transformation at the microlevel is an autonomous praxis. Its relationship to the macrostructure is fundamental in this transformation.

Soup Kitchens and Grass-roots Organizations

It is important, in the first place, to look at organizations, such as the Maria Goretti Soup Kitchen, within the context of the *poblaciónes*. The grass-roots organizations existing in the *poblaciónes* could be classified according to different criteria. A clear differentiation among them is the type of action they predominantly develop. Espinoza (1983) has made a distinction between (1) actions oriented to the satisfaction of basic needs, such as survival initiatives like soup kitchens;[12] (2) community action initiatives such as popular education activities, Christian communities, and so on;[13] and (3) action toward the maintenance, conquest, or recuperation of basic improvements in the quality of life of the *pobladores*, such as housing. These types of activities are known as *acción reivindicatoria*.[14] The problem with these categories is that they usually rigidify what is being described. And sometimes the rigidification makes categories useless when one is trying to understand social phenomena. This precaution is particularly relevant in the discussion of the urban reality of the popular sectors, for one of their fundamental characteristics is heterogeneity.

The analysis of any organization will suggest that the boundaries between categories are very diffused and difficult to define. The difficulties in determining such boundaries are related to the heterogeneity found in the shanty towns. There are several organizations with different but coexisting histories, origins, and objectives. The popular education experiences being implemented in these groups are also numerous and different from each other. An important implication of this heterogeneity is that an analysis that focuses on one type of action will be relevant for other types. Another significant implication, however, is that it is difficult both to generalize and to draw conclusions applicable to all experiences. The "strengths" in analyzing the action of a soup kitchen, which is predominantly oriented to survival, are various. First, the number of soup kitchens have increased during the last five years, and forecasts for the next ten years

[12]Other examples of these organizations are productive workshops developed by unemployed workers (comités de cesantes; "commando juntos;" consumers' cooperatives to reduce costs of food; family gardens cultivated in small areas, usually in part of the family's lot and intended to provide vegetables. Most of these initiatives were created in response to the economic recession, which has severely affected the country since 1981).

[13]Espinoza (1983) argues that these initiatives stress the idea that the popular sectors must develop their own capacities as much as possible, promoting a development from the bottom up instead of the other way around as has historically been the case. Other groups that may fall into this category are human rights committees, women's refection groups and workshops on women's issues, and health community groups.

[14]The *acción reivindicatoria* has been historically centered in the housing demands of shanty towns. Land take-overs and other urban improvements have been its most distinctive features.

are likely to include high unemployment due to the financial deterioration of the economy. Hence, it is expected that these organizations will continue to expand through strategies that will probably take new forms to reduce the cost of basic needs. Second, since these organizations depend on external aid such as that provided by the Church, their development depends on the development of an external support network. The direction of the last few years, especially that of the Vicariate, indicates that external aid is being progressively understood in relation to its social and organizational effects. There is a movement away from paternalism, promoting instead the responsibility, the commitment, and the relative autonomy of organizations in facing their own problems. A good example is the Vicariate's policy regarding financial aid to soup kitchens. We consider this relation a strength because the support of external institutions (or individuals) is an essential part of the possibilities of transformation and development in the shanty towns. Third, the participants in organizations oriented to survival are usually in the most marginal situations in an already marginal world. Theirs is an extreme situation characterized not only by the worst of economic conditions but also by apathy and despair, and there are many reasons to believe that there is a large percentage of the population in this situation. From a quantitative point of view, an understanding of this type of action opens the door for the understanding of the situation and prospects of a great number of people. Finally, the previous point has led us to consider that this understanding had demanded the questioning of old categories of interpretation and the development of new ones. The traditional way of conceiving political discourse and action totally ignored the existence of a political life for marginal people like the members of the Maria Goretti Soup Kitchen; the private and the personal spheres were disregarded as apolitical. Since most grass-roots organizations are built around survival, and since mainly women comprise them, it is possible to develop a new approach. In fact, understanding the cultural implications of this type of organization demands a new framework of interpretation.

However, there are "weaknesses" as well, one of which is the transitory character of these organizations. Since participation is contingent on an urgent need, once the emergency is over, participants withdraw. It is difficult to assign some degree of stability to these groups. Perhaps it would be appropriate to think that the organizations exist as an insurance reserved for emergencies. In this case, survival forms persist over time but participants do not necessarily. In addition, the concern about the satisfaction of basic needs leads to an emphasis on local and immediate objectives. The experience of immediacy makes it difficult for participants to relate their concrete problems to broader structures of domination. Thus, the relation between short- and long-term projects is precarious and usually nonexistent. This makes it more difficult to imagine how these organizations would relate to a popular project. Educational processes of consciousness raising must take this transitory situation, which characterizes the participation of a large number of members, as an important reason to emphasize throughout the educational process the everyday expression of relations of domination. In this sense, the political participation in a popular project is not necessarily restricted to participating in a specific organization.

The Maria Goretti Soup Kitchen is not intended to be representative of the shanty town organizational reality. Sheer survival is the main problem underlying its practices and contradictions. However, as we have argued, the action and discourse go beyond survival. In this sense, the analysis of the soup kitchen may be useful for other analyses that have as their primary reference other types of organizations. The above clarification has direct implications in the discussion of a popular project that follows in the next section.

The Transformation of Organizational Practices

It is not only difficult but also mistaken to talk about any popular project as an abstract category, particularly when the study of organizational practices is constrained by the analysis of concrete situations. Furthermore, there is no conception of "project" that will accommodate reality, although we frequently attempt this. Our approach here is to look at these concrete practices and see what aspects of them might be conceived as projects. Hence, we are from the beginning discouraging those who might think that by doing this we are outlining the Project of the Popular Sectors of Chile. We are only analyzing a specific situation—organizations for survival—which exist in a particular space and time within the history of the marginal sectors living in the shanty towns of Santiago. Therefore, the concept of project has another constraint: its relation to a particular situation within the marginal sectors (i.e., that of the dwellers of the *poblaciónes*). Considering the boundaries we are setting up for the use of the word "project," it might be more appropriate to talk about an urban project for shanty town dwellers.

Several approximations to a definition of project should be articulated. A recapitulation will be helpful for a continuation of the discussion. *Project* can be defined as a set of practices in which human action and its transformative intentionality become a reality. This meaning assumes a basic articulation that makes everyday practices transcend a mere responsive action (*accíon reivindicatoria*) toward injustice, challenging the hegemony of the dominant class. It has also been defined in terms of the development of critical consciousness, as a collective movement able to reach a significant degree of acceptance as an alternative praxis transcending both the local level and those most active as a liberating praxis questioning a situation of oppression arising from social and gender relations of domination.

The idea of project becomes clearer when contrasted to the idea of habitus. Habitus has been defined by Bourdieu (1977) as follows:

> The habitus is precisely this immanent law, *lex insita*, laid down in each agent by his earliest upbringing, which is the precondition not only for the coordination of practices but also for practices of co-ordination. (p. 81)
>
> The habitus, the durably installed generative principle of regulated improvisations, produces practices which tend to reproduce the regularities immanent in the objective conditions of the production of their generative principle. (p. 78)

Thus, habitus is represented by the existence of a present order maintained through its cultural reproduction. The reproduction involves those ideas, values, attitudes, systems of communication, cultural significations, and everyday practices that contribute to structural relations of domination but are conceived as taken for granted, unproblematic reality. It is important, though, not to understand habitus as just an inevitable force of adjustment to life making people comfortable with what exists; nor is it to be understood as conservative socialization. Fundamentally, habitus must be understood in structural terms, that is, in terms of class, gender, and other structural relations (see Chapter 4). Neither should it be understood as an external force imposed on people determining their being. It is in everyday life where habitus is expressed, locally and historically. Structural relations are not just structured out there but are in a process of structuring by all of us, every day. Our responsibility in reproduction and transformation is primarily being worked out through our everyday practices. The project will be informed by human practices, which challenge the habitus and transform it.

In Chapter 4, I have characterized the tension between "habitus" and "project" by looking at both as parts of a dialectical relationship. We will provide a brief characterization of each side of this dialectic, using the example of the Maria Goretti Soup Kitchen. An outline of the habitus–project relation is provided in the following chart where there are enumerated the dimensions of what we have been calling the "personal world."

Integrative Polarities of a Personal World

Socialization (Habitus)	Transformation (Project)
1. Social self (me)	Intentional self (I)
2. Identity	Individuation
3. Order (reproduction)	Change (transformation)
4. Preconscious	Conscious
5. Past (history)	Future
6. Ideological symbols	Utopian symbols
7. Determinism	Freedom

1. *Social Self/Intentional Self.* The *social self* is that aspect of each person that in the context of his or her relationship to his or her culture is likely to be maintained. It is the aspect

of the self that reproduces that which he or she sees as a reflection of his or her culture. It is the image (mirror relation) between culture and subject. The *intentional self* is that other aspect of being a person that reacts to the culture intending its transformation. The reference here is oneself.

2. *Identity/Individuation: Identity* is defined as the identification of the subject with a group or class with a common culture. It is a sense of belonging and acceptance of the most predominant features of the cultural order. *Individuation* is the expression of resistance to the dominant culture. In the process of belonging there is a possibility of distancing oneself from the culture and developing a critique and alternative view that challenge dominant concepts of identity. The reference here is the culture.

3. *Order/Change: Order* is represented by those practices oriented toward the reproduction of the existing order. It is an adherence to what exists in its fundamental features. *Change* is represented by the transformation of the system while assuming a critical view of the foundations of the existing order.

4. *Preconscious/Conscious:* This tension is expressed in the dialectical relationship between consciousness as it is expressed concretely in the present time and the foundations upon which that consciousness has been developed. The preconscious is a characteristic of the past.

5. *Past/Future:* The habitus relies on the history of human events and their continuity in the present. Our *past* is in a way determining our present. The *future*, on the other side, could be different in that it may break with the past in transforming the present order.

6. *Ideological Symbols/Utopian Symbols: Ideological symbols* are understood here as representations of reality that negatively distort the possibility of transformation. They make cultural reality appear as a natural dimension of human life. They naturalize experience. We use ideological symbolism to justify the maintenance of things the way they are. A *utopian symbol*, by contrast, represents an alternative of transformation. Justification is grounded in the cultural dimension of human experience obscured by ideological representation. Utopian symbols are in Sullivan's (1984) terms "symbolic images of the future that challenges the ultimacy and total legitimacy of the present order." (p. 70)

7. *Determinism/Freedom:* The weight that determinism has in the human consciousness is a factor that contributes to the development and consolidation of the habitus. There are different types of determinism that influence our way of looking at reality. Historical and economic determinisms have usually been active in preventing social change. *Freedom* is used here to indicate that there is always a possibility for transformation that will change the habitus through an emancipatory movement.

The seven faces of the dialectics of "habitus" and "project" allow us to elaborate upon a description of the dynamics of cultural reproduction and transformation among the members of the Maria Goretti Soup Kitchen. These dynamics, however, exist in a context in which structural relations ultimately define the development of cultural action. The degree of oppression of a specific group or class in society is related to the amount of power that group holds with respect to the dominant class. It also depends on the degree of hegemony of the dominant class and to the degree of mobilization of the oppressed. As Giddens (1979) argues, it is only within a structural context where subjects are more or less agents. The development of agency—central to a project—is related to the development of certain socioeconomic, cultural, and political conditions in which action becomes transformative (see Chapters 4 and 6).

The analysis of the dynamics of cultural reproduction and transformation presents two clear expressions. On one side, there is an "affirmative dynamic" representing the process in which a social class or a social group consolidates their commitment to the existent structural situation. A study of the habitus under this dynamic shows, for example, how poverty would be accepted as a natural given and would be explained in, say, mythical terms. The habitus, in these circumstances, is characterized by a process in which the group or class will look at itself in terms of traditional explanations tending to justify the present order. There is no critical consciousness about their relation to the dominant sectors. On the contrary, there is a noncritical recognition of socioeconomic differences and a search, in expressions belonging to other groups and classes, of values, ideas, and practices that provide a justification of their view of the world. The "project," under these circumstances, is the realization of action and discussion of alternatives that intend to improve the quality of life without challenging the hegemony of the dominant project. Usually, in an affirmative dynamic, oppressed groups and classes adopt the project of those who are dominating them, which might end up helping them improve their own situation.

However, there are several historical examples of "transformative dynamics." In these, the habitus is characterized by the "valorization" of what is positive in the group and the rejection, to those "penetrations" in Willis's (1977) terms, of the dominant ideology into the popular culture. The project, in this dynamic, is constituted by a mobilization that proposes creative alternatives threatening the structural order; the practices of transformation are counter-hegemonies.

Historically, both dynamics have coexisted. Nevertheless, in specific historical situations, one may be more prominent. There was little doubt that the Chilean society engaged in a transformative dynamic under the last two democratic governments, the Christian Democrats (1964–1970) and the Popular Unity (1970–September, 1973). After the coup, the popular sectors turned to an affirmative dynamic, which was only seriously challenged in 1983 when the national mobilization of the opposition began.

The story of the Maria Goretti Soup Kitchen shows bits of everything. The intention of the discussion above is thus not to rigidify the soup kitchen's practices as affirmative or transformative, but to emphasize that they must be looked at in relation to the dynamics of the group and class to which they belong, which is in turn directly related to macroprocesses of transformation. We believe that looking at Maria Goretti's experience in terms of habitus and project provides a means to visualize the experience in terms of a project for the shanty town dwellers. More specifically, it provides the background needed for an accurate understanding of the role that education may play in it.

TABLE 3.   Maria Goretti's Practices in the Perspective of Habitus and Project

1. *Social Self*

The participants reproduce a traditional understanding of the role they play in the world. This is primarily characterized by being mothers/wives/housewives. As part of their role as women they must begin to provide for the family's food when there is not enough due to the unemployment of men. They join the soup kitchen to satisfy this need.

1. *Intentional Self*

The participation in the soup kitchen provides the opportunity for collectivizing the personal experience in the home, and for engaging in new activities that demand new responsibilities. Participants begin to look at themselves differently, finding that they are asking new questions about those aspects they had taken for granted. The new self is able to engage in practices with new significations which challenge others. A contradictory self-image arises.

2. *Identity*

Participants identify with some of the distinctive features of their culture. First, there is an apathetic tendency stimulated by the opposition of husbands or *convivientes* to participation, repression, and social stigmatization. Second, there is an identification with patriarchal relations.

2. *Individuation*

The organizational development has questioned relations of domination. The questioning of *machismo*, for example, has led women to reject the participation of men in the group.

3. *Order*

The situation of being in extreme need is transitory. There is a hope that the government will improve salaries in POJH. Meanwhile, there is a dependent relationship to the Church.

3. *Change*

Extreme poverty is related to a socioeconomic system consolidated by the Pinochet government. It is important to struggle against the government and the system. Thus, organizations engage in a process that transcends survival. It implies the development of critical consciousness. Although aid from the Church is needed, organizations seek independence. The participant's responsibility to struggle for the solution of their problems is emphasized.

4. *Preconscious*

Both class and gender oppression, experienced through poverty and male domination, have been lived with as natural throughout a process of socialization.

4. *Conscious*

Both class and gender oppression become realities that could be transformed. This awareness has been developed through a process of "conscientization" stimulated in the last years by the popular education programs.

5. *Past*

Past is represented for many by a rural past where traditions are strong. It is also represented by a process of personal suffering in the condition of women. In terms of national events, references only go back as far as the Allende years.

5. *Future*

There is a more "realistic" notion of the future expressed in the improvements of life through changes in the established institutions such as POJH. There is also a dream of a more radical change, which is rarely made explicit. Overall, there is a strong sense of the present and the immediate.

6. Ideological Symbols

There are strong justifications for *machismo*, *apoliticism*, and *dependency* that become obstacles for the possibilities of transformation.

6. Utopian Symbols

There are symbols that challenge the present order. These are collective organization solidarity, independence, autonomy, liberation of women, and participation.

7. Determinism

The future of our children will be like our own present. We were born poor and now we are even poorer. The same will continue to happen. Changes always favor the ones at the top.

7. Freedom

If we get together, among ourselves, with other organizations, we can do something to change the world. In Puente Alto we have a Soup Kitchens' Coordinating Committee. This is a new step, which shows us that there are things we can do.

Each of these seven faces (see Table 3) of the dialectics of "habitus" and "project" has been characterized by one statement intended to summarize the main dynamics in the Maria Goretti Soup Kitchen's story. The construction of a project must take these into account. We do not intend to give the impression that our formulation of a project is a pure abstraction of a future's dream, something that is distant from what goes on every day. Rather, the characterization of a habitus and a project intends to stress a praxis of transformation that is locally situated, based on the realization that local change is ultimately possible if there is global change.

A praxis of transformation is conceived here as a process in which subjects are constituted by the resolution of conflicts that resist a situation of domination. This is the constitution of historical agents of change. Two examples of this kind of praxis in the story of the Maria Goretti Soup Kitchen are the struggle against husbands or *convivientes* and the struggle against the *encargada* for participation and independence. It is, as stressed above, through the resolution of conflicts that transformation becomes a reality. This is why it is very important to recognize new forms of conflict in the marginal areas.

Traditionally, social subjects have been considered to be in conflict just because they occupied a position regarding the ownership of the modes of production. Orthodox Marxism has argued that the poor were part of a project of liberation because they were poor. Depending on how social structure is conceived, subjects are thought to have this or that characteristic. This way, subjects are preconstituted according to a model. In the Marxist determinist approach people are categorized as proletarian or bourgeoisie according to a model defined by the conflict characterized by the ownership of the capitalist means of production. This line of thinking is not helpful in understanding the situation of the oppressed in the marginal areas of Third World countries. It is necessary, on the contrary, to look at what is happening in reality to establish who is in conflict with whom and what the contents of those conflicts are. The organizational struggle of the Maria Goretti Soup Kitchen would be totally disregarded by traditional theorists because their essential conflicts, as their position within the working class, are not expressed in traditionally recognized categories. Their conflict as women, for example, not part of what is considered "class conflict," would be omitted from study. As well, the political character of the struggle of the soup kitchen would go unrecognized, for the *political* must be located in the public sphere. Everyday struggle is invisible unless expressed in established forms identified as political in the public realm.

It still remains a question as to how the experience of the Maria Goretti Soup Kitchen transcends its particularity and gains the broader perspective that makes a project possible. I believe this question is relevant for all organizations existing in the *poblaciones*. This heterogeneous world needs to articulate a *direction*. We will argue that materialization of the idea of local development (LD) provides an adequate framework for the articulation of a project.

Local Development: A Perspective for the Construction of a Project

More than any other concept, LD, as a perspective in this study, takes on an educational connotation. This is our bias in looking at popular projects, which is one way of saying that the purpose of this work is not to analyze the economic possibilities of such ventures. We will, rather, take into account the possibilities for the development of a critical consciousness as our main issue.

By LD, we understand the development of a reflection-action process whose main purpose is the improvement of the quality of life in a particular locality. Such a process is conceived as a struggle that empowers grass-roots organizations in decision making regarding their own development projects. This process of empowerment is directly related to the development of a social movement where local initiatives and experiences are coordinated and centralized at a macrolevel. The following discussion attempts to explain the sources of this definition.

The recent conceptualizations of the *local* have been a consequence of the years of dictatorship, for the repression and isolation of the popular sectors have been opposed by actions attempting to bring people together again at a local level, in a *manzana*,[15] *población*, or county. The notion of "similar people living nearby with similar problems" is gradually coming back, ending a period of time where most people in the *poblaciónes* stayed in their own homes. From the point of view of the rearticulation of a social movement, there are several examples of initiatives circumscribed by the place where people live rather than by centralized initiatives. For example, the most significant expression of resistance to the dictatorship, the national days of protest, has been primarily local demonstrations (i.e., the neighborhood, *población*, or county).

The notion of the local as a level for development fits our understanding

---

[15]*Manzana* is a term used by urbanists to define a square block of housing.

of a process of consciousness-raising based on everyday practices. It is at the local level where these practices are primarily lived. A relation between organizations and social and gender relations, for example, is clearly established when the idea of development is grounded in structures of domination embedded in everyday practices. In this sense, both the philosophy and methodology of popular education are focusing the attention on the dynamics of transformation of the everyday life. For example, popular education programs have been emphasizing the leadership-organization relation to transform authoritarian practices into democratic relations. It is expected that new practices will have a positive influence in consolidating the organization, and thus in its capacity for mobilizing people for social transformation. The emphasis of popular education must be pursued, for it provides a framework that links the problem of hegemony to the consolidation of structures of domination through taken for granted, everyday experiences.

Hence, LD is directly related to the redemocratization of Chilean society. Although it is difficult to imagine such a process after twelve years of consolidated military rule, a redemocratization process has already taken off. Our participation in this process (as educators, as grass-roots organizations) must inevitably be clarified. From this point of view, it is important to conceive such redemocratization as a process lived and managed by social organizations, including those existing in the private sphere such as the family. In this process, the development of programs of action, the appropriation of old instruments, and the creation of new ones by the organizations themselves are crucial; and these may be best implemented at the local level. From an educational point of view, for example, it is necessary to support critical reflection on grass-roots organizational practices to generate democratic action that opens new grounds for negotiation with those in power. Negotiation today may be a new face of democratic action. Planning, implementation of programs, and evaluation may be organized around processes of negotiation with local authorities for the solution of basic problems.

None of the aspects discussed above can be fully understood, however, if we do not take into account the institutional reforms that are being implemented by the Chilean government. The one that concerns us here is the administrative decentralization of the country, which confers a new role to local governments. They now have the power to make decisions regarding the administration of the counties and to directly manage the financial resources for development programs. This was approved by the junta and published as a law in 1979. The process of "municipalization," as it is called in Chile, offers multiple new possibilities for local development requiring examination with an open mind. From the point of view of financial resources, it appears to be easier to negotiate with local authorities, for they are closer to where the problems are occurring and have the power to decide upon the allocation of available funds. However, the current situation makes municipalization look like a strategy of the centralized state to strengthen its power in the local communities through new means of control and repression. Hence LD, within the Chilean context, must not be seen as a mere pragmatic step nor as an immediate one. It must be seen as a perspective. As such, one must start considering the new possibilities that the negotiations between the *pobladores* and their mayors may have as an outcome. There is a possibility of a better rationalization in the use and distribution of local resources, of improving the planning for local activities, and, central to our study, of increasing the participation of neighbors and their organizations in planning and developing action. In a large study that looks at economic and social development in global terms, Galilea (1983) argues for the importance of a participatory planning in Latin America and the Caribbean. But such planning requires a high level of organization. When this is achieved, it is likely that planning at the local level will offer better possibilities of reaching a higher degree of efficiency. After all, as pointed out by Galilea, to a large extent the planning experience in Latin America is developed within a local context, although the local community is not typically a protagonist.

However, the emphasis on LD also raises questions regarding the micro–macro relationship. LD must be coordinated at a macrolevel. Local participation must find means of expression and influence at a national level to address issues of macro and structural transformation. Galilea (1983) argues that the local–national relation is crucial, for there are limited things that may be done at the local level. It is important to avoid the tendency of believing that at the local level all problems are solved. Such an understanding would presuppose a narrow association between popular representation and the local realm. Thus the idea of LD suggests a new relation to the macrolevel structure in which the participation at the bottom constitutes the foundations of the system and the coordination, promotion, and implementation of structural transformation are ultimate responsibilities of the top.

It will be helpful to provide some examples of programs being implemented in Chile today along the lines of LD. During field work, the first author researched groups' experiences where both their praxis and their purpose showed a way of working with the grass roots in an LD perspective. He visited these groups and met with the professionals in charge and with some of the participants. Finally, he organized a one-day seminar in which these experiences were presented and discussed.

Example 1: Primary Health Care and Education Program. This is a basic health care program. Its services are offered to a population of 8,000 people in a semirural area. This infrastructure is a polyclinic comprising five health care centers. The program depends on the Health Department of the Municipality of Pirque. In addition to its health services, the program has some educational objectives such as the promotion of organizations to implement action regarding health consciousness. The purpose is to integrate health and educational aspects through the joint effort of technical personnel and members of the local community. From the beginning, the community has been involved in the implementation of a diagnosis of their main problems, which has promoted participation and furthered the organization. Several concrete actions have been developed as an outcome. In addition, some of their activities have been coordinated with other programs implemented by the municipality such as one helping parents deal with problems their children are having at school.

Example 2: Primary Health Care Program in Consultorio Villa O'Higgins. This has been implemented in a *población*, Villa O'Higgins, located in a poor urban area of southern Santiago. Community participation is the central aspect of the health polyclinic, which reaches a population of 80,000. From the beginning, both the center and the community have worked jointly. The polyclinic's director invited the four *Juntas de Vecinos* of the area to discuss the improvements of the health services. The *Juntas de Vecinos* suggested the initiation of a training program for health coordinators who could simply be members of the community interested in forming part of a joint team on a volunteer basis. The personnel of the polyclinic offered the workshop, and their first task was the implementation of a diagnosis. About 20,000 people were surveyed. The diagnosis was a good means to mobilize the community. Today, three health centers are being built by the community.

Example 3: Technical Assistance for Urban Development Programs. This project is focused on the improvement of both housing and the urban environment and on promoting the development of grass-roots organizations as the conductors of local development. It is attempting to change the reactive character of organizations by advocating involvement in planning and action. To achieve this, the project claims, a methodology is needed that promotes a continuous, "horizontal" technical assistance. A planned action, in their view, requires the utilization of internal (community) and external (municipality) resources to be used in development programs. Organizations have to negotiate their plans with the community and then, as their representatives, with the municipal authorities. This strategy has been implemented in both *poblaciónes*, Nuevo Amanecer, and Ampliacion La Higuera, two organizations interpreters located in La Florida county. As a result, several committees of *pobladores* have been created, each of them being responsible for the implementation of a specific improvement program. What has been most successful is the control, by the organization, of the resources that the municipality has allocated for POJH, the government employment program. Instead of the municipality deciding on what to do with the resources, the *Junta de Vecinos* has negotiated the use of such resources to solve problems which they have identified, thus controlling the way they have spent the monies. In this process, the architects are professionals "hired" by the organization.

Example 4: Preschool Centers Project. This project's main objective was to open four centers for 1,800 children of the nearby *poblaciónes*. The centers were run by 140 women of the community trained as coordinators by a professional team hired by the municipality. The three-month training workshop placed an emphasis on basic skills required for preschool education as well as on the problems of women. The methodology provided an opportunity for these problems to be expressed and reflected upon by group members. Both the training and work at the center were processes of consciousness-raising. The final evaluation conducted by the directors of the program revealed the extent to which preschool education could promote the active participation of the community as well as mobilization around women's issues.

Out of these experiences of LD we learned all of them had a basic concern with the satisfaction of basic needs. They all had as a starting point the identification of the most urgent needs to be satisfied (*accíon reivindicatoria*). Hence, they all required the presence of professionals with a solid preparation in the technical aspects involved. But overall, there is a clear attempt to place technology in a framework of development of participation and organization. As well, they all attempt the involvement of community members in the identification and solution of their problems. There is a concern for the development of a social consciousness based on specific problems but linked to a global structure. Finally, they are all linked to the administrative apparatus of the municipality.

There is also much to learn from their differences. One extreme is Example 4 which originated in the municipality. The other extreme, represented by Example 3, is a program originated in an organization and moved on to negotiate with the authorities for financial resources. In the middle, Examples 1 and 2 are programs that have been inserted into an official structure; but due to the nature of the problem (health), they have a relative independence from the political fluctuations that so greatly affect the "municipalization" process today. In other words, health projects have existed, but now they may acquire new characteristics due to the decentralization of resources. There are no recipes for work today with local authorities. What is clear is that there are contradictions within the official system that must be explored and spaces to be occupied for the promotion of redemocratization.

There are also differences as to how the projects are legitimized in the community, which correlate with the extent to which the community assumes responsibility for implementation. Example 3 is a good example of a project strongly legitimized in the community. On the other hand, Example 4, according to the information provided by the staff, failed in making links with other community groups and some influential community organizations questioned the professional qualifications of the preschool coordinators.

The role played by the professionals involved was also different in each experience. In the case of Example 3, the architects are not hired by the municipality, which gives them more autonomy. Furthermore, the fact that they are "hired" by the organization has made them critically question their professional role. Their situation has required an openness toward popular cultural and educational relationships with their "employers." Both organizations and professional staff have been working jointly in the elaboration of the development plans.

Regarding the administration of resources, one must say that in spite of the differences between socioeconomic models, Chile has and will have limited resources to satisfy the basic needs of the popular sectors. Hence, community resources are needed to complement those coming from elsewhere. Some experiences put more emphasis on the role of the community in the planning of the use of external resources. Others emphasize the use of their own resources. Traditionally, the centralized system had promoted an apathetic attitude toward the contribution of resources as supporting the belief that everything has to be provided by the "State." LD questions this idea. The responsibility in the transformation of everyday-life situations is taken by the community in a more protagonistic way.

However, in these examples, it is not clear how such notions as community participation, organizational empowerment, and participatory methodology are reconceptualized in terms of a process of development of critical consciousness. The above examples do constitute successful cases of community organization that have resulted both in the improvement of local services and in the satisfaction of basic needs. There still remains a question to what extent these processes are engaged in consciousness-raising. The professional emphasis—on medical, architectural, and preschool education—although required for resolving specific problems demanding technical solutions, must be complemented with an educational perspective. Such a perspective will reconceptualize problems of development by relating them to a process of consciousness-raising where structures of domination, embedded in everyday practices, constitute the focus of a transformative praxis.

The perspective of LD offers both an institutional structure and a conceptual framework that facilitates the development of organization, participation, and consciousness-raising in the context of redemocratizing Chilean society. It is a framework of transformation in which popular education has a central contribution to make.

CONCLUSION

This chapter on "critical pedagogy" has attempted to show the reader that a "critical psychology" can be fruitfully applied to pedagogical issues both in the formal and informal sectors of education. The four examples given draw heavily from the concepts of a critical psychology developed in the preceding chapters. As I stated at the outset of this chapter, my examples are in no sense exhaustive. They were given to illustrate to the reader that a critical psychology has definite concrete possibilities in the development of a "critical pedagogy." It is my hope that the reader who has followed me this far will find it useful to develop his or her critical work in education with the help of a critical psychological orientation. As a discipline, psychology has been very heavily implicated in social practices of interpretation in education, which can only be considered as a form of domination and maintenance for groups in social power and at the expense of marginal groups. It is my deep desire that my present attempt will be seen and utilized with a growing form of social science that has human emancipation and freedom as its abiding passion.

APPENDIX

I have extensively discussed two studies in Chapter 7 to illustrate, in detail, what a critical psychology might look like and what it is not. It is important for the reader to understand that the Willis study is one minute example of what a critical psychology might look like. Other studies may be, and are, radically different from this one yet can be considered critical in intent. What is important is that the study incorporate the features of a critical study that I have developed in this book.

My major critical concerns in this book were directed toward structures of domination based on class differences in economic opportunity, sexism, racism, and adultocentrism. Other critical theories may not have the same focal concerns. In fact, one can analyze some studies that do not issue from a critical theoretical orientation and consider some of the critical features that these studies exemplify. This is important at first, since there are very few psychological studies having an explicit critical orientation. I would like to conclude by giving several examples to round out my treatment.

1. *Let Us Now Praise Famous Men.* This work by James Agee with photographs by Walker Evans focuses on a poor white family living in the American South during the 1930s (Agee & Evans, 1974). It is an intensive study of their personal world and also depicts how the researcher–writer (Agee) was affected by his stay with them. Instead of blaming the victims, Agee attempts to show by detailed description how people work and live under oppressive social conditions. While not sidestepping the oppression these people suffer, he nevertheless establishes their tremendous power in working together. This is a very moving ethnography of the personal world of the participants and the researchers. It brings to the fore the best of liberal sympathies. What is absent in this ethnography is the relation of the personal cultural world to the larger economic conditions which enforce poverty as a way of life among these people. It is, thus, lacking the agency–structure dialectic.

2. *Darwin on Man.* This exploration of scientific creativity by Howard Gruber (1974) is an intensive psychological study of Darwin's formative development that views his discovery as a communal enterprise. Particularly, this study brings out the notion of project or enterprise discussed in an earlier chapter. What is clear from this psychohistory is the relation of Darwin's lifelong project to the people around him. Darwin's personal agency is agency in relation. The notebooks indicate the tremendous personal support that Darwin received from the women who surrounded him. One never gets the impression from biology textbooks that the theory of evolution also owes something to women,

273

who gave up their project for its author. Gruber's study is important because it dramatizes the notion a project within the context of creative scientific theorizing.

3. *The Privileged Ones.*   This work by Robert Coles (1977) differs from most of the studies discussed in this book, which have focused on the working class or racial underclasses. This approach, however, represents only a partial understanding of the ethnography of class. If Willis tries to comprehend why lower-class children come to accept working-class jobs, Coles takes the middle-class child and tries to understand why "children cultured in affluence" come to see themselves as deserving wealth and luxury. This extensive ethnography of affluent children attempts to understand the development of the "project of affluence" (i.e., I expect to be as rich as or richer than my parents) and outlines the concept of "entitlement," which is a pervasive psychological expectation that things must go your way (i.e., no resistance is expected). Coles's study, therefore, gives one an insight into how upper-class children are socialized into power roles in our society. To use a Hegelian phrase, the study helps us understand the master in the master-slave relation. What is totally absent is the agency–structure dialectic, which would make it a critical account.

4. *The Hidden Injuries of Class.*   This study by Richard Senett and Jonathon Cobb (1973) seeks to understand how the class structure and nature of work affect the lives of adult working-class males. It shows how class structure is reproduced in the personal lives of these men. Gone is the rebellion and resistance that seem to characterize their youthful counterparts in the Willis study. What seems to be indicated is that the lads will eventually be subdued by the class system by disintegrating working conditions. What is dramatized here is not the presence of personal agency and cultural solidarity but the full working out of "alienated labor" and the presence of psychological liabilities that make these men accept the system and their lives within it as inevitable. The victims blame themselves. One senses here how the structural conditions of capitalism, and the alienated labor that Marx claims ensues, affect and subdue the lives of working-class men. They "buy the system" without benefiting from it. I am suspicious of the pervasive pessimism of this study. It seems that there is no resistance in these males, and yet Stanley Aronowitz, in his *False Promises* (1973), makes it very clear that there is a considerable amount of resistance in the work force that shows up in subtle ways. In this, Aronowitz sides with Willis, risking to err on the side of optimism.

5. *World of Pain: Life in the Working-Class Family.*   This work by Lillian B. Rubin (1976) is an intensive study of a group of white lower-middle-class families. Based on interviews with men and women who make up these working-class families, the study aims to link the interiority of family life (i.e., microcosm of a personal world) with the work that these people do. In other words, it assesses their place in the class structure and the effect it has on their personal lives within the family. As the author states herself, "Indeed, while there are hundreds of studies of marriage and the family each year, few even mention the word "class"—an indication of how invisible the class structure has been to those who conceptualize and carry out those projects" (Rubin, 1976, p. 5).

What is dramatized in this study is how the family of working-class individuals are subdued by the cultural and economic system. This study, like the previous one, captures the limitations and liabilities of personal lives under capitalism. What seems totally absent is the possibility of "personal project," which holds out the possibility of social transformation.

Like the Senett and Cobb study, it appears to characterize the total victory of ideology (habitus) over utopia (project). In spite of its obvious merits and sensitivities, I hold it suspect for its total eclipse of projective quality of human action.

6. *The Life of the Self.* Robert Jay Lifton's study (1976) concerns American soldiers who turned against the war they were fighting (Vietnam). There are many interesting things about this study, but most important for our purpose is how the researcher assumes an advocate role for the people he is studying. By *advocate,* I mean that this psychiatrist shares the moral rejection of the war that his participants express. He purposefully resists calling his sessions with these veterans "psychotherapy" because he considers their war guilt a moral sensitivity rather than the focus for psychiatric diagnosis. He calls his group a "rap group" and he intentionally attempts to enter into a reflexive–dialogical relation with the participants. He assumes a critical stance toward his own profession of psychiatry, which is aiding the cause of an immoral war by treating resistance to this war by some veterans as "deviance."

7. *Sane Asylum.* In this work, Charles Hampden-Turner (1976) studies a community of reformed addicts and alcoholics. The study is an *ethnography* with no discussion of the effects of social structure outside of the small groups considered. Nevertheless, it focuses on a microcosm of seemingly hopeless and wasted people and shows how, through a certain type of communal living, their lives are transformed from almost total "liability" to "project". In this study, one gets a feel for the notion of interdependence, which is what I mean by the enhancing power of a personal world. If the study errs, it will do so on the side of optimism. It captures the "utopian symbolism" released by human solidarity and shows how it can transform seemingly hopeless lives. One really gets the impression of a movement from oppression to liberty in the lives of a specific group of people. For all of its shortcomings, which I have failed to discuss, its interest and ability in capturing human emancipation is laudatory.

I have just given a small sampling of studies as examples to help orient the reader to a world of critical interpretation. The reader must now take the initiative to provide further examples. My selection reflects some of my own idiosyncrasies.

BIBLIOGRAPHY

Abel, T. The operation called Verstehen. *American Journal of Sociology*, 1948, 54, 211–218.

Agree, J., & Evans, W. *Let us now praise famous men*. New York: Ballantine Books, 1974.

Althusser, L. Ideology and the state. In *Lenin and philosophy and other essays*. London: New Left Books, 1971.

Anyon, J. Social class and the hidden curriculum of work. *Journal of Education*, Winter, 1980, 162(1).

Anyon, J. Social class and school knowledge. *Curriculum Inquiry*, Spring, 1981, 1(1). (a)

Anyon, J. Elementary schooling and the distinctions of social class. *Interchange*, 1981, 3, 118–132. (b)

Apple, M. *Ideology and curriculum*. Boston: Routledge and Kegan Paul, 1979.

Apple, M. Curricular form and the logic of technical control: Building the possessive individual. In L. Barton, R. Meighan, & S. Walker (Eds.), *Schooling, ideology and the curriculum*. Sussex, England: Falmer Press, 1980.

Apple, M. The political economy of text publishing. In *Excellence, reform and equality in education: An international perspective*. Buffalo and Toronto: State University of New York, Buffalo and OISE, 1981.

Apple, M., & Weis, L. (Eds.). *Ideology and practice in schooling*. Philadelphia: Temple University Press, 1983.

Archer, M. *Social origins of educational systems*. London: Sage Publications, 1979.

Aries, P. *Centuries of childhood*. New York: Vintage, 1962.

Aronowitz, S. *False promises*. New York: McGraw-Hill, 1973.

Ausubel, D. P., & Sullivan, E. V. *Theory and problems of child development* (2nd ed.). New York: Grune & Stratton, 1970.

Ausubel, D. P., Sullivan, E. V., & Ives, W. S. *Theory and problems of child development* (3rd. ed.). New York: Grune & Stratton, 1980.

Bakan, D. *The duality of human existence*. Chicago: Rand McNally, 1966.

Baum, G. *Religion and alienation*. Toronto: Paulist Press, 1975.

277

Bauman, Z. *Hermeneutics and social science*. New York: Columbia University Press, 1978.

Becker, E. *Escape from evil*. New York: Free Press–Macmillan, 1975.

Belaval, Y. Vico and anti-Catesianism. In G. Tagliacozzo (Ed.), *Giambattista Vico: An international symposium*. Baltimore: Johns Hopkins University Press, 1969.

Berg, L., & Bramble, W. Computers and the future of education. In *Applications of micro computers for instruction and educational management*, 17. 1–2, Fall-Winter, 1983, 101–188.

Berlin, I. *Four essays on liberty*. New York: Oxford University Press, 1969.

Berlin, I. *Vico and Herder: Two studies in the history of ideas*. New York: Viking, 1976.

Berlyne, D. E. *Structure and direction in thinking*. New York: Wiley, 1966.

Bernstein, D. *Class, codes and control*. London: Routledge, 1975.

Bernstein, R. *Praxis and action*. Philadelphia: University of Pennsylvania Press, 1971.

Bernstein, R. J. *The restructuring of social and political theory*. Philadelphia: University of Pennsylvania Press, 1978.

Black, M. *Models and metaphors: Studies in language and philosophy*. Ithaca, N.Y.: Cornell University Press, 1962.

Bleich, D. *Subjective criticism*. Baltimore: Johns Hopkins University Press, 1978.

Bluestone, B., & Harrison, D. *The De-industrialization of America*. New York: Basic Books, 1982.

Bourdieu, T. Outline of a theory of practice. In *Cambridge studies in social anthropology*. London: Cambridge University Press, 1977.

Bourdieu, T., & Passeron, J. C. *Reproduction in education, society and culture*. Beverly Hills, Calif.: Sage Publications, 1977.

Bowles, S., & Gintis, H. *Schooling in capitalist America: Education reform and the contradictions of economic life*. New York: Basic Books, 1976.

Braverman, H. *Labor and monopoly capital: The degradation of work in the twentieth century*. New York: Monthly Review Press, 1974.

Brenner, H. *Mental illness and the economy*. Cambridge, Mass.: Harvard University Press, 1973.

Brenner, H. *Estimating the social costs of national economic policy: Implications for mental and physical health and criminal aggression*. Washington, D.C.: U.S. Government Printing Office, 1976.

Bronfenbrenner, U. *The ecology of human development*. Cambridge, Mass.: Harvard University Press, 1979.

Broughton, J. Developmental structuralism: Without self, without history. In H. K. Betz (Ed.), *Recent approaches to the social sciences*. Calgary, Alberta, Canada: University of Calgary Press, 1979.

Brown, A. L. Knowing when, where and how to remember: A problem of meta cognition. In R. Glaser (Ed.), *Advances in instructional psychology* (Vol. 1). Hillsdale, N.J.: Erlbaum, 1978.

Brown, B. *Marx, Freud, and the critique of everyday life: Toward a permanent cultural revolution*. New York: Monthly Review Press, 1973.

Buber, M. *I and thou*. New York: Scribner, 1970.

Buck-Morse, S. Socioeconomic bias in Piaget's theory and its implications for cross-cultural studies. *Human Development*, 1975, *18*, 35–49.

Buss, A. R. The emerging field of the sociology of psychological knowledge. *American Psychologist*, 1975, *30*, 988–1002.

Cagan, E. Individualism, collectivism, and radical educational reform. *Harvard Educational Review*, 1978, *48*, 227–266.

Campbell, D. On the conflicts between biological and social evolution and between psychology and moral tradition. *American Psychologist*, 1975, *30*, 1103–1126.

Campbell, D. Science's social system of validity: Enhancing collective belief change and the problems of the social sciences. In D. W. Fiske and R. A. Shweder (Eds.), *Metatheory in the social sciences*. Chicago: University of Chicago Press, 1986.

Campbell, P. *Computers in education: A question of access*. Paper presented to the Annual Meeting of the American Educational Research Association, Montreal, Canada, April 1983.

Campbell, P. The computer revolution: Guess who's left out. *Interracial Books for Children Bulletin*, 1984, *15*(3), 3–6.

Canada. Department of Labour. *In the chips: Opportunities, people, partnerships*. Report of Labour Canada Task Force on Microelectronics and Employment. Ottawa: Queen's Printer, 1982.

Canada. Economic Council of Canada. *In short supply: Jobs and skills in the 1980s*. Ottawa, Canada: Supply and Services Canada, 1982.

Caplan, A. L. *The sociobiology debate*. New York: Harper & Row, 1978.

Chein, I. *The science of behaviour and the image of man*. New York: Basic Books, 1972.

Chodorow, M. *The reproduction of mothering: Psychoanalysis and the sociology of gender*. Berkeley: University of California Press, 1978.

Chomsky, N. *Language and mind*. New York: Harcourt, Brace, & World, 1968.

Chomsky, N. *Problems of knowledge and freedom*. New York: Random House, 1971.

Coleman, J. *Coleman report: Equality of educational opportunity*. Technical Report, Washington, D.C.: U.S. Government Printing Office: M66, 1966.

Coles, R. *Privileged ones*. Boston: Little, Brown, 1977.

The computer moves in. *Time*. January, 1983, pp. 3–5.

Connell, R. W. *Ruling class, ruling culture*. London: Cambridge University Press, 1977.

Connell, R. W., et al. *Making the difference*. Sydney Australia: Allen & Unwin, 1982.

Connell, R. W. *Which way is up? Essays on sex, class and culture*. Sydney Australia: Allen & Unwin, 1983.

Connell, R. W. *Teachers' work*. Sydney, Australia: Allen & Unwin, 1985.

Cornforth, M. *Materialism and the dialectical method*. New York: International Publishers, 1971.

Cover, J. Theological reflections: Societal effects of television. *Religious Education*, 1983, *78*(1), pp. 38–49.

Dagenais, J. *Models of man: A phenomenological critique of some paradigms in the human sciences*. The Hague: Nijhoff, 1972.

Danziger, K. The social origins of modern psychology. In A. Buss (Ed.), *Positivist sociology in the context of psychological theory*. New York: Irvington, 1978.

Davis, G. *Childhood and history in America*. New York: Psychohistory Press, 1976.

Dawe, A. Theories of social action. In T. Bottomore & R. Nisbet (Eds.), *A history of sociological analysis*. New York: Basic Books, 1978.

De Charms, R. *Enhancing motivation: Change in the classroom*. New York: Wiley, 1976.

De Lone, R. *Small futures*. New York: Harcourt Brace Jovanovich, 1979.

De Mause, L. The evolution of childhood. In L. De Mause (Ed.), *The history of childhood*. New York: Psychohistory Press, 1974.

Descartes, R. *Discourse on method*. Baltimore: Penguin Books, 1960. (Originally published, 1637).

Dickason, A. Anatomy and destiny: The role of biology in Plato, as Plato's views on women. In C. C. Gould & M. W. Wartofsky (Eds.), *Women in philosophy: Toward a theory of liberation*. New York: Putnam, 1976.

Dorfman, A., & Mattelhart, A. *How to read Donald Duck*. New York: International General Press, 1975.

Dyer, K. The dialogic of ethnology. *Dialectical Anthropology*, 1979, *14*, 205–224.

Education Ontario: The computer age and education. Toronto, Canada: Ontario Ministry of Education and Colleges and Universities, January 1982.

Edwards, R. *Contested terrain*. New York: Basic Books, 1979.

Eichler, M. The origins of sex inequality. A comparison and critique of different theories and their implications for social policy. *Women's Studies International Quarterly*, 1979, *2*, 329–346.

Eichler, M. *The double standard: A feminist critique of feminist social science*. London: Croom Helm, 1980.

Ellul, J. *The technological society*. Toronto, Canada: Vintage Books, 1964.

Erikson, E. Identity in the life cycle. *Psychological Issues*, 1959, *1*(1).

Espinoza, V. *Tipas de acción poblaciónal y movimiento popular urbano en Chile y Santiago*, SUR (mimeo), 1983.

Ewen, S. *Captains of consciousness*. New York: McGraw-Hill, 1976.

Ewen, S., & Ewen, E. *Channels of Desire*. New York: McGraw-Hill, 1982.

Favreau, O. E. Sex bias in psychological research. *Canadian Psychological Review*, 1977, *18*, 56–65.

Fay, B. *Social theory and political practice*. London: G. Allen, 1975.

Feinberg, W., & Rosemount, K. *Work, technology and education: Dissertation essays on the intellectual foundations of American education*. Urbana: University of Illinois Press, 1975.

Fowler, J. W. Faith, liberation and human development. *The Foundation*. Atlanta: Gammon Theological Seminary, Spring, 1974.

Freire, P. *The pedagogy of the oppressed*. New York: Seabury, 1970.

Freire, P. *Cultural action for freedom*. Baltimore: Penguin Books, 1974.

Fullan, M. *The meaning of educational change*. Toronto, Canada: OISE Press, 1982.

Gadamer, H. G. Hermeneutics and social science. *Cultural Hermeneutics*. 1975, *2*(4), 307–316. (a)

Gadamer, H. G. *Truth and method*. New York: Seabury, 1975. (b)

Gadlin, H., & Ingle, G. Through the one-way mirror: The limits of experimental self-reflection. *American Psychologist*, 1975, *30*, 1003–1009.

Gagné, R. M. Contributions of learning to human development. *Psychological Review*, 1968, *75*, 177–191.

Galilea, S. *Planificación de los Asentamientos humanos en America Latina y el Caribe*.

Santiago: Centro de investigación del Desarrollo Urbano, Universidad Catolica de Chile, 1983.

Garcia-Huidobro, J. G. *Aportes para el análisis y la sistematization de experiencias no formales de educación de adultos.* Santiago, Chile: UNESCO, 1980.

Garcia-Huidobro, J. G., & Pina, C. Obstáculos, facilitadores, aciertos y errors: comentarios a la marcha de los proyectos. Seminario Sistematization, Documento No. 2. Santiago, Chile: CIDE-FLASC, 1984.

Gardner, H. *The quest for mind.* New York: Random House, 1972.

Gaskell, J. Sex inequalities in education for work. *Canadian Journal of Education,* April 1981, *6,* 54–72.

Gaskell, J. Gender and course choice: The orientations of male and female students. *Journal of Education,* March, 1984, *166*(1), 89–102.

Gauld, A., & Shotter, J. *Human action and its psychological investigation.* London: Routledge, 1977.

Geertz, C. *The interpretation of culture.* New York: Basic Books, 1973.

Gerth, H., & Mills, C. W. *Character and social structure: The psychology of social institutions.* New York: Harcourt Brace Jovanovich, 1964.

Giddens, A. *New rules for sociological method.* London: Hutchinson University Library, 1977.

Giddens, A. *Central problems in social theory: Action, structure and contradiction in social analysis.* London: Macmillan, 1979.

Gilligan, C. *Integrating women's thinking into theories of moral development and education.* (Sound Recording) Toronto, Canada: OISE Press, 1985.

Giorgi, A. *Psychology as a human science.* New York: Harper & Row, 1970.

Giorgi, A., Fischer, C., & Murray, E. *Phenomenological psychology* (Vol. 2). Pittsburgh: Duquesne University Press, 1975.

Giroux, H. *Theory and resistance in education: A pedagogy for the opposition.* South Hadley, Mass.: Begin and Garvey, 1983.

Glasgow, D. G. *The black underclass.* San Francisco: Jossey-Bass, 1980.

Goldsen, R. *The show and tell machine.* New York: Delta Paperback, 1975.

Gould, C. C. Philosophy of liberation and the liberation of philosophy. In C. C. Gould & M. W. Wartofsky (Eds.), *Women and philosophy: Toward a theory of liberation.* New York: Putnam, 1976.

Gramsci, A. In P. Hoare & G. Smith (Eds. and trans.), *Selections from prison notebooks.* New York: International Publishers, 1971.

Grant, G. *Technology and empire.* Toronto, Canada: Anansi Press, 1967.

Gruber, H. E. *Darwin on man: A psychological study of scientific creativity.* New York: Dutton, 1974.

Gutierrez, G. *A theology of liberation.* New York: Orbis, 1973.

Habermas, J. *Toward a rational society.* Boston: Beacon, 1970.

Habermas, J. *Knowledge and human interests.* Boston: Beacon, 1972.

Habermas, J. *Theory and practice.* Boston: Beacon, 1974.

Habermas, J. *Communications and the evolution of society.* Boston: Beacon, 1979.

Hall, D. L. Biology, sex, hormones and sexism in the 1920s. In C. C. Gould & M. W. Wartofsky (Eds.), *Women in philosophy: Toward a theory of liberation.* New York: Putnam, 1976.

Hampden-Turner, C. *Radical man.* New York: Doubleday, 1971.

Hampden-Turner, C. *Sane asylum.* San Francisco: San Francisco Book Co., 1976.

Harp, J. & Hofley, J. (Eds.). *Structural inequality in Canada.* Scarborough, Ontario, Canada: Prentice-Hall, 1980.

Harré, R., & Secord, P. E. *The explanation of social behaviour.* Oxford, England: Blackwell, 1972.

Hart, H. L. A. Description of responsibility and rights. In A. C. N. Flew (Ed.), *Logic and language,* first series. Oxford, England: Blackwell, 1951.

Hartmann, H. The unhappy marriage of marxism and feminism. In L. Sargent (Ed.), *Women and revolution.* Black Rose, 1979.

Hilgard, E. R., & Bower, G. H. *Theories of learning* (3rd ed.). New York: Appleton Century Crofts, 1966.

Hirsch, E. D. *The aims of interpretation.* Chicago: University of Chicago Press, 1976. (a)

Hirsch, E. D. *Validity in interpretation.* New Haven, Conn.: Yale University Press, 1976. (b)

Hodges, H. W. Vico and Dilthey. In G. Tagliacozzo (Ed.), *Giambattista Vico: An international symposium.* Baltimore: Johns Hopkins University Press, 1969.

Horner, M. The motive to avoid success and changing aspirations of college women. In J. Bardwick (Ed.), *Readings on the psychology of women.* New York: Harper & Row, 1970.

Hudson, L. *The cult of the fact.* London: Jonathan Cape, 1972.

Hull, C. *Principles of behavior.* New York: Appleton Century Crofts, 1943.

Humphries, E. *Privacy in jeopardy: Student records in Canada.* Toronto, Canada: OISE Press, 1980.

Hunt, D., & Sullivan, E. V. *Between psychology and education.* Hinsdale, Ill.: Dryden, 1974.

Hunt, J. Mc. V. *Intelligence and experience.* New York: Ronald, 1961.

Ingleby, D. Psychology of child psychology. In M. P. M. Richards (Ed.), *The integration of a child into a social world.* London: Cambridge University Press, 1974.

Innis, H. A. *The bias of communication.* Toronto: University of Toronto Press, 1951.

Jacoby, R. *Social amnesia.* Boston: Beacon, 1975.

James, W. *Varieties of religious experience.* New York: Modern Library, 1936. (Originally published, 1902.)

Jameson, F. *The prison house of language.* Princeton, N.J.: Princeton University Press, 1972.

Jamison, P., Suppes, P., & Wells, S. Effectiveness of alternative instruction media: A survey. *Review of Educational Research,* 1974, *44,* 1–67.

Jencks, C., *et al.* Who gets ahead? The determinants of economic success in America. New York: Basic Books, 1979.

Jensen, R. How much can we boost IQ scholastic achievements? *Harvard Educational Review,* 1969, 39, 1–123.

Kamerman, S. B. Work in family in industrialized societies. *Science—Journal of Women in Culture and Society,* 1979, 4, 632–650.

Kamin, L. *The science and politics of I. Q.* Hillsdale, N.J.: Erlbaum, 1974.

Kavanaugh, J. F. *Following Christ in a consumer society*. Maryknoll, New York: Orbis Books, 1981.

Kavanaugh, J. Capitalist culture as a religious and educational formation system. *Religious Education*, 1983, 78(1), pp. 50–60.

Kellner, D. Ideology, marxism and advanced capitalism. *Socialist Review*, 1978, 8(6), 57–58.

Keniston, A. *Young radicals*. New York: Harcourt, Brace, & World, 1968.

Kessen, W. J. Commentary in insight of the child development movement in the United States. *Monographs of the Society for Research in Child Development*, 1975, 40, Serial #161.

Kuhn, T. *The structure of scientific revolutions*. Chicago: University of Chicago Press, 1962.

Laing, R. D., & Cooper, D. C. *Reason and violence*. London: Tavistock Publications, 1964.

Leiss, W. *The limits to satisfaction*. Toronto: University of Toronto Press, 1976.

Lifton, R. J. *The life of the self: Toward a new psychology*. New York: Simon & Schuster, 1976.

Livingstone, D. *Ideologies and educational futures*. Sussex, England: Falmer Press, 1983.

Lock, A. *Action, gesture and symbol*. New York: Academic Press, 1978.

Logan, R. *The axiomatics of the Innis-McLuhan School of Communications*. Unpublished paper presented to the Culture and Technology Seminar, University of Toronto, Canada, December, 1982.

Lonergan, B. *Insight*. London: Longmans, 1957.

Lonergan, B. *Method of theology*. New York: Herder & Herder, 1972.

McCarthy, T. *The critical theory of Jurgen Habermas*. Cambridge, Mass.: M.I.T. Press, 1978.

Maccoby, M. *The gamesman*. New York: Simon & Schuster, 1976.

McLuhan, M. *Explorations: Studies in culture and communications*. Nos. 1–9. 1953–1959. Toronto, Canada: University of Toronto Press, n.d.

McLuhan, M. *The Guttenberg galaxy: The making of typographic man*. New York: New American Library, 1969.

MacMurray, J. *The self as agent*. London: Faber & Faber, 1957.

MacMurray, J. *Persons in relation*. London: Faber & Faber, 1961.

McNeill, D. Developmental psycholinguistics. In F. Smith & G. A. Miller (Eds.), *The genesis of language*. Cambridge, Mass.: M.I.T. Press, 1966.

Malone, Thomas, Toward a theory of intrinsically motivating instruction. *Cognitive Science*, 1981, 4, 333–69.

Mander, J. *Four arguments for the elimination of television*. New York: William Morrow, 1978.

Mannheim, K. Conservative thought. In P. Kecskemeti (Ed.), *Essays on sociology and social psychology*. London: Routledge & Kegan Paul, 1953. (a)

Mannheim, K. *Ideology and utopia*. New York: Harcourt, Brace and World, 1953. (b)

Markovic, M. Women's liberation and human emancipation. In C. Gould & M. Wartofsky (Eds.), *Women and philosophy: Toward a theory of liberation*. New York: Putnam, 1976.

Marris, P., *Loss and change*. London: Routledge & Kegan Paul, 1978.

Marsh, P., Rosser, E., & Harré, R. *The rules of disorder*. London: Routledge, 1978.

Martin, J. *Telematic society: A challenge for tomorrow*. Englewood Cliffs, N.J.: Prentice-Hall, 1981.

Martinic, S. *Educación y cambio social*. Santiago, Chile: C.I.D.E., 1984.

Martinic, S. *La perspectiva de los participantes en los proyectos de educación popular: Propuesta de investigation*. Unpublished manuscript, Santiago, Chile, September, 1985. (a)

Martinic, S. *Mediaciónes sociales del saber*. Paper presented to the First Congress of Chilean Anthropology. Santiago, Chile, November 20–23, 1985. (b)

Marx, K. *Early writings*. (T. Baltimore, Ed.). New York: McGraw-Hill, 1963. (Originally published, 1844.)

Marx, K. & Engels, F. *The German ideology*. New York: International Publishers, 1960.

Mead, G. H. *A social psychology: Selected papers*. Chicago: University of Chicago Press, 1914.

Merleau-Ponty, M. *The structure of behavior*. Boston: Beacon, 1963.

Mills, C. W. *The sociological imagination*. New York: Oxford University Press, 1959.

Mitchell, J., & Oakley, A. *The rights and wrongs of women*. Hamondsworth, England: Penguin Books, 1976.

Morgan, R. *Sisterhood is powerful: An anthology of writing from women's liberation movement*. New York: Random House, 1970.

Neisser, U. *Cognitive psychology*. New York: Appleton Century Crofts, 1967.

Neisser, U. *Cognition and reality*. San Francisco: Freeman, 1976.

Nelson, J. Fine-living: TV and the brain. *In-Search*, 1980, pp. 26–32.

Newell, A., & Simon, H. A. Computer simulation of human thinking. *Science*, 1961, *134*, 2011–2017.

Noble, D. *America by design: Science, technology, and the rise of corporate capitalism*. New York: Knopf, 1977.

Oakley, A. A case of maternity: Paradigms of women as maternity cases. *Science—Journal of Women in Culture and Society*, 1979, *4*, 607–631.

Olson, C. P. Labouring to learn: How working theory gets down classrooms and kids. *Interchange*, 1981, *12*(2), 252–269.

Osgood, C. E., Suci, G., & Tannenbaum, T. H. *The measurement of meaning*. Urbana, Ill.: University of Illinois Press, 1957.

Papert, S. *Mindstorms: Children, computers, and powerful ideas*. New York: Basic Books, 1980.

Parsons, T., & Shils, E. A. (Eds.). *Toward a general theory of action*. Cambridge, Mass.: Harvard University Press, 1951.

Peirce, C. S. *Collected papers* (Vol. 5): *Pragmatism and pragmaticism*. Cambridge, Mass.: Belknap, 1934.

Petit, P. *The concept of structuralism: A critical analysis*. Berkeley: University of California Press, 1975.

Piaget, J. *The origins of intelligence in children*. New York: Norton, 1963.

Piaget, J. *Insight and illusions of philosophy*. New York: World Publishing Co., 1971.

Piore, M. P. In R. C. Edwards, M. Riech, & D. M. Gordon (Eds.), *Notes for a theory of labor stratisfactions*. Boston: Heath, 1973.

Pirandello, L. Six characters in search of an author. In E. Bentley (Ed.), *Naked masks*. New York: Dutton, 1952.

Polanyi, M. *Personal knowledge*. Chicago: University of Chicago Press, 1968.

Prentice, A. *The school promoters: Education and social class in mid-nineteenth century upper Canada*. Toronto, Canada: McClelland and Stewart, 1977.

Radnitzky, G. *Contemporary schools of medi-science*. Chicago: Regnery, 1973.

Richards, H. *The evaluation of cultural action*. Hong Kong: Macmillan Press, 1985.

Richards, M. *The integration of a child into a social world*. London: Cambridge University Press, 1974.

Rickman, H. P. Vico and Dilthey's methodology of the human studies. In G. Tagliacozzo (Ed.), *Giambattista Vico: An international symposium*. Baltimore: Johns Hopkins Press, 1969.

Ricoeur, P. *Freud and philosophy: An essay on interpretation*. New Haven, Conn.: Yale University Press, 1970.

Ricoeur, P. The model of a text. *Social Research*, 1971, 38, 529–555.

Ricoeur, P. The hermeneutical function of distanciation. *Philosophy Today*, 1973, 17, 129–143.

Ricoeur, P. Explanation and understanding: On some remarkable connections among the theory of text, theory of action and theory of history. In C. Reagan, & D. Stewart (Eds.), *The philosophy of Paul Ricoeur*. Boston: Beacon Press, 1978.

Riegel, K. *Psychology mon amour: A countertext*. Boston: Houghton, Mifflin, 1978.

Ruben, L. *World of pain: Life in the working-class family*. New York: Basic Books, 1969.

Ryan, J. Early language development: Towards a communicational analysis. In M. P. M. Richards (Ed.), *The integration of a child into a social world*. London: Cambridge University Press, 1974.

Ryan, W. *Blaming the victim*. New York: Random House, 1971.

Sahlens, M. D. *The use and abuse of biology*. Ann Arbor: University of Michigan Press, 1976.

Sampson, E. Psychology and the American ideal. *Journal of Personality and Social Psychology*, 1977, 35, 767–782.

Sampson, E. Cognitive psychology as ideology. *American Psychologist*, 1981, 36, 730–743.

Sarason, S. B. *The psychological sense of community*. San Francisco: Jossey-Bass, 1974.

Sarason, S. B. *Psychology misdirected*. New York: Free Press, 1981.

Sartre, J. P. *Search for method*. New York: Vintage Books, 1968.

Schafer, R. *A new language for psychoanalysis*. New Haven, Conn.: Yale University Press, 1976.

Scheman, N. *Individualism and the objects of psychology: Feminist perspectives on epistemology, metaphysics, and the philosophy of Simons*. (S. Hardin & M. Hintikko, (Eds.), Netherlands: Reidel, 1981.

Schiller, H. *The world crisis and the new information technologies: A way out or deeper in?* University of California at San Diego, unpublished paper, 1983.

Schon, D. *The reflective practitioner*. New York: Basic Books, 1983.

Science Council of Canada. *Planning now for an information society: Tomorrow is too late*. Ottawa: Science Council of Canada, Report 33, 1982.

Sennett, R., & Cobb, J. *The hidden injuries of class.* New York: Vintage Books, 1973.

Sennett, R. *The fall of public man.* New York: Random House, 1976.

Sève, L. *Man in Marxist theory and the psychology of personality.* Atlantic Highlands, N.J.: Humanities Press, 1978.

Sharon D., & Mehler, A. *Microcomputers in teaching and learning: An inventory of Canadian research.* Toronto, Canada: T.V. Ontario, 1985.

Shields, S. Functionalism, Darwinism and the psychology of women. *American Psychologist,* 1975, 30, 739–754.

Shotter, J. *Images of man in psychological research.* London: Methuen, 1975.

Skinner, B. Are theories of learning necessary? *Psychological Review,* 1950, 57, 193–216.

Slinger, P. Television commercials: Mirror and symbol of societal values. *Religious Education,* 1983, 78(1), pp. 29–37.

Smythe, D. W. *Dependency road.* New Jersey: Ablex Co., 1980.

Stephenson, B. Computers in Ontario Education: Technical Report. Toronto, Canada: Ontario Ministry of Education, 1982.

Sullivan, E. V. *Piaget in the school curriculum: A critical appraisal.* OISE Monograph, Toronto, Canada, 1966.

Sullivan, E. V. *Kohlberg's structuralism: A critical appraisal.* OISE Monograph, Toronto, Canada, 1977. (a)

Sullivan, E. V. A study of Kohlberg's structural theory of moral development. *Human Development,* 1977, 20, 252–276. (b)

Sullivan, E. V. Structuralism in a psychological context. In H. K. Betz (Ed.), *Recent approaches to the social sciences.* Calgary, Alberta, Canada: University of Calgary Press, 1980. (a)

Sullivan, E. V. The scandalized child: Children, media and commodity culture. In J. Fowler & Brusselmans (Eds.), *Toward a moral and religious maturity.* Morristown, New Jersey: Silver-Burdett Co., 1980. (b)

Sullivan, E. V. The career and legacy of Jean Piaget. *Queen's Quarterly,* Summer, 1981, pp. 341–352.

Sullivan, E. V. Mass media and religious values. *Religious Education,* 1983, 78(1), pp. 13–24. (a)

Sullivan, E. V. Computers, culture and educational futures: A critical appraisal. *Interchange,* 1983, 14/31, Toronto, Canada. (b)

Sullivan, E. V. Commonsense and valuing. *Religious Education,* 1983, 78(1), pp. 5–12. (c)

Sullivan, E. V. Common sense: The foundations for social science. In F. Van Holthon & D. Olson (Eds.), *Common Sense.* Maryland: University Press of America, 1987.

Sullivan, E. V., Olson, C. P., & R. Logan. *The development of policy and research projections for computers in education: A comparative ethnography.* (Report submitted to the Social Science and Humanities Research Council of Canada), Ottawa, October, 1986.

Takanishi, R. Childhood as a social issue: Historical roots of contemporary child advocacy movement. *Journal of Social Issues,* 1978, 34, 8–28.

Taylor, C. *Explanation of social behaviour.* New York: Routledge, 1964.

Taylor, C. Interpretation and the sciences of man. *Review of Metaphysics*, 1971, p. 51.

Television: Corporate America's Game. A Study Conducted by International Association of Machinists and Aerospace Workers, the International Union of Operating Engineers and Bakery Confectionary and Tobacco Workers, 1979.

Te Selle, S. *Speaking in parables: A study of metaphors and theology.* Philadelphia: Fortress, 1975.

Touraine, A. Toward a sociology of action. In A. Giddens (Ed.), *Positivism and sociology.* Toronto, Canada: Heinmann, 1974.

Touraine, A. Eight ways to eliminate the sociobiology of action. In J. W. Freiberg (Ed.), *Critical sociology.* New York: Irvington, 1979.

Touraine, A. *The voice and the eye.* New York: Cambridge University Press, 1981.

Trevarthen, C. The foundations of intersubjectivity: Development of interpersonal and cooperative understanding in infants. In D. Olson (Ed.), *The social foundations of language and thought.* New York: Norton, 1980.

Turkel, S. *The second self.* New York: Simon & Schuster, 1984.

Unger, R. M. *Knowledge and politics.* New York: Free Press, 1975.

Unger, R. M. *Law and modern society: A criticism of social theory.* New York: Free Press, 1976.

United States. National Commission on Excellence in Education. *A nation at risk: The imperative for educational reform. A report to the nation and the secretary of education.* Washington, D.C.: U.S. Department of Education, 1982.

Venn, A., & Walkerdine, V. The acquisition and production of knowledge. *Ideology and consciousness,* Spring, 1978, pp. 67–94.

Vico, G. *The new science of Giambattista Vico.* Ithaca, N.Y.: Cornell University Press, 1970. (Originally published, 1725.)

Von Wright, G. H. *Explanation and understanding.* Ithaca, N.Y.: Cornell University Press, 1971.

Walker, H. *La evaluación iluminativa del Programa Padres e Hijos: Fundamentos teóricos y procedimientos methodologicos.* Unpublished manuscript, Santiago, Chile, 1983.

Walker, Larrain H. *The transformation of practices in grass-roots organizations: A case study.* Doctoral dissertation, University of Toronto, Canada, 1986.

Weil, S. *The need for roots.* New York: Harper & Row, 1971.

Whitteck, C. Theories of sex differences. In C. C. Gould & M. W. Wartofsky (Eds.), *Women and philosophy: Toward a theory of liberation.* New York: Putnam, 1976.

Whitty, G., & Young, M. (Eds.). *Society, state and schooling.* Sussex, England: Falmer Press, 1977.

Wilden, A. *Structure and transformation* (Vol. 3): *Developmental and historical aspects* (C. Riegel, & G. C. Rosenthal, Eds.). New York: Wiley, 1975.

Wilden, T. *The imaginary Canadian.* Vancouver: Pulp Press, 1980.

Williams, R. Base and superstructure in Marxist cultural theory. *New Left Review,* December, 1973, 82, 3–16. (Reprinted in Dale *et al., Schooling and capitalism: A sociological reader.* London: Routledge, 1976.) (a)

Williams, R. *Key words: A vocabulary of culture and society.* London: Fontana Croom Helm, 1976. (b)

Willis, P. *Learning to labour.* Hampshire, England: Teakfield Limited, 1977.

Wilson, E. O. *Sociobiology: The new synthesis*. Cambridge, Mass.: Harvard University Press, 1975.

Wine, J. D., Moses, B., & Smye, M. Female superiority in sex difference competence comparisons: A review of the literature. In C. Stark-Adamac (Ed.), *Sex roles: Origins, influences, and implications*. Montreal: Eden Press, 1980.

Winter, G. *Elements for a social ethic*. New York: Macmillan, 1966.

Wishy, B. *The child and the republic*. Philadelphia: University of Pennsylvania Press, 1968.

Wolff, R. P. There is nobody here but us persons. In C. C. Gould & M. W. Wartofsky (Eds.), *Women in philosophy: Toward a theory of liberation*. New York: Putnam, 1976.

Wootton, A. *Dilemmas in discourse: Controversies about the sociological interpretation of language*. London: Allen & Unwin, 1975.

Wright, E. O. Class boundaries in advanced capitalist societies. *New Left Review*, July–August 1976, pp. 3–41.

Zuniga, R. B. The experimenting society and radical social reform. *American Psychologist*, 1975, 30(2), 99–115.

Zuniga, R. B. *Investigación científica y practica profesionales: Una reflexión epistemologica*. Paper presented at the University of Puerto Rico in a seminar on scientific epistomology and social practices. March, 1986. (a)

Zuniga, R. B. *Evaluateurs, chercheurs et travailleurs sociaux*. Unpublished paper. University of Montreal. Montreal, Canada, 1986. (b)

INDEX

Abstract universality, 133–136
Active structures, human action and, 37–38
Adequate account
  as argument, 146, 168
  comparisons of, 166–173
  critical nature of, 149, 171
  as emancipatory praxis, 147–148, 170
  negotiated, 167
Adultocentric interpretation, 121
Age, class dynamics and, 106–108
Agency, structure and, 128–130
Agency sense, in nondominant classes, 81
Agent
  intentional project of, 123
  interventional capacity of, 126
Agent-patient dialectic, 45, 116
Agent-structure dynamics, 141
Age-related institution, legitimacy of, 107
Aggression, vs. violence, 152
Aggro concept, 152–156
Agnosticism, methodological, 20
Ambiguous expressions, 19, 21
American psychology. See also
  Psychology
  as administrative science, 4
  new vocabulary of, 11
  Piaget's influence on, 9
Analysis, instrument rationality and, 4–6
Assimilation, 2
Atomism, of Descartes, 20

Behaviorism, as science, 5–6, 9, 26
Bias, as interpretative horizon, 143

Biological metaphor, in gender
  dominance, 100
Black nationalism, 90. See also Watts
  youth
Black Underclass, The (Glasgow), 91
Bourgeois hegemony, 90
Brute datum, subjective interpretation at
  level of, 22

Capitalism
  gender, class, and reproduction of
    social relations under, 101–105
  habitus of, 70
  nuclear family and, 103–104
  patriarchy under, 99–100
Caretaker-child interaction, 56
Cartesian legacy, 22
Cartesian mind-body dialectic, 21
Cartesian synthesis, Vico's criticism of, 23
Cause, intention and, 141
Child development, environment of, 55
Children
  psychohistory of, 107
  socialization of, 101
Class
  as cultural form, 88
  defined, 78
  as structure of domination, 77–88
Class dynamics
  age and, 106–108
  ethnicity and, 91–99
Classical liberalism, synthesis of, 52

About the Author

EDMUND V. SULLIVAN is Professor of Applied Psychology and Community Development at The Ontario Institute for Studies in Education. He has written extensively on the subjects of educational psychology and child development and is co-author with Thomas Berry of *Educational Essays on Creative Planetary Survival*.

www.ingramcontent.com/pod-product-compliance
Ingram Content Group UK Ltd.
Pitfield, Milton Keynes, MK11 3LW, UK
UKHW020654280225
455688UK00004B/117